SURROGACY IN CANADA

Surrogacy in Canada

Critical Perspectives in Law and Policy

Vanessa Gruben, Alana Cattapan, & Angela Cameron

EDITORS

IRWIN LAW

Published in 2018 by

Irwin Law Inc
Suite 206, 14 Duncan Street
Toronto, ON M5H 3G8
www.irwinlaw.com

ISBN: 978-1-55221-488-6 e-book ISBN: 978-1-55221-489-3

Library and Archives Canada Cataloguing in Publication

Surrogacy in Canada : critical perspectives in law and policy / Alana Cattapan, Vanessa Gruben, & Angela Cameron, editors.

Includes bibliographical references and index.
Issued in print and electronic formats.
ISBN 978-1-55221-488-6 (softcover). — ISBN 978-1-55221-489-3 (PDF)

1. Surrogate motherhood—Law and legislation—Canada. 2. Surrogate mothers—Legal status, laws, etc.—Canada. 3. Human reproductive technology—Law and legislation—Canada. I. Cattapan, Alana, editor II. Gruben, Vanessa, editor III. Cameron, Angela (Angela Jane), editor IV. Title.

KE3660.5.S94 2018 344.7104'196 C2018-905385-2
KF3830.S94 2018 C2018-905386-0

Canada

Ontario
Ontario Media Development Corporation
Société de développement de l'industrie des médias de l'Ontario

Printed and bound by CPI Group (UK) Ltd, Croydon, CR0 4YY
1 2 3 4 5 22 21 20 19 18

Contents

Foreword

Glenn Rivard

It has been over a decade since Parliament addressed the issue of commercial surrogacy in the *Assisted Human Reproduction Act* (*AHRA*)[1] and some provinces and territories brought into effect family law measures to address parental status issues arising from surrogacy arrangements.

I was the Department of Justice senior legal adviser to Health Canada during the development and adoption of the *AHRA*. I continued in that role as Health Canada developed the extensive regulations required by the legislation, and was co-counsel for the Government of Canada in its defence of the constitutionality of the Act (the *Reference re Assisted Human Reproduction Act*)[2]. In response to the 2010 Supreme Court of Canada decision, extensive amendments were adopted to the statute prior to my retirement from the Department of Justice. My experience has given me a window on the evolution of reproductive technologies and the law that governs them.

As the chapters in the present book indicate, key issues pertaining to surrogacy remain the subject of debate, including commercial surrogacy, parental status, and globalization and cross-border surrogacy arrangements, which is as it should be.

1 SC 2004, c 2.

2 2010 SCC 61.

Distrust of commercial surrogacy has a long history in Canada. In its 1993 report (*Proceed with Care*), the Royal Commission on New Reproductive Technologies considered commercial surrogacy to be a "basic affront to human dignity occasioned by the commodification of children and the commercialization of reproduction." This concern was echoed by the House of Commons Standing Committee on Health in its 2001 report on the first Assisted Human Reproduction bill (*Assisted Human Reproduction: Building Families*). The House Committee concluded, "Commercial surrogacy treats children as objects and treats the reproductive capacity of women as an economic activity." The recommendations of the royal commission and those of the House of Commons Committee were, with respect to commercial surrogacy, somewhat more restrictive than those that were eventually adopted by Parliament in 2004 as part of the *AHRA*. Nonetheless, the general concerns regarding commercialization of surrogacy and the commodification of women's reproductive capacities were reflected in the provisions of the new law.

Section 6 of the *AHRA* prohibits payment to a surrogate mother and for conduct in furtherance of commercial surrogacy. The restrictive nature of the section is somewhat eased, however, by section 12, which allows for the reimbursement of expenditures incurred by a surrogate mother, including reimbursement for loss of work-related income. The failure of the federal government to adopt the regulations necessary to make section 12 operational, however, has created ongoing uncertainty for surrogate mothers and commissioning parents. It is hoped that the regulatory consultation launched by Health Canada in 2016 will lead to the development of these necessary regulations and the proclamation into force of section 12 (as well as the other inoperative provisions of the Act).

Historically, the practice of surrogacy has also raised concerns regarding the legal status of the resultant child. Who is to be considered the child's parent—the surrogate mother or the commissioning person/couple? If the former, how and when can parental rights be transferred to the intended parent(s)? How are custody disputes to be resolved when they arise? These related issues were addressed in the reports of both the royal commission and the House of Commons Committee. Both bodies recommended that the provinces adopt legislation to provide certainty regarding the status of the child, and that disputes be resolved with the best interest of the child in mind. Provinces and territories have acted to address these issues, though the adequacy of these provincial laws remains up for debate.

The values we apply to surrogacy arrangements can, of course, change over time. The early discomfort with assisted reproductive technologies, as reflected in both the royal commission report and that of the House of Commons Committee, has, I would argue, eased somewhat. Both the public and the medical profession have grown increasingly used to the existence of these procedures, and Canada has had relatively few scandals in this field.

The essays in the present book look at surrogacy in the light of today's experiences. Both commercialization and the adequacy of laws pertaining to the status of the child are examined, as are more recent issues. The extent to which increasing international mobility has led to Canada's becoming a destination nation for surrogacy, and the concerns arising from that, is reviewed. Also evaluated is the ongoing lack of sufficient information regarding the practice of surrogacy, and the impacts this has on our ability to develop public policy in this area.

The present book performs an invaluable service in examining these and other matters related to surrogacy agreements, and I recommend it to anyone with an interest in the ongoing legal, ethical, and policy challenges raised by surrogacy in Canada. The essays contained herein provide valuable insights, and I commend the authors for their contributions to this timely examination of the many issues pertaining to surrogacy as practised in Canada today.

Glenn Rivard, LLB

Acknowledgements

This book is the result of a great deal of work by many great people. First, we would like to thank the contributors to this volume for sharing their outstanding work. You have been a pleasure to work with, and your chapters—individually and collectively—make an important contribution to knowledge in this field.

This book was conceived in conjunction with a workshop of the same name, held at the University of Ottawa in May 2017, and we owe a debt of gratitude to the participants and volunteers whose work at the workshop inspired a lot of what appears in the book.

We would also like to thank the research students who worked on this text (and the workshop), Victoria Paton, Karen Chow, Stephanie Tadeo, and Melanie Snow for their hard work and dedication to this volume. You have persisted through our many requests, and we thank you for your patience. Thank you also to Megan Poole for providing research assistance as we neared the end of this project.

Finally, we would like to acknowledge the financial support of the Social Sciences and Humanities Research Council and the Shirley Greenberg Chair in Women and the Legal Profession.

Introduction

REGULATORY PASTS AND FUTURES

Alana Cattapan, Vanessa Gruben, & Angela Cameron

Surrogacy—where a woman bears a child expressly for the purpose of surrendering custody of that child upon birth to another person or persons[1]—is on the rise. Reported surrogacy cycles in Canada have increased from less than one hundred a year when data were first collected in 2001, to more than six hundred a year in 2016.[2] Yet, despite the increasing numbers of women engaging in surrogacy, we still know little about who surrogates are and their experiences of surrogacy in the Canadian context.[3] The scarcity of data has been attributed to a lack of clarity in the 2004 *Assisted Human Reproduction Act* (*AHRA*), whose provisions prohibiting payment (but allowing for the reimbursement of expenditures) make those engaged in surrogacy wary of disclosure.[4] Even less is known about how Canadians engage in surrogacy abroad.

The media tells us a little. In an article for *Hazlitt*, on online magazine, freelance journalist Alison Motluk describes an experience of a surrogacy

1 Ontario Law Reform Commission, *Report on Human Artificial Reproduction and Related Matters* (Toronto: Ontario Law Reform Commission, 1985) at 91 [OLRC Report].

2 Canadian Fertility and Andrology Society, News Release, "Multiple Pregnancy Rate Resulting from IVF at an All-Time Low of 9.7% in Canada" *Cision* (2 November 2017), online: www.newswire.ca/news-releases/multiple-pregnancy-rate-resulting-from-ivf-at-an-all-time-low-of-97-in-canada-654686493.html.

3 See, for example, Pamela M White, Chapter 2, this volume.

4 *Assisted Human Reproduction Act*, SC 2004, c 2 [*AHRA*].

in Canada as undermining the autonomy of the woman acting as a surrogate and causing stress and financial hardship.[5] Against her wishes and clinical guidelines, the surrogate had four embryos implanted in her uterus, later undergoing a surgical procedure (selective reduction) to reduce the number of fetuses to two.[6] Throughout her pregnancy, the intended parents raised concerns about the health care expenses she was incurring, which suggests that tradeoffs were being made between the best interests of the surrogate and the family's finances.[7] A recent series on international surrogacy for the *Toronto Star* painted a different picture, focusing on the kindness of Canadian surrogates in enabling families from all over the world to have the children they desired, and portraying Canada positively as a destination for international surrogacy.[8]

While our empirical knowledge of surrogacy in the Canadian context comes largely from media reports[9] and a selection of master's theses and doc-

---

5 Alison Motluk, "Anatomy of a Surrogacy" (6 November 2017), *Hazlitt*, online: https://hazlitt.net/longreads/anatomy-surrogacy [Motluk, "Anatomy"].

6 *Ibid.*

7 *Ibid.*

8 Robert Cribb & Emma Jarratt, "Canadian Surrogates and Their Extraordinary Altruism" *Toronto Star* (17 January 2016), online: www.thestar.com/news/world/2016/07/17/canadian-surrogates-and-their-extraordinary-altruism.html.

9 Alison Motluk, "The Baby-Making Business: On the Front Lines of Toronto's Booming, Semi-legal Surrogacy Market" (3 February 2014), *Toronto Life* (blog), online: https://torontolife.com/city/baby-making-business-surrogacy-market-toronto [Motluk, "Baby-Making"]; Scott Tracey, "Surrogates Will Continue, With or Without Government Endorsement" *Guelph Mercury* (29 April 2004) A3; Hilary Stead, "Guelph Woman Has Womb for Hire" *[Brantford] Expositor* (31 July 1999) B6; Robert Matas, "Surrogate Mother Tells Her Opponents to Respect Decision" *Globe and Mail* (29 May 1987) E12; Hamida Ghafour, "Netting a Newborn: Infertile Couples Are Shopping the Internet for Surrogate Mothers to Carry Their Child" *Toronto Star* (16 February 2001) 1; Andrew Duffy, "Couple Risks Prison to Hire Surrogate Mom" *Edmonton Journal* (2 November 1996) A3; Dennis Bueckert, "Plenty of Wombs for Rent: Surrogate Motherhood Phenomenon Growing in Canada, Advocates Say" *Winnipeg Free Press* (31 May 1999) B1; Tom Blackwell, "Illegal Purchase of Sperm, Eggs and Surrogacy Services Leads to 27 Charges against Canadian Fertility Company and CEO" *National Post* (15 February 2013), online: http://nationalpost.com/news/illegal-purchase-of-sperm-eggs-and-surrogacy-services-leads-to-27-charges-against-canadian-fertility-company-and-ceo [Blackwell, "Illegal Purchase"]; Paula Adamick, "Surrogate Mother Defends Her Role" *Toronto Star* (27 May 1988) A3; Laura Pratt, "Womb Service: An Inside Look at Surrogate Motherhood" *Today's Parent* (June 2000) at 66.

toral dissertations,[10] an extensive literature exists about surrogacy around the world that spans across fields as diverse as philosophy,[11] law,[12] social work,[13]

10 Ann Muriel Fisher, *A Narrative Inquiry: How Surrogate Mothers Make Meaning of the Gestational Surrogacy Experience* (MA Thesis, School of Child and Youth Care, University of Victoria, 2012) [unpublished]; Shireen Kashmeri, *Unraveling Surrogacy in Ontario, Canada: An Ethnographic Inquiry on the Influence of Canada's Assisted Human Reproduction Act (2004), Surrogacy Contracts, Parentage Laws, and Gay Fatherhood* (MA Thesis, Department of Sociology and Anthropology, Concordia University, 2008) [unpublished]; Scott J Duggan, *Factors Relating to Parenting by Non-heterosexual Fathers* (Doctoral Dissertation, Ontario Institute for Studies in Education, University of Toronto, 2007) [unpublished]; Sophia Fantus, *The Path to Parenthood Isn't Always Straight: A Qualitative Exploration of the Experiences of Gestational Surrogacy for Gay Men in Canada — Perspectives of Gay Fathers and Surrogates* (Doctoral Dissertation, Faculty of Social Work, University of Toronto, 2017) [unpublished].

11 See, for example, Amrita Bannerjee, "Reorienting the Ethics of Transnational Surrogacy as a Feminist Pragmatist" (2010) 5:3 *The Pluralist* 107; Christine Overall, *Ethics and Human Reproduction: A Feminist Analysis* (Boston: Allen and Unwin, 1987); Vida Panitch, "Surrogate Tourism and Reproductive Rights" (2013) 28:2 *Hypatia* 274 at 274.

12 See, for example, Glenn Rivard & Judy Hunter, *The Law of Assisted Human Reproduction* (Markham, ON: LexisNexis/Butterworths, 2005); Erin Nelson, *Law, Policy and Reproductive Autonomy* (Oxford: Hart, 2013); Karen Busby & Delaney Vun, "Revisiting *The Handmaid's Tale*: Feminist Theory Meets Empirical Research on Surrogate Mothers" (2010) 26:1 *Canadian Journal of Family Law* 13; Stefanie Carsley, "Tort's Response to Surrogate Motherhood: Providing Surrogates with a Remedy for Breached Agreements" (2013) 46:1 *University of British Columbia Law Review* 1; Maneesha Deckha, "Situating Canada's Commercial Surrogacy Ban in a Transnational Context: A Postcolonial Feminist Call for Legalization and Public Funding" (2015) 61:1 *McGill Law Journal* 31; Régine Tremblay, "Surrogacy in Quebec: The Good, the Bad and the Foreigner" (2015) 27:1 *Canadian Journal of Women and the Law* 94.

13 See, for example, Eric Blyth, "Children's Welfare, Surrogacy and Social Work" (1993) 23:3 *British Journal of Social Work* 259; George Palattiyil et al, "Globalization and Cross-Border Reproductive Services: Ethical Implications of Surrogacy in India for Social Work" (2010) 53:5 *International Social Work* 686.

psychology,[14] and women's studies.[15] Much of this research comes from the feminist tradition, as feminist scholars have historically been concerned about surrogacy, taking issue with the potential exploitation of one woman's body for the reproductive purposes of another person or couple and with the commercial gains that might be exacted on and through women's bodies in a highly profitable market in assisted human reproduction.[16] And although many important scholars remain opposed to the practice,[17] if the use of surrogates is here to stay in Canada, we need both new ways to understand surrogates as autonomous actors within well-established, and potentially exploitative, marketplaces, and regulatory mechanisms that address current practices.

---

14 Janice C Ciccarellli & Linda J Beckman, "Navigating Rough Waters: An Overview of Psychological Aspects of Surrogacy" (2005) 61:1 *Journal of Social Issues* 21; Susan Golombok et al, "Families Created through Surrogacy Arrangements: Parent Relationships in the 1st Year of Life" (2004) 40:3 *Developmental Psychology* 400; Susan Golombok et al, "Surrogacy Families: Parental Functioning, Parent-Child Relationships and Children's Psychological Development at Age 2" (2006) 47:2 *Journal of Child Psychology and Psychiatry* 213; Susan Golombok et al, "Families Created Through Surrogacy: Mother-Child Relationships and Children's Psychological Adjustment at Age 7" (2011) 47:6 *Developmental Psychology* 1579; Vasanti Jadva et al, "Surrogates and Intended Parents in the UK" (2016) 4:3 *Journal of Medical Law and Ethics* 215; Amrita Pande, *Wombs in Labor: Transnational Commercial Surrogacy in India* (New York; Columbia University Press, 2014); Elly Teman, "The Social Construction of Surrogacy Research: An Anthropological Critique of the Psychosocial Scholarship on Surrogate Motherhood" (2008) 67:7 *Social Science and Medicine* 1104; Olga van den Akker, *Surrogate Motherhood Families* (London: Palgrave Macmillan, 2017).

15 GKD Crozier, Jennifer Lane Johnson, & Christopher Hajzler, "At the Intersections of Emotional and Biological Labor: Understanding Transnational Commercial Surrogacy as Social Reproduction" (2014) 7:2 *International Journal of Feminist Approaches to Bioethics* 45; Serene Khader, "Intersectionality and the Ethics of Transnational Commercial Surrogacy" (2013) 6:1 *International Journal of Feminist Approaches to Bioethics* 68; Katy Fulfer, "Cross-Border Reproductive Travel, Neocolonialism and Canadian Policy" (2017) 10:1 *International Journal of Feminist Approaches to Bioethics* 225; Jenni Millbank, "Rethinking 'Commercial Surrogacy' in Australia" (2015) 12:3 *Bioethical Inquiry* 477; Jennifer Parks, "Care Ethics and the Global Practice of Commercial Surrogacy" (2010) 24:7 *Bioethics* 333; Miranda Davies, ed, *Babies for Sale? Transnational Surrogacy, Human Rights and the Politics of Reproduction* (London: Zed Books, 2017).

16 Susan Sherwin, "Some Reflections on 'Surrogacy'" in Gwynne Basen, Margrit Eichler, & Abby Lippman, eds, *Misconceptions: The Social Construction of Choice and the New Reproductive and Genetic Technologies* (Hull, QC: Voyageur, 1994); Christine Overall, *Human Reproduction: Principles, Practices and Policies* (Toronto: Oxford University Press, 1993).

17 See, for example, Maria De Koninck, Afterword, this volume.

This volume brings together a range of critical perspectives on the governance of surrogacy in Canada, with a focus on public policy and law. Despite existing work on the theoretical implications of commercialization, commodification, and exploitation, limited scholarship addresses the particularity of the Canadian case, where only "altruistic" surrogacy is legal but there is limited enforcement of the relevant law, the *AHRA*.[18] As described below, Health Canada has recently taken steps to revisit this law and to create regulations related to the reimbursement of expenditures paid to surrogates, which is often theorized as a loophole in the law that might enable compensation.[19] The contributions collectively provide understandings of how to address the challenges of regulation, to (re)think broadly about the governance of surrogacy, and to address the health, well-being, and autonomy of surrogates in the Canadian context and elsewhere. Some contributors also provide much-needed and long-awaited empirical data about how surrogacy in Canada is currently occurring. In this critical period in which the regulations on reimbursement are being developed — and with pressures mounting to re-examine the law in its entirety — this book identifies important concerns about the experience of surrogacy in Canada and makes recommendations for change.

A. REGULATING SURROGACY IN CANADA

Works tracing the history and governance of surrogacy often include biblical references that indicate that surrogacy has always existed, citing the story of Sarah, who had a child borne by a surrogate, who was also her handmaiden.[20] The lines between servant and surrogate are not clear in

18 See, for example, Alana Cattapan, "Risky Business: Surrogacy, Egg Donation and the Politics of Exploitation" (2014) 29:3 *Canadian Journal of Law and Society* 361 [Cattapan, "Risky Business"]; Suze Berkhout, "Buns in the Oven: Objectification, Surrogacy, and Women's Autonomy" (2008) 34: 1 *Social Theory and Practice* 95; Jennifer Damelio & Kelly Sorenson, "Enhancing Autonomy in Paid Surrogacy" (2008) 22:5 *Bioethics* 269; Stephen Wilkinson, "The Exploitation Argument Against Commercial Surrogacy" (2003) 17:2 *Bioethics* 169; *AHRA*, above note 4.

19 See Section B(3), below in this chapter.

20 See, for example, Avi Katz, "Surrogate Motherhood and the Baby-Selling Laws" (1986) 20:1 *Columbia Journal of Law and Social Problems* 1 at 1–2; Debora L Spar, "For Love and Money: The Political Economy of Commercial Surrogacy" (2005) 12:2 *Review of International Political Economy* 287 at 291.

the telling and retelling, raising still-relevant questions about the tangled web of exploitation, labour, and joy bound up in many historical and contemporary experiences of surrogacy. It has largely been since the advent of *in vitro* fertilization, however—and the possibility that a woman might carry a pregnancy and bear a child with whom she shares no genetic relationship—that surrogacy has proliferated. The use of *in vitro* fertilization coupled with the work of a surrogate means that a woman can give birth to a child created with the egg and sperm of the intended parents, or gamete donors, or some combination thereof. The relatively new and complex ways that children can be created in this context has resulted in anxiety about how the state would or should respond, leading to a range of inquiries, litigation, and regulatory developments.

In Canada, public policy and law began to consider surrogacy seriously in the early 1980s, when concerns about lack of regulation of the practice and lack of direction for professionals were raised by both the Ontario Law Reform Commission and the Canadian Medical Association. On 5 October 1982, the attorney general of Ontario, Roy McMurtry, called for an inquiry into "the legal issues relating to the practice of human artificial insemination, including 'surrogate mothering' and transplantation of fertilized ova to a third party."[21] Within the year, the Canadian Medical Association raised concern about the "legal, social, and psychological implications of surrogacy," adopting a resolution in its annual general meeting to advise physicians to "become associated with the procedure [surrogacy]" only with "great caution," in part because the legality of the procedure was not yet clear.[22]

Other reports ensued. The Law Reform Commission of Canada, for example, issued a working paper that recommended that surrogacy arrangements be considered null and void and, further, that commercial surrogacy be criminalized.[23] The recommendations of the working paper were based,

21 OLRC Report, above note 1, vol 1 at 1.

22 Canadian Medical Association, "Proceedings of the 116th Annual Meeting, Including the Transactions of General Council" (1983) at 128, resolution 83-23 as cited in OLRC Report, above note 1, vol 2 at 221.

23 Law Reform Commission of Canada, "Medically Assisted Procreation," Law Reform Commission of Canada Working Paper No 65 (Ottawa: Minister of Supply and Services Canada, 1992); see also Royal Commission on New Reproductive Technologies, *Proceed with Care: Final Report of the Royal Commission on New Reproductive Technologies* (Ottawa: Minister of Government Services Canada, 1993) at 668 [*Proceed with Care*].

in part, on research conducted by Margrit Eichler and Phebe Poole for the Law Reform Commission, which indicated that (in the cases for which information was available) there were often socio-economic disparities between intended parents and surrogates. Eichler and Poole's finding is particularly notable, as this study, conducted in 1988, constituted a significant part of the limited empirical research on surrogates in the Canadian context, and thus has long been used as evidence of exploitation in surrogacy arrangements.[24] In 1991, the Uniform Law Conference of Canada supported the idea that the "woman who gives birth, not the woman who produced the egg, [is] the mother."[25]

Despite these early interventions, those chronicling the history of surrogacy and other forms of assisted reproduction in Canada most often begin with the report of the Royal Commission on New Reproductive Technologies.[26] At the urging of feminist scholars and activists concerned about the implications of reproductive technologies for women's bodies, the federal government called a royal commission in 1989 to study "current and potential medical and scientific developments related to new reproductive technologies, considering in particular, their social, ethical, health, research, legal, and economic implications and the public interest, recommending what policies and safeguards should be applied."[27] Four years, and a great deal of controversy later, the commission issued its report, calling for an approach to surrogacy vested in the commission's principle of non-commercialization.[28]

---

24 Cattapan, "Risky Business," above note 18.

25 *Proceed with Care*, above note 23 at 668; Uniform Law Conference of Canada, *Uniform Child Status Act* (1992); *Uniform Child Status Act* (2010) (the uniform statute was updated in 2010, reinforcing the idea that surrogacy arrangements are null and void, and further, that this is a matter to be governed by provinces under family law); see also Susan G Drummond, "Fruitful Diversity: Revisiting the Enforceability of Gestational Carriage Acts" in Trudo Lemmens et al, *Regulating Creation: The Law, Ethics, and Policy of Assisted Human Reproduction* (Toronto: University of Toronto Press, 2017) 274 at 277.

26 Bernard Dickens, "A Historical Introduction of the Supreme Court's Decision on the *Assisted Human Reproduction Act*" in *Regulating Creation, ibid* at 23.

27 Canada, *Speech from the Throne* (1989). See also Canada, Order in Council PC 1989; *Proceed with Care*, above note 23 at 2.

28 Charlotte Gray, "Controversial 'Reprotech' Royal Commission Faces Growing Criticism" (1991) 145:10 *Canadian Medical Association Journal* 1371 at 1371; see also the discussion of the royal commission and subsequent developments in Glenn Rivard's Foreword to this volume.

In their chapter on "preconception arrangements" (i.e., surrogacy), the commissioners laid out a framework for the governance of surrogacy that was opposed to the practice—commercial or otherwise—insofar as the "best interests of children ... lie in not being the object of a contract, agreement, or paid transaction."[29] The approach to surrogacy taken in the commission's recommendations aimed not to "signal acceptance or encouragement" of surrogacy while ensuring that any legal or regulatory interventions did not add to the potential vulnerability that women acting as surrogates might be experiencing.[30] The commissioners were entirely opposed to payment for surrogacy and recommended prohibitions on payment as well as on assisting people in making commercial arrangements.[31]

Although the framework for the governance of surrogacy recommended by the royal commission eventually found its way into law, the road from the commission to legislation was a circuitous one. The commission's report was tabled in 1993, and it was not until two years later that the federal government issued a response, in the form of a voluntary moratorium on nine reproductive technologies seen by the government to be especially egregious. These included commercial (but not unpaid/altruistic) surrogacy.[32] Reports quickly emerged from clinicians planning to ignore the moratorium because their "patients need[ed] the service,"[33] despite strong opposition from some members of the public.[34] In 1996, the federal government introduced legislation that would enact the criminal prohibitions that the voluntary moratorium had proposed, although the bill ultimately died on the Order Paper.[35]

29 *Proceed with Care*, above note 23 at 688.

30 *Ibid* at 689.

31 *Ibid* at 489–90.

32 Health Canada, News Release, "Health Minister Calls for Moratorium on Applying Nine Reproductive Technologies and Practices in Humans" (27 July 1995); Éric Montpetit, "Policy Networks, Federalism and Managerial Ideas: How ART Non-decision in Canada Safeguards the Autonomy of the Medical Profession" in Ivar A Bleiklie, Malcolm L Goggin, & Christine Rothmayr, eds, *Comparative Biomedical Policy: Governing Assisted Reproductive Technologies* (New York: Routledge, 2004) 64 at 66–67.

33 Canadian Press, "Fertility Industry Defiant: Won't Observe Ban on High-Tech Baby-Making Techniques" *Hamilton Spectator* (28 July 1995) A1.

34 "Voluntary Restraint Won't Stop Baby Sales" *Kitchener-Waterloo Record* (29 July 1995) A14; "Cowardly Inaction on Baby Trade" *Toronto Star* (29 July 1995) SA2/B2.

35 Rivard & Hunter, above note 12 at 20.

There were subsequent, unsuccessful attempts at legislation, and it was not until 2001 that the federal government moved the process along by taking the unprecedented step of having a draft of the *AHRA*—rather than a bill—considered by a subcommittee of the Standing Committee on Health.[36] The subcommittee listened to the testimony of nearly one hundred witnesses (including just one surrogate) between May and November 2001, which informed a report entitled *Assisted Human Reproduction: Building Families* that was tabled in December 2001.[37] On the whole, the report reiterated the position on surrogacy taken by the royal commission, recommending that commercial surrogacy arrangements be prohibited and that altruistic/non-commercial arrangements be permitted but discouraged.[38] The report was also clear that there should not be any compensation "to any party involved, directly or indirectly, in any surrogacy arrangement," including "those parties who provide medical, legal, and psychological services," and it recommended changes to the draft legislation to prohibit payment to these groups, except in cases where health care services were needed to care for the pregnant woman.[39] Further, to advance the principle of non-commercialization to which the draft legislation and the subcommittee were committed, *Building Families* also recommended the elimination of provisions that would permit the reimbursement of expenditures to surrogates (as well as gamete donors).[40]

The recommendations in *Building Families* had little impact, however: regarding surrogacy, the version of the *AHRA* tabled in the House of Commons in 2002 was strikingly similar to the draft legislation. The Act took two more years to work its way through the House of Commons and Senate, ultimately resulting in the passage of the *AHRA* in 2004. The Act, as passed, followed a structure very similar to the 2001 draft legislation.

36 For an overview of the *AHRA*'s legislative history, see Alana Cattapan, *Controlling Conception: Citizenship and the Governance of Assisted Reproductive Technologies in Canada (1989–2004)* (Doctoral Dissertation, York University, 2015) [unpublished] at 159; Bonnie Brown, Nancy Miller Chenier, & Sonya Norris, "Committees as Agents of Public Policy: The Standing Committee on Health" (2003) 26:3 *Canadian Parliamentary Review* 4.

37 Canada, Standing Committee on Health, *Assisted Human Reproduction: Building Families* (Ottawa: Standing Committee on Health , 2001) [*Building Families*].

38 *Ibid.*

39 *Ibid* at 12–13.

40 *Ibid* at 37.

Its provisions related to surrogacy fall roughly into two sections: criminal prohibitions and controlled activities (i.e., activities that are permitted in accordance with regulations). In terms of criminal prohibitions, as proposed by the royal commission, the *AHRA* bans payment for surrogacy while permitting surrogacy performed altruistically.[41] The law also includes prohibitions on "arranging for the services of a surrogate mother, offer[ing] to make such an arrangement for consideration, or advertis[ing] the arranging of such services," although the suggested expansive restrictions on payment for relevant legal and psychological services are not included.[42] The penalties for contravening the criminal prohibitions are a fine of up to $500,000 or up to ten years in jail, or both.[43] Regarding activities permitted in accordance with regulations, the *AHRA* includes provisions about the development of regulations for the reimbursement of receipted expenditures—for costs incurred by surrogates over the course of their pregnancy.[44] These provisions were included despite the clear opposition to the reimbursement of expenses that was articulated in *Building Families*, and they were seen at the time (and since) to be a loophole in the law that might permit payment to surrogates.[45] At the time the Act was passed, the implementation of the regulatory provisions of the Act was jointly tasked to Health Canada and Assisted Human Reproduction Canada, an arm's-length agency established by the Act.[46]

41 *AHRA*, above note 4, s 6.

42 *Ibid*.

43 *Ibid*, ss 60 & 61 (as per the Act, the penalties associated with the contravention of these prohibitions is up to $500,000 or "imprisonment for a term not exceeding ten years" or both for an indictable offence. The penalties associated with a summary conviction are a "fine not exceeding $250,000" or "imprisonment for a term not exceeding four years," or both.) See *ibid*, s 60.

44 *Ibid*, ss 2 and 12.

45 See, for example, the discussion of reproductive technologies in: Canada, Parliament, *House of Commons Debates*, 37th Parl, 1st Sess, Vol 137, No 186 (9 May 2002). (The potential for the reimbursement of expenses to be a loophole through which payment could occur was discussed frequently in the legislative process that followed the publication of *Building Families*, above note 37); Canada, Parliament, House of Commons, Standing Committee on Health, *Evidence*, 37th Parl, 2nd Sess, No 013 (9 December 2002); see, for example, Letter and Submission from the Canadian Bar Association on Bill C-56; Blackwell, "Illegal Purchase," above note 9.

46 Rivard & Hunter, above note 12 at 182–84.

B. THE *AHRA*: PATCHING A LEGAL VOID

Although change in the area of surrogacy has been slow since the passage of the Act in 2004, there have been a number of important developments in terms of its implementation and enforcement—the first, and perhaps most important, being the constitutional challenge to a large number of the *AHRA*'s provisions and their subsequent removal from the Act.[47] The amendment of the Act also signalled the closure of the Assisted Human Reproduction Canada, tasked with managing the Act's licensing provisions, ensuring its implementation, and generally making certain that the spirit of the Act was maintained.[48] This closure has created a regulatory void that, until recently, has enabled an expansion of the market in fertility services, including surrogacy, in Canada. The proliferation of surrogacy and relevant services has been the second major development, as surrogacy has become increasingly commonplace. Alongside this proliferation have been calls for clear governance of the practice, either to enable altruistic surrogacy to continue in a transparent legislative environment or to enable expanded arrangements, in ways that stand in stark contrast to the concerns of feminists that were heard in the 1980s when surrogacy first came to be considered as a matter of law and public policy. There have also been significant developments in provincial family laws, which have sought to address the parentage issues arising from surrogacy arrangements.

1) Constitutional Challenges and Amending the *AHRA*

Even prior to the royal commission, the federal government's authority to govern reproductive technologies had been an important point of contention.[49] The *Constitution Act, 1867* does not assign health to either level of

47 *Reference re Assisted Human Reproduction Act*, 2010 SCC 61 at paras 227 and 285 [*Reference re AHRA*].

48 *Jobs, Growth and Long-Term Prosperity Act*, SC 2012, c 19, s 713.

49 See, for example, Barbara von Tigerstrom, "Federal Health Legislation and the *Assisted Human Reproduction Act Reference*" (2011) 74:1 *Saskatchewan Law Review* 33; Dave Snow, "Explaining a Policy Failure: Jurisdictional Framing, Federalism, and Assisted Reproductive Technologies in Canada" (2015) 41:2 *Canadian Public Policy* 124; Ian B Lee, "The *Assisted Human Reproduction Act Reference* and the Federal Criminal Law Power" (2012) 90:2 *Canadian Bar Review* 469; Patrick Healy, "Statutory Prohibitions and the Regulation of New Reproductive Technologies under Federal Law in Canada"

government, and therefore both the federal and provincial governments have legislative authority to make laws in this area.[50] Parliament has relied primarily on its criminal law power to make laws relating to health. The Supreme Court of Canada has adopted a broad approach to these powers: "The scope of the federal power to create criminal legislation with respect to health matters is broad, and is circumscribed only by the requirements that the legislation must contain a prohibition accompanied by a penal sanction and must be directed at a legitimate public health evil."[51] Nevertheless, many matters of health fall within provincial jurisdiction, and the lines between federal and provincial jurisdiction in health are critical points of intergovernmental contention.

Members of the Bloc Québécois[52] have long articulated opposition to the federal government's attempts to regulate in the health field. Following the passage of the *AHRA*, the attorney general of Quebec filed a reference with the Quebec Court of Appeal on the constitutionality of certain provisions of the *AHRA*, including section 12, which prohibits the reimbursement of expenditures to surrogates and gamete donors except in accordance with the regulations.[53] The Court of Appeal found that all of the thirty-two contested provisions were within provincial jurisdiction and, therefore, were constitutionally invalid.[54] The Attorney General of Canada appealed

(1995) 40:4 *McGill Law Journal* 905; Timothy A Caulfield, "Clones, Controversy, and Criminal Law: A Comment on the Proposal for Legislation Governing Assisted Human Reproduction" (2001) 39:2 *Alberta Law Review* 335; Canada, Parliamentary Research Branch: Political and Social Affairs Division, *Intergovernmental Consultations on Health: Toward a National Framework on Reproductive Technologies*, by Nancy Miller Chenier (Ottawa: Library of Parliament, 2002), online: www.res.parl.gc.ca/Content/LOP/ResearchPublicationsArchive/bp1000/prb0234-e.asp#Background; Montpetit, above note 32.

50 *Schneider v British Columbia*, [1982] 2 SCR 112.

51 *RJR-MacDonald Inc v Canada (Attorney General)*, [1995] 3 SCR 199 at para 32.

52 The Bloc Québécois is a federal political party dedicated to political sovereignty for the province of Quebec. Part of its mandate is to create the legal conditions for Quebec to separate from Canada, including clarifying the roles of the provinces and federal government under the *Constitution Acts* of 1867 and 1982.

53 *Reference Re: Assisted Human Reproduction Act*, 2008 QCCA 1167.

54 *Ibid*. See also Angela Cameron & Vanessa Gruben, "Quebec's Constitutional Challenge to the *Assisted Human Reproduction Act*: Overlooking Women's Reproductive Autonomy" in Stephanie Paterson, Francesca Scala, & Marlene Sokolon, eds, *Fertile Ground: Exploring Reproduction in Canada* (Montreal and Kingston: McGill-Queen's University Press, 2014) 125 at 129–30.

the decision and, in a deeply divided judgment issued in 2010, the Supreme Court of Canada found most of the impugned provisions to fall outside the legislative authority of Parliament on the basis that they sought to regulate "assisted human reproduction as a health service" and were therefore constitutionally invalid (*ultra vires*).[55] Among the few sections that were found to be constitutional was section 12. Chief Justice McLachlin, writing for four judges, concluded that the purpose of section 12 was "to ensure that credited expenses are confined to actual outlays, and do not cross the line into commercialized reproductive activities ... which is considered inappropriate reimbursement."[56] The chief justice reasoned that section 12 was rooted in the same concerns as the sections prohibiting the payment of surrogates and the purchase of gametes (sections 6 and 7), which the attorney general of Quebec conceded were rooted in a criminal law purpose.[57] Justice Cromwell agreed.[58] He concluded that section 12 "is a form of exemption from the strictness of the regime which [sections 6 and 7] impose and, to some extent, defines the scope of the prohibitions in those sections."[59] As such, it was a valid exercise of the federal criminal law power.[60]

In light of the Supreme Court decision, the Government of Canada took steps to amend the Act. A 2012 omnibus budget bill—one widely criticized for its heft and for overreaching the regular parameters of a budget bill—included provisions amending the *AHRA* and removing the impugned provisions.[61] Although the sections of the *AHRA* establishing the Assisted Human Reproduction Agency of Canada and calling for periodical parliamentary review of the Act as a whole survived constitutional scrutiny, the federal government set a timeline for the closure of the agency (see below) and repealed the requirement for parliamentary review of the Act.[62]

The closure of Assisted Human Reproduction Canada was an important loss. The Act—as passed in 2004—called for the establishment of

55 *Reference re AHRA*, above note 47.

56 *Ibid* at para 111.

57 *Ibid* at para 112.

58 *Ibid.*

59 *Ibid* at para 290.

60 *Ibid.*

61 "Omnibus Budget: Bill C-45 Is an Affront to Democracy," Opinion Editorial, *Toronto Star* (19 October 2012), online: www.thestar.com/opinion/editorials/2012/10/19/omnibus_budget_bill_c45_is_an_affront_to_democracy.html.

62 *Jobs, Growth and Long-Term Prosperity Act*, above note 48, s 713.

the oversight agency to "promote and protect the health and safety, and the human dignity and human rights, of Canadians" and "to foster the application of ethical principles."[63] The agency was to work in collaboration with the minister of health and Health Canada to ensure that the licensing and regulatory functions of the Act were in good order and that the ethical commitments of the Act were upheld.[64] It was slow to be established, and its was tenure short, beginning its operations in 2007 and ceasing in 2012 following the Supreme Court decision and the omnibus budget bill.[65] Its operations were controversial, and it was criticized for doing little with a lot of public funds, even though its capacity was limited, as it could do little without Health Canada's engaging in the regulatory processes that would allow many of the Act's provisions to come into force.[66] One of the agency's important activities, however, was stakeholder consultations on the reimbursement of expenditures under the *AHRA*, including the distribution of a relevant consultation document in 2007, although little came of this work.[67] Following the omnibus budget bill, the agency was shuttered in March 2013.[68]

2) An Expanding Market and a Lack of Political Will

From the royal commission's recommendations to discourage altruistic surrogacy, to the recommendation in *Building Families* to eliminate related prohibitions in the draft legislation, to the failure to develop regulations more than a decade after the Act's passage, the reimbursement of expenses to surrogates has been one of the most hotly contested of the *AHRA*'s provisions. The federal government failed to make regulations while the constitutional challenge wove its way to the Supreme Court and while Assisted Human Reproduction Canada was established and subsequently shut down. As a result, there was a lack of clarity about how the regulatory

63 *AHRA*, above note 4, s 22.

64 Rivard & Hunter, above note 12 at 182–84.

65 *Jobs, Growth and Long-Term Prosperity Act*, above note 48, s 713.

66 Françoise Baylis & Jocelyn Downie, "The Tale of Assisted Human Reproduction Canada: A Tragedy in Five Acts" (2013) 25:2 *Canadian Journal of Women and the Law* 183 at 183.

67 See the archived consultation, online: http://web.archive.org/web/20140806061625/http://www.consultations.hc-sc.gc.ca/public-consult/consultations/past-anterieures/consultation-eng.php?id=81.

68 Canada, Public Works and Government Services Canada, *Jobs Growth and Long-Term Prosperity: Economic Action Plan 2012* (Ottawa: Government of Canada, 2012) at 5.

provisions of the *AHRA*—particularly those pertaining to the reimbursement of expenditures—should or could be used.

Scholars and journalists working in this field report cases in which the law has been openly flouted. They chronicle the ways that surrogates have been paid in a grey market, "underground" and "under the table," and document ways that participants have avoiding outright or open contravention of the law by paying expenses through agencies, going abroad, or otherwise.[69] While scholars have argued that the reimbursement of expenditures cannot occur in the absence of regulations (as they are to occur "in accordance with regulations" that do not yet exist), Health Canada has indicated—without providing any policy statement—that surrogates can be reimbursed while waiting for regulations to come into effect.[70] Health Canada's website has indicated—at least since 2013—that "you can reimburse a donor or surrogate for actual expenses they have related to the donation or pregnancy."[71] However, if reimbursement is legally permissible only "in accordance with the regulations" and those regulations do not yet exist, it is simply poor legislative interpretation to understand any reimbursement as permitted.[72] Until section 12 regulations are promulgated, the grey market in surrogacy services remains outside of the *AHRA*.

While outright payment is prohibited, this is not to say it has not been occurring. The federal government, it seems, is refusing to consistently enforce the legislation as it is written. Numerous media reports have indicated that payment is an ongoing (if not frequent) practice and that the federal government has been reluctant to implement the Act when it has

69 See, for example, Motluk, "Anatomy," above note 5; Motluk, "Baby-Making," above note 9; Blackwell, "Illegal Purchase," above note 9.

70 Françoise Baylis, Jocelyn Downie, & Dave Snow, "Fake It Till You Make It: Policymaking and Assisted Human Reproduction in Canada" (2014) 36:6 *Journal of Obstetrics and Gynaecology Canada* 510 at 511; Françoise Baylis & Jocelyn Downie, "Wishing Doesn't Make It So" (17 December 2013), *Impact Ethics* (blog), online: https://impactethics.ca/2013/12/17/wishing-doesnt-make-it-so; Jocelyn Downie & Françoise Baylis, "Transnational Trade in Human Eggs: Law, Policy, and (In)Action in Canada" (2013) 41:1 *Journal of Law, Medicine and Ethics* 224 [Downie & Baylis, "Transnational Trade"].

71 Government of Canada, "Using Donors or Surrogates" (4 February 2013), online www.canada.ca/en/health-canada/services/egg-sperm-embryo-donation/using-donors-or-surrogates.html.

72 Downie & Baylis, "Transnational Trade," above note 70 at 227.

been aware of its contravention.[73] There was one case in which a surrogacy broker was investigated and charged for violating the Act's prohibitions on the payment of both ova donors and surrogates — she reimbursed "expenses" without opening envelopes that were, apparently, filled with receipts — as well as for receiving financial consideration for arranging surrogacy services.[74] The penalties imposed ($60,000 total), however, fell far short of the maximums under the Act and, according to Baylis and Downie, were "so low that others involved in similar activities might just consider fines a 'cost of doing business.'"[75] Several years later, "business is booming" for that same surrogacy agency. At the same time, the advent of a new federal government in 2015 has meant new interest in the development of regulations that will finally bring the *AHRA* into force.[76]

3) Recent Public Consultation by Health Canada Contemplating Law Reform

In September 2016, the Government of Canada released a notice of intent announcing that it intended to "strengthen and clarify the regulatory framework governing assisted human reproduction in Canada."[77] Health Canada asked Canadians for feedback on the pre-publication of the policy proposals, including potential regulations on the reimbursement of expenditures to surrogate, the administration and enforcement of the *AHRA*, and the role of

73 See, for example, Motluk, "Baby-Making," above note 9; Motluk, "Anatomy," above note 5; Blackwell, "Illegal Purchase," above note 9; Alison Motluk, "The Human Egg Trade: How Canada's Fertility Laws Are Failing Donors, Doctors, and Parents" *The Walrus* (12 April 2010), online: https://thewalrus.ca/the-human-egg-trade.

74 *R v Picard and Canadian Fertility Consulting Ltd* (Agreed Statement of Facts); Tom Blackwell, "'Business Has Boomed': Canadian Surrogacy Agent Facing 27 Charges Continues Her Controversial Work" *National Post* (17 March 2013), online: http://news.nationalpost.com/2013/03/17/business-has-boomed-canadian-surrogacy-agent-facing-27-charges-continues-her-controversial-work.

75 Baylis & Downie, "Wishing Doesn't Make It So," above note 70.

76 Alison Motluk, "After Pleading Guilty for Paying Surrogates, Business Is Booming for This Fertility Matchmaker" *Globe and Mail* (28 February 2016), online: www.theglobeandmail.com/life/health-and-fitness/health/business-is-booming-for-fertility-matchmaker-leia-swanberg/article28930242.

77 Government of Canada, News Release, "Government of Canada Plans to Introduce Regulations to Support the *Assisted Human Reproduction Act*" (30 September 2016), online: www.canada.ca/en/health-canada/news/2016/09/government-canada-plans-introduce-regulations-support-assisted-human-reproduction-act.html.

inspectors.[78] Notably, this notice of intent was filed roughly eighteen months after Health Canada contracted the Canadian Standards Association (CSA) to create a task force to develop an annex regarding the reimbursement of expenses for donors and surrogates. The timing raised important questions about the relevance of the CSA annex in the development of the regulations under the *AHRA*.[79]

Consultations on Health Canada's regulatory process continued in 2017, when it released a discussion document entitled "Toward a Strengthened *Assisted Human Reproduction Act*: A Consultation with Canadians on Key Policy Proposals."[80] The discussion document outlined the federal government's intended approach to the relevant regulations (i.e., sections 10, 12, and 45–58 of the *AHRA*), inviting feedback on eight specific questions.[81]

---

78 Government of Canada, Department of Health, "Notice to Interested Parties — Intent to Develop Regulations under the *Assisted Human Reproduction Act*" (2016) C Gaz I, Vol 150 (1 October 2016), online: www.gazette.gc.ca/rp-pr/p1/2016/2016-10-01/html/notice-avis-eng.html.

79 Note, prior to the announcement of the notice of intent, Health Canada asked the Canadian Standards Association (CSA) to develop an annex to its standards on Tissues for Assisted Reproduction (CSA-Z900.2.1-12). After an online (and relatively short) consultation process, the CSA published the annex in October 2016, three weeks after the Government of Canada's announcement requesting public feedback on its proposal (which directly mentioned the CSA annex). Health Canada's direction to the CSA raises important concerns about the possibility that the CSA annex — in its current form or otherwise revised — will be incorporated as a regulation under the *AHRA*. See McLeod, Chapter 4, this volume.

80 Government of Canada, Health Canada, "Toward a Strengthened *Assisted Human Reproduction Act*: A Consultation with Canadians on Key Policy Proposals" (Ottawa: Health Canada, 12 July 2017), online: www.canada.ca/en/health-canada/programs/consultation-assisted-human-reproduction/document.html [Health Canada, "Strengthened *AHRA*"].

81 *Ibid*. The discussion document included the following eight items to elicit feedback from "stakeholders" on specific issues:

1) Please explain any other circumstances that should be exempt, conditionally or unconditionally, from section 10 of the *AHR Act*.
2) Please explain, and support with scientific rationale, what level of regulatory oversight would be considered appropriate for fertility clinics that solely process directed donations. Should it differ from the processor registration framework proposed above?
3) Please explain if any of the establishment requirements listed above should not be applied equally for all persons engaged in regulated activities (processing, importing, and distributing) and why.

In February 2018, Health Canada released a summary of the public feedback ("What We Heard" Report) in response to the discussion document, incorporating the feedback of the fifty-seven individuals and groups that participated.[82] The "What We Heard" Report suggests that stakeholders want greater clarity around the categories of expenses that might be reimbursed to surrogates, the mechanisms for reimbursement, and the enforcement of any new reimbursement regulations.[83] Other concerns included the need for a complaints mechanism in the event of a disagreement over expenses, and more clarity on the economic parameters of an altruistic model.[84]

There have been some concerns about the process Health Canada has undertaken to develop policy proposals in this area. First, the consultation process has not facilitated the substantive participation of surrogates. Submissions on the pre-publication process were obtained from "health professionals, industry members, fertility lawyers . . . academics, researchers" and others with the professional and organizational capacity to provide written feedback on a relatively technical area of public policy.[85] And,

---

4) As part of the donor suitability assessment, should anonymous sperm and ova donors be excluded based on their upper age? If so, what is a reasonable upper age limit beyond which sperm and ova donations should no longer be accepted? (Note: Section 9 of the *AHR Act* already prohibits obtaining sperm or ovum from a donor under 18 years of age, except in narrowly prescribed circumstances.)
5) Please explain whether or not Health Canada should provide additional criteria on genetic disease screening, including a list of serious genetic diseases that a donor of sperm or ova should be screening for and why.
6) Please list any additional infectious disease agents that should be tested for and explain the scientific interpretation for why they should be included.
7) Please explain whether or not cases of suspected transmission of a genetic disease from donor sperm or ova should be reported to Health Canada and why. What would be the expectation for Health Canada's role in assessing and taking action for such cases?
8) Please identify any other categories of expenditure that should be considered for reimbursement and explain why.

82 Health Canada, "What We Heard Report: A Summary of Feedback from the Consultation: Toward a Strengthened *Assisted Human Reproduction Act*" (Ottawa: Health Canada, 2018) [Health Canada, "What We Heard"].

83 See Petropanagos, Gruben, & Cameron, Chapter 5, this volume.

84 Health Canada, "What We Heard," above note 82 at 1.

85 Health Canada, "Strengthened *AHRA*," above note 80 at 3.

while the executive summary of the "What We Heard" Report suggests that "surrogates" participated in the consultation process,[86] the document itself states that the interests of surrogates were instead raised by "stakeholders advocating on behalf of surrogates."[87] Surrogates and their interests appear to be underrepresented in the consultation process in the same ways that occurred in the consultation processes leading up to the *AHRA*.

Second, the consultation process has drawn attention to issues that fall "outside of the scope" of the regulations under consideration.[88] The discussion document mentions calls to address a number of provisions outside of the regulatory process, including "the policy underpinning sections 6 and 7 of the Act, which prohibit payment for surrogacy" as well as the penalties for violating the law.[89] While the discussion document indicates that these concerns are not part of the "current regulatory project, they will be considered in the future when amendments to the AHR Act may be contemplated."[90]

The "What We Heard" Report takes issues considered to fall "outside of the scope" even further. It indicates that stakeholder submissions addressed the regulation of surrogacy consultants and the role of contracts in surrogacy arrangements, although these issues fall beyond the constitutional jurisdiction of the federal government. The report also identified cross-border surrogacy practices as a topic of concern for stakeholders.[91] Respondents pointed to the impact of reproductive tourism within Canada on the health care system and expressed concern that Canada's altruistic model might attract increasing numbers of intended parents from outside the country.[92]

Third, the notion of "reasonable compensation" is integrated into the "What We Heard" Report's discussion of reimbursing donors and surrogates (i.e., section 12), despite that issue's being beyond the scope of the policy proposals laid out in the September 2016 call for consultation.[93] While the report

86 Health Canada, "What We Heard," above note 82 at 1.

87 *Ibid* at 4.

88 *Ibid* at 7, see also Health Canada, "Strengthened *AHRA*," above note 80 at 9.

89 Health Canada, "Strengthened *AHRA*," *ibid* at 9.

90 *Ibid*.

91 A number of these concerns are addressed by Pamela M White in Chapter 2 of this volume.

92 See Busby & White, Chapter 7, this volume.

93 Health Canada, "What We Heard," above note 82 at 5. It is worth noting that, while the report does have a section specifically for feedback that would "[f]all outside the scope

goes to some lengths to characterize some of the other concerns raised by the submissions as being outside of the federal regulatory project, the notion of "reasonable compensation" was incorporated in several places without caveat. A "reasonable compensation" approach is presented as a replacement for the current altruistic model. Here, Health Canada notes that while "some stakeholders asserted that '. . . altruistic donation and surrogacy should continue to be the guiding principle . . .' behind the *AHRA*; 'many stakeholders advocated for a model that would allow for reasonable compensation.'"[94] The notion of "reasonable compensation" runs counter to the *AHRA* as it is currently constructed, yet it is mentioned throughout the report. While it is unclear if Health Canada is considering such a drastic change, it is noteworthy that these terms are used throughout the report without context, raising the spectre of future legislative reform.

These consultations on surrogacy-related provisions of the *AHRA* by Health Canada seem to be a harbinger of change, although it is difficult, given the lack of transparency up to this point, to predict what kinds of changes (if any) will be made. It seems clear that regulations under section 12 (providing a list of allowable receipted expenses) will be forthcoming. However, given the ongoing discussion in the consultation process of issues outside the scope of the regulatory process, medical and legal practitioners, scholars, and advocates are speculating on whether more drastic changes to the *AHRA* are in the air, including the possibility of reconsidering the restrictions on commercial surrogacy.

C. SURROGACY AND THE PROVINCES/TERRITORIES: CONTRACT LAW AND FAMILY LAW

Shifts in law and policy on this issue at the federal level have been the focus of much scholarly and activist attention, in large part because the *AHRA* plays such an important role in governing the core principles of surrogacy: maintaining altruism, setting penalties, and contemplating enforcement. The constitutional division of powers between the federal and provincial/territorial governments means that governance of all aspects of surrogacy

of the current regulatory project" (at 7) the argument by stakeholders for "reasonable compensation" did not appear in this section; rather it was treated as within the scope of comments related to section 12 "reimbursement of donors and surrogates."

94 *Ibid.*

must, by necessity, stretch across these Canadian jurisdictions. Perhaps most notable is the role of provincial/territorial laws, in particular family and contract law. Each province/territory has its own laws treating surrogacy contracts and parentage, and in some cases the legal approaches differ greatly, which in turn has a significant impact on one's decisions about family building.

The legal treatment of private agreements between women acting as surrogates and intended parents has been uneven in Canada. As the *AHRA* prohibits payment for surrogacy services, any monetary provisions in surrogacy contracts are unenforceable; however, other aspects of the relationship between surrogates and intended parents are frequently the subject of such contracts.[95] While the enforceability of some types of provisions remains unclear (e.g., what kinds of food the surrogate can eat during pregnancy), many provinces have passed legislation to make more clear the role of contracts in parentage disputes. In Ontario, for example, recent legislative changes dictate that a surrogacy agreement, signed before the birth of the child, can be used as evidence of parental intent in the event of a dispute.[96] In stark contrast, the Quebec *Civil Code* declares all surrogacy contracts to be completely unenforceable.[97]

In many provinces, family law has been reformed in recent years to regulate parentage in altruistic surrogacy arrangements, as permitted by the *AHRA*. Ontario[98] and British Columbia[99] have legislative schemes that allow intended parents to appear on birth registrations as parents, once certain conditions are met, and time periods elapsed, without a court appearance or an adoption order. Nova Scotia,[100] Newfoundland and Labrador,[101] Prince Edward Island,[102] Alberta,[103] Quebec,[104] Manitoba,[105] Saskatchewan,[106] and

95 Carsley, above note 12.
96 *All Families Are Equal Act*, SO 2016, c 23, s 10(2).
97 CQLR c CCQ-1991, art 541 [CCQ].
98 *Children's Law Reform Act*, RSO 1990, c C.12.
99 *Family Law Act*, SBC 2011, c 25, s 29.
100 *Vital Statistics Act*, RSNS 1989, c 494.
101 *Children's Law Act*, RSNL 1990, c C-13.
102 *Child Status Act*, RSPEI 1988, c C-6.
103 *Family Law Act*, SA 2003, c F-4.5, s 8.2.
104 CCQ, above note 97.
105 *Vital Statistics Act*, CCSM c V60, ss 3(2) and 3(6).
106 *Vital Statistics Act*, SS 2009, c V-7.21; *The Children's Law Act*, SS 1997, c C-8.2.

New Brunswick, however, do not facilitate parentage through a streamlined birth-registration process, and require instead a formal adoption proceeding or a court order to transfer parentage from the surrogate mother to the intended parents. These schemes vary in complexity and required waiting times. Importantly, same-sex couples who are intended parents are treated equally under provincial/territorial parentage laws around surrogacy and adoption. These laws are a response to decades of activism by same-sex couples and multi-parent families.[107]

The differences in family law across provinces and territories produce different legal outcomes for families built using surrogacy across jurisdictions. In some cases, such as Ontario and British Columbia, the law allows for fast and inexpensive recognition of the intended parents as legal parents following the birth of a child to a surrogate, while protecting the legal and social interests of the surrogate in relation to the child.[108] In other jurisdictions, such as Quebec, intended parents must spend considerable time and money, and submit their families to judicial scrutiny, in order to adopt the child.[109] The period of time awaiting an adoption order places stress and strain on both the intended parents and the surrogate, as legal rights and responsibilities during this time are unclear. Further, Ontario and British Columbia allow for more than two legal parents, while other jurisdictions, such as Nova Scotia, restrict parentage to two people.[110] While the *AHRA* may soon facilitate consistent treatment of some aspects of surrogacy, such as receipted expenses, there is no similar consistency in family

107 See, for example, Angela Cameron, "A Chip off the Old (Ice) Block? Women-Led Families, Sperm Donors and Family Law" in Jennifer Kilty, ed, *Within the Confines: Women and the Law in Canada* (Toronto: Women's Press, 2014); Rachel Epstein, ed, *Who's Your Daddy? And Other Writings on Queer Parenting* (Toronto: Sumac Press, 2009); Fiona Kelly, *Transforming Law's Family: The Legal Recognition of Planned Lesbian Motherhood* (Vancouver: UBC Press, 2012); Vanessa Gruben, Angela Cameron, & Fiona Kelly, "De-anonymising Sperm Donation: Some Doubts and Directions" (2010) 26:1 *Canadian Journal of Family Law* 95; Karen Busby, "Of Surrogate Mother Born: Parentage Determinations in Canada and Elsewhere" (2013) 25:2 *Canadian Journal of Women and the Law* 284.

108 BC *Family Law Act*, above note 99, s 29 and *All Families Are Equal Act*, above note 96, s 10.

109 Stefanie Carsley, "Reconceiving Quebec's Laws on Surrogacy" (2018) 96 *Canadian Bar Review* 121.

110 BC *Family Law Act*, above note 99, *Children's Law Reform Act*, above note 98, ss 9 & 10, NS *Vital Statistics Act*, above note 100.

law across the provinces. Each province and territory retains its individual constitutional jurisdiction to make family law, subject to the *Charter*, making coordination a matter of political pressure and will.

D. CRITICAL INTERVENTIONS

The background provided thus far in this introduction is only a small part of the history of surrogacy (and its governance) in Canada. Surrogacy is an understudied field of public policy and law, governed through the messy and complex interactions of professional/medical associations, the federal government, provinces, and independent, often for-profit clinics that experience relatively little oversight. The much-debated and carefully negotiated *Assisted Human Reproduction Act* was never really implemented, and the ongoing lack of well-funded, systematic data collection on how surrogacy occurs means that evidence-based law- and policy-making is a distant goal. The contributions to this volume work to address these concerns and shine a light on persistent gaps in the literature.

1) The Ongoing Struggle to Address Women's Autonomy

Feminist scholars continue to be concerned with the potential exploitation of women who act as surrogates, the commodification of their bodies, and the status of the children that result from surrogacy arrangements. In Chapter 1, Christine Overall, while accepting that the practice of surrogacy may be here to stay, considers the troubling moral issues that arise with respect to women who act as surrogates and the resulting children. She argues that, in any surrogacy arrangement, paid or unpaid, the resulting baby belongs to the woman who gestated him rather than to the individual(s) who commission the pregnancy. As a result, Overall argues that the woman who gives birth is the mother—she is responsible for the baby and has the authority to make decisions about the baby at the time of birth and at least shortly thereafter. She raises four arguments in defence of her claim: the baby is the outcome of the pregnant woman's labour; the child's identity is founded upon his or her connection to the woman who gestated him; in other cases of gestation and delivery, the birthing woman is the person who has responsibility for and authority over the baby; and in almost every other case (in the West) where an infant is born and does not stay with the person who gestated him or her, the transfer of authority and responsibility is through a formal process, from the birthing woman to the new parent(s). Overall also raises potential counter-arguments to her claim and offers several replies. Based on this analysis, she makes several recommendations regarding the formation of social policy arising from recognizing the gestating woman as the mother of the infant.

Importantly, in the Afterword to this volume, Maria De Koninck presents a commentary on surrogacy that is a revised version of a submission made to Health Canada in September 2017 as part of the consultation process on the development of regulations under the *AHRA*. This commentary builds on a previous submission De Koninck wrote with the late Abby Lippman in response to the Government of Canada's announcement regarding the development of regulations under the *AHRA*. Here, in recognition of Lippman's contributions to the debates on surrogacy, De Koninck expresses that both she and Lippman oppose the legitimation of surrogacy and consider it to be contrary to human dignity, arguing that neither the mother nor the child can be the objects of a contract. The commentary addresses three areas: the infringement on Canadian values by the proposed orientation of the government's regulations; the continued "pathologization" of the desire to have children; and the danger of redefining social practices—in this case, surrogacy—in terms of commercial exchange. De Koninck concludes that regulating surrogacy legitimates it and that, ultimately, market forces and competition will erode efforts to protect the rights of women and children. She therefore calls for a ban on surrogacy in Canada.

2) A Troubling Lack of Research

Several authors in this volume lament the lack of empirical research on surrogacy and underscore the need for this type of research in developing effective and responsive law and policy in Canada. As noted above, we know very little about the lived experiences of women who act as surrogates, the intended parents, and the children conceived as a result of surrogacy arrangements. Pamela M White, in Chapter 2, spells out what we don't know about surrogacy practices and outcomes in Canada and explores why these gaps exist. She identifies a number of cultural, historical, political, legal, and regulatory factors that have resulted in a shortage in data about assisted reproduction and surrogacy in Canada. One significant shortcoming is the focus on quantitative, rather than qualitative, research, and she notes that the latter would provide important insights into the lived experiences of surrogates, intended parents, and resulting children. White also identifies a number of gaps in the quantitative data, many of which arise because the intended parent, rather than the surrogate, is erroneously categorized as the "patient" for registry purposes. White concludes that a number of changes are needed to ensure there is a comprehensive and accurate understanding of surrogacy practices and outcomes in Canada.

In Chapter 3, Kévin Lavoie and Isabel Côté respond to this call for more empirical data and present their findings from a series of interviews in Quebec. Their chapter describes a series of interviews with people in Quebec who engaged in surrogacy as a form of family building, including surrogates as well as intended parents (focusing on gay fathers, and heterosexual mothers). The authors identify four principal themes running through these interviews: the negotiation and formalization of surrogacy agreements; medical considerations; financial considerations; and the establishment of filiation or parentage. Based on these interviews, they conclude that "legal vagueness"—namely, the absence of a coherent and reliable legal framework in the province—is a critical factor that exacerbates the vulnerability of parties involved in surrogacy arrangements. They call on both the federal and provincial governments to embark on a thorough reform of surrogacy practice in Quebec and Canada.

3) Complex Governance

At the time of writing (2018), we are at a critical moment in terms of the governance of assisted reproduction in Canada. This is the first time in a decade that Health Canada has taken steps to introduce regulations under the *AHRA*, and there are important questions about the process for promulgating such regulations. Mark C McLeod, in Chapter 4, addresses the possible use of incorporation by reference to promulgate the regulations regarding eligible reimbursable expenses under the *AHRA*. This possibility has arisen as a result of the task force of the Canadian Standards Association (CSA), a third-party organization, which drafted an annex, "Reimbursement of Expenses for Donors and Surrogates," at the request of Health Canada in 2015. While the *AHRA* permits regulation making to be delegated to bodies such as the CSA, McLeod concludes that such an approach is inappropriate in this context and falls short of what Canadians deserve. He raises several concerns in support of this conclusion, including that such an approach reduces transparency in the policy-making process, may result in ineffectual policy, creates barriers to public participation during the development of the regulations, and creates barriers to public accessibility to the law. These concerns raise questions about whether regulations arrived at through such a process will be reasoned and democratically responsive.

There are also important questions about whether the current reimbursement model established under section 12 of the *AHRA* is the most effective to ensure that women who act as surrogates are appropriately reimbursed. In Chapter 5, Angel Petropanagos, Vanessa Gruben, and Angela Cameron propose an alternative reimbursement model that is intended to address a number of practical, ethical, and legal concerns about the receipted-expense model established under section 12. Their proposed flat-rate reimbursement model would capture three categories of surrogacy-related expenses. First, a flat fee, likely paid monthly, would be provided to a woman who acts as a surrogate in order to cover base expenses that are expected to be incurred by all women who act as a surrogate (e.g., vitamins, medications, travel and accommodation, dependent care). Second, potential surrogates would be provided with a mandatory, flat-rate, one-time reimbursement payment for legal and counselling fees that would be provided once the woman and the intended parent(s) were considering a surrogacy arrangement together. Finally, this model would provide a mechanism for claiming exceptional expenses that may arise as a result of the pregnancy. These payments would be made on a case-by-case basis and might arise from a long period of bed rest because of a high-risk pregnancy or from complications after pregnancy.

Many have responded to Health Canada's request for input on the regulations under the *AHRA* by calling for more sweeping reforms to the regulation of assisted reproduction in Canada. Erin Nelson is among those who believe that the *AHRA* should be reformed. In Chapter 6, she urges us to consider a significant overhaul to the regulation of surrogacy in Canada, including decriminalizing commercial surrogacy. She argues that the current regulation of assisted reproduction cannot be justified, as it is neither effective nor necessary. Nelson takes the position that both altruistic and commercial forms of surrogacy should be permitted, but she advocates careful oversight to minimize the potential for harm and to promote the interests of children, surrogate mothers, and intended parents. Such oversight could be accomplished by an arm's-length oversight body that reviews and monitors surrogacy agreements and/or the provision of services by surrogacy consultants or agencies.

4) Issues of Internationalization

There is no doubt that transnational surrogacy, whether it be Canadians seeking surrogates abroad or foreign intended parents seeking surrogates in Canada, is a pressing issue that requires the attention of Canadian lawmakers. Karen Busby and Pamela M White, in Chapter 7, consider why Canada is emerging as a preferred jurisdiction for those seeking surrogates outside their home country. They identify a number of factors contributing to Canada's emergence as a surrogacy destination and conclude that the international demand for Canadian surrogates should give us cause for concern. Busby and White, after considering various arguments for restricting surrogacy arrangements to citizens or residents of Canada, ultimately recommend that Canadian law should prohibit non-residents from participating in surrogacy arrangements in this country. They also make several recommendations for research, such as better empirical research into surrogacy in Canada, and for law reform, including the possibility of permitting commercial surrogacy in Canada, which would have an important impact on international demand.

Katy Fulfer, in Chapter 8, argues that Canada has a moral and political responsibility to address the ethical challenges raised by transnational surrogacy and takes the position that self-sufficiency is an important mechanism for taking responsibility for this practice. She explains that "self-sufficiency" refers to meeting a community's needs for a medical product or service, usually with unpaid donations from community members rather than commercial payments or from services outside the community. Fulfer argues for a relational approach to self-sufficiency and for broadening the scope of collective responsibility to include responsibilities for global structural injustice. She takes the position that self-sufficiency provides a mechanism for Canada to take responsibility for its role in maintaining injustices in the area of transnational surrogacy. She notes that her advocacy of the principles of self-sufficiency is consistent with the principle of non-commercialization entrenched in the *AHRA*, although she acknowledges that her approach may result in tensions with the current receipted expense model in the Act.

Ultimately, this book offers a much-needed assessment of the status of surrogacy in Canada. Written at a time when the regulatory environment is in flux, contributions to this volume take up some of the most pressing issues of the moment as regards surrogacy—including commercial surrogacy, parental status, globalization, the need for empirical data, and cross-border surrogacy arrangements—from a critical perspective. While changes to the federal *AHRA* may provide solutions to some of the issues raised in these chapters, others (such as Canada's place in the global surrogacy market) will require both policy and legal responses from a number of levels of government as well as the private sector. We hope this volume will stimulate much-needed discussions and debates among law- and policy-makers, women who act as surrogates, intended parents, children conceived through surrogacy arrangements, health care professionals, scholars, lawyers, ethicists, and the Canadian public on the future regulation of surrogacy in Canada.

1

Whose Child Is This?

"SURROGACY," AUTHORITY, AND RESPONSIBILITY

Christine Overall[*]

A. INTRODUCTION: THE CASE OF MELISSA COOK

Melissa Cook is a California resident who took part in a formal "surrogacy" arrangement through Surrogacy International, Inc, a California-based "surrogacy" broker. On 17 August 2015, when she was forty-seven years old, three male embryos were implanted in her uterus. The eggs came from an anonymous "donor"; the sperm was from a fifty-year-old postal worker, CM, who was single and deaf and living with his elderly parents and had used Surrogacy International to obtain a "surrogate."[1] CM requested that multiple embryos be implanted.[2]

Cook never met CM and did not talk with him via telephone. During the pregnancy, they communicated first via email and then, by the end of November, through their respective lawyers. What followed is described in detail in *Cook*:

* I am grateful to Alana Cattapan and two anonymous reviewers for their helpful guidance and comments on an earlier draft of this chapter. I also thank Alana Cattapan for her work in providing additional references for this chapter.

1 I put "donor" in quotation marks to signal the fact that the woman who provided the ova was very likely paid.

2 *Cook v Harding*, 190 F Supp 3d 921 (CD Cal 2016) [*Cook*] (subsequent descriptions of the *Cook* case are from this decision, except where otherwise indicated).

> On September 16, 2015, C.M. emailed Cook and mentioned the possibility of her reducing the pregnancy, and asked her how much longer she would have to obtain a legal abortion. The next day, C.M. emailed the fertility clinic monitoring Cook's pregnancy, requesting that Cook's medical visits be "less often, because [he] gets a bill that costs [him] a lot of money." He also expressed his concern that he may not be able to afford triplets, or perhaps even twins. The clinic insisted that Cook's high-risk pregnancy required weekly visits. On September 18, 2015, C.M. emailed [Robert] Walmsley [his counsel] at Surrogacy International to reiterate his financial concerns about the cost of the medical visits. While he said that he did not want to reduce two of the pregnancies, his financial situation left him considering terminating all three pregnancies.[3]

Melissa Cook offered to care for the three babies for some months after their birth, to enable CM to improve his finances. Citing their surrogacy contract's "selective reduction" clause, CM responded by asking Cook to abort, via selective reduction, one of the three developing fetuses. Cook replied that the three fetuses were all healthy and refused to have an abortion. On 28 October 2015, CM informed Cook that he was thinking of seeking adoptive parents for one or more of the three babies. Cook responded that she would raise one of the babies herself. CM sent several more requests for selective termination, saying that her refusal to reduce was in breach of her contract and that she was liable for money damages under the terms of the agreement. Cook reiterated her refusal to abort and her willingness to raise one of the children. CM reiterated his intention to put one baby up for adoption.

On 9 February 2016, the California Children's Court granted CM's petition to terminate Cook's legal relationship with the babies and named CM as the sole parent. Three male babies were born via caesarean very prematurely on 22 February 2016. The babies remained in the Neonatal Intensive Care Unit at Panorama City Medical Center for seven weeks, and Cook was not allowed to see them or to be told anything about their condition.

Having serious doubts about CM's ability to care for three premature infants, Cook sought custody of one baby and a hearing to determine the best interests of the other two. These requests were refused, and CM was

3 *Ibid* at 928.

given custody and legal parenthood of all three.[4] In April 2016, the babies were released from intensive care and turned over to CM. Cook never saw her babies.[5]

My interest in the *Cook* case is not primarily in the legal decisions made about it but rather in the relationship of Cook to CM, and his interactions with her, along with the fact that the babies she gestated were taken away from her despite the doubts she voiced about CM's capacity to be their parent. The Melissa Cook case illustrates the serious moral problems that can arise in the practice of "surrogacy," particularly when the woman who gestates is not acknowledged as the mother of the baby. In general, I regard "surrogacy" arrangements as raising troubling moral issues, primarily with respect to the women who participate in them as "surrogates" and the babies who are created. However, despite my reservations about it, I recognize that the practice of "surrogacy" may be here to stay.[6] This chapter explores one area in which the practice may be improved.

I argue for the following central claim: in any "surrogacy" arrangement, whether formal or informal, paid or unpaid, the baby belongs to the woman[7] who gestated him[8] rather than to the individual(s) who "commission" the pregnancy. This does not, of course, mean that she owns him: no parent owns their child. Nor does it mean that she will or must necessarily raise him. Just as some other people who gestate one or more fetuses sometimes do not raise their offspring, but instead give up their child(ren) for adoption, so also saying that the woman who gestates in "surrogacy" is the infant's mother does not imply that she either will or should necessarily keep him and raise him. To say that she is the mother is simply to say that she *is responsible for him and has the authority to make decisions about him at*

4 *CM v MC*, 7 Cal App 5th 1188 (2017).

5 Brendan Pierson, "California Surrogate Loses Bid to Be Named Mother of Triplets" *Thomson Reuters* (8 June 2016), online: http://reut.rs/218jPml.

6 See Christine Overall, *Ethics and Human Reproduction: A Feminist Analysis* (Boston: Allen & Unwin, 1987); Christine Overall, *Human Reproduction: Principles, Practices, Policies* (Toronto: Oxford University Press, 1993); and Christine Overall, "Reproductive 'Surrogacy' and Parental Licensing" (2015) 29:5 *Bioethics* 353.

7 I recognize that a few gestators identify as men. But, for the sake of simplicity, I will refer to any person who gestates as a "woman," and to the parental status of the gestator as "mother."

8 I will use the masculine pronoun for the baby, simply to distinguish him from the pregnant woman.

his birth and at least shortly thereafter. In this sense, she is the baby's mother (not his "surrogate mother").

To defend this claim, I first explain my use of quotation marks with the words "surrogacy" and "surrogate." I next offer four arguments in defence of my claim. I present four potential counter-arguments to my claim and give my response to each of them. I then discuss what I take to be five important policy implications of my claim. Finally, I show how the adoption of my approach to "surrogacy" would have changed the outcome of the Melissa Cook case—for the better.

B. REASONS FOR USING "SURROGACY" AND "SURROGATE"

I use quotation marks to draw attention to the questionable presuppositions behind the terms "surrogate" and "surrogacy." The word "surrogate" means "substitute," "deputy," or "representative."[9] I believe, as some feminists argued years ago, the term "surrogate" undermines the gestating woman, her labour, her rights, and her relationship to the baby.[10] It implies, *a priori*, that the woman is not the child's mother and is only a stand-in; that the "real mother," if any, is elsewhere.

We should not assume that the woman who gestates is a substitute or stand-in. There are genuine questions as to who should be designated the parent of any children born of these arrangements, and the answers need to be arrived at by means of careful argument (which I attempt here), not settled *a priori* by virtue of terminology.

C. FOUR ARGUMENTS IN DEFENCE OF MY CLAIM

1) Continuity of Creation and Care by the Woman

My central claim is that, in "surrogacy" arrangements, the gestating woman is the mother of the baby. The baby belongs to her, in the sense that she is responsible for him and has the authority to make decisions about him.

9 *Collins Thesaurus*, *sub verbo* "surrogate," online: www.collinsdictionary.com/dictionary/english-thesaurus/surrogate.

10 See, for example, Phyllis Chesler, *Sacred Bond: The Legacy of Baby M* (New York: Vintage Press, 1988); Rita Arditti et al, *Test Tube Women* (London: Pandora Press, 1989) at xvii; Thelma McCormack, "Public Policies and Reproductive Technology: A Feminist Critique" (1988) 14:4 *Canadian Public Policy* 361 at 362.

My first argument in support of this claim is based on the fact that the baby is the outcome of the pregnant woman's labour. The pregnant woman—unlike anyone else—provides continuous and intimate creation of and the continuous and intimate care for the fetus/baby from the moment the embryo is implanted in her uterus until he is born.

This is *not* an argument about the "bonding" that allegedly occurs between a pregnant woman and her fetus, or between a newly delivered woman and her infant. Bonding may occur in some, or even many, pregnancies, but, even if so, it is irrelevant to my argument. This argument is not about psychological ties or the pregnant woman's feelings. The feelings of "surrogates," like those of other pregnant women, may vary greatly from one to another. Instead, the argument appeals to what I suggest are the material and social processes that actually occur during pregnancy.

During the course of gestation, the pregnant woman literally creates the physical body of the fetus. Whether or not the fetus is genetically related to her, her body engages in the physical labour that brings it into existence. As Tim Bayne and Avery Kolers put it, "First, the foetus is *physically contained* within its gestational mother. Second, the foetus is *physiologically integrated* with the gestational mother—she provides its nutrients and eliminates its waste . . . ."[11] Third, the foetus is *materially derived* from the mother's body.

However, gestation is not a passive, merely biological development. It is also an agentic, thoughtful process, involving the woman's active learning, self-care, and care for the fetus. For example, the pregnant woman often learns new information about pregnancy, fetal development, her own nutritional and exercise needs, appropriate health care, rest and sleep, environmental and workplace safety, and the process of labour and birth. In most pregnancies, the pregnant woman engages in creative thinking and activity about how much domestic, unpaid, or paid work to do; what domestic or leisure activities to engage in; whom to consult for pregnancy care; how to prepare for the birth; and where to give birth. The pregnant woman also makes deliberate choices about nutrition, sleep, medications (if any), exercise, medical care, and maternity clothes. The pregnant woman develops an awareness of the fetus in her body and actively responds to it. She learns to adjust to the constant changes, physical and psychological, generated by her pregnancy.

---

11 Tim Bayne & Avery Kolers, "Toward a Pluralist Account of Parenthood" (2003) 17:3 *Bioethics* 221 at 229.

Pregnancy may not be exactly like this in every single instance. In "surrogacy" arrangements, of course, the scope of the pregnant woman's choices may be circumscribed in particular ways by the terms of her contract. But *most* pregnant women's choices are not unlimited; they are constrained by their social, economic, religious, geographic, and familial environments. My point here is just that the pregnant woman is engaged in the real, active, autonomous work of fetal creation. This is certainly the case in "surrogacy" arrangements, where the woman is and must be especially deliberative about the gestation—even if and when her choices involve acquiescing in her doctor's, the commissioners', or the contract's requirements. Through her deliberate, and deliberative, choices, the "surrogate" brings the fetus into being and engages in the most intimate possible physical care of the fetus for nine months. No one else but the pregnant woman has anything like such a close connection with the fetus, and no one else but her provides the labour that actually creates the baby who will be born.

2) Continuity of Identity of the Fetus/Infant

The child's identity as the offspring of the woman who gestated is clear. His identity is founded upon his connection to the woman who gestated him. Even though the woman in a "surrogacy" case conceives and gestates with the purpose of handing over the infant to other persons, she has a nine-month connection to her baby both materially (via gestation) and intentionally (by virtue of choosing conception and continued pregnancy). The fetus, and the infant it will become, comes into being in her body, develops in her body, and is identifiable for its first nine months of existence as the creation of her body. The fetus is the fetus of the gestating woman, the baby is born of that woman, and his identity is constituted through his continuous relationship to her, not to anyone else.

3) The Widespread Practice of Treating the Birthing Woman as the Mother

In almost every other case (in the West) of gestation and delivery, we take the birthing woman (along with her partner, if any) to be the person who has responsibility for and authority over the baby. In other words, in every other situation in which a woman gives birth, we regard her as the mother of the baby. I cannot think of any cases where the pregnant woman's moral status as mother is denied at the birth of her baby—except, possibly, in cases of extreme youth or a demonstrated record of severe child abuse. Otherwise, the baby is deemed to belong to the woman who births him.

This is *not* an argument about the alleged "sacredness" of motherhood. To affirm this argument, one need not subscribe to any romantic and unsubstantiated notions about the spiritual aspects of motherhood, or about the alleged inviolability of the mother-child relationship. This argument is a simple one: it is an empirical observation about social practices governing the moral role of the birthing woman and her relationship to the infant she delivers. It is also, of course, a normative claim: that the woman who births an infant is best situated, by virtue of her ongoing relationship with the fetus that the infant previously was, to have responsibility for and authority over the baby.

In making this argument, I am not saying that the woman cannot transfer responsibility for the baby through the process of adoption. Of course she can. The point is that putting the child up for adoption is a decision that the woman is allowed to make. And not only is she allowed to make it—it is assumed that whether or not to keep the baby and raise him is no one else's decision to make.

Moreover, in making this claim, I am not denying that in extreme cases infants may be legitimately removed from their mother independent of her own will, if the woman is demonstrably abusive or incompetent. Certainly, caring societies need to reserve this right in order to ensure the safety of infants in extreme cases where the birthing woman either will not or cannot care for the infant, or where she is a demonstrated danger to children. I am simply saying that the justified default assumption in Western societies is that the baby belongs to the woman who births him, by which I mean that she has responsibility for and authority over the baby.

If the birthing woman has a partner (of any sex/gender), we often regard the partner as having similar responsibility for and authority over the baby. But that person's responsibility and authority are morally derived primarily from their relationship with the gestating woman.[12] During the pregnancy,

12 The partner's moral responsibility and authority are not necessarily always derived from merely providing a gamete. To see this, consider the case of sperm "donors," who—by virtue of the agreement that transfers authority over the use of their sperm to a woman—are understood to have no responsibility for or authority over children

the partner's relationship to the fetus is mediated through the pregnant woman; the woman's relationship to the fetus is direct, but the partner's relationship is indirect. The partner acquires responsibility and authority by virtue of the relationship with the pregnant woman, the partner's commitment to and support of the pregnant woman, and the partner's demonstration of commitment to and responsibility for the future infant.

What role, then, might the partner of the birthing woman in a "surrogacy" arrangement have in regard to the fate of the infant? Could he or she, by virtue of the relationship with the birthing woman, somehow veto the decision either to keep the child or to hand him over to the commissioners?[13] These questions are difficult. On the one hand, it is essential to preserve and protect the birthing woman's responsibility for and authority over the infant. On the other hand, the very real role that a partner can and often does play, both in supporting a woman's pregnancy and then in raising the subsequent child, must be recognized. Nonetheless, the situation of "surrogacy" is unique in certain ways and significantly different from ordinary cases where a pregnant woman's partner either helps to raise the child or shares in a decision to surrender the child for adoption. If "surrogacy" is institutionalized within a society, then, clearly, special arrangements will have to be made with respect to the "surrogate's" partner, if any. That is, it would be both ethically and pragmatically inappropriate for the partner to retain responsibility for and authority over the infant if the "surrogate" herself is willing to surrender the baby to the commissioners. So the contract would have to explicitly specify that the gestational mother's partner, if any, acquires no rights with respect to the infant (although it is, of course, desirable that the partner be supportive of the pregnancy and the "surrogacy" arrangement). At the same time, if a "surrogate" has a partner at the time she signs the contract, it would be desirable for the partner to signify his/her willingness to share in raising the child if the woman changes her mind and keeps the infant.

---

created via their sperm. That agreement acknowledges that the "donor" has no further relationship with the woman or her offspring, should she become pregnant. Consider, by contrast, the female partners of gestational mothers. I suggest that they *do* acquire responsibility for and authority over their partner's offspring, even though they do not provide a gamete from which the offspring is created, by virtue of their relationship to the gestational mother and their mediated relationship to the fetus.

13 I am grateful to María J Pietrini for raising these questions.

4) The Role of the Birthing Woman in Transferring Authority for Her Baby

In almost every other case (in the West) where an infant is born and does not stay with the person who gestated him, the transfer of authority and responsibility is through a formal process, from the birthing woman to the new parents.[14] The woman who gestates—along with her partner, if any—cannot just give the baby away to anyone she chooses. Although the responsibility and authority are the birthing woman's to assert and to transfer, the persons to whom they are formally transferred must *qualify* to become the infant's parents.[15] Those who are going to receive the baby are formally evaluated for fitness to parent and are approved to care for the infant. In other words, an official adoption process, in which the prospective parents' qualifications and minimum competency are assessed, is taken to be an essential prerequisite to handing over the infant from the woman who gestated him to other persons.[16]

Even in cases where the child is adopted by a relative, the transfer of the child is rightly subject to legal oversight. For example, in British Columbia, the legal requirements for adoption by a relative or step-parent are governed by the provincial *Adoption Act*, and potential adopters must apply to the provincial court, which will evaluate the child's best interests.[17]

---

14 See, for example, United Nations, Department of Economic and Social Affairs, Population Division, *Child Adoption: Trends and Policies* (New York: United Nations Publications, 2009) at 29, online: www.un.org/esa/population/publications/adoption2010/child_adoption.pdf.

15 See Carolyn McLeod & Andrew Botterell, "'Not for the Faint of Heart': Assessing the Status Quo on Pregnancy and Parental Licensing" in Françoise Baylis & Carolyn McLeod, eds, *Family-Making: Contemporary Ethical Challenges* (New York: Oxford University Press, 2014).

16 This is a departure from the much less formal arrangements that occurred in the past (and still occur today). For example, when her mother died a few weeks after giving birth in 1901, my maternal grandmother Hazel Bayes was "taken" (to use her own word) by her aunt, with the informal approval of her father. The aunt, who was childless and unmarried before "taking" Hazel, seems to have been a good parent. But there was no legal oversight of the process by which Hazel was transferred from her father to her aunt. Such unregulated transfers were, and are, potentially risky for children.

17 Government of British Columbia, "Adoption by a Relative or Step Parent," online: www2.gov.bc.ca/gov/content/life-events/births-adoptions/adoptions. Mary L Shanley describes a situation in the United States that is an exception to the general rule of transfer of the infant via formal adoption processes. In this case, the woman is

In light of my defence of the birthing woman's authority and responsibility, one might think that I should argue that she herself should have the right to choose who the best parents of her future child will be and who is entitled to rear the child. For, it might be argued, if I support the birthing mother's moral position vis-à-vis her baby, I should also assume that, in entering into a "surrogacy" arrangement, the woman will fully take into consideration the future child's welfare and choose the commissioners on that basis.

But, even though the gestational mother has authority over and responsibility for her child at birth, there are several reasons for not assigning her the sole right to choose the infant's future parents if she chooses not to rear him. First, in "surrogacy" arrangements, the gestating woman does not necessarily have full information about the commissioners, and in particular about their stability, integrity, and capacity to care for the future infant and child he will become. She is even less likely to be able to assess the characteristics of a range of potential parents and to choose among them. In other words, she lacks an adequate epistemic basis for assessing prospective commissioners.

Second, her motives in undertaking the pregnancy are unlikely to be entirely disinterested and unbiased. She is not becoming pregnant solely out of concern for the well-being of the future baby, who does not even exist at the point when she signs the contract. (In fact, it probably does not even make sense to say that she gets pregnant for the sake of the interests of her future child.) And while she may be inspired to help other persons to have a child, in many cases she is undertaking the arrangement at least partly in order to earn money.[18] Given that commercial "surrogacy" arrangements are fundamentally *financial* transactions,[19] an assessment process by which

estranged from the genetic father of the baby, and he nonetheless applies for custody of the baby whom she seeks to give up for adoption. I would argue that, in such a case, if the estranged genetic father is simply given the baby, without (at least) his prior demonstration of his commitment to the pregnancy and the infant and without evaluation of his parental capacities, the well-being and rights of the infant are unjustifiably disregarded. See Mary L Shanley, "Fathers' Rights, Mothers' Wrongs? Reflections on Unwed Fathers' Rights and Sex Equality" (1995) 10:1 *Hypatia* 74 at 75.

18 See, for example, France Winddance Twine, *Outsourcing the Womb: Race, Class and Gestational Surrogacy in a Global Market* (New York: Routledge, 2011).

19 Debora L Spar, "For Love and Money: The Political Economy of Commercial Surrogacy" (2005) 12:2 *Review of International Political Economy* 287 at 290. See also Debora L Spar, *The Baby Business* (Boston: Harvard Business School Press, 2007).

new prospective parents are evaluated is essential for the protection of the interests of the infant. Indeed, if we were to say simply that the gestational mother can choose the future parents of her baby with no other oversight, this provision could lead to a practice in which women—especially those who are impoverished or vulnerable in other ways—are incentivized by tempting financial offers to sell their babies to whoever will pay them the best.

Societies rightly endorse the adoption process as a legitimate requirement, because it recognizes and defends the rights and interests of the infant. Unlike the birth mother, prospective adoptive parents lack the direct gestational relationship to him that the woman had during her pregnancy. Nor are they likely to have the kind of intimate, supportive, committed relationship with the pregnant woman that her partner has. Hence, the prospective parents do not have the moral status possessed by the birth mother and her partner. In order to acquire that status, they must be assessed to ascertain that they have at least minimal capacities to raise the infant, who is a stranger to them. Merely wanting to raise a child is not considered a sufficient qualification for being given someone else's baby.

In making this argument, I do not assume that the vetting process for potential adoptive parents is perfect, that it is always fairly applied, or that it cannot be improved. Like any social process, adoption procedures can certainly be enhanced, to ensure that they focus on and evaluate characteristics that identify competent parents.[20] In any adoption arrangement, the gestational mother's child-rearing values should be taken into account, because, as I have argued, she is the person who knows the baby best at birth. Nonetheless, the gestational mother's views, by themselves, should not be determinative. An independent screening process for prospective parents is both morally and practically essential, in all cases—including "surrogacy"—in which an infant is transferred away from the woman who birthed him.

D. FOUR COUNTER-ARGUMENTS AND MY RESPONSES

1) Some "Surrogates" Do Not Regard Themselves as Mothers

Counter-argument: *Some, perhaps most, "surrogates" do not regard themselves as mothers, and do not wish to be called the mother of the baby whom they gestate. Some "surrogates" may choose to regard themselves as incubators, hot*

20 See McLeod & Botterell, above note 15.

houses, inns, or ovens.[21] *To them, the commissioning woman is the mother of the baby, while they (the "surrogates") are merely* pro tem *caregivers, nannies, or baby-sitters.*[22]

Response: "Surrogates" are, of course, free to take any view of themselves and their role that they choose. Like Barbara Katz Rothman, I would be curious to know how and why they come to have these self-perceptions, especially since some such self-perceptions seem to underestimate their own importance and the value of their own labour.[23] But my claim is not related to how "surrogates" feel about themselves—it is not about their self-perceptions. Regardless of their views of themselves, in my *technical* sense of the term, they are mothers. That is, regardless of their self-perception, they play an important moral role vis-à-vis the baby, one of responsibility for and authority over the infant, when they give birth to him—even if they eventually hand over the baby to the commissioners, even if they do not raise the child, and even if they never see the child again. To say that they are mothers in this sense is entirely consistent with their participation, in good faith, in the "surrogacy" arrangement, with the intention of transferring the infant to the commissioners.

2) The Role of the Contract

Counter-argument: *The contract (along with the money paid) gives the commissioners, not the birthing woman, the responsibility for and authority over the baby.*

Response: There is something deeply morally questionable about treating the contract and payment as sufficient, in themselves, for the commissioners to acquire responsibility for and authority over the baby born of a "surrogacy" arrangement. Handing over the baby just because there was a

21 I am grateful to Elly Teman for drawing this objection to my attention. The women who refer to themselves as incubators, hot houses, inns, or ovens seem to regard this language as both an accurate and a positive way of conceptualizing their role. Elly Teman, *Birthing a Mother: The Surrogate Body and the Pregnant Self* (Berkeley: University of California Press, 2010) at 36.

22 *Ibid* at 22, 57, and 78.

23 Barbara Katz Rothman, "Review of *Birthing a Mother: The Surrogate Body and the Pregnant Self*" (2012) 34:3 *Sociology of Health and Illness* 475 at 475–76.

contract and the commissioners paid looks suspiciously like baby selling,[24] an arrangement in which the rights and interests of the infant play no part.

Some argue that such an arrangement can't be baby selling, because human beings can't (legally) be sold.[25] But that argument begs the question, for such an arrangement could very well be an *illegal* form of selling human beings. Others argue that the infant is, in effect, manumitted after the sale and then is treated well.[26] This latter fact, if it is a fact, does not explain why selling infant human beings is acceptable in the first place. After all, if selling newborns is morally permissible, why not also sell older children or teenagers? The burden of defence must be on those who claim that "surrogacy" contracts and the attendant exchange of money do not constitute baby selling, and also on those who say that, if the arrangement *is* baby selling, there is nothing wrong with it.

Some argue that the "surrogacy" arrangement is a way of buying not a baby, but parental entitlement (rights), which enables the commissioners to acquire a parental relationship with a baby and exercise responsibility for and authority over him.[27] But, even if this interpretation of the function of the contract and the money paid is correct, the rights and interests of the infant are still being treated as if they are irrelevant to the arrangement. The rights to the baby are transferred only because doing so suits the commissioners and the gestational mother. Only their well-being and interests are considered. Such an approach, in which the most vulnerable person involved is not protected, is surely unjustified. And it is also, surely, unjust to the child himself. For this reason, it is not morally justified to claim that the contract and the money paid give the commissioners responsibility for and authority over the infant.

These objections apply even in cases where there is no fee paid, but just the expenses of the gestating woman are reimbursed. For in such cases there is still the transfer of an infant with no particular attention to and protection of the infant's rights and well-being.

---

24 See, for example, Nancy Machinton, "Surrogate Motherhood: Boon or Baby-Selling: The Unresolved Questions" (1987) 71:1 *Marquette Law Review* 115; Richard J Arneson, "Commodification and Commerical Surrogacy" (1992) 21:2 *Philosophy & Public Affairs* 132.

25 Avi Katz, "Surrogate Motherhood and the Baby-Selling Laws" (1986) 20:1 *Columbia Journal of Law and Social Problems* 1. See also Spar, *The Baby Business*, above note 19.

26 See R Jo Kornegay, "Is Commercial Surrogacy Baby-Selling?" (1990) 7:1 *Journal of Applied Philosophy* 45.

27 See, for example, Jason KM Hanna, "Revisiting Child-Based Objections to Commercial Surrogacy" (2010) 24:7 *Bioethics* 341.

3) The Role of the Genetic Connection

Counter-argument: *The genetic connection gives the commissioners, not the birthing woman, the responsibility for and authority over the baby.*

Response:[28] The most immediate problem with this geneticist counter-argument is that it has implications that are likely to be highly undesirable and even self-defeating for those who wish to enforce "surrogacy" contracts and facilitate the handover of infants to commissioners. For notice that, in the case of "traditional 'surrogacy,'" the geneticist claim would make the male commissioner who supplies sperm equal to the "surrogate," since she provides just as much genetic material as he does. This equality would also prevail if a donor ovum was used; then, the male commissioner who supplies sperm would have no more than a half-entitlement to the infant, along with the ovum provider, who would have the other half-entitlement. Thus, if the geneticist counter-argument is applied consistently, it gives rights either to the gestating woman or to the gamete donor; it does not give parental entitlements *exclusively* to the commissioners. For that reason, the objection seems at least unwise, and probably also inconsistent with the views of those who seek to defend the sole entitlement of the commissioners. In most cases, the geneticist approach would fail to give responsibility for and authority over the infant exclusively to the commissioners.

But let's assume, for the sake of thoroughly assessing this counter-argument, that we are dealing with a situation where the commissioners provide both gametes. The geneticist counter-argument seems to resolve the question of parenthood in this case entirely in favour of the commissioners. Yet before accepting this outcome, it is necessary to consider the strength of geneticism by analyzing the assumption that the genetic connection gives anyone the responsibility for and authority over a baby. Following Avery Kolers and Tim Bayne, I distinguish between two different interpretations of this assumption: 1) it is a claim about the *material constitution* of the baby; or 2) it is a claim about the *genetic structure* of the baby.[29]

28 I also respond to this objection in Overall, "Reproductive 'Surrogacy' and Parental Licensing," above note 6.

29 See Avery Kolers & Tim Bayne, "'Are You My Mommy?' On the Genetic Basis of Parenthood" (2001) 18:3 *Journal of Applied Philosophy* 273.

First, if the idea that the genetic connection gives the commissioners the entitlement to the baby is a claim about the *material constitution* of the baby, then the response is that a baby is simply not equivalent or reducible to the gametes from which he grew:

> A new object comes into being with the creation of a zygote, and claims over its ingredients are not necessarily claims over it . . . . [Moreover] the extent to which the genetic parents' gametes compose even a newborn infant is already minuscule. The genetic material is a negligible part of the *material* constitution of the child or even the foetus.[30]

In fact, an argument for parental entitlement based on the material constitution of the infant wholly favours the gestating woman, who, through her nine months' work of gestation, has created the infant as he exists at birth.

Second, if the idea that the genetic connection gives the commissioners the entitlement to the baby is a claim about the *genetic structure* of the baby, then the problem is that a human being's genetic structure is a permanent fact about that human being. To make it the basis for imputing authority over and responsibility for the baby to the supplier(s) of gametes would imply that a gamete supplier continues to have authority over and responsibility for his or her genetically related child for all the child's life, and such a claim is incompatible with the child's growing authority over and responsibility for himself, as he develops. In addition, this interpretation of the geneticist claim possesses a very awkward implication. An identical twin possesses a genetic structure identical to that of his or her twin, but neither one has authority over or responsibility for the other.[31] So the claim is refuted: Genetic connections do not give the commissioners authority over and responsibility for the baby created through "surrogacy."[32]

30 *Ibid* at 276.

31 *Ibid* at 276 & 277. For similar reasons, it also does not work to argue that, since one owns one's genetic information, and "since this genetic information partly structures one's genetic children, one has . . . rights" over these children.

32 In drawing this conclusion, I am not saying that genetic connections have or should have no importance whatsoever within families. What I am saying is that a genetic connection of commissioners with an infant is, by itself, insufficient to nullify the essential material and moral role of the woman who gestates the baby.

4) The Role of the Commissioners' Intentional Connection

Counter-argument: *The commissioners of the pregnancy, not the birthing woman, have the responsibility for and authority over the baby by virtue of their intentional connection to him: they initiated the pregnancy. And, in some cases, they may also have remained socially connected to the pregnant woman during the pregnancy.*

Response: Contracting with (and paying) a woman to gestate is not primarily a relationship with her baby; it is, primarily, a *commercial* relationship with the woman. Moreover, any intentional relationship the commissioners may have with the fetus/baby is necessarily mediated by and through the pregnant woman. Their relationship with the woman—such as it is—is much less morally significant than the relationship the pregnant woman has with the fetus/baby. Unlike the mother, the commissioners have neither continuity of connection with respect to the infant nor continuity of care for him. Therefore, even if the commissioners have sincerely tried to stay in touch with the gestating woman, their connection to her cannot morally trump her relationship to the infant whom she gestates and delivers and her moral status with respect to him.

E. POLICY RECOMMENDATIONS

Based on the four arguments I have offered, and in light of the failure of counter-arguments, I conclude that, in any "surrogacy" arrangement, whether formal or informal, paid or unpaid, the baby belongs to the woman who gestated him rather than to the individual(s) who "commission" the pregnancy. To say that she is the mother is simply to say that she *is responsible for him and has the authority to make decisions about him.* I shall now suggest five recommendations for the formation of social policy with respect to "surrogacy" that arise from recognizing the gestating woman as the mother of the infant. The presumed social context for these recommendations is a legal, publicly regulated system of surrogacy (and not one conducted as a private business) within the context of Canada only—that is, a context where the gestating woman and the commissioners are citizens or permanent residents who all live, work, and receive medical care in Canada.

1) The commissioners of the "surrogacy" arrangement should not be granted automatic authority over or responsibility for the infant, whether by virtue of the "surrogacy" contract, by virtue of providing one or both gametes, or by virtue of paying the pregnant woman. There should be no automatic "right to a baby" gestated by another woman.

2) Since the baby is the gestating woman's responsibility, and she has authority over him, he should not simply be transferred to the commissioners without a formal adoption procedure. Before the baby is handed over, there should be an appropriate evaluation of the commissioners to determine whether or not they are at least minimally qualified to be adoptive parents. Introducing this evaluation would properly recognize the importance of the infant's rights and interests. Probably the assessment should take place even before the pregnancy is initiated. "Surrogacy" would thereby become a type of adoption—preconception adoption.[33] Minimum qualifications could include having no record of abuse or violence, having minimally adequate resources to financially support the child, and other characteristics as required in the best practices that govern adoption. Ability to pay as required by the "surrogacy" contract is not, by itself, a reflection of fitness to parent. Likewise, supplying gametes is not a reflection of fitness to parent.

   It might be objected that, since people who conceive conventionally do not have to be assessed to determine their fitness to parent, those who resort to "surrogacy" should not have to go through an adoption vetting process. My response is that formal screening and licensing are necessary and justified because in the "surrogacy" case—unlike cases of procreation in which the gestating woman raises her child—the baby changes hands. He is transferred from his birth mother to the commissioners, and the continuity of care and connection is severed through that transfer. "Surrogacy" is therefore like adoption, in that the authority over and responsibility for the child is reassigned. It is important for societies to be particularly careful in situations where a child is transferred, because the child is vulnerable, helpless, needy,

33 This suggestion is, of course, not novel, as it dates back to Steinbock's work in 1988. See Bonnie Steinbock, "Surrogate Motherhood as Prenatal Adoption" (1988) 16:1–2 *Journal of Law, Medicine and Ethics* 44.

and utterly dependent. When an infant is separated, shortly after his birth, from the woman whose body has nourished and cared for him, it is essential to ensure that the caring arrangements that replace the maternal-infant relationship be at least adequate and competent.

3) If the commissioners fail to qualify as adoptive parents, then, in the ideal case, no pregnancy would be initiated. If, however, the pregnancy has already been initiated, and the gestating woman does not want an abortion, then, after the birth, the commissioners should not be given the baby. In such a case, if the woman who gestated also does not want the baby, he should be put up for adoption by genuinely qualified and screened adoptive parents. Likewise, if the commissioners somehow change their minds (for whatever reason) about wanting to be parents, and if the woman who gestated does not want the baby, he should be put up for adoption by genuinely qualified parents. A clause in the contract could provide that commissioners who change their minds are required to provide at least some minimal financial support for the child—not because they may be the genetic parents (in some cases they are not), but because they instigated the social arrangement through which the child came into existence and then failed to assume parental responsibility for him.

4) If a "surrogate" changes her mind and wants to keep her baby, then she ought not to be held to the contract. She should be able to change her mind, just like any other pregnant woman who may have planned to have her infant adopted and then changes her mind. The contract should provide for a period of time after the birth during which she is legally entitled to change her mind and keep her baby.[34] The length of that period should be consistent with best practices in the regulation of adoption. Throughout the period in which the woman is entitled to change her mind, she should retain authority over and responsibility for the child—although, of course, if she is not inclined to change her mind, she could hand over the baby before her time for reconsideration is over. Moreover, it should not be possible (barring extreme unfitness on the woman's part) to legally force her to surrender the child against her will.

34 I thank Ruth Macklin for making this point.

In making this recommendation, I am *not* claiming or assuming that women are incapable of making informed decisions about entering into "surrogacy" arrangements, or that they are incapable of foreseeing the consequences of their actions or their own likely feelings at the conclusion of their pregnancy. I am simply extending to them the same right that every other woman has who plans to surrender her infant for adoption. Such a woman always has a grace period, after birth, in which she can change her mind and keep her baby.

5) Some people might be concerned that, if she changes her mind, some commissioners will lose the money they paid the "surrogate." The contract could specify that, if the woman changes her mind, all or some fees (beyond those covering her expenses) will be refunded. Such a provision would likely deter "frivolous" changes of mind by "surrogates"—although I regard it as unlikely that these would occur in the first place.

   Other than such a provision, there is no reason to elevate the finances of the commissioners over the well-being of babies and the women who gestate them. If "surrogacy" as a practice is permitted, then it ought to be a case of *caveat emptor*: let the buyer beware. Not every (attempt to) purchase brings satisfaction. Under these circumstances, potential commissioners might be less motivated to enter into a "surrogacy" arrangement, but I do not regard that decline in motivation as a drawback of my policy recommendations. Under the conditions that I advocate, commissioning a "surrogate" pregnancy might be somewhat riskier than it is now, but at least the commissioners would be aware of the risks. As Bonnie Steinbock points out, the fact that the commissioners would not be sure the baby is theirs to raise until after the grace period is over would be hard on them, but their situation would be no different than that of adoptive parents generally.[35]

F. APPLICATION TO THE MELISSA COOK CASE

I do not seek to defend Melissa Cook's decision to enter into a "surrogacy" contract. I believe that entering into a contract to serve as a "surrogate" at

---

35 Steinbock, above note 33 at 49.

the age of forty-seven is foolhardy at best and possibly immoral at worst.[36] Moreover, I believe that she should have insisted on having only one embryo implanted in her uterus.[37] I do not, however, pursue these problems here, because my aim in this chapter is not to defend Cook's participation in the "surrogacy" contract with CM.

Rather, my aim has been to demonstrate that there were very good reasons, once she became pregnant and then gave birth, to respect Cook's authority over and responsibility for the three infants. As their gestational mother, Cook provided continuity of care: her body created and sustained the fetuses from their earliest days. By virtue of their connection with her, the triplets' identity is constituted as the children of Melissa Cook. I have shown that there are no good reasons to treat "surrogates" like Cook differently from other mothers (particularly women who plan to put their children up for adoption) who are regarded as having authority over and responsibility for their babies.

Most importantly, I contend that an adoption procedure to assess the fitness of CM to parent should have been undertaken. The necessity for this assessment arises primarily because, in this "surrogacy" arrangement as in all of them, the infants were transferred from the woman who created

36 I say this because retrospective studies of pregnancy via oocyte donation and *in vitro* fertilization indicate that patients forty-five and older have statistically significant lower rates of implantation of the embryo, achievement of clinical pregnancy, and successful live birth compared to those of women in younger groups. Jason S Yeh et al, "Pregnancy Outcomes Decline in Recipients over Age 44: An Analysis of 27,959 Fresh Donor Oocyte In Vitro Fertilization Cycles from the Society for Assisted Reproductive Technology" (2014) 101:5 *Fertility and Sterility* 1331. More problematically, studies of spontaneously conceived pregnancies in women older than forty-five indicate that they result in increased maternal morbidity, higher rates of caesarean section, higher rates of neonatal prematurity, and a higher incidence of admission of babies to special care units. Pregnancy over forty-five is risky for both women and their babies. Li-An Wong-Taylor et al, "Maternal and Neonatal Outcomes of Spontaneously Conceived Pregnancies in Mothers over 45 Years: A Review of the Literature" (2012) 285:4 *Archives of Gynecology and Obstetrics* 1161.

37 The reason is that implanting more than one embryo increases the risk of multiple pregnancy, and multiple pregnancy is hazardous. The dangers include gestational hypertension, anemia, miscarriage, pre-term labour and birth, caesarean delivery, congenital abnormalities in the infants, and post-partum hemorrhage. University of Rochester Medical Center, "Complications of Multiple Pregnancy" in *Health Encyclopedia*, online: www.urmc.rochester.edu/encyclopedia/content.aspx?ContentTypeID=85&ContentID=P08021.

and nurtured them to someone else who lacked any continuous relationship with them. In addition, of course, the specific facts of the case raise questions about both CM's motivations and his ability to parent any baby. But, independent of those facts, it would have been important to ascertain whether he was able to care for not just one but as many as three infants, who were very likely to be premature.[38] If he had then been found to be unfit to function as a parent, particularly in such difficult circumstances, the assumption that he would become the infants' parent should have been voided immediately.

In addition (and even if CM had, contrary to fact, been assessed and shown to be a fit parent), Melissa Cook should have been permitted, within a period of time after the birth, to change her mind about surrendering her babies. At that point, part or all of the fees paid to Cook (outside of her expenses) could have been reimbursed.

But above all, her responsibility for and authority over the babies should have been recognized and respected. Melissa Cook was, and is, the babies' mother.

38 According to the University of Rochester Medical Center, *ibid*, "Over 60% of twins and nearly all higher-order multiples are premature (born before 37 weeks). The higher the number of fetuses in the pregnancy, the greater the risk for early birth."

2

"Why We Don't Know What We Don't Know" About Canada's Surrogacy Practices and Outcomes

Pamela M White

> Despite the fact that the success of procedures generates the statistics, the statistics justify the carrying out of infertility medicine — the choice of a particular treatment for a particular patient.[1]

A. QUESTIONING WHAT WE KNOW AND DON'T KNOW ABOUT SURROGACY

Canada's initial foray into the emerging medical arena of assisted reproduction occurred when the country's first "test-tube baby" was born in 1983, some five years after the birth in the United Kingdom of Louise Brown.[2] Yet for all of the study undertaken since by a royal commission,[3] parliamentary committees,[4] courts,[5] ethicists, and policy analysts,[6] Canadians continue to know

1 Charis Thompson, *Making Parents: The Ontological Choreography of Reproductive Technologies* (Cambridge, MA: MIT Press, 2005) at 109.

2 Wayne Williams, "Canada's Very Own Test Tube Baby" *CBC Digital Archives* (10 February 1984), online: www.cbc.ca/archives/entry/canadas-very-own-test-tube-baby.

3 Royal Commission on New Reproductive Technologies, *Proceed with Care: Final Report of the Royal Commission on New Reproductive Technologies* (Ottawa: Minister of Government Services Canada, 1993).

4 House of Commons, Standing Committee on Health, *Assisted Human Reproduction: Building Families* (Ottawa: Standing Committee on Health, 2001).

5 Décret 1177-2004 (15 December 2004) in GOQ (5 January 2005) 137 année, n 1, partie 2 at 62–63; Décret 73-2006 (14 February 2006) in GOQ (8 March 2006) 138 année, n 10, partie 2 at 1290; *Reference re Assisted Human Reproduction Act*, 2010 SCC 61.

6 See, for example, Parliamentary Research Branch, *Legislative Summary: Bill C-13 Assisted Human Reproduction Act*, by Monique Hébert, Nancy Miller Chenier, & Sonya Norris, LS-434E (Ottawa: Library of Parliament, 2002) [revised 16 April 2003]; Margrit Eichler, "Frankenstein Meets Kafka: The Royal Commission on New Reproductive Technologies"

very little about the practices and outcomes of fertility medicine. Even less is known about what some consider to be one of its more contentious practices: surrogacy.[7] But lack of empirical evidence about surrogacy's outcomes has not hindered governments and medical organizations from prohibiting some practices, regulating others, and privileging certain professional protocols.[8] Perhaps we should not be surprised at this state of affairs: reproductive health information, be it about contraception, abortion, or birthing, has frequently been hidden from women, a circumstance that denies women and girls their full human rights.[9]

This chapter traces my journey to uncover what we know and do not know about surrogacy and fertility medicine practices and outcomes in Canada. In so doing, it asks: "Why don't we know what we don't know?" I query why is it so difficult to obtain reliable and consistent information about assisted reproduction and the practice of surrogacy. I seek to understand whether there is something unique about fertility medicine—and, in particular, surrogacy—that belies rigorous measurement and information-based decision

in Gwynne Basen, Margrit Eichler, & Abby Lippman, eds, *Misconceptions: The Social Construction of Choice and the New Reproductive and Genetic Technologies*, vol 1 (Hull, QC: Voyageur, 1993) 1; Timothy Caulfield, "Underwhelmed: Hyperbole, Regulatory Policy, and the Genetic Revolution" (2000) 45 *McGill Law Journal* 437.

7 Karen Busby & Delaney Vun, "Revisiting *The Handmaid's Tale*: Feminist Theory Meets Empirical Research on Surrogate Mothers" (2010) 26:1 *Canadian Journal of Family Law* 13; Erin Nelson, "Global Trade and Assisted Reproductive Technologies: Regulatory Challenges in International Surrogacy" (2013) 41:1 *Journal of Law, Medicine and Ethics* 240; Françoise Baylis, Jocelyn Downie, & Dave Snow, "Fake It Till You Make It: Policy Making and Assisted Human Reproduction in Canada" (2014) 36:6 *Journal of Obstetrics and Gynaecology Canada* 510; Kristin Lozanski, "Transnational Surrogacy: Canada's Contradictions" (2015) 124 *Social Science and Medicine* 383.

8 *Assisted Human Reproduction Act*, SC 2004, c 2; Bill C-38, *An Act to implement certain provisions of the budget tabled in Parliament on March 29, 2012 and other measures*, 1st Sess, 41st Parl, 2012; Notice (Department of Health), (1 October 2016) C Gaz I, 2818 (*Assisted Human Reproduction Act*, SC 2004, c 2, ss 6, 12(2)); Health Canada, "Toward a Strengthened *Assisted Human Reproduction Act*: A Consultation with Canadians on Key Policy Proposals" (2017), online: www.canada.ca/en/health-canada/programs/consultation-assisted-human-reproduction/document.html [*Toward a Strengthened AHR Act*]; *Regulation respecting clinical activities related to assisted procreation*, CQLR c A-5.01, r 1, s 27; *All Families Are Equal Act (Parentage and Related Registrations Statute Law Amendment), 2016*, SO 2016, c 23.

9 Lynn P Freeman, "Censorship and Manipulation of Reproductive Health Information" in Sandra Coliver, ed, *The Right to Know: Human Rights and Access to Reproductive Health Information* (Philadelphia: University of Pennsylvania Press, 1995) at 1.

making. In attempting to answer these questions, I examine how the strategic management of information shapes what we know and don't know about surrogacy, and how it influences decisions about what practices and outcomes are worthy of research, policy attention, and clinical best practice protocols. I assess the implications of not knowing for patients, policy, and law.

I contend that continuation of the status quo will not fill our knowledge gaps about Canadian surrogacy practices and outcomes. Reconsideration of what is collected by Canada's assisted reproduction registry, known as the Canadian Assisted Reproductive Technologies Register Plus (CARTR Plus), who has access to this information, and how the data system is managed is seriously overdue. There is clearly considerable work to be done to make CARTR Plus a reliable and useful database. A concerted research effort aimed at including the voices of surrogates, intended parents, and children conceived using fertility techniques is also needed so that infertility health care can be based on sound evidence. For too long, various levels of government have strategically ignored the need for these data. The implications of not knowing have set the stage for misplaced policy and law.

In Section B, I examine the absence of information about surrogacy in Canada and identify the various cultural, historical, and political factors, as well as the legal, social, and regulatory parameters, that influence current Canadian data collection regarding surrogacy. In Section C, I look in detail at the current information that is and is not available about surrogacy practices and outcomes in the Canadian context, including both qualitative and quantitative data. I focus on assisted reproduction registries in Section D, describing the development of Canada's registry, CARTR Plus, as well as identifying both the shortcomings and potential of this registry to provide the public with access to much-needed quantitative data. Following that, I argue in Section E that data collection and analysis needs to shift its focus so that the surrogate, rather than the intended parent, is considered the patient. Finally, in Section F, I make a number of recommendations for designing a suitable assisted reproduction and surrogacy information system for Canada.

B. KNOWING AND NOT KNOWING: THE ART OF STRATEGIC IGNORANCE

Medical advancement and the delivery of effective and efficient health care are predicated on the principle that knowledge is valued and, indeed, is required in order to make informed decisions about patient care and clinical efficacy.[10] Evidence-based medicine involves the integration of clinical expertise, patient preferences, and the best scientific evidence.[11] The necessity to "do no harm" demands that clinicians undertake their activities in the knowledge that they are acting in the best interests of their patients. This is a positive obligation, whereby clinicians must endeavour to use both the relevant information and the best practices available to them when providing advice and care to patients.

We actually know very little about Canadian surrogacy practices and outcomes. Only minimal and incomplete information is available about gestational surrogacy, a practice where a woman conceives and gives birth to a child that is not genetically related to her.[12] Even less information exists about traditional surrogacy, which occurs when the surrogate is the ovum donor and, as a result, is genetically related to the child. Likewise, very few studies have been undertaken in Canada about the psychosocial outcomes for surrogates, children, and intended parents, although recently some work on queer families has emerged.[13] In short, little has changed over the past ten years since Busby and Vun identified Canada's surrogacy information lacuna and its implications for policy and law.[14]

It is difficult to believe that this long-standing information deficit on surrogacy has come about because of a lack of interest in the topic. Nor can it be suggested that our not knowing about surrogacy and reproductive medicine is merely a product of an inexact and under-examined science of assisted reproduction data collection. Nor should it be implied that a lack

10 David L Sackett, R Brian Haynes, & Peter Tugwell, *Clinical Epidemiology* (Boston: Little, Brown, 1985) ch 3.

11 Sharon Strauss et al, *Evidence-Based Medicine: How to Practice and Teach It*, 4th ed (Edinburgh: Churchill Livingston, 2011) at 1.

12 Shir Dar et al, "Assisted Reproduction Involving Gestational Surrogacy: An Analysis of the Medical, Psychosocial and Legal Issues — Experience from a Large Surrogacy Program" (2015) 30:2 *Human Reproduction* 345; Pamela M White, "Hidden from View: Canadian Gestational Surrogacy Practices and Outcomes, 2001–2012" (2016) 24:47 *Reproductive Health Matters* 205 [White, "Hidden from View"].

13 Stu Marvel et al, "Listening to LGBTQ People on Assisted Human Reproduction: Access to Reproductive Material, Services, and Facilities" in Trudo Lemmens et al, eds, *Regulating Creation: The Law, Ethics, and Policy of Assisted Human Reproduction* (Toronto: University of Toronto Press, 2016) at 406.

14 Busby & Vun, above note 7.

of data implies an absence of risk.[15] I argue that the management of what we know and do not know about surrogacy arises from cultural, historical, and political factors that act to sequester information and to influence what gets collected and measured (or *not* collected or measured), by whom, and for what purposes.[16] For example, the science of embryology and practice of reproductive medicine play a pivotal role in the structure of assisted reproduction data registries and the administration of knowledge about fertility treatment. Other factors, including the Supreme Court of Canada decision in *Reference re Assisted Human Reproduction Act*,[17] lack of provincial involvement, and limited research funding,[18] have also shaped what we know and do not know about fertility treatment and surrogacy.

I argue that strategic management of what we know and do not know about surrogacy operates in a more nuanced manner than, for example, has been described by Robert Proctor, who writes about acts of deliberate misrepresentation of medical information that were committed by tobacco companies.[19] Proctor showed that rejection of scientific evidence linking smoking to lung cancer delayed regulation of tobacco products, promoted the continued recreational use of tobacco, and denied policy-makers and the public vital evidence-based information necessary to make decisions about health, safety, and personal behaviours. Nor am I suggesting that our lack of knowledge arises merely due to a data deficiency[20] or data gap—a

---

15 See Diane Beeson & Abby Lippman, "Gestational Surrogacy: How Safe?" in Miranda Davies, ed, *Babies for Sale? Transnational Surrogacy: Human Rights and the Politics of Reproduction* (London: Zed Books, 2017) at 82.

16 Londa Schiebinger, "Agnotology and Exotic Abortifacients: The Cultural Production of Ignorance in the Eighteenth-Century Atlantic World" (September 2005) 149:3 *Proceedings of the American Philosophical Society* 316; Steven Hilgartner, "Selective Flows of Knowledge in Technoscientific Interaction: Information Control in Genome Research" (2012) 45:2 *British Journal for the History of Science* 267; Jennifer L Croissant, "Agnotology: Ignorance and Absence or Towards a Sociology of Things That Aren't There" (2014) 28:1 *Social Epistemology* 4.

17 Above note 5.

18 I refer specifically to lack of funding for ethics and health research. See *Investing in Canada's Future: Strengthening the Future of Canada's Research* (Ottawa: Advisory Panel for the Review of Federal Support for Fundamental Science, 2017), online: www.sciencereview.ca/eic/site/059.nsf/vwapj/ScienceReview_April2017.pdf/$file/ScienceReview_April2017.pdf [Naylor Report].

19 Robert N Proctor, *Cancer Wars: How Politics Shapes What We Know and Don't Know about Cancer* (New York: Basic Books, 1995).

20 Nelson, above note 7.

problem that, on first glance, would appear to be easy to rectify, especially if it came about as a result of a careless oversight or omissions in data collection. Instead, I believe our problem lies with the mechanisms used to manage and organize knowledge and its converse — the preservation of ignorance. In examining these mechanisms, we can explore how data are organized and we can examine what is collected as well as that which is not measured, published,[21] or analyzed.[22]

Canadian data collection mechanisms regarding surrogacy are influenced by a number of noteworthy legal, social, and regulatory parameters. In examining these parameters, it is necessary, first, to look at the funding instruments that promote knowledge about assisted reproduction and surrogacy, as these instruments play a role in shaping what we know and do not know. Second, it is important to consider the privacy and access regimes that have been put in place, as these mechanisms filter and silo information as well as protect the confidentially of patients and clinicians. Third, we need to examine the socio-political processes that deem certain information to be of value and uncontested while, at the same time, ignore other sources of knowledge. For example, the experiences of surrogates, intended parents, and children conceived as a result of assisted reproduction have rarely been heard; even more rarely are these voices factored in at the decision-making table when determinations about types of data collection and analysis projects are made. The ongoing lack of patient representation on assisted reproduction registry boards and committees is a case in point, although it must be noted that a measure of change is occurring in this regard.[23]

Regulation also influences the management of what we know and do not know. For example, Health Canada's lack of transparency regarding the auditing of fertility clinics and its failure to fulfill its responsibility to inform the public about assisted reproduction frustrate the public's awareness of

---

21 Hilgartner, above note 16 at 276.

22 Daniel Legates, Willie Soon, & William M Briggs, "Learning and Teaching Climate Change Science: The Perils of Consensus Knowledge Using Agnotology" (2013) 22:8 *Science and Education* 2007 at 2009.

23 See, for example, Conceivable Dreams, an Ontario-based patient advocacy group, described in the article by Isabel Teotonio, "Let's Talk about Male Infertility" *Toronto Star* (12 August 2017), online: www.thestar.com/news/canada/2017/08/12/lets-talk-about-male-infertility.html.

benefits and risks, and weaken consumer protection.[24] In Canada, the rise of unelected self-governance bodies[25] such as Accreditation Canada and the Canadian Standards Association (CSA) have come to play important roles in the determination of what aspects of assisted reproduction should be quantified, measured, evaluated, and made public. For example, accreditation compliance scores generated by these bodies are sometimes advertised by clinics, usually on their websites or in office waiting rooms,[26] although clinics are not required to publicize this information.[27] Further, the criteria by which compliance is assessed are self-determined by the professional group being accredited.[28] The unelected CSA, in the absence of regulation, has influenced fertility clinic practices, and, in so doing, it has recommended criteria that may be translated into regulatory drafting.[29] This direct line between unelected bodies and the legislature, especially in the absence of basic tools for evidence-based law reform, raises serious questions about law-making processes and transparency.

C. HIDDEN FROM VIEW: CANADIAN SURROGACY PRACTICES AND OUTCOMES

The published research on surrogacy practices and outcomes both in Canada and internationally reveals a piecemeal approach to data collection and a lack of qualitative research examining the lived experiences of surrogates,

24 See the websites of Health Canada (www.canada.ca) or the Public Health Agency of Canada (www.phac-aspc.gc.ca), where very little assisted reproductive information is provided online to Canadians.

25 Frank Vibert, *The Rise of the Unelected: Democracy and the New Separation of Powers* (Cambridge: Cambridge University Press, 2007).

26 Example from the Ottawa Fertility Clinic, one Canadian clinic that does post its pregnancy rates. Ottawa Fertility Centre, "2015/2016 Success Rates by Treatment Type," online: www.conceive.ca/patient-resources/pregnancy-rates.

27 Tom Blackwell, "The Fertility Clinic Guessing Game: Canadians Have No Way to Find Out Success Rates of Pricey IVF Treatments" *National Post* (22 June 2014, last updated 24 January 2015), online: nationalpost.com/health/the-fertility-clinic-guessing-game-canadians-have-no-way-to-find-out-success-rates-of-pricey-ivf-treatments.

28 See Accreditation Canada, "Health and Social Service Standards," online: https://accreditation.ca/standards.

29 See McLeod, Chapter 4, this volume. See also Canadian Standards Association, *CAN/CSA-Z900.2.1: Tissues for Assisted Reproduction* (Toronto: CSA Group, December 2012 and subsequent updates), online: www.scc.ca/en/standards/notices-of-intent/csa/tissues-for-assisted-reproduction; *Toward a Strengthened AHR Act*, above note 8.

intended parents, and resulting children. A systematic review of surrogacy published in 2016 by Söderström-Anttila et al examined over fifty peer-reviewed international articles and studies.[30] It reveals a spotty research record worldwide on the topic of surrogacy, with many of the reviewed papers demonstrating an over-reliance on case studies and small population samples. One notable exception was the Toronto CReATE fertility clinic database study, which was one of very few to track gestational surrogacy practices and outcome trends over time.[31] Another set of studies of significant value was that led by Susan Golombok, which examined longitudinal psychological implications for surrogates, children, and intended parents. It showed that regulated traditional and gestational surrogacy practices in the United Kingdom exhibited positive outcomes, and it confirmed the existence of harmonious relationships between those involved in surrogacy arrangements.[32]

Regarding pregnancy experiences and reproductive health, the Söderström-Anttila review found that surrogates experienced levels of hypertensive disorders and placental complications similar to those of other

30 Viveca Söderström-Anttila et al, "Surrogacy: Outcomes for Surrogate Mothers, Children and the Resulting Families — A Systematic Review" (2016) 22:2 *Human Reproduction Update* 260.

31 Dar et al, above note 12.

32 Susan Golombok et al, "The European Study of Assisted Reproduction Families: Transition from Infancy to Adolescence" (2002) 17:3 *Human Reproduction* 830; Susan Golombok et al, "Non-Genetic and Non-Gestational Parenthood: Consequences for Parent-Child Relationships and the Psychological Well-Being of Mothers, Fathers and Children at Age 3" (2006) 21:7 *Human Reproduction* 1918; Susan Golombok et al, "Families Created Through Surrogacy: Mother-Child Relationships and Children's Psychological Adjustment at Age 7" (2011) 47:6 *Developmental Psychology* 1579; Susan Golombok et al, "Children Born Through Reproductive Donation: A Longitudinal Study of Psychological Adjustment" (2013) 54:6 *Journal of Child Psychology and Psychiatry* 653; Sarah Imrie & Jadva Vasanti, "The Long-Term Experiences of Surrogates: Relationships and Contact with Surrogacy Families in Genetic and Gestational Surrogacy Arrangements" (October 2014) 29:4 *Reproductive BioMedicine Online* 424; Jadva Vasanti & Sarah Imrie, "Children of Surrogate Mothers: Psychological Well-Being, Family Relationships and Experiences of Surrogacy" (2014) 29:1 *Human Reproduction* 90; Jadva Vasanti et al, "Surrogacy: The Experiences of Surrogate Mothers" (2003) 18:10 *Human Reproduction* 2196; Jadva Vasanti et al, "Surrogacy Families 10 Years On: Relationship with the Surrogate, Decisions over Disclosure and Children's Understanding of Their Surrogacy Origins" (2012) 27:10 *Human Reproduction* 3008; Jadva Vasanti, Sarah Imrie, & Susan Golombok, "Surrogate Mothers 10 Years On: A Longitudinal Study of Psychological Well-Being and Relationships with the Parents and Child" (2015) 30:2 *Human Reproduction* 373.

patients undergoing *in vitro* fertilization (IVF)—a worrisome risk, given that surrogate mothers tend to be younger than other women who become pregnant through IVF.[33] Findings of studies published since the systematic review show higher levels of multiple birth and multiple embryo transfers among surrogates, raising questions about differing treatments that surrogates appear to be receiving compared to other fertility patients.[34]

Importantly, few of the studies examined in this systematic review followed a qualitative research methodology, an approach that enables the participants' voices and perspectives to be accorded empirical value.[35] Publication in the field is changing quickly, with recent studies examining surrogate chatlines and social media sites, places where surrogates share experiences, exchange information about fertility techniques and clinics, and provide support to one another.[36] There are also recently published findings from Australian-based research on surrogates[37] as well as a number of studies on gay intended parents.[38]

In the Canadian context, clinic and registry database research, through CARTR Plus, predominates.[39] In addition, some research has been published about the implications for members of Canada's queer community

---

33 Söderström-Anttila et al, above note 30.

34 Kiran M Perkins et al, "Trends and Outcomes of Gestational Surrogacy in the United States" (2016) 106:2 *Fertility and Sterility* 435; White, "Hidden from View," above note 12; Jenni Millbank, "Rethinking 'Commercial' Surrogacy in Australia" (2015) 12:3 *Journal of Bioethical Inquiry* 477.

35 David Silverman, *Qualitative Research: Issues of Theory, Method and Practice*, 3d ed (Los Angeles: Sage, 2011).

36 Zsuzsa Berend, "Surrogate Losses: Understandings of Pregnancy Loss and Assisted Reproduction among Surrogate Mothers" (2010) 24:2 *Medical Anthropology Quarterly* 240; Zsuzsa Berend, "The Romance of Surrogacy" (2012) 27:4 *Sociological Forum* 913; Zsuzsa Berend, "We Are All Carrying Someone Else's Child: Relatedness and Relationships in Third-Party Reproduction" (2016) 118:1 *American Anthropologist* 24; Heather Jacobson, *Labor of Love: Gestional Surrogacy and the Work of Making Babies* (New Brunswick, NJ: Rutgers University Press, 2016).

37 Millbank, above note 34.

38 Marcin Smietana, "Affective De-Commodifying, Economic De-Kinning: Surrogates' and Gay Fathers' Narratives in US Surrogacy" (2017) 22:2 *Sociological Research Online* 1; Amy May & Kelly Tenzek, "'A Gift We Are Unable to Create Ourselves': Uncertainty Reduction in Online Classified Ads Posted by Gay Men Pursuing Surrogacy" (2016) 12:5 *Journal of GLBT Family Studies* 430; Lucy Blake at al, "Gay Father Surrogacy Families: Relationships with Surrogates and Egg Donors and Parental Disclosure of Children's Origins" (2016) 106:6 *Fertility and Sterility* 1503.

39 Dar et al, above note 12; White, "Hidden from View," above note 12.

of laws and regulations related to assisted reproduction, surrogacy, and gamete donation.[40] And there are a few Canadian qualitative studies of note. One study focusing on the donation of surplus eggs and embryos for research collected a few comments from participants about surrogacy being an option should IVF fail.[41] A recently published work interviewed altruistic Canadian, American, and Australian surrogates about their relationships with intended parents, all of whom were family or friends of the surrogate.[42] Further, Lavoie and Côté in Chapter 3 of this volume, discuss their findings from two sets of interviews from Quebec: the experiences of parents (mostly gay fathers) who started their families with the help of surrogates and an ongoing study of women who acted as surrogates.

Many holes remain. We know little about the durability of post-birth relationships between Canadian surrogates and intended parents. Nor do we understand how Canadian surrogates view the value of the counselling they receive, although findings from a US-based study show that many consider available counselling to be inadequate.[43] We have little to no evidence on cross-border surrogacy, whether it is undertaken by Canadians who obtain surrogacy services abroad or by international intended parents using Canadian surrogates.[44]

In Canada, the most comprehensive source of information about gestational surrogacy practices and outcomes is CARTR Plus, a database maintained and governed by Canadian clinic directors—that is, persons who operate and manage for-profit fertility clinics. It contains fertility treatment

---

40 Marvel et al, above note 13.

41 Pamela M White, "Life on the Liminal Bridge Spanning Fertility and Infertility: A Time to Dream and a Time to Decide" (2017) 24:4 *Journal of Law and Medicine* 886; Alana Cattapan & Ashley Doyle, "Patient Decision-Making About the Disposition of Surplus Cryopreserved Embryos in Canada" (2016) 38:1 *Journal of Obstetrics and Gynaecology Canada* 60.

42 Sarah Jane Toledano & Kristin Zeiler, "Hosting the Others' Child? Relational Work and Embodied Responsibility in Altruistic Surrogate Motherhood" (2017) 18:2 *Feminist Theory* 159.

43 Erika L Fuchs & Abbey B Berenson, "Screening of Gestational Carriers in the United States" (2016) 106:6 *Fertility and Sterility* 1496.

44 Busby & White, Chapter 7, this volume. See also Aaron D Levine et al, "Contribution of Assisted Reproductive Technology to Overall Births by Maternal Age in the United States, 2012–14" (2017) 317:12 *Journal of the American Medical Association* 1272; Edward G Hughes & Denise Dejean, "Cross-Border Fertility Services in North America: A Survey of Canadian and American Providers" (2010) 94:1 *Fertility and Sterility* e16.

information spanning over fifteen years.[45] Yet, as is discussed below, data inaccessibility and a lack of database documentation have meant that the information on surrogacy IVF treatments available from this registry has been under-utilized.[46]

Despite the existence of the CARTR Plus database, there is still a serious dearth of information on Canadian surrogacy practices and outcomes. For example, we do not know much about the characteristics of women who become surrogates, their parity, family background, or income. Nor do we know which type of practice — traditional or gestational — is more common in Canada. (It is often reported that gestational surrogacy occurs in about 95 percent of US cases;[47] in contrast, in the United Kingdom, about 45 percent of surrogates engage in traditional surrogacy.[48]) In addition, we don't know how surrogates respond to fertility treatments compared with other IVF patients.[49] Curiously, because of the way that assisted reproductive registries, including CARTR Plus, are structured we know more about intended parents than we do about surrogates, a phenomenon that I discuss in greater detail below.

D. ASSISTED REPRODUCTION REGISTRIES: HISTORY, FOCUS, AND RESULTS

1) The Development of Canada's Assisted Reproduction Registry

Most countries where fertility medicine is practised have established assisted reproduction registries. The form these registries take, the information that is collected, and how they are governed vary by jurisdiction. In Europe, for example, considerable effort has been made to ensure comparability of data fields, and member states are asked to comply with the definitions published

45 Joanne Gunby & Salim Daya, "Assisted Reproduction Technologies (ART) in Canada: 2002 Results from the Canadian ART Register" (2006) 86:5 *Fertility and Sterility* 1356 [Gunby & Daya, "ART in Canada, 2002"].

46 Dar et al, above note 12; White, "Hidden from View," above note 12.

47 Diane S Hinson & Maureen McBrien, "Surrogacy across America" (Fall 2011) 34:2 *Family Advocate* 32.

48 Kirsty Horsey, *Surrogacy in the UK: Myth Busting and Reform — Report of the Surrogacy UK Working Group on Surrogacy Law Reform* (London: Surrogacy UK, November 2015).

49 Beeson & Lippman, above note 15.

by the World Health Organization (WHO) and recommended by the International Committee Monitoring Assisted Reproduction Technologies (ICMART).[50] ICMART acknowledges that assisted reproduction definitions used by nations can reflect available medical treatment as well as cultural, regulatory, and religious differences.[51] While these differences play a role in all attempts to harmonize international data collection, ICMART nonetheless advocates for registry standardization, as a harmonized approach facilitates monitoring of the efficacy, safety, and quality of procedures, and enables international comparative research.[52]

Fertility experts from Canada and the United States participate in ICMART. Both countries use a registry system developed by the American-based Society for Assisted Reproduction Technology (SART). However, not all of the ICMART recommendations have been adopted by the fertility clinic directors who control Canada's assisted reproduction registry, CARTR Plus.[53] To a lesser degree, this situation also exists with the National ART Surveillance System (NASS) in the United States, which is managed by the Centers for Disease Control and Prevention (CDC).

Canada's assisted reproduction registry, initially known as CARTR and now called CARTR Plus, adopted the SART registry layout and software system in 1999.[54] Yet the history and governance of Canada's assisted reproduction registry, and its subsequent ability to influence policy and law, differ considerably from its American counterpart, NASS. In 1992, the

50 The European IVF-Monitoring Programme (EIM) for the European Society of Human Reproduction and Embryology (ESHR); "Assisted Reproductive Technology in Europe, 2000: Results Generated from European Registers by ESHRE," by Anders Nyboe Andersen, Luca Gianaroli, & Karl G Nygren (2004) 19:3 *Human Reproduction* 490; Karl G Nygren et al, "Cross-Border Fertility Care: International Committee Monitoring Assisted Reproduction Technologies Global Survey — 2006 Data and Estimates" (2010) 94:1 *Fertility and Sterility* e4.

51 Fernando Zegers-Hochschild et al, on behalf of ICMART and WHO, "The International Committee for Monitoring Assisted Reproductive Technology (ICMART) and the World Health Organization (WHO) Revised Glossary on ART Terminology" (2009) 24:11 *Human Reproduction* 2683. In a telephone call 26 October 2017, staff at BORN declined to discuss with the author their involvement with the ICMART committee.

52 Zegers-Hochschild et al, *ibid*.

53 For a list of CARTR Plus variables, see BORN Ontario, "CARTR Plus," online: www.bornontario.ca/en/partnership-projects/cartr-plus/.

54 Joanne Gunby & Salim Daya, "Assisted Reproduction Technology (ART) in Canada: 2001 Results from the Canadian ART Register" (2005) 84:4 *Fertility and Sterility* 590.

US federal government took steps to protect American fertility treatment consumers by passing the *Fertility Clinic Success Rate and Certification Act of 1992*.[55] All fertility clinics located in the United States are required by law to send detailed information about IVF treatments and outcomes to the CDC, which is mandated by law to publish an annual summary report describing IVF treatment outcomes and trends along with a statement showing success rates per clinic by type of treatment and patient.[56] This federal law overrides the individual fertility clinic's propriety right to protect IVF success rates, an intervention that many American IVF clinic directors view as an unwanted intrusion.

The US federal legislation mandating the creation of an assisted reproduction registry is predicated on the assumption that the "consumer" is the ultimate beneficiary of the data collection.[57] It is assumed that, by having knowledge about clinic success rates, the consumer will be able to make informed reproductive health decisions. However, this aspect of the US law has been quite controversial, as IVF success rates depend on many factors, which may include clinics choosing patients on the basis of the probability of a successful outcome. For example, patient characteristics, including age and complex infertility problems, as well as the use of donor gametes, affect the "success" of transfer cycles. Indeed, Thompson, in her study of several American fertility clinics, observed how outcome measures could be manipulated as a result of inclusion or exclusion of patients and treatments.[58]

Nonetheless, the NASS data allow CDC analysts to publish complex statistical studies focusing on a variety of topics ranging from surrogacy outcomes, uptake of new techniques and procedures, and change in multiple

---

55 *Fertility Clinic Success Rate and Certification Act of 1992*, Pub L No 102-493, 106 Stat 3146 (24 October 1992).

56 Centers for Disease Control and Prevention, "Archived ART Reports and Spreadsheets" (2014), online: www.cdc.gov/art/reports/archive.html.

57 Eli Y Adashi & Ron Wyden, "Public Reporting of Clinical Outcomes of Assisted Reproductive Technology Programs: Implications for Other Medical and Surgical Procedures" (September 2011) 306:10 *Journal of the American Medical Association* 1135 at 1135. Ron Wyden is the US senator who championed the US federal legislation requiring IVF clinics to report assisted reproduction treatment information to the CDC.

58 Thompson, above note 1; Andrea Preisler, "Assisted Reproductive Technology: The Dangers of an Unregulated Market and the Need for Reform" (2013) 15:2 *DePaul Journal of Health Care Law* 213 at 225–28.

births rates.[59] These studies, along with those produced by independent researchers, have influenced the development of treatment guidelines recommending the number of embryos to transfer, supported the adoption of new techniques, and revealed unexpected outcomes of policy measures associated with insurance mandates. In this latter instance, research has shown that insurance funding increased the incidence of IVF, which, paradoxically, contributed to higher multiple births. This outcome—a finding that has worrisome health implications—had not been foreseen: it had initially been predicted that lowered costs would result in fewer multiple embryo transfers.[60] Recently, topics of cross-border reproduction and surrogacy have been the subjects of in-depth research analysis based on data from NASS.[61]

Canada does not have a complete picture of fertility treatments that are provided to patients. When it comes to tracking IVF procedures, the best national database appears to be CARTR Plus. No pan-Canadian registry records information on artificial insemination (AI), although ICMART recommends that such data be collected as does a 2014 report by Quebec's Commissaire à la santé et au bien-être.[62]

In contrast to the United States and the United Kingdom, no legislation requires Canadian fertility clinics to report fertility treatment information to a public health organization. Individual fertility clinics submit their treatment data on a voluntary basis to CARTR Plus, which is governed by Canada's IVF Directors. Since 2013, the Better Outcomes Registry

59 See, for example, Dmitry M Kissin et al, "Embryo Transfer Practices and Multiple Births Resulting from Assisted Reproductive Technology: An Opportunity for Prevention" (2015) 103:4 *Fertility and Sterility* 954; Sara Crawford et al, "Assisted Reproductive Technology Use, Embryo Transfer Practices and Birth Outcomes after Infertility Insurance Mandates: New Jersey and Connecticut" (2016) 105:2 *Fertility and Sterility* 347; Levine et al, above note 44.

60 J Ryan Martin et al, "Insurance Coverage and In Vitro Fertilization Outcomes: A U.S. Perspective" (2011) 95:3 *Fertility and Sterility* 964; Kasey S Buckles, "Infertility Insurance Mandates and Multiple Births" (July 2013) 22:7 *Health Economics* 775; Sheree L Boulet et al, "Embryo Transfer Practice and Perinatal Outcomes by Insurance Mandate Status" (2015) 104:2 *Fertility and Sterility* 403; Crawford et al, above note 59.

61 Perkins et al, above note 34; Levine et al, above note 44.

62 Regarding International Committee Monitoring Assisted Reproductive Technologies (ICMART), see KG Nygren et al, *The ICMART Tool Box for ART Data Collection* (Palo Alto, CA: ICMART, 2011) at 23; Commissaire à la santé et au bien-être, *Avis détaillé sur les activités de procréation assistée au Québec* (Quebec: Gouvernement du Québec, 2014) ch 3.

and Network (BORN), a prescribed registry under the Ontario *Personal Health Information Protection Act*,[63] has hosted and managed the CARTR Plus registry. With the recent funding of assisted reproduction by Ontario, information for patients receiving publicly funded treatments, including IVF and artificial insemination (AI), is now being sent to the Ontario Ministry of Health and Long-Term Care by fertility clinics. However, the information gained as a result of provincially funded fertility programs forms but a subset of assisted reproduction treatments undertaken in the province: not everyone who needs fertility treatments is eligible to receive them under the funded program.[64] Regrettably, Ontario does not disaggregate the information pertaining to treatments received by surrogates, even though the Ontario program provides IVF and AI services to them.[65] When Quebec funded fertility treatments, fertility clinics located in the province were also required to send billing and IVF and AI treatment information to the Ministère de la santé et des services sociaux.[66] As a result, in both the Ontario and Quebec examples, different sets of information are being collected by different organizations. And, paradoxically, provincial funding for fertility treatments could produce a deterioration in the national registry, with the creation of parallel provincial data silos that reflect differing administrative processes and the funding of different treatments.[67]

The piecemeal approach to data collection in Canada is due, in part, to the constitutional division of powers. When the *Assisted Human Reproduction Act* (*AHRA*) was passed in 2004, it had been expected that Canada's registry (CARTR, as it was called at the time) would be replaced or possibly merged into a federally mandated personal health information registry (PHIR) that was to have been established by Assisted Human

63 *Personal Health Information Protection Act, 2004*, SO 2004, c 3. For a history of BORN, see BORN Ontario, "History of BORN Ontario," online: www.bornontario.ca/assets/documents/History%20of%20BORN%20Ontario_May%202014.pdf.

64 For example, women over the age of forty-three are not eligible for a funded cycle of IVF in Ontario.

65 FOI Request A-2017-00-00166 made by Pamela M White to Ontario Ministry of Health and Long-Term Care, 1 September 2017.

66 Commissaire à la santé et au bien-être, *Avis détaillé sur les activités de procréation assistée au Québec* (Quebec: Commissaire à la santé et au bien-être Québec, 2014) ch 3.

67 Participation by Quebec-based IVF clinics in CARTR (as it was called at that time) dropped slightly during the period that Quebec directly funded fertility treatments, suggesting that imposition of a data response burden on IVF clinics can contribute to decreased data quality in the CARTR Plus national database.

Reproduction Canada (AHRC).[68] The 2010 Supreme Court of Canada's *Reference* decision ended the ability of the federal government to establish a PHIR and donor registry, as the Court concluded that this fell within the legislative authority of the province.[69] No similar opportunity now exists within the remit of the amended *AHRA*.[70]

Provincial governments could regulate mandatory record keeping and, through the auspices of co-operative federalism, transmit provincially collected health information to a national statistical organization such as the Canadian Institute for Health Information (CIHI) or Statistics Canada.[71] Provinces could also work toward the creation of provincial donor registries, though this approach could result in the creation of database silos.

The current registry, CARTR Plus, arose from collaboration between fertility clinic directors, who fund and govern the CARTR registry, and Ontario's BORN registry. In 2013, CARTR faced financial and human resources challenges, which put in question its sustainability. Subsequently, the fertility clinic directors negotiated an agreement with BORN[72] to replace CARTR with a new database system called CARTR Plus. The previously collected information found in CARTR continues to be maintained by BORN, and enables the linkage of CARTR Plus data to Ontario prenatal databases held by BORN as congenital disabilities and birth registration.[73] Apart from Ontario, no other provincial health organization has adopted a similar approach or become a partner in BORN. Quebec fertility clinic directors have recommended that Quebec emulate the BORN model, although this has not yet occurred.[74]

---

68 *Assisted Human Reproduction Act*, SC 2004, c 2, ss 17–18 [*AHRA*].

69 *Reference re Assisted Human Reproduction Act*, above note 5.

70 *Jobs, Growth and Long-Term Prosperity Act*, SC 2012, c 19, s 718 (Division 56: *Assisted Human Reproduction Act*) (Royal Assent 29 June 2012), repealed the sections mandating the PHIR and donor registry.

71 For example, provincial cancer data are transmitted to Statistics Canada to form a national registry on cancer. Provincial information on provincial hospital and ambulatory care is sent to the Canadian Institute for Health Information.

72 Mari Teitelbaum, "CARTR 2.0: Enhancing Outcomes Ascertainment through a Partnership with BORN Ontario for Improved Quality Assurance and National Reporting" (Paper delivered at the CFAS Annual Meeting, Victoria, BC, 26–29 September 2013).

73 Ontario IVF clinic directors pass along patient OHIP information to BORN to enable record linkage. See BORN website: www.bornontario.ca/en/born-information-system.

74 Quebec, National Assembly, *Journal des débats (Hansard)*, 41st lég, 1st sess, No 44 (17 March 2015) at 29–30, Commission permanent de la santé et des services sociaux,

I argue that CARTR's joining forces with BORN was a prudent decision, especially given the Court's *Reference* decision. It demonstrates the dedication of the fertility clinic directors to continue and further develop an assisted reproduction registry that can be used for population health research purposes. In 2016, for example, the Canadian Fertility and Andrology Society (CFAS) directed some of its limited research funding toward improvements in data collection.[75] Regarding longitudinal database research opportunities, there exists the possibility of linking CARTR Plus data for Ontario-based patients to other registry data holdings, an approach modelled on methodologies implemented by NASS in association with several US states. For example, NASS records are linked to state vital statistics records and health registries for the purposes of health research. Studies published from these linked databases reveal interesting differences and similarities in reporting coverage, especially for states such as Massachusetts and Florida that include assisted reproduction information on the health data portion of birth certificates.[76]

While the BORN venture holds much promise, it remains difficult for researchers to access CARTR Plus information. Public access to CARTR and CARTR Plus information has changed considerably over the past fifteen years. Between 2001 and 2007, detailed CARTR data showing type of treatment, use of donor gametes and embryos, and number of pregnancies and births were published in the journal *Fertility and Sterility*. From 2008 to 2012, the CARTR annual data reports showing results in the same manner as in the previous years were available to CFAS members only. Reports during this period were posted on the organization's website. A redesign of the CFAS website in 2015 saw their removal.[77] Since 2013, a press release

testimony of Dr François Bissonnette, Société Canadienne de fertilité et d'andrologies, online: www.assnat.qc.ca/en/travaux-parlementaires/commissions/csss-41-1/journal-debats/CSSS-150317.html#_Toc430348608.

75 Canadian Fertility and Andrology Society, "Research Seed Grant Program," online: https://cfas.ca/about-cfas/appropriations-committee/research-seed-grant.

76 Bruce Cohen et al, "Accuracy of Assisted Reproductive Technology Information on Birth Certificates: Florida and Massachusetts, 2004–2006" (2014) 28:3 *Pediatric and Perinatal Epidemiology* 181.

77 Gunby & Daya, "ART in Canada, 2002," above note 45; Joanne Gunby & Salim Daya, "Assisted Reproduction Technologies (ART) in Canada: 2003 Results from the Canadian ART Register" (2007) 88:3 *Fertility and Sterility* 550; Joanne Gunby et al, "Assisted Reproduction Technologies (ART) in Canada: 2004 Results from the Canadian ART Register" (2008) 89:5 *Fertility and Sterility* 1123; Joanne Gunby et al, "Assisted Reproduction Technologies (ART) in Canada: 2005 Results from the

has been used to announce a summary of the yearly IVF treatment information, and a detailed presentation is given at the CFAS annual conference.[78] Researchers requesting access to CARTR Plus information held by BORN must obtain approval from fertility clinic directors, a lengthy process that can take over six months for a simple data tabulation; moreover, high fees are imposed on those seeking even the most simple of data requests.[79]

Further, there continues to be a question about the reliability and accuracy of the registry's data. One of the long-standing problems with the CARTR Plus registry is that it relies on a voluntary data reporting system: most, but not all, fertility clinics report in every year, although in recent years there has been an uptick in compliance. The registry also lacks rigorous oversight and independent governance. IVF patients are not involved in CARTR Plus governance, research review, data analysis, and results publication, even though patients indirectly fund such work through the fees they pay for their fertility treatments.

Nor are the CARTR Plus findings widely distributed to the public in a manner that would help patients understand the risks or advantages or fertility treatments, or the level of success of such treatments.[80] Canadian fertility clinic directors have refused to publicly release clinic-level data showing pregnancy rates per type of procedure. Provincial-level IVF data are also suppressed, on the basis that they may lead to the identification

Canadian Assisted Reproductive Technologies Register" (2009) 91:5 *Fertility and Sterility* 1721; Joanne Gunby et al, "Assisted Reproduction Technologies (ART) in Canada: 2006 Results from the Canadian ART Register" (2010) 93:7 *Fertility and Sterility* 2189; Joanne Gunby et al, "Assisted Reproduction Technologies (ART) in Canada: 2007 Results from the Canadian ART Register" (2011) 95:2 *Fertility and Sterility* e1; Joanne Gunby et al, "Assisted Reproduction Technologies (ART) in Canada, 2008–2012" [unpublished]. These reports are available to members only. From 2013 onwards, only a presentation deck has been made available, and only to CFAS members.

78 Canadian Fertility and Andrology Society, series of CARTR Plus annual media releases, "ART Live Birth Rates," online: https://cfas.ca/public-affairs/canadian-art-register.

79 Author's experience over the period 2013–17. BORN is not well resourced to address data requests. Cost-recovery fees are imposed on requests for data. Had the assisted reproduction registry been held by CIHI or Statistics Canada, the data that I requested would have been in the public domain and hence available to all users. Similar data requests made to the CDC have been answered in less than forty-eight hours and at no cost.

80 Blackwell, above note 27. See commentary about how to make NASS data more consumer friendly: Ryszard J Chetkowski, "Consumer-Friendly Reporting of In Vitro Fertiltization Outcomes" (2014) 101:1 *Fertility and Sterility* e7.

of individual IVF clinics, although Quebec has made detailed information available.[81] Nonetheless, annual data from CARTR Plus are used to provide the Canadian fertility clinic success rates that feed into Accreditation Canada certification and fertility clinic publicity. As a result, it can be argued that, compared to the United States and the United Kingdom,[82] consumer protection afforded to Canadian patients is weaker and considerably more reliant on the goodwill of professional, for-profit, fertility clinics. It is noteworthy that Bill C-38, which amended the *AHRA*, mandated a fiduciary responsibility to Health Canada (an obligation that could also be fulfilled by the Public Health Agency of Canada) to inform Canadians about assisted reproduction procedures and outcomes.[83] However, little has been undertaken in this area since the federal ministry assumed this duty following the demise of the AHRAC in 2012.

Yet, for all of its deficiencies, CARTR Plus avoids some of the problems that would have plagued the proposed PHIR had it been created pursuant to the now defunct provisions of the *AHRA*. The *AHRA* envisaged a regulatory data system similar to the one currently in operation by the UK Human Fertilisation and Embryology Authority (HFEA). It would have been a costly exercise and one devoted largely to the collection of data for regulatory and licensing purposes. For the envisaged PHIR to have been used for regulatory actions, it would have needed a complement of auditors and clinic licencee inspectors as well as data analysts. Based on the actions of the AHRAC, it is clear that it was not prepared to take on such a role.[84]

---

81 Commissaire à la santé et au bien-être, above note 66.

82 See *R (Assisted Reproduction and Gynecology Centre and another) v Human Fertilisation and Embryology Authority*, [2013] EWHC 3087 (Admin), [2013] WLR (D) 416 (case of IVF clinics resisting the action of the Human Fertilisation and Embryology Authority to impose a clinic licence condition of an annual target of multiple births of 15 percent or less).

83 *Jobs, Growth and Long-Term Prosperity: 2012 Economic Action Plan* (Ottawa: Department of Finance, 29 March 2012) at 219, online: www.budget.gc.ca/2012/plan/pdf/Plan2012-eng.pdf ("Health Canada undertakes responsibility for the remaining federal functions in AHR, such as compliance and enforcement, and outreach").

84 Between January 2009 and March 2010, the author was assigned to Assisted Human Reproduction Agency of Canada by Statistics Canada to develop a strategic plan for the creation and management of a personal health information registry and donor registry. This work package never progressed beyond initial meetings held with IVF directors. The Supreme Court decision in late 2010 struck down the areas of the *Assisted Human Reproduction Act, 2004* that sought to use federal *Criminal Code* powers to legislate in

The *AHRA* also imposed restrictions on the use of the PHIR for population health research purposes.[85] It did not enable the AHRAC to permit statistical organizations such as the CIHI, Statistics Canada,[86] or provincial statistical agencies to provide data stewardship or access to the database for population health research purposes. Moreover, the *AHRA* prevented data linkage, thereby inhibiting research use.[87] Such restrictions on public use are not limited to Canada. The primacy of the regulatory mandate has been an issue with the UK HFEA, for example. The Human Fertilisation and Embryology Authority produces an annual overview report and data spreadsheets that have been made publicly available. However, a special research committee was established only in 2013, with a mandate to produce in-depth detailed studies based on the data.[88]

While NASS, the US fertility data collection system, exhibits limitations — notably the focus on pregnancy rates, which some researchers argue increases pressure on clinics to transfer multiple embryos[89] — it is an authenticated data system covering the majority of American fertility clinics. In retrospect, the American approach, which involves a unique public–private partnership between the CDC and SART,[90] might have been a more appropriate registry model for Canada to have adopted. Indeed, these types of arrangements between provinces/territories and institutions/businesses exist in other contexts in Canada.[91] Had Canada adopted a similar model, a public health organization such as Statistics Canada or the CIHI could

areas of provincial responsibility, with the result that the PHIR and donor registries, as had been envisaged by the 2004 Act, were ruled non-constitutional.

85 Vanessa Gruben, "Assisted Reproduction without Assisting Over-Collection: Fair Information Practices and the Assisted Human Reproduction Agency of Canada" (2009) 17 *Health Law Journal* 229.

86 One could make the legal argument Statistics Canada, had it considered it to be in the public interest to obtain information on IVF treatments collected by IVF clinics, could have used its powers under section 13 of the *Statistics Act*.

87 *AHRA*, above note 68, s 18(2).

88 Consult the Human Fertilisation and Embryology Authority website, online: www.hfea.gov.uk.

89 Robert Klitzman, "Deciding How Many Embryos to Transfer: Ongoing Challenges and Dilemmas" (2016) 3 *Reproductive Biomedicine and Society Online* 1 at 7–8; Thompson, above note 1.

90 Stan Williams et al, "Public Reporting of Assisted Reproductive Technology Outcomes: Past, Present and Future" (February 2015) 212: 2 *American Journal of Obstetrics and Gynaecology* 157 at 157.

91 See, for example, Canadian Institute for Health Information (CIHI), online: www.cihi.ca.

have managed the population health elements of an assisted reproduction registry for Canada. This would have resulted in improved data accuracy and facilitated the updating of registry elements to better measure changing fertility treatment advancements.[92] It would have also better promoted public information and consumer protection or awareness. However, this approach would not have solved the problem of a donor registry, which remains an outstanding and unfulfilled promise of the *AHRA* and is beyond the scope of this chapter.

2) Adapting Assisted Reproduction Registry Data to Better Understand Surrogacy Practices and Outcomes

Although there are many shortcomings in the current CARTR Plus registry, one of the most critical is the lack of information about surrogacy practices and outcomes. Under the current approach, the focus is on the intended parent rather than the surrogate, which leads to significant information deficits. One of the major challenges encountered in the presentation of information on assisted reproduction is rendering the technical embryological, medical, and statistical success measures in a relevant and user-friendly manner. Much of this difficulty stems from the way in which fertility treatment data are structured and managed. For example, it is convenient for fertility clinics to organize patient encounters by IVF cycle. This situation occurs for two reasons. First, procedure billing and medical treatments usually occur on a per–IVF cycle basis. However, the term "IVF cycles" means very little to the general public or the newly initiated IVF patient. Second, using the IVF cycle as the unit of observation focuses attention on results achieved by the

92 There has been considerable debate about the need to update the NASS data fields. See, for example, Williams et al, above note 90; David Meldrum, "Society for Assisted Reproductive Technology/Centers for Disease Control and Prevention In Vitro Registry 2.0" (2013) 100:5 *Fertility and Sterility* 1212; Marcelle J Ceders, "National Reporting of In Vitro Fertilization Success Rates: How Do We Get Patients Useful Information?" (2013) 100:5 *Fertility and Sterility* 1210; David R Meldrum, "Pregnancies and Deliveries per Fresh Cycle Are No Longer Adequate Indicators of In Vitro Fertilization Program Quality: How Should Registries Adapt?" (2013) 100:3 *Fertility and Sterility* 620; Vitaly A Kushnir et al, "The Status of Public Reporting of Clinical Outcomes in Assisted Reproductive Technology" (2013) 100:3 *Fertility and Sterility* 736; Dmitry M Kissin, Sara Crawford, & Sheree L Boulet, "The Status of Public Reporting of Official Outcomes in Assisted Reproductive Technology" (2013) 100:3 *Fertility and Sterility* e16.

ova, sperm, and embryo rather than on the outcomes for the patient, client, or surrogate. For the embryologist studying success rates and examining differing techniques, the focus is appropriate. However, the measure renders analysis at the level of the patient difficult, as one patient often experiences multiple cycles of IVF transfer or ovarian stimulation. As a consequence, CARTR Plus, like all assisted reproduction registries, reveals more about the embryo than it does about the IVF clinic, the client, or the surrogate. Moreover, the statistical focus of the fertility clinic shapes the patient–clinician relationship.[93] This aspect of the clinic–patient interface has very specific implications when registries are used as the information source about surrogacy practices and outcomes.

Given that assisted reproduction information in a registry such as CARTR Plus is organized at the level of the embryo or gamete, we need to ask: who is the patient? At one level, it would be easy to argue that the "paticnt" is the embryo, as its implantation success is the focus of the data collection system. However, CARTR Plus, like NASS, considers the patient to be the individual undergoing the fertility treatment, which is consistent with the view that a patient is a person. But what about in cases of gestational surrogacy: Is the patient the intended parent or the surrogate? CARTR Plus and NASS consider intended parents, rather than surrogates, to be the patients. This may be because intended parents are the persons who require access to fertility treatments. Moreover, the intended parents are the clients of the fertility clinic.

The research implications of classifying the intended parent as the patient are considerable. For example, all of the fertility treatment intervention data involving gestational surrogates are recorded from the perspective of the intended parent. This approach situates the surrogate as the infertility treatment practice used to overcome the childlessness of the intended parents. It should not be surprising, then, that the term "surrogate carrier" has gained prominence in fertility circles, as this term aptly describes the surrogate's non-patient role and function. A similar sleight of hand occurs with respect to the third-party ovum donor who, like the surrogate, may not be considered to be a patient for the purposes of the database.[94]

93 Thompson, above note 1.

94 Vanessa Gruben, "Women as Patients, Not Spare Parts: Examining the Relationship between the Physician and Women Egg Providers" (2013) 25:2 *Canadian Journal of Women and the Law* 249.

The separation of the patient from the treatment options becomes clearly evident when one unpacks the classification system used by NASS and CARTR to describe IVF treatments received by surrogates. For example, the gestational surrogate receives either an "own ovum" embryo or a "donor ovum" embryo. However, a gestational surrogate, by definition, does not use *her own ovum* embryo. Rather, the ovum used for the embryo(s) transferred to the gestational surrogate are not from the surrogate; rather, they originate from the intended mother, confirming that the intended mother, not the surrogate, is the fertility treatment patient.[95]

Another important consequence of classifying the intended parent as the patient is that very little information is recorded about "non-patients": ova donors and gestational surrogates. A recent paper on surrogacy trends based on NASS data[96] tells us a lot about the parity, age, infertility issues, racial background, and place of residence of intended parents. But no comparable information exists about the surrogate. This data deficiency means that it is very difficult to interpret outcomes, assess harms, or determine the usefulness of recommended practice guidelines for the surrogate undergoing fertility treatments on behalf of intended parents.

Further, the limited data on surrogates that do exist exhibit important omissions that suggest less attention has been paid to these data fields compared with other variables. For example, it has been acknowledged that over 30 percent of the age data for surrogates were missing (2007–14) and that a similar problem existed for donated ova.[97] In the US, efforts are being made to improve data reporting, and information on the racial background of surrogates is to be collected.[98]

In Canada, as we have seen, CARTR Plus adopted the American SART database structure. Yet Canadian fertility clinic directors have been much less transparent than their American counterparts about data deficiencies and their intentions regarding data improvement.

95 Donor ovum embryos transferred to a gestational surrogate contain the ovum obtained from a third party — i.e., someone who is not the gestational surrogate.

96 Perkins et al, above note 34; Magdalina Gugucheva, *Surrogacy in America* (Cambridge, MA: Council for Responsible Genetics, 2010), online: www.councilforresponsiblegenetics.org/pagedocuments/kaevejoa1m.pdf.

97 Email from Sheree Boulet to Pamela M White, 11 December 2016. See also Perkins et al, above note 34.

98 *Ibid.*

It is important to note that considerably more information about the surrogate exists in clinic medical records than is transferred to CARTR Plus.[99] Information about the characteristics of the surrogate and ovum donor, often shown on detailed profiles that intended parents eagerly peruse to make decisions that will affect the genetic and epigenetic heritages of their surrogate-born child, is not included in the assisted reproduction registry. These donor and surrogate profiles are derived from a personal survey and contain information about family medical history and surrogate health characteristics. This type of information is no more sensitive than other data already included on the registry. In my view, there is an argument to be made for including this information on a population health registry used for research purposes, provided that appropriate privacy, confidentiality and data security provisions are in place.

E. SHIFTING THE FOCUS: THE SURROGATE AS PATIENT

What would happen if the paradigm of an assisted reproduction registry was changed to make the surrogate the patient and thereby the focus of the data collection and analysis? Researchers could then shed light on outcomes, best practices, and adherence to soft governance guidelines[100] related to the gestational surrogate. This approach would make it possible to step outside of the ontology of the fertility clinic concept of treatment success and the science of embryology. Taking this perspective, one could investigate whether surrogates receive similar fertility treatments and whether there has been an uneven application of recommended treatment guidelines. Such an approach would give recognition to the duty of care owed to her and that her fully informed consent to treatment is required.[101]

My attempts to situate the surrogate as the subject of analysis using existing data obtained from CARTR Plus and NASS has had limited success: the data are inadequate and the scope for analysis is narrow. I have been able to compare surrogate and non-surrogate IVF embryo transfer patterns to reveal that surrogates have a greater statistical risk than other

99 Dar et al, above note 12.

100 Embryo transfer guidelines have been developed: Jason Min & Camille Silvestre, *Guidelines on the Number of Embryos to Transfer* (Montreal: Canadian Fertility and Andrology Society, 2013).

101 See, for example, *Health Care Consent Act, 1996*, SO 1996, c 2, Schedule A.

patients of receiving two or more embryos, a worrisome outcome given the known health risks of a multi-fetal pregnancy.[102] The difference is especially pronounced when donor ovum embryos are used. In the United States and Canada, recommended embryo transfer guidelines are more likely to be followed when the patient is not acting as a surrogate and she uses her own ovum embryos. For gestational surrogates, embryo transfer guidelines are followed in less than 50 percent of the donor ovum embryo transfer cycles.[103] While this finding may be of statistical significance, it will not be possible to fully understand the factors that influence this observed treatment outcome unless research is conducted that asks surrogates how they make treatment decisions, including the number of embryos to transfer. Factors such as intended parents' preference for twins, the high cost of IVF, and a desire among both parties to achieve success on the first cycle are likely to influence embryo-transfer decisions. No information about these considerations are to be found in CARTR Plus. It is only through in-depth surrogate-focused qualitative research that insights will be gained about the factors influencing treatment decision-making.[104]

Another data deficiency working to impair our knowledge about treatment practices relates to the age of women acting as surrogates. An examination of American fertility clinic compliance with the embryo-transfer guidelines from the Association Society for Reproductive Medicine and the Society for Assisted Reproduction Technology reveals that clinics may be using age of the surrogate rather than the genetic age of the ovum donor to determine the number of embryos to transfer. Following such a clinical

102 Laura A Schieve et al, "Low and Very Low Birth Weight in Infants Conceived with Use of Assisted Reproductive Technology" (2002) 346:10 *New England Journal of Medicine* 731; Peter OD Pharoah, "Risk of Cerebral Palsy in Multiple Pregnancies" (June 2006) 33:2 *Clinical Perinatology* 301; David Johnston, *Raising Expectations: Recommendations of the Expert Panel on Infertility and Adoption* (Toronto: Ontario Ministry of Children and Youth Services, 2009); Andrea P MacKay et al, "Pregnancy-Related Mortality among Women with Multifetal Pregnancies" (2006) 107:3 *Obstetrics and Gynecology* 563; Antonia Sazonova et al, "Neonatal and Maternal Outcomes Comparing Women Undergoing Two In Vitro Fertilization (IVF) Singleton Pregnancies and Women Undergoing One IVF Twin Pregnancy" (2013) 99:3 *Fertility and Sterility* 731.

103 Pamela M White, "Comparison of Altruistic and Commercial Surrogate Embryo Transfer Experiences: California and Canada" (2018) *Women's Health Issues*, online: https://doi.org/10.1016/j.whi.2018.01.004.

104 Examples of this type of research are found in the work of Berend, 2010, 2012, 2016, above note 36; Jacobson, above note 36; and Klitzman, above note 89.

practice will result in a higher number of embryos being transferred per cycle, as ovum donors tend to be under age thirty-five; the age range for which one embryo per transfer is recommended. Regrettably, it is not possible to undertake a similar line of enquiry using CARTR Plus, as surrogate age data are not made available to researchers, a circumstance that might lead one to ask whether the failure to provide the data is a deliberate attempt to mask non-compliance with accepted practice guidelines. Or is this situation one of managed ignorance? Of course, the data deficiency may simply reflect poor data reporting practices, a matter that could be rectified by requiring reporting fertility clinics not to leave data entry cells blank, undertaking automated validation checks, and increasing the number of data fields to accommodate new data requirements.

These examples of data insufficiency reveal how data management regimes shape what we know and do not know about the practice of surrogacy and its outcomes. They also lead to the question of whether CARTR Plus can address the population health challenges posed by internationally footloose fertility medicine. The global expansion of reproductive technologies is neither predictable nor consistent. In an expanding transnational world of fertility travel, permeable boundaries of space, time, and bodies erode, enabling new possibilities to emerge and transform. Since its inception, cross-border assisted reproduction has been a feature of fertility medicine.[105] Twenty-first-century IVF is a globally based, multimillion dollar medical industry.[106] Bodies, embryos, medical knowledge, and treatments flow with few restrictions across international borders and within nations, remaking normative and culture-based notions of kinship and family.[107]

Canada is not well equipped to track the rise of international surrogacy occurring within its borders. Contrary to the recommendations of ICMART, CARTR Plus does not record the place of residence of intended

---

105 Robert Forman, "Cross-Border Reproductive Care: A Clinician's Perspective" (2011) 23:7 *Reproductive BioMedicine Online* 808 at 808.

106 Bob Simpson & Kate Hampshire, "Introduction: Assisted Reproductive Technologies — A Third Wave?" in Kate Hampshire & Bob Simpson, eds, *Assisted Reproductive Technologies in the Third Phase: Global Encounters and Emerging Moral Worlds* (New York: Berghahn Books, 2015) 1 at 10–11.

107 Michal Rachel Nahman, "Reproductive Tourism: Through the Anthropological 'Reproscope'" (2016) 45 *Annual Review of Anthropology* 417 at 418–19; Sarah Franklin, "Not a Flat World: The Future of Cross-Border Reproductive Care" (2011) 23:7 *Reproductive BioMedicine Online* 814.

parents, making it impossible to obtain a count of the number of international intended parents. Among the provinces, British Columbia can provide vital statistics on residence of intended parents, and it is expected that Ontario will soon be able to do likewise, but it is unclear whether this will be possible for other provinces.[108] Further, it is not possible for CARTR Plus to measure what has come to be referred to as the blended Canadian/US option. This occurs when Australian, UK, European, or other non-Canadian resident international parents arrange with a Canadian surrogate to have the IVF treatments conducted in the United States although the pregnancy and delivery takes place in Canada.[109]

Similarly, Canadian data systems do not track cross-border fertility treatment undertaken by Canadian residents, though a recent study of US registry data reveals that Canadian fertility patients are the most numerous non–US resident group using American fertility clinics.[110] However, because NASS does not consider surrogates to be patients, it cannot tell us about the number of Canadian surrogates going to the United States for donor ova treatment cycles or to receive other fertility treatments: this information is simply not collected.[111]

Further, it is not possible for Canadians to study interprovincial flows of surrogates, intended parents, and other IVF patients, as CARTR Plus holds no data on this phenomenon. For example, it is not possible to determine if intended parents residing in Quebec seek surrogates living in other provinces. Yet evidence obtained from BC parentage court documents indicates that such practices are occurring. In the case of *Family Law Act (Re)*, a same-sex couple (DD and ML) from Quebec travelled to the United States for an ovum donor (ME, the sister of ML) and then used a BC surrogate (EM) to carry and give birth to their child (È).[112] Whether this is an exceptional or common occurrence is not discernible using data made available from CARTR Plus, although provincial vital statistics registries

108 Pamela M White, "Canada's Surrogacy Landscape Is Changing: Should Canadians Care?" (2017) 39:11 *Journal of Obstetrics and Gynecology Canada* 1046.

109 The author has spoken with international intended parents who have engaged in the Canada/US blended option. See Busby & White, Chapter 7, this volume.

110 Levine et al, above note 44. Hughes & Dejean, above note 44.

111 Email exchanges between NASS analysts and the author, 11 December 2016.

112 *Family Law Act (Re)*, 2016 BCSC 22.

may be able to shed light on this topic.[113] By contrast, research conducted using NASS data to show utilization of surrogacy between US states reveals considerable interstate mobility of fertility patients, which is not surprising given differing state surrogacy laws.[114]

Finally, another type of data deficiency is the failure to collect data about artificial insemination. Assisted reproduction registries were designed to collect information about IVF practices. And yet AI is more common and less expensive than IVF. If we look at the information available from assisted reproduction programs recently funded in Ontario, from 31 December 2015 to the end of May 2017, the relationship of AI to IVF is 3:1.[115] ICMART recommends that AI be included in a national registry, a position echoed by the report of the Quebec Commissaire à la santé et au bien-être.[116] Availability of such data could help address important issues. In Ontario, for example, surrogates are permitted to have an unlimited number of AI treatments, raising the question as to whether this could lead to an increase in traditional surrogacy, along with an increase in multiple births.[117] To date, there is no way to measure if such a change is occurring. Unless in-depth qualitative research is also funded, we will not know if the supports provided to this group of surrogates meet their needs.

F. DESIGNING SUITABLE ASSISTED REPRODUCTION AND SURROGACY INFORMATION SYSTEMS FOR CANADA

In this chapter, I have argued that political, legal, and professional factors have resulted in Canada's not having a comprehensive and accessible assisted reproduction registry. One consequence of strategically ignoring how assisted reproduction and surrogacy information management structures are evolving is that we may face a decrease rather than an increase in

113 The British Columbia and Ontario vital statistics registries are likely candidates. Birth registrations in these two provinces reflect assisted reproduction births and parentage.

114 Kiran M Perkins et al, "Differences in the Utilization of Gestational Surrogacy Between States in the USA" (April 2018) 5 *Reproductive Biomedicine and Society Online* 1.

115 FOI Request, above note 65.

116 Commissaire à la santé et au bien-être, above note 66.

117 FOI Request, above note 65. See also evidence from Quebec: Leah Hendry, "Quebec's Axing of Fully Funded IVF Leads to Increase in Multiple Pregnancies" *CBC News* (29 December 2017), online: www.cbc.ca/news/canada/montreal/quebec-s-axing-of-fully-funded-ivf-leads-to-increase-in-multiple-pregnancies-1.4461148.

information in the future. Change is sorely needed, and in the balance of this chapter I provide several recommendations to guide such change.

First, CARTR Plus needs to be expanded to include more information about surrogacy practices and outcomes. Not only does the focus need to shift toward the surrogate, rather than the intended parent, as patient, but also more demographic and psychosocial information needs to be included in the database. Further, more data about international surrogacy need to be collected to shed light on some of the various factors that make Canada a desirable surrogacy destination. Finally, more in-depth qualitative studies are needed to understand the lived experiences of surrogates, intended parents, and the resulting children.

Second, the present governance structure of CARTR Plus, which relies on fertility clinic directors to determine access, content, and public dissemination, should no longer control the scope and extent of Canada's assisted reproduction registry. We can admire the determination of IVF directors to continue this registry in the face of relatively little interest expressed by any level of government. However, it is now time for provincial and federal health agencies, in association with statistical agencies such as the CIHI or Statistics Canada and provincial vital statistics registries, to work together with all IVF patients and clinic directors to create a national assisted reproduction registry that meets WHO standards and the information needs of Canadians.

Third, in tandem with such an initiative, there needs to be a concerted effort to determine overarching assisted reproduction and surrogacy research priorities, dissemination strategies, and access options. Existing funding forums could be used to scope out priority research areas and increase the participation of those involved in surrogacy and fertility treatments. Improved data availability through the use of Data Research Centres funded by the Canadian Institutes of Health Research would see the CARTR Plus registry used by a wider group of analysts in secure data safe havens.[118]

The privileging of a particular database epistemology and the normalization of particular statistical categorization has shaped the dimensions of what is currently known and not known about surrogacy and assisted

118 For a description about how the Data Research Centres function, see the Canadian Research Data Centre Network, online: www.crdcn.org, and www.cihr-irsc.gc.ca/e/48922.html.

reproduction. The exposé of Canada's surrogacy and assisted reproduction data systems presented in this chapter highlights a range of factors that have functioned to strategically manage what is known and conveniently left off the table when it comes to understanding Canada's surrogacy practices and outcomes. These factors include the statistical denial of the surrogate's patient status, the embryological focus of embryo success/failure, competitive delivery of fertility medicine, and private-sector data governance operating absent the government oversight that would ensure adherence to data quality standards and adoption of recommended international guidelines. Without a significant opportunity by surrogates, children, intended parents, counsellors, and clinicians to provide input into the research and data collection frameworks, control of the research and data systems will remain in the hands of those who currently get to shape what we know, do not know, and will know about surrogacy. Any discussions about remaking Canada's surrogacy law and regulations must give priority to consideration of the information systems and the research frameworks and, most importantly, to who gets to set what we know and how we know about surrogacy.

3

Navigating in Murky Waters

LEGAL ISSUES ARISING FROM A LACK OF SURROGACY REGULATION IN QUEBEC

Kévin Lavoie & Isabel Côté

A. INTRODUCTION

The use of surrogacy as an assisted reproduction practice in Quebec raises several legal, ethical, and social issues. The lack of a legislative framework complicates this practice, which has been fuelling debate for several years.[1] Although the Quebec government recognizes the use of third-party donors as an assisted reproduction technique for the realization of a parental project carried out by a single person or a couple, contracts involving surrogacy are not valid and are considered "null and void."[2] Legally speaking, the woman who gives birth is the mother of the child, according to the Roman law maxim of *semper certa est*, regardless of the reproductive context or the interests of the persons involved.[3] In the event that their child is born in Quebec, members of an intended couple who have an agreement

1 Isabel Côté & Jean-Sébastien Sauvé, "Homopaternité, gestation pour autrui: No man's land?" (2016) 46:1 *Revue générale de droit* 27; Louise Langevin, "Réponse jurisprudentielle à la pratique des mères porteuses au Québec: Une difficile reconciliation" (2010) 26:1 *Revue canadienne de droit familial* 171 [Langevin].

2 Art 541 CCQ.

3 Michelle Giroux, "Le recours controversé à l'adoption pour établir la filiation d'un enfant né d'une mère porteuse: Entre ordre public contractuel et intérêt de l'enfant" (2011) 70 *Revue du Barreau* 509; Andréanne Malacket, "Maternité de substitution: quelle filiation pour l'enfant à naître?" (2015) 117:2 *Revue du Notariat* 229.

with a woman who will act as a surrogate cannot be recognized from the outset as the child's parents. They have no legal recourse if the surrogate changes her mind and decides to keep the child. Similarly, the courts cannot force an intended parent who is not genetically linked to adopt and care for the child if the agreement is dissolved during pregnancy or at the birth of the baby.[4]

The first parents of a child born of a surrogate pregnancy in Quebec are the surrogate woman and the man responsible for conception. To regularize the situation — that is, to establish the child's filiation with the other intended parent — the route used is adoption by special consent. To do this, the woman who has given birth must first relinquish her parental rights and responsibilities. The courts must then render a decision on the basis of the existing rules on filiation and applicable jurisprudence. With regard to decisions rendered since 2007, there are two opposing lines of jurisprudence on this issue. The majority position holds that placement for adoption is in the best interests of the child. Conversely, the second position is that to allow placement for adoption in such a context is contrary to public policy.[5] In 2014, the Quebec Court of Appeal, in the decision *Adoption — 1445*,[6] held that a heterosexual couple could proceed to have the filiation of a child born by surrogacy recognized through adoption by special consent, although it considered the measure to be the "least unsatisfactory solution." The use of this solution was more recently confirmed by another decision, *Adoption — 161*,[7] rendered in January 2016.

4 Marie-France Bureau & Ève Guilhermont, "Maternité, gestation et liberté: Réflexions sur la prohibition de la gestion pour autrui en droit Québécois" (2011) 4:2 *Revue de droit et santé de McGill* 45; Langevin, above note 1.

5 Michelle Giroux, *Filiation de l'enfant né d'une procréation assistée*, JurisClasseur Québec coll "Droit civil — Personnes et famille" Fascicule 30, Montreal, LexisNexis Canada, 2010 (updated 15 August 2014).

6 *Adoption — 1445*, 2014 QCCA 1162. For an analysis of this situation, see Louise Langevin, "La Cour d'appel du Québec et la maternité de substitution dans la décision *Adoption — 1445*: quelques lumières sur les zones d'ombre et les conséquences d'une solution la moins insatisfaisante" (2015) 49:2 *Revue juridique Thémis* 451.

7 *Adoption — 161*, 2016 QCCA 16. In this situation, the surrogate had not declared her maternal filiation to the directeur de l'état civil (the Quebec registrar of civil status). For the court of first instance, this meant that it could not consent to adoption by special consent, since she was undeclared. In this case, the surrogate had clearly expressed her desire not to be recognized as the child's mother, whereas the intended parents wanted the biological father's spouse also to be recognized as the child's

At the federal level, the *Assisted Human Reproduction Act* (*AHRA*) does not prevent the realization of a parental project using surrogacy as long as the surrogate is over twenty-one years of age. It prohibits remuneration for such services as well as compensation for anyone advertising them.[8] Although it authorizes the reimbursement of expenses incurred, upon presentation of receipts,[9] the regulations governing eligible expenses have not yet been adopted.[10] This situation contributes to false representations of the practice, by equating surrogacy with a criminal act in the popular imagination and suggesting that intended parents "buy" a child or that surrogate women engage in such a project to enrich themselves.

Considering the complexity and risks associated with the process of procreation by surrogacy in Quebec, some people choose to cross borders to realize their parental project and/or call on the services of specialized agencies to guide them through the process.[11] The use of a private intermediary

father. However, for the court, this would have constituted an "evasion of the law" allowing for a "procedure that was illegal and contrary to public policy" because the mother did not appear on the child's birth certificate. The Court of Appeal, however, held that this reading was incorrect and that the best interests of the child required that a placement order for its eventual adoption be issued.

8 *Assisted Human Reproduction Act*, SC 2004, c 2, s 6 [*AHRA*].

9 *Ibid*, s 12.

10 Since section 12 of the *AHRA* is still not in force, eligible expenses are not regulated (see Petropanagos, Gruben, & Cameron, Chapter 5, and McLeod, Chapter 4, this volume). Thus, a woman cannot be paid to carry a child for someone else but can be reimbursed for expenses related to her pregnancy, such as maternity clothes, medication, and travel for medical appointments. She may also be reimbursed for lost wages during pregnancy if she has to be bedridden in order to preserve her health or that of the fetus. In such cases, a signed medical opinion must be obtained from a physician. The specific terms and conditions of each surrogacy agreement make it difficult to determine which expenses are eligible or ineligible and under what circumstances receipts are required. In practice, there is no formal procedure to guide those involved, whether surrogates or intended parents, in drafting their agreement and its monetary provisions.

11 With the abolition of the Assisted Human Reproduction Canada in 2012, Health Canada became the federal authority responsible for the development and enforcement of policies under the *AHRA*. However, this institution does not have control mechanisms in place to verify that surrogacy agreements comply with the provisions of the Act. According to several observers, the authorities' inaction and the "vagueness" regarding reimbursement of expenses has led to the emergence of a market for commercial intermediaries specializing in surrogacy. The role of these private agencies is to manage surrogacy projects by accompanying intended parents and surrogates throughout the whole process, while also coordinating the actors involved (medical clinics, law firms, hospitals, etc.). For a critical analysis of the situation, see Françoise Baylis & Jocelyn

(i.e., a broker or agent) as an access channel to surrogacy can have several advantages for intended parents, including physical and psychological evaluation of women who apply and matching services to find a surrogate to carry out their project. The clinics at which the related medical procedures occur may also intervene to facilitate the legal aspects related to the filiation of children born in this way, while sometimes offering mediation between the intended parents and the women carrying the baby in case of disagreement.[12] However, the costs associated with the use of a private intermediary are high, thus limiting its use to individuals or couples who have substantial financial means or are willing to take on debt.

Although a body of theoretical work on surrogacy has built up over the past twenty years, particularly in the fields of law and bioethics, empirical research on the subject is scarce.[13] The few available studies have focused on the links between surrogates and intended parents, and mainly their psychological aspects.[14] Our objective is to report on the practice of surrogacy and the legal issues arising from the lack of legislative framework in Quebec, through the experiences and concerns expressed by intended parents and surrogates. We believe it is important to add their voices to the collective discussion, in order to reflect on social and legal responses that could lead to an appropriate regulatory framework.

This chapter is divided into three parts. The first part describes the two Quebec research projects from which this contribution is derived. In addition to an overview of the methodological considerations (regarding data collection and analysis), this section describes the characteristics of the intended parents and surrogates who were interviewed. The second part presents the results, which are broken down into four main themes associated with the process of reproduction through surrogacy: negotiation and formalization of an agreement; medical considerations; financial considerations; and

---

Downie, "The Tale of Assisted Human Reproduction Canada: A Tragedy in Five Acts" (2013) 25:2 *Canadian Journal of Women and the Law* 183; Françoise Baylis, Jocelyn Downie, & Dave Snow, "Fake It Till You Make It: Policymaking and Assisted Human Reproduction in Canada" (2014) 36:6 *Journal of Obstetrics and Gynaecology Canada* 510.

12 Dean A Murphy, *Gay Men Pursuing Parenthood Through Surrogacy* (Sydney: University of New South Wales Press, 2015).

13 See White, Chapter 2, this volume.

14 Elly Teman, "The Social Construction of Surrogacy Research: An Anthropological Critique of the Psychosocial Scholarship on Surrogate Motherhood" (2008) 67:7 *Social Science and Medicine* 1104.

the establishment of filiation. Legal issues are thus problematized in light of participants' experiences. Finally, considering the current debate on the regulation of this practice, we identify the implications for public policy and family law in Quebec.

B. METHOD

This chapter draws on two sets of data from Quebec research documenting the experiences of people affected by surrogacy. One study focuses on the parenting trajectories of gay fathers who started their families with the help of a surrogate,[15] while the other is an ongoing doctoral study that looks at the relationship of motherhood among women involved in a surrogacy arrangement.[16] Given the complexity of the subject and its exploratory nature, as well as the material made up of individuals' subjective experiences, a qualitative approach was preferred in both cases. This choice is justified by the desire to understand and apprehend the perspective of participants considered to be key informants.[17] We draw on their experiences to describe assisted reproduction practices and the difficulties associated with the absence of regulation in Quebec, with a view to making their voices heard, voices that are often ignored in discussions on the reform of parentage law.

Three complementary strategies were deployed to recruit our participants. First, various Quebec organizations offering services to families, either for the gay community or infertile couples, were approached so that they could solicit their members who fit the desired profile. Second, our calls for participation were distributed through social media, notably through

---

15 The study *Représentations des rôles parentaux de couples gais ayant eu leurs enfants grâce à la gestation pour autrui* was funded by a grant from the Fonds institutionnel de recherche de l'Université du Québec en Outaouais and was approved by the research ethics committee of that same institution.

16 The MATRICES study (maternités assistées par tierces reproductrices [maternity through surrogacy]), conducted as part of a PhD in applied social sciences, is funded by the Social Sciences and Humanities Research Council (SSHRC) through a Vanier Canada Graduate Scholarship. This study was approved by the arts and science research ethics committee of the Université de Montréal.

17 Pierre Paillé & Alex Mucchielli, *L'analyse qualitative en sciences humaines et sociales*, 3d ed (Paris: Armand Colin, 2012).

various Facebook groups dedicated to assisted reproduction and family issues. Finally, we completed our sample using the snowball method.[18]

The data presented in this chapter were collected through semi-structured individual interviews[19] conducted at individuals' residences or in a university space. During the interviews, several themes were discussed, including parents' motivation to realize their dream of starting a family through surrogacy or women's desire to participate in such a project, their representations of paternal and maternal figures, the impact of these representations on the relational dynamics existing—or not existing—between the persons concerned, and, finally, the procreation process and its legal stakes, which is the subject of this chapter. Interviews (averaging two hours in length) were transcribed in full, coded using NVivo software, and then interpreted using content analysis.[20]

---

18 This is a technique by which subjects and our key informants referred us to other participants who fit the desired profile until we obtained the required sampling. This method is frequently used in studies whose focus is a relatively marginal phenomenon and whose environment is difficult to access. See Alvaro Pires, "Échantillonnage et recherche qualitative: Essai théorique et méthodologique" in Jean Poupart et al, eds, *La recherche qualitative: Enjeux épistémologiques et méthodologiques* (Montreal: Gaëtan Morin, 1997) 113.

19 Semi-structured interviewing is a method of data collection in which the researcher is guided by what emerges from the interview, while at the same time following an outline for the discussion, to reach a better understanding of the phenomenon under study. See Lorraine Savoie-Zajc, "L'entrevue semi-dirigée" in Benoît Gauthier, ed, *Recherche sociale: De la problématique à la collecte de données*, 5th ed (Quebec: Presses de l'Université du Québec, 2010) 337.

20 Content analysis is used to analyze a body of research consisting of interviews, as is the case with this research. The analysis technique used here includes various stages, including pre-analysis (which allows the researcher to absorb the collected material to let first impressions emerge), a phase of exploitation of the material (where statements are divided into thematic units and then categorized in order to extract their meaning), and the analysis itself. For this last stage, the material was first submitted to vertical analysis, in which each participant's discourse is taken independently of that of the others, and then cross-sectional analysis, which compares each participant's discourse to the others. This approach has the advantage of allowing the researcher to have an overall view of the problem while facilitating the identification of invariant, consensual, and divergent elements raised by each participant with respect to the themes in the interviews. See Laurence Bardin, *L'analyse de contenu* (Paris: Presses universitaires de France, 2007).

1) Characteristics of the Persons Interviewed

Our sample consisted of twenty-eight participants, whom we chose to divide into two distinct groups, according to their respective roles in the procreation process. The first group corresponded to intended parents ($n = 13$)—that is, those who formulated a parenting plan by surrogacy in Canada. This group comprised nine gay men, who were interviewed between November 2012 and April 2013, and four heterosexual women, who were interviewed between September 2016 and April 2017. Our sample was relatively homogeneous: they were all Caucasian people aged twenty-six to forty-nine (the average age was thirty-eight) living in urban areas. All had a postsecondary education, and most were employed in professions that allow them to enjoy a relatively affluent standard of living. They had all been in couples for several years. Their children born through surrogacy were between a few weeks and four years of age at the time of the interviews, except in the case of one intended mother whose surrogate was pregnant. Two couples had asked a friend to carry their child, thus carrying out their surrogacy project within a pre-existing friendship. One couple turned to an online Facebook community to connect with surrogates. The others sought the services of private Canadian agencies to help them find a surrogate.

The second group consisted of Canadian surrogates ($n = 15$) who were involved in surrogacy projects formulated by Québécois intended couples. Participants were women aged twenty-three to forty-two (the average age was thirty-four). Ten were heterosexual, while the other five identified with one of the constellations of sexual diversity. Twelve women had a post-secondary diploma (college or university) and three had a high school or vocational diploma. Five participants had a relatively high personal income ($70,000 or more); seven women had highly variable personal incomes between $30,000 and $70,000; and three women, all single mothers, earned less than $20,000 a year. At the time of their first surrogacy project, all were multiparous, except one woman who had never been pregnant before. Most of these women had been surrogates once previously, although four had been surrogates several times (from two to four surrogate pregnancies at the time of the interviews). Five women went through this experience with an Ontario agency, while four of them had made contact with couples through social networks. Six women already knew the intended parents before the process began, with five having agreed to bear a child for a couple with whom they were friends and one for a gay cousin and his spouse. Nine surrogates went through gestational surrogacy, meaning that the embryo implanted into their uterus after *in vitro* fertilization was conceived using the sperm of the biological father and the eggs of the intended mother or a donor other than the surrogate. Six women bore a fetus conceived using their own gametes as part of a traditional (or genetic) surrogacy.

C. RESULTS

Analyzing the experiences of adults involved in surrogacy enables us to document their understanding of the current state of the law and policies on assisted reproduction, as well as the strategies used to implement their plans and navigate through the legal system and the system of medical assistance for reproduction. In this section, we identify the legal issues raised throughout the procreation process, basing our presentation on four elements: (1) negotiation and establishment of a surrogacy agreement, whether formally by contract or informally through verbal agreement between the parties; (2) medical considerations (i.e., restrictions imposed on surrogates arising from potential risks to the fetus and the role of perinatal professionals during pregnancy); (3) financial considerations (i.e., the issue of reimbursement of expenses incurred and the flow of money between the parties); and (4) filiation of the child, which focuses on the, provincial rules that apply depending on the place of birth.

1) Negotiation and Formalization of an Agreement

After the initial contact between the intended parents and the surrogate, whether arranged by a specialized agency, occurring on digital social networks such as Facebook, or as part of a pre-existing friendly or family relationship, the parties negotiate their surrogacy agreement. Our objective here is not to enumerate the elements under negotiation but rather to identify issues related to the agreement, whether formal or not.

a) Establishing a Formal Contract Agreement

Considering the current situation in Quebec regarding the absolute nullity of surrogacy agreements and the fears associated with them, several Québécois intended parents turned to specialized agencies located in other

Canadian provinces, mainly Ontario, to establish an agreement with a surrogate. In most of these cases, the legal procedures were managed by the agency. Others also crossed borders to sign a contract, but without necessarily going through a private intermediary. The intended parents' need for security, especially with respect to ensuring that the child would be delivered to them at birth, was their primary motivation.

> We were not interested in having a surrogate in Quebec because here, there is always the primacy of the maternal bond, the possibility that the child may be taken back by the mother. (Simon, intended father)

For surrogates who formalized their agreement with the intended parents, the contract represented the certainty that their gesture—bearing a child for others—was carried out legitimately and was not a criminal or illegal act, which gave them some peace of mind.

> In New Brunswick, a surrogate mother is legal, it's not child trafficking! It's done with contracts, and both sides are protected. I could never have decided to keep the baby. They had already made their will, they had already chosen the people who would take care of the baby, no matter what happened during my pregnancy. And for the surrogate mother, it's the same thing. She's protected. If my future pregnancies became at risk, if there were problems for my uterus, if there were problems for my personal health, I had the right 100 percent to terminate the pregnancy, to terminate the contract. (Virginie, surrogate)

Contrary to popular belief, the women interviewed who had chosen to go ahead with the surrogacy project had given thought to the ins and outs of the process. Moreover, the notion of "power" was central to their thinking, as they soon realized that the service of bearing a child for a couple is in great demand. Partly due to the scarcity effect, this gave them the freedom to negotiate the surrogacy agreement within their parameters, which increased their sense of control over the situation. This was particularly significant in the discourse of women who had been surrogates more than once.

> [For my second surrogacy], I told them, "Here's the contract I used the first time, these are my terms and conditions. Take it or leave it." It was non-negotiable. I didn't use lawyers, because I didn't need one,

> the contract was already made. They tried to negotiate certain points, trivialities. It seems to me it was more about the terminology used. For me it was, "No, I'm familiar with this terminology and I won't change anything." I felt at that time that I really had the big end of the stick, but for me it was really important to protect myself. (Claudine, surrogate)

Although the need for protection was shared by both parties, for some surrogates the framework imposed by the contract appeared to be inadequate for their needs. In such cases, they had the impression that this legal document had been prepared on the basis of a pre-defined template that did not take into account the particularities of each situation or the aspirations of the triad they formed with the couple, particularly if the surrogate woman wished to assume a certain parental role with the child or if the project was the result of a friendly agreement.

> I started to wonder as I saw the wording of the legal agreement take shape, because it seemed so cold and so formal. But I think that's just because it was based on a template where the surrogate would not have any relationship with the child. I think that's where they started from, and they just kind of made a few changes here and there. That process, I found a little bit uncomfortable. Because as soon as everything starts to be in the legal language, I started to feel as if my role was being limited in a way .... It had to be very clear, that the fathers were going to be the legal parents. And the lawyers didn't want to sort of leave any grey area about me, possibly having some sort of parenting role, because I think that might have interfered with the judge's ability to make a clear decision and say yes, that this couple is the parents. (Kate, surrogate)

Certain clauses listed in the contract were considered superfluous or even inappropriate. The confidentiality clause was frequently mentioned as an example of an "absurd" measure included in contracts, especially in the era of digital social networks. Surrogates' pregnancy and their visibility as pregnant women made it difficult for them to comply with this provision, contrary to the freedom of action enjoyed by intended parents when it came to disclosing the project to their friends and colleagues, for example.

> The idea is that it's up to them to tell the child who her biological mother is. So, they didn't want me to be talking too much about it, or posting on social media, for example, because that would impair their ability to be

> the ones who would decide when and how to tell their child . . . . I feel like I take the confidentiality clause more seriously than they do. I just don't want to do the wrong thing. But obviously, everyone in their community knows that I am the mother of the baby. So, I don't even know if it was their idea necessarily to put the confidentiality clause, or if it was just something their lawyer recommended. (Kate, surrogate)

Although meant to preserve the privacy rights of both parties, this clause was, in the view of these surrogates, entirely to the benefit of intended parents, since the burden of visibility of the surrogacy project rested entirely on the shoulders of the surrogate, not on those of the couple. Many felt that this clause undermined their freedom of action or, at least, considerably reduced the scope of possibilities, since their prominent belly raised many questions from members of their community, which sometimes were impossible to dodge without lying. Nonetheless, for the sake of the intended parents, surrogates were generally careful to respect the confidentiality clause, even if they were not very familiar with its real scope and limitations.

b) Establishing an Amicable Informal Agreement

In the case of an unregulated surrogacy project, mutual trust is of particular importance, since it is the only assurance of compliance with the agreement between the parties. Several reasons were put forward by the participants to explain their choice of making the project a reality in Quebec and thus relying on the honour and word of the other party: difficulty in travelling to another province, insufficient financial resources to pay a lawyer's fees, a lack of interest in legal issues, a desire to maintain an adaptable and flexible agreement, and a desire to preserve the authenticity of the pre-existing relationship. In such cases, dialogue was a way to ensure consensus among the people concerned.

> Yes, we talked about it a lot, but it was just verbal. We really agreed on all points. We thought the same, we saw it the same way. We didn't sign any papers, nothing. Anyway, it's not legal. It's of no value. (Denis, intended father)

In these circumstances, establishing a bond of trust meant validating a shared vision of the surrogacy project. Intended parents and surrogates, the latter often accompanied by their husbands and children, would therefore generally plan an occasion, such as a supper, to discuss the agreement. People's aspirations, needs and fears, as well as medical and financial considerations, were then addressed more or less explicitly.

> Because even if you start the process, at the end of the day, if I decide that I'm going to keep it, I'll keep it. They have no guarantees. So, we were talking about this fear, about everything and nothing . . . . It was so simple. We're a bunch of friends, you talk, you talk, and everything's easygoing. It wasn't complicated. I wouldn't have set out on an adventure that was complicated from the start. (Sandrine, surrogate)

During this three- or four-way discussion, the stated objective was for participants to familiarize themselves with each other's values and temperament, verify whether their personalities were compatible enough to go through the adventure together, and set down the broad outlines of the agreement. Given the absence of models and the uniqueness of the process, the negotiation represented a relational approach in the moment when everyone's role was under construction. In such a context, identifying potential problems and formulating courses of action in response were not part of the initial discussion.

> We didn't want to jinx ourselves, so we thought we'd cross the bridge when we got there. If [it] comes to it, we'll talk it out together and we'll make our decision then. But we didn't want to plan ahead. And, really, all four of us mutually agreed on that. (Sofia, intended mother)

Despite the trust and common vision that united them, many participants who had reached an informal agreement nevertheless pointed to the lack of protection in the event of problems. They recognized the candour with which they had engaged in the project, and they crossed their fingers, hoping that no disagreement would occur during pregnancy. For them, the overall vision of the surrogacy project was more important than the sum of the elements that could be subjected to a formal contract.

> It's because they're close friends, and we have a bond of trust that is very intense. Of course that makes all the difference. I've known them for five years, but I'm aware that trust . . . you know, life, it changes, there are so many things. It's not necessarily a breach of trust. Sometimes it's

> personality, there are a lot of things that can break when it comes to trust. (Marilyne, surrogate)

2) Medical Considerations

One of the issues discussed extensively by the parties at the time of establishing the agreement was medical considerations—that is, the implications of a surrogacy project for the lives of surrogates and their bodily autonomy. Overall, surrogates adopted a facilitative attitude toward the presence of future parents at their side, choosing to delegate some decision-making power to them during pregnancy.

> I always gave them free rein in almost everything, if they wanted a screening test, if they wanted this, if they wanted that. They would consult me, but I would tell them: "You're the one who's steering this ship, and if there's something I really disagree with, I'll tell you. But otherwise, the rest is your decision." I didn't give them 100% of the rights over my body, but as much as they could have, I gave them. (Élise, surrogate)

However, it seems that the boundaries between the intended parents' parental project, the fetus that the woman is carrying for them for nine months, and the pregnant body of the woman were not easy to map or establish. Two areas of particular concern were the restrictions placed on surrogate women during pregnancy and medical decision-making; they highlight the ambiguity of the current context and the variability of interpretations among those interviewed regarding their rights and responsibilities.

a) Restrictions on Surrogate Women

In an informal agreement, requirements in terms of nutrition or activities to be avoided were defined through discussions between the parties and were respected at the discretion of the surrogate. The parties all agreed on certain basic points (no drugs, alcohol, or tobacco, for example), and the intended parents trusted the woman to go through the pregnancy while caring for both her own health and that of the fetus, as was the case for her previous pregnancies.

> All I wanted was for her to take care of the child during pregnancy. I didn't even express it because she had three children, and I know that

> she doesn't drink when she's pregnant, that she eats very well, doesn't smoke and doesn't take drugs . . . . I wasn't worried about that at all, we trusted her completely. (Sofia, intended mother)

Within the framework of a formal agreement, the restrictions imposed on the surrogate were carefully listed and described in the contract signed between the parties. In addition to the usual prescriptions related to the consumption of alcohol, tobacco, and drugs, other specifics were added according to the wishes of the intended parents, such as maintaining a daily dietary log, avoiding certain foods or beverages (seafood, certain cheese, fast food, coffee, soft drinks, etc.), giving up sports during pregnancy, or undertaking not to fly or travel beyond a certain distance from her place of residence. The list of restrictions can vary greatly from one situation to another. For intended parents, the restrictions delimit the course of the pregnancy by identifying things that are obvious but that must be spelled out in black and white to clarify as much as possible their agreement with the surrogate.

> Sometimes I would tell her [the surrogate]: "Don't forget, you can't eat raw milk cheese or seafood, and be careful with sushi." Things like that, but we've never poked into her life, searching, or making lists of what she eats. She wasn't a prisoner, we trusted her. But sometimes I used to make little jokes like, "Are you sure you're allowed to eat this?" I wasn't saying it to be mean. (Richard, intended father)

In fact, it was the feeling of being monitored that annoyed the surrogates most, as they perceived it as a lack of trust on the part of the intended parents. The restrictions specified in the contract gave them the feeling that the parents were restricting their freedom and interfering excessively in their daily life. The majority of them did not hesitate to point out that it was "*their* child, *my* pregnancy," drawing a clear line between the gestating fetus and their experience as a pregnant woman.

> There are parents who practically want you to come and live with them. They have a long list of things they don't want you to do. There are parents who are real control freaks and think it gives them the right to tell us what to do. They are anxious parents who have experienced many setbacks and really want to be parents so much. (Claudine, surrogate)

While the surrogates interviewed undertook to follow the doctor's recommendations and do what was necessary to ensure the health of the unborn child, certain clauses "crossed the line," according to them, especially when they negatively affected their family life.

> There was a couple who no longer wanted me to hold my daughter in my arms; it was important that I didn't lift any weight, my daughter included. You can be sure I never would have put my family aside to carry a child. Of course, I wouldn't go parachuting while pregnant. There are common-sense limits. Except there are some things I wasn't ready to give up. I wasn't willing to put my life on hold to carry out someone else's pregnancy. (Virginie, surrogate)

Regardless of the quantity or content of the restrictions, the fear of reprisals led some women, particularly those selected by an agency, to comply with the terms of the contract. The fear of being blamed and prosecuted in the event of a problem during pregnancy or at birth meant that these women changed their behaviour or lifestyle to comply with the agreement at all costs.

> So, my last family, they were super strict on everything. Not the fact that they're not going to know, but what about if something happens; they do their best and then it comes back on me? They know that I've done something wrong. That's the only reason why I stick so close to the contract, is because I don't want anything to fall back on me, in the way that I did something wrong. (Karen, surrogate)

b) Decision Making: What Rights for Which Patient?

During pregnancy, several medical examinations and screening tests are performed by health professionals. The latter must designate their interlocutor (i.e., their patient) during these perinatal meetings in a context where three people are involved in the surrogacy project and perhaps present for appointments.

> I have the right to be accompanied [to appointments] by just one person. We insisted: "I don't mind, but if I have to choose between the two parents, I prefer you take both of them and I won't be there" [laughs]. I always say it as a joke, to make them understand the situation. I try to redirect the doctor to the parents. Of course, the technical questions—do you

> have nausea, weight gain and all that—those are mine, but everything else, I want it to really be them. They [professionals] do it as a matter of course, most of the time. (Élise, surrogate)

Surrogacy requires providing "a space for each person concerned, which means communicating our needs throughout the process," summarized one surrogate. In this sense, surrogacy is a process in which the common aspirations of intended parents and women surrogates come together, but where their respective interests occasionally diverge.

> In the event that only one person was admitted to the operating room, I wanted it to be my husband, but she [the intended mother] wanted it to be her. I finally let her win. I warned her: "If there are medical decisions to be made and I can't make them, I want my husband to take them, not you. It's going to be spelled out very clearly in the contract and in my birth plan. You're not my spouse, you're not there for me." (Claudine, surrogate)

During perinatal support, professionals can, with a view to mediation, influence the process and prompt a discussion between the parties as to the rights and responsibilities of each party.

> During pregnancy follow-up, there are more or less invasive tests to be done. They [the intended parents] always left the choice to me. They would say to me, "You decide, it's your body." My midwife gave her take on it, saying, "Yes, but it's not always just about her body. I advise you to talk about it together, longer than just trying to make a quick decision based on 'It's her body,' because it can have more serious consequences that will directly affect the baby." (Manon, surrogate)

The experiences reported by participants regarding perinatal support were relatively positive. However, the issue of the exclusive rights of the surrogate as a designated patient, particularly in terms of access to information about fetal health, remained controversial, particularly from the perspective of the intended parents.

> We were really worried. We were wondering, but why aren't we important? In the end, it's our parental project, not that of [name of the surrogate]. We were never kept informed of what was happening by the doctor or nurses. That was disappointing on their part. (Sofia, intended mother)

> My obstetrician made this clear to them: "My patient is Claudine, not you. If I see that your presence hinders [my work], I will ask you to leave. It's going to be the same thing during childbirth. Even if your contract says something, my role as a doctor is to look after my patient. That's my priority." (Claudine, surrogate)

While the surrogate is always the designated patient during pregnancy and receives recognition as such from perinatal care providers, the situation changes suddenly at the birth of the baby, according to the statements of intended parents and surrogates interviewed. According to the intended parents, as soon as the umbilical cord is cut, they took on the rights and responsibilities pertaining to the child.

> When they give birth, until they cut the cord, she makes the medical decisions. If the doctors ask her questions, she decides, because it's her body, that's normal. Once they cut the cord, the babies are no longer in her body, so we decide for the children. Now she's no longer connected. It's logical. She is no longer responsible and has no further rights. (Alexandre, intended father)

This immediate transfer of the rights of the surrogate woman to the intended parents means that the parents then have exclusive control over information concerning the welfare of the child. That can create potentially anxiety-provoking situations for the surrogate, as recounted by a participant who gave birth to a baby with no vital signs at birth.

> It was the worst scene I've ever seen in my life, it was like a horror movie: the baby had zero vital signs .... But since in New Brunswick I had no connection with the child, I had no right to know. So them [the intended parents], they were gone, it must have been about an hour. It seemed like an eternity to me. I had no way of knowing if he was dead; I knew absolutely nothing. They [the professionals] were not allowed to tell me. (Virginie, surrogate)

c) Respect the Contract at All Costs?

To what extent should a surrogacy agreement be respected and its clauses imposed? This questioning highlights the discomfort and upheavals that can be caused by "catastrophic scenarios," among which termination of pregnancy is likely to raise the greatest fears. The issue of abortion directly affects women's sovereignty over their bodies, which may conflict with a clause in the contract that stipulates, for example, that the doctor's recommendations must be followed, notwithstanding the woman's own opinion.

> Our agreement was that if a doctor were to recommend an abortion, we would accept it. We wanted her to accept it. I think it would have been a huge trial for her. Now that I know her well, I can see that it would have been very challenging for her. I think she would have done it. It would have taken her a lot of work, it would have been hard for her, but it was the agreement. (Louis, intended father)

> So I went for the test, and the results came back saying yeah: there's a likelihood of the child having Down syndrome. I was crying, and talking to the fathers about it, and one of them was like: "yeah . . . I don't know . . . ." He was sort-of suggesting that they wouldn't want to keep the child if it had the syndrome . . . . I was not going to get an abortion. I just really had no intention of that, at this point. (Kate, surrogate)

Besides abortion, participants mentioned other clauses in the surrogacy contract that might restrict the rights of surrogates over their bodies, such as requiring that consent from the intended parents be obtained before carrying out certain interventions. This was the case, for example, for certain procedures during childbirth.

> She asked us if we'd allow her to have an epidural. I thought it was nice of her to ask us that question, but I can't imagine a situation where one could deny a woman an epidural. I draw the line at the fact that it's her body. (Antoine, intended father)

Even if childbirth has gone well and the child is in perfect health, the surrogate may come out of the experience wounded—for example, by having agreed to a caesarean section on the doctor's advice, to comply with the contract clause to this effect. The following situation reported by an intended father highlights the obstetric violence experienced in the delivery room and, more broadly, the notion of consent in a context where the surrogate woman fears being blamed for a problem with the baby when everyone is acting in an excessively cautious manner, to her disadvantage.

> The doctor made the decision to proceed with a cesarean section. It was not an emergency C-section, in the sense that there was no fetal distress or

> problem with the placenta. It wasn't a planned C-section either because, clearly, there was nothing planned! What we learned later was that she [the surrogate] had a very bad experience with the caesarean section. She really experienced it as an assault. She considered that it was unnecessary and that they [the medical team] could have allowed her labour to continue for several hours. She had not been given time. I think it's a typical case for surrogates, where the doctor suggested a caesarean section and she accepted for our sake, not for hers. (Louis, intended father)

3) Financial Considerations

The monetary issue is a sensitive and controversial subject, but it highlights the legal "vagueness" associated with the reimbursement of expenses, their eligibility, and the amounts that may be associated with them in accordance with federal law.

a) Reimbursement of Expenses

Although complex in appearance, the issue of reimbursement can be summed up succinctly: no one knows exactly what can be reimbursed or how much the amounts are, regardless of the path of access to surrogacy (with or without intermediaries) or the type of agreement (formal or informal) that binds people together. Indeed, the apparent "grey area" regarding the reimbursement of eligible expenses was subject to numerous interpretations by participants.

> Since it's grey, there's no "yes" or "no," it's "maybe." There is no real limitation on what can be reimbursed. It's a rather vague subject, you could say. (Geneviève, surrogate)

> She [the surrogate] has to provide receipts because the law says you only have the right to reimburse her expenses. It is not very clear in the law what she has the right to submit or not, but it basically covers everything that allows her to provide for her needs and those of the unborn child. (Louis, intended father)

The absence of a list of eligible expenses opens the door to different ways of doing things, some more exhaustive or creative than others, to reach the agencies' target horizon of $20,000 offered to the surrogate. In addition to expenses related to food, medication, clothing, and transportation, other bills can also be added: babysitting, housekeeping, body care or massage therapy services, and so on. The vagueness of this aspect of the process left many interviewees perplexed:

> I found myself faced with her expenses for work, hotel, gifts. It wasn't really part of the surrogacy project, but we still paid because we were building a relationship and we felt like doing it. [sigh] I stopped counting at that point. (Antoine, intended father)

In addition to the challenge of identifying eligible expenses, it is also necessary to determine the amounts. The participants noted that, at that point, they had to "play with numbers and words" to navigate through the ambiguity of the law and the practices established in recent years by the agencies and lawyers who guided them through the process.

> There's still a huge legal vagueness, so it's like a lottery. My lawyer used to tell me, "Ask for that amount." I would reply: "Yes, but I don't want to ask for half a million dollars if I have a caesarean section." She would say, "If they [the intended parents] don't agree, they'll make a counteroffer." It had more to do with my lawyer than with the couple. All we had to do was agree on what was reasonable and what was not. (Élise, surrogate)

b) The Transfer of Money

Another aspect of the monetary dimension concerned the movement of money between the parties, which was distinguished by whether or not an agency was used as a private intermediary dealing with financial management. Those who had done business with an agency pointed out the positive effects of this choice, allowing them to avoid discussing money among themselves and thus avoid potential disputes:

> For us, the advantage is that the agency takes care of this part, they are the ones who manage the receipts. The first time Vanessa was a surrogate, she had to handle all the receipts herself. She told us that she had trouble doing everything. They [the people at the agency] set up a scanner for her to scan all her receipts. Then the agency keeps track. (Antoine, intended father)

> The financial side of surrogacy is the agency's responsibility. As a surrogate, you just have to develop a good relationship with the intended

> parents and not worry about the financial side of things that might lead to conflicts or misunderstandings. (Isabelle, surrogate)

For many surrogates associated with an agency, discussing money with their couple would have had the effect of "distorting" the beauty of their gesture or blurring the altruistic nature of their motivations. In addition, the agency's managerial role gave participants the impression that they were doing things correctly and not doing something illegal or criminal. The responsibility to make sure that everything was in accordance with the law then fell on the intermediary's shoulders, which reassured them and gave participants the freedom to move forward with the project.

For those who instead opted for an amicable agreement without going through an agency, reimbursement procedures had to be established by the surrogates and the intended parents themselves. Although the discussion cannot be avoided, many preferred to talk about it briefly, without making a fuss about it.

> I shared my needs with them, we talked. Neither of us like to talk about money; we were very uncomfortable. You know, I wish I could really offer them . . . you know, have a job where I can take a leave of absence the entire time I'm pregnant, have money coming in. They just said, "We'll pay your rent, we'll pay your living expenses." (Marilyne, surrogate)

The participants all tried to make things as simple as possible from the beginning of the project, by setting up a system of reimbursement or money transfer to avoid having to bring the subject up again during the pregnancy.

> They gave me a credit card right away. So, any expenses that would have related to the pregnancy, "just put it on the credit card and we'll pay it." They decided that it would be the simplest way. And they just said, "keep your receipts." So, every time that I needed to have multivitamins or something, I just would put it on their credit card, and just put the receipt in the envelope. (Kate, surrogate)

An amicable agreement did not mean that the intended parents were the only ones to get involved financially. Several surrogates showed ingenuity in reusing maternity items and clothing, thereby reducing the costs associated with pregnancy for the couple. Recognizing the economic burden that the surrogacy project places on intended parents, surrogates—many supported by their spouses, depending on the case—did not hesitate to cover certain expenses or, at least, to use the means at their disposal to reduce costs.

c) The Sensitive Issue of Remuneration

The participants all had an opinion on the subject of remuneration for surrogates or, at least, expressed some reservations about certain positions on the topic. Our objective here is not to add any more arguments to the debate but rather to highlight the impact of the current legal framework and preconceptions about surrogacy on the experiences of those directly concerned. In this regard, being subjected to the judgment of others coloured the journey of intended parents and surrogates:

> I think it forces people to be dishonest, to find ways to get around the system. I don't like that. I also don't like being forced to say, "My expenses are reimbursed" and as soon people find out I've been reimbursed $18,000, they say, "You did it for cash." I didn't do it for cash, but I wouldn't have done it completely for free either. (Claudine, surrogate)

> I can see this discomfort .... [A]nytime money is associated with a human life, I can see how that makes people uncomfortable. But I don't see paying a surrogate as purchasing a human life. I see it as remunerating her for the risks and the inconveniences that she takes on. I really think it's up to a woman to decide if this is something that works for her; then, she has the right to make that decision. (Kate, surrogate)

Beyond ideological positions on remuneration and the stigma attached to it, in the current context surrogates carry a definite economic burden, since the expenses associated with the project are not limited to the nine months of pregnancy alone, but include a host of other costs, including lost wages and, in some cases, a delay in contributing to their pension plan during maternity leave. Although not part of generally recognized "direct expenses," because it is associated with a form of remuneration, this amount can be used to make up for the loss of income that a woman experiences for a few months, but also, potentially, for the rest of her career.

> There should be some compensation for everything she [the surrogate] loses by agreeing to do this for us. Yes, she is entitled to maternity leave

> after [the birth of the child], but during that leave she is paid 55%[21] of her salary . . . . [S]he still loses 45% of her income! She puts her life on hold for a year, that's worth something, after all. But then, if we want to provide a framework . . . how much is that worth? (Josée, intended mother)

> If I take a step back, it's obvious that it cost me more [than what I received in compensation]. At the end of the day, I dug myself into a pretty good hole. It was a beautiful gesture, but financially . . . . If I were to do it again, I wouldn't do it for just any price. It cost me a lot in that sense [financially]. But look, I got through it. (Sandrine, surrogate)

4) Establishing Filiation

Having children thanks to a surrogate is not the easiest way for Quebec couples who cannot conceive without outside help. Several reservations expressed by the participants stem from current family law in Quebec, more specifically the status of mother attributed to the surrogate and the procedures required to establish filiation with the non-biological parent. Additional sources of concern for the persons involved are the place of delivery and problems that may arise if the agreement is dissolved during pregnancy or at the birth of the child.

a) Place of Delivery

The civil law principle that "[t]he woman who gives birth is the mother," which prevails in Quebec, was unanimously criticized by the participants. Indeed, they consider that this unnecessarily complicates the surrogacy process for intended parents, in addition to not reflecting the identity and feelings of the surrogate, who does not consider herself to be the mother of the child she has borne. While the birth of the child is a joyful moment for everyone, it is nevertheless fraught with legal hassles if it occurs in "la Belle Province."

---

21 The income replacement rate is in fact 70 percent under the Quebec Parental Insurance Plan. This error on the part of the participant illustrates our point that ignorance, not only of the law but also of social policies, is often a preponderant element among people who engage in surrogacy. Nevertheless, the excerpt presented remains relevant, since women who carry a child endure financial losses when they give birth.

> After birth, it was hell. Usually, when a woman gives birth, she fills out a simplified form that ensures everything is done in the same form: social insurance number, health insurance card, tax credits from both governments, and so on. But we couldn't fill that out, because it couldn't be in the name of [name of surrogate], it had to be in the name of my boyfriend, who is the father. That's what I find difficult in Quebec, things are complicated for no reason. (Sofia, intended mother)

To avoid these inconveniences, many people—intended parents, obviously, but also surrogates who want to simplify the process and not be recognized as mothers—choose other Canadian provinces for childbirth, such as Ontario or New Brunswick. With legal frameworks perceived as "surrogacy friendly," that is to say, simpler and more predictable than that of Quebec, these provinces are sometimes chosen by couples who have the necessary resources to implement their reproductive project in this way. As the interviewees suggested, this option is also strongly suggested by intermediaries, both agencies and lawyers.

> There was a little bit of concern about the fact that I was working in Quebec and travelling to Montreal every week, because they said: "If you give birth in Quebec, it would really complicate things for us." I wasn't due until January. So, it was unlikely that I was going to be in Quebec when I was near the time to give birth. But it was something that the lawyers emphasize many times: "Don't give birth in Quebec if you can avoid it!" (Kate, surrogate)

Crossing borders to another Canadian province does not necessarily mean that the process will be without complications or risks. As one Quebec surrogate who gave birth in a neighbouring province put it, "Everything we do in Ontario, Quebec does not understand, and everything we do in Quebec, Ontario does not understand. It's completely disorganized. We're navigating through that." Other intended parents have chosen to delay the signing of legal papers until they return home with their children.

> The children were born in Ontario. They left the hospital for Quebec by train and had no names or certificates at that time, they were in a "grey zone." No legal paperwork could be signed at the hospital, to facilitate the lawyers' work. We needed a lawyer to represent us in court to legalize it all with a "parentage" declaration. (Gabriel, intended father)

Lack of awareness of surrogacy as an assisted reproduction practice and the absence of hospital protocols to handle it can also lead to confusion among psychosocial and health professionals, or even to pitfalls that constrain the roles of the persons involved and their freedom of action, particularly that of the surrogate and the child's biological father.

> I wanted to go home [after childbirth]. "If you leave, we're going to have to file a complaint with child services," the hospital social worker told me. I said, "It's not as if the child is being abandoned, all alone: his father is there." But they treated [father's name] as if he weren't the father. (Zoé, surrogate)

b) Establishing Filiation with the Non-biological Parent

Parents reported having to deal with various difficulties in establishing filiation with their child. One challenge stems from a lack of awareness of the legal considerations surrounding the practice of surrogacy in Quebec and the apparent inconsistency of the courts when it comes to recognizing the non-biological parent. For example, while some couples were able to establish their children's filiation with both parents in Quebec, others encountered some resistance. The lesson these couples learned was to not mention that they used surrogacy.

> In the papers, it was not clearly stated that she was a surrogate, because it is a grey area. We said that I was adopting my spouse's child, which is true. It's just that we didn't say he was born to a surrogate. (Josée, intended mother)

Given the complexity of the process in Quebec and their lay understanding of the law, many couples must rely entirely on the expertise of lawyers in this area to guide them through the legal maze leading to the recognition of the non-biological parent.

> She [the surrogate] had to sign a paper stating that she was abandoning her parental rights. She had a month to reconsider her decision and, after that, we would adopt the child. There are people who say that the judge could refuse to accept that I should adopt the child. Personally, it wouldn't have bothered me not having my name, just my boyfriend's. But it bothered him more. He was thinking about school enrolment, doctor's appointments and everything . . . . If we separated, we would have

> had a notarial document drawn up stating that he considered me to be the mother of that child, and that I had as many rights as he did. The lawyer talked to us about that. (Élisabeth, intended mother)

In addition to filiation issues, welcoming a child brings with it concerns related to childcare and, consequently, the adoption leave that non-biological intended parents want to benefit from. The granting of this leave is contingent on the submission of an application for adoption to the Youth Chamber. At that point, the surrogate is registered on the birth certificate of the child and must first dispose of her parental rights.[22] Combined with differing rules of filiation from one province to another, the cumbersome and unpredictable administrative and legal procedures make families emotionally and economically fragile, requiring them to evaluate the different scenarios and make calculations in order to adequately predict the first few months of the post-partum period.

> Because of the legal vagueness, what we could do is ask that their names [of the intended parents] be directly on the child's birth certificate in Ontario, and avoid passing through adoption here in Quebec. But if we do that, she [the intended mother] will have no maternity leave, no parental benefits, no adoption leave. She will just be declared the mother of the child. The rest is unpaid. Whereas if I give birth in Ontario, I revoke my rights, my name is on the certificate and I will be entitled to maternity leave [as the woman who gave birth]. (Élise, surrogate)

The relationship with public institutions also complicates matters. The dissociation of biological, social, and legal links brought about by surrogacy is difficult to reconcile with the current state of the organization of services and social policies on parenting. In many cases, the issue of government benefits remains unresolved for several months, further complicating the post-birth period for all parties.

> I received automatic benefits. My benefits were adjusted "You have a new child . . . ." I called them to tell them I didn't have custody. Usually governments communicate with each other, but not at all in this case. I received a lot of stuff, and I hadn't made any requests. I even got the health insurance card. They [the intended parents] made the application,

22 Giroux, above note 3.

> but the government sent everything . . . to the mother, that is, me. (Anne, surrogate)

c) In Case of Dissolution of the Agreement

In the event of dissolution of the intended parents' parental project during pregnancy or at delivery, the child suddenly becomes the responsibility of the surrogate. From an agreement on assisted reproduction, it becomes a case of natural filiation, which then rests entirely on the shoulders of the surrogate. This risk, which hangs over surrogates' heads like a sword of Damocles, exacerbates their sense of vulnerability:

> Of course, the law here doesn't recognize the contracts. So if I go to court and say, "They [the intended parents] swore to me that they would take the disabled child" or "They said they would pay for the funeral expenses and they didn't pay them," I'm the one who ends up with the expenses if the child dies at birth. (Anne, surrogate)

To plan for such eventualities, the surrogates draft several scenarios. Some would take the child home and raise it as their own, while others would give it up for adoption. This was the option chosen by Anne, who was pregnant with her second surrogate pregnancy:

> I made myself a plan B. If they [the intended parents] ever died in a plane crash, or if the family didn't want the baby, or whatever, I figured I'd find another couple to give it up for adoption. Once you're pregnant, you can always add a father or mother in the documents. So one of the two is always there and that makes it an adoption by spouse. (Anne, surrogate)

D. CONCLUSION

Given the absence of regulation and the variability of interpretations of the current legal framework regarding surrogacy in Quebec, legal concerns were a major part of the discourse of surrogates and intended parents who were interviewed. The "vagueness" that persists with respect to surrogacy in Quebec forced them to navigate blindly through the administrative and bureaucratic maze, particularly with respect to the establishment of filiation and reimbursement of eligible expenses. Confronted with evasive, inconsistent, or unsatisfactory responses from government officials and health professionals, intended couples and surrogates quickly turned to social and digital networks for answers to their questions or advice from experienced individuals on the internet.[23] This obviously raises questions as to the validity of the legal information that circulates in these forums and its interpretation by the persons concerned. These are concerns not only in Quebec, but in the rest of Canada as well.[24]

Social science research shows that people with poor or erroneous knowledge of the law tend to rely on beliefs about and representations of *what they believe to be* the current legislative framework, with all the potentially negative consequences that may result.[25] However, it appears that a better understanding of the laws and rules affecting the couple or family does not necessarily facilitate a preventive response to potential problems, since emotional considerations also come into play.[26] This was indeed the case in several examples reported by the interviewed surrogates and intended parents, where the relational aspect of their amicable agreement was highly valued, as opposed to a formal agreement by contract, which, despite providing greater protection, was perceived as cold and distorted.

Our observations echo the experiences of other socio-legislative contexts in the West, while the empirical knowledge that emerges testifies to the inclusion of surrogates, not only in the genesis of the intended parents' family story, but also in the kinship system of the child thus born.[27] As for the surrogates, research shows that it is the link between themselves and the intended parents that they highlight in their stories, more so than the

23 Zsuzsa Berend, *The Online World of Surrogacy* (New York: Berghahn Books, 2016).

24 Regarding the challenges of establishing legal filiation/parentage, see Nelson, Chapter 6, this volume. Regarding the reimbursement of eligible expenses, see Petropanagos, Gruben, & Cameron, Chapter 5, and McLeod, Chapter 4, this volume.

25 Hélène Belleau & Pascale Cornut St-Pierre, "Pour que droit et familles fassent bon ménage: Étude sur la conscience du droit en matière conjugale" (2012) 25:1 *Nouvelles pratiques sociales* 62.

26 Hélène Belleau, "D'un mythe à l'autre: De l'ignorance des lois à la présomption du choix éclairé chez les conjoints en union libre" (2015) 27:1 *Canadian Journal of Women and the Law* 1 [Belleau].

27 Lucy Blake et al, "Gay Father Surrogacy Families: Relationships with Surrogates and Egg Donors and Parental Disclosure of Children's Origins" (2016) 106:6 *Fertility and Sterility*, 1503; Jérôme Courduriès, "Ce que fabrique la gestation pour autrui" (2016) 144–45 *Journal des anthropologues* 53; Susan Golombok, *Modern Families: Parents and Children in New Family Forms* (Cambridge: Cambridge University Press, 2015).

one with the child they have carried.[28] The reciprocity of the links between adults is emphasized, while the child is seen as the sum of this relationship and the contributions of each person involved—the intended parents, the surrogate, and, where applicable, her spouse and children.[29]

While most research tends to show that the practice appears to be positive and satisfactory to all parties, we have no desire to depict a romanticized vision of surrogacy. Indeed, the law appears as a significant potential means to guarantee the protection and safety of those involved in such a process. The lack of framework in Quebec currently places all parties in a position of vulnerability. Intended parents must live with the fear that their child will not be given to them at birth or that it will be difficult to establish parentage. They are also subject to various administrative burdens, in addition to the adaptation associated with welcoming a newborn child. The lack of framework also fosters the emergence of transnational reproductive support networks, which casts a certain social stigma on their parental project and helps to portray them as couples who instrumentalize women to help them to have a child, when the reality is much more complex and nuanced.[30] As for women who are surrogates, they are not assured that the parents will take care of the child at birth. They must also submit to various nutritional or behavioural requirements during pregnancy that impede their autonomy and freedom. Since women have a right to reproductive autonomy in Canada, we believe it is imperative to reaffirm that women who are surrogates must be able to refuse any medical treatment, as well as any intervention with respect to the fetus they are carrying. They must also remain free in any decision regarding their pregnancy—including to terminate it without having to justify their decision—and delivery.

---

28 Vasanti Jadva, Susan Imrie, & Susan Golombok, "Surrogate Mothers 10 Years On: A Longitudinal Study of Psychological Well-Being and Relationships with the Parents and Child" (2015) 30:2 *Human Reproduction* 373; Elly Teman, *Birthing a Mother: The Surrogate Body and the Pregnant Self* (Berkeley: University of California Press, 2010).

29 The collective work, *Perspectives internationales sur la gestation pour autrui: expériences des personnes concernées et contextes d'action,* edited by Isabel Côté, Kévin Lavoie, & Jérôme Courduriès (Québec, QC: Presses de l'Université du Québec, 2018), brings together various empirical studies conducted in different national and legislative contexts reflecting these more or less close relationships between intended parents and surrogates.

30 Amrita Pande, *Wombs in Labor: Transnational Commercial Surrogacy in India* (New York: Columbia University Press, 2014).

The taboos and ideological positions surrounding remuneration, or at least the payment of some form of compensation, preclude any collective discussion to ensure that surrogates do not find themselves at a financial disadvantage when they agree to collaborate in the parental project of others. Anchored in the institution of motherhood, the rhetoric of donating a "gift of life" gives precedence to selfless dedication and the altruistic aspect of carrying a child for others, while relegating to the background the financial and material considerations of surrogacy, which are essential for the well-being of women who choose to engage in this reproductive work.[31] Any reference to the monetary aspect immediately leads to a counter-discourse that degrades the gesture, comparing it to the "purchase" of a child reified as a consumer good or to the "rental of the wombs" of women. These criticisms drive women to develop a discourse based on the qualities of altruism and generosity that are linked to female identity.[32] The reading of some judgments shows that judges are also sensitive to this representation that associates surrogacy with the self-denial of the surrogate while the vocabulary used in their decisions emphasizes the iconography of the gift.[33] This position seems all the more paradoxical because no one seems to denounce the fact that intermediaries who sometimes participate in the realization of a parental project by surrogacy — lawyers, fertility clinic professionals, agency employees — receive a fee for their services.[34]

When a great disparity between social values and those underlying the law is observed, a degree of confusion compromising the effectiveness of existing laws is also noted.[35] This discrepancy could explain the trajectory of couples who still choose surrogacy as a means to access parenthood, despite the lack of regulation in Quebec and the legal issues that entails. The recent proposals[36] made by the Comité consultatif sur la réforme du

31 Heather Jacobson, *Labor of Love: Gestational Surrogacy and the Work of Making Babies* (New Brunswick, NJ: Rutgers University Press, 2016); Helena Ragoné, *Surrogate Motherhood: Conception in the Heart* (Boulder, CO: Westview Press, 1994).

32 Teman, above note 14.

33 Régine Tremblay, "Surrogates in Québec: The Good, the Bad, and the Foreigner" (2015) 27:1 *Canadian Journal of Women and the Law* 94.

34 Katherine Drabiak et al, "Ethics, Law and Commercial Surrogacy: A Call for Uniformity" (2007) 35:2 *Journal of Law, Medicine and Ethics* 300.

35 Belleau, above note 26.

36 Quebec, Ministère de la justice, *Pour un droit de la famille adapté aux nouvelles réalités conjugales et familiales*, by Comité consultatif sur le droit de la famille [Family Law

droit de la famille [Advisory Committee on Family Law Reform] and the Conseil du statut de la femme [Council for the Status of Women], which have the merit of initiating the discussion, are to be welcomed. The same is true of the public consultation recently conducted by Health Canada on proposals for regulations to strengthen the enforcement of certain provisions of the *AHRA*, particularly with respect to reimbursable expenditures. In the light of the experiences of those directly concerned, we believe it is necessary to reflect on mechanisms to protect those involved in a surrogacy agreement, without falling into the trap of antagonizing their respective needs and interests. It is therefore to be hoped that both the federal and provincial levels of government will take note of these proposals and of the empirical evidence on the subject to embark on a thoroughgoing reform on this issue. The legislature's timidity in this regard has lasted far too long.

Advisory Committee], chaired by Alain Roy (Quebec, Ministère de la justice du Québec, 2015); Quebec, Conseil du statut de la femme, *Avis: Mères porteuses — réflexions sur des enjeux actuels* (Quebec: Conseil du statut de la femme, 2016).

4

Reimbursement of Expenditures and Possible Sub-delegation of the Assisted Human Reproduction Regulations

Mark C McLeod

A. INTRODUCTION

Governance by the promulgation of regulations has become a central form of state action and the core of much national law-making.[1] Indeed, the concept of governance by the promulgation of regulations has dramatically evolved in recent years. Specifically, there is now an increased propensity on the part of national governments to incorporate by reference documents that have been drafted by foreign governments, private sector organizations, or other entities in order to achieve government objectives. Incorporation of documents by reference is a drafting technique whereby the regulation-maker may bring the content of an incorporated document into a regulation by simply referring to the title of the document, without the need to reproduce it word for word in the regulation itself.[2]

1 Francesca Bignami & David Zaring, *Comparative Law and Regulation: Understanding the Global Regulatory Process* (Cheltenham, UK: Edward Elgar, 2016).

2 See, for example, Government of Canada, Standing Committee for the Scrutiny of Regulations, 39th Parliament, 2nd Session, "Second Report" (2008) at para 2, online: www.parl.gc.ca/HousePublications/Publication.aspx?DocId=3204106&Ses=2 ["Second Report"]; *Incorporation by Reference in Regulations Act*, SC 2015, c 33, summary. "This enactment amends the *Statutory Instruments Act* to provide for the express power to incorporate by reference in regulations."

In Canada, for example, the *Aviation Occupational Safety and Health Regulations*,[3] the *Canada Occupational Health and Safety Regulations*,[4] and the *Food and Drug Regulations*[5] utilize incorporation by reference. In this way, the Government of Canada maintains that it can achieve several goals related to regulatory management, including effective and responsive regulations.[6] Nonetheless, there are significant pitfalls to this form of collaborative governance.[7] In this chapter, I explore the nature and scope of this concern with particular reference to the Government of Canada's plans to enact regulations to clarify eligible reimbursable expenses under section 12 of the *Assisted Human Reproduction Act* (*AHRA*).[8]

In September 2016, the federal government announced that it intended to "strengthen and clarify the regulatory framework governing assisted

3 *Aviation Occupational Health and Safety Regulations*, SOR/2011-87, s 6.5(1).

4 *Canada Occupational Health and Safety Regulations*, SOR/86-304, s 2.2(1).

5 See, for example, *Food and Drug Regulations* CRC, c 870, B.01.045; Health Canada, "Incorporation by Reference" (2016), online: www.hc-sc.gc.ca/fn-an/legislation/acts-lois/ibr-ipr-eng.php.

6 See, for example, Liberal MP Kevin Lamoureux, Winnipeg North, MB, on Bill S-2 (Historical), *Incorporation by Reference in Regulations Act* (2015), online: https://openparliament.ca/bills/41-2/S-2/?singlepage=1. Lamoureux expressed lack of support for Bill S-2, which provided for the express power to incorporate by reference in regulations, stating, "It is something that has caused . . . the *Liberal Party to express our concern, and it is the reason we will not be supporting Bill S-2* . . . . The current government . . . cannot be trusted to use this power responsibly. We have seen that time and time again. Its willingness to abuse oversight mechanisms . . ." [emphasis added]; Canadian Food Inspection Agency, "Incorporation by Reference Policy" (2016), online: www.inspection.gc.ca/about-the-cfia/acts-and-regulations/incorporation-by-reference/policy/eng/1450356693608/1450356805085.

7 Kevin Lamoureux, Winnipeg North, MB, above note 6: "It is important at the get-go to recognize that incorporation by reference enables the federal government or agencies to give legal effect to material that has been published elsewhere. We should all be concerned about that."

8 SC 2004, c 2 [*AHRA*]; Government of Canada, "Government of Canada Plans to Introduce Regulations to Support the *AHRA*" (2016), online: www.canada.ca/en/health-canada/news/2016/09/government-canada-plans-introduce-regulations-support-assisted-human-reproduction-act.html [Government of Canada, "Plans to Introduce"]; Health Canada, "Assisted Human Reproduction: Legislation and Guidelines" (2016), online: www.hc-sc.gc.ca/dhp-mps/brgtherap/legislation/reprod/index-eng.php; Center for Genetics and Society, "Canada: The *Assisted Human Reproduction Act*" (2007), online: http://geneticsandsociety.org/article.php?id=335; Mavis Jones & Brian Salter, "Proceeding Carefully: Assisted Human Reproduction Policy in Canada" (2010) 19:4 *Public Understanding of Science* 420 at 425–42.

human reproduction in Canada."[9] More specifically, it intended to "update the regulations for the safety of donor semen . . . [, to] develop regulations for testing and screening the donors of ova, . . . and [to] *clarify eligible reimbursable expenses* for parties involved in surrogacy arrangements, and semen and ova donation."[10] At the same time, the government announced that it would allow stakeholders to provide feedback following pre-publication of the regulatory proposals in the *Canada Gazette* while developing a regulatory framework governing assisted reproduction.[11] These announcements were then followed by an invitation from the government to comment on policy proposals in a consultation document in July 2017.[12]

Despite these public proclamations, it is possible the government intends to promulgate regulations with respect to eligible reimbursable expenses under section 12 of the *AHRA* using incorporation by reference. Circumstantial evidence supports this theory. When Ottawa announced that it would "strengthen and clarify the regulatory framework,"[13] it stipulated that it would "clarify" eligible reimbursable expenses.[14] Arguably, the term "clarify" is ambiguous and contrasts markedly with the commitment to "update" pre-existing regulations for the safety of donor semen and to "develop" regulations for testing and screening ovum donors.[15] Due to this dissimilarity in language, donors, surrogates, fertility clinics, and other interested parties[16] may be unsure as to whether the government will (1) update existing directives published by Health Canada,[17] (2) develop regulations

9 Government of Canada, "Plans to Introduce," above note 8.

10 *Ibid* [emphasis added].

11 *Ibid*.

12 Government of Canada, "Toward a Strengthened *Assisted Human Reproduction Act*: A Consultation with Canadians on Key Policy Proposals" (2017), online: www.canada.ca/en/health-canada/programs/consultation-assisted-human-reproduction/document.html ["Toward a Strengthened *AHRA*"].

13 Government of Canada, "Plans to Introduce," above note 8.

14 *Ibid*.

15 *Ibid*.

16 Other interested parties may include sperm and egg banks, importers and exporters of sperm and eggs, as well as brokers.

17 Government of Canada, "Prohibitions Related to Purchasing Reproductive Material and Purchasing or Selling In Vitro Embryos" (2013), online: www.hc-sc.gc.ca/dhp-mps/brgtherap/legislation/reprod/purchasing-achat-eng.php; Government of Canada, "Prohibitions Related to Surrogacy" (2013), online: www.hc-sc.gc.ca/dhp-mps/brgtherap/legislation/reprod/surrogacy-substitution-eng.php [Government of Canada, "Prohibitions"].

internally, as it has unequivocally stated with respect to testing and screening the donors of ova, or (3) merely clarify provisions drafted by a third party that are thereafter incorporated by reference.

Coupled to the dissimilarity in language, further circumstantial evidence supports this theory. A Task Force of the Canadian Standards Association Group ("CSA Group"), a third-party for-profit organization that develops leading-edge, consensus-based standards,[18] first drafted an informative annex entitled "Reimbursement of Expenses for Donors and Surrogates" at the request of Health Canada in June 2015. Following a voluntary "inquiry stage" consistent with its own internal document-development process, the CSA Group published the annex (the "CSA Group standards") in October 2016.[19] This publication occurred only three weeks after the federal government announcement about its intent to clarify eligible reimbursable expenses under the *AHRA*. Importantly, Health Canada has never requested or contracted a third party, including the CSA Group, to draft and publish a document on such a specific area of the *AHRA*. For example, the only promulgated regulations since the enactment of the *AHRA* in 2004, namely, the *Consent Regulations*, were drafted by Health Canada.[20]

This chapter will address select concerns with respect to both the possible use of incorporation by reference to promulgate regulations related to eligible reimbursable expenses under the *AHRA*, as well as concerns related to the Task Force of the CSA Group. Importantly, current literature has never explored the intersection between incorporation by reference and provisions of the *AHRA*. Drawing on the background of the relevant provisions of the *AHRA* and the Supreme Court of Canada case of *Reference re Assisted Human Reproduction Act*,[21] I will argue that incorporation by reference has inherent risks and should not be undertaken with respect to regulations related to eligible reimbursable expenses. These risks include, but are not limited to, allowing a non-elected body to determine the content of regulations, undermining the transparency of the policy-making

18 See, for example, CSA Group, "About the CSA Group," online: www.csagroup.org/about-csa-group.

19 CSA Group, *Annex A (Informative) Reimbursement of Expenses for Donors and Surrogates* (Toronto: CSA Group, 2016) [CSA Group standards].

20 *Assisted Human Reproduction (Section 8 Consent) Regulations*, SOR/2007-137 [*Consent Regulations*].

21 2010 SCC 61 [*Reference re AHRA*].

process, developing ineffectual policy, abating public access to Canadian law, as well as diminishing public participation and parliamentary control over sub-delegated law-making. In order to highlight these risks, I will explore select concerns in relation to transparency and membership of the task force that was charged to draft the CSA Group standards, the process of developing the CSA Group standards, and their content. Following a discussion of the various risks, I argue that these risks can be negated by undertaking an extensive public consultation akin to that previously undertaken in the development of the *Consent Regulations* under the *AHRA*.[22] By enacting regulations governing eligible reimbursable expenses through established drafting processes spearheaded by Health Canada, important democratic and ethical principles will not be undermined.

With the possibility the government may be deliberating whether to promulgate regulations related to eligible reimbursable expenses using incorporation by reference,[23] there is a critical time issue with respect to bringing concerns to the public's attention prior to enactment. The aim of this chapter is to bring these concerns to the attention of the minister of health, "professional, non-partisan . . . public servants,"[24] provincial and territorial officials, professional associations, experts in the field of assisted reproduction, and bioethicists, as well as the donors, surrogates, fertility clinics, and other interested parties who will ultimately be governed by these regulations.[25] These stakeholders have interests in, and positions on, regulatory oversight that are deserving of respect and deliberation by the Government of Canada.

B. A BRIEF HISTORY OF ASSISTED HUMAN REPRODUCTION IN CANADA

In order to frame the concerns about promulgating regulations related to eligible reimbursable expenses by incorporation by reference, this section undertakes an examination of the *AHRA* as well as the Supreme Court

22 *Consent Regulations*, above note 20.

23 *Ibid*.

24 In "Minister of Health Mandate Letter" (4 October 2017) at para 17, Prime Minister Justin Trudeau notes that "Our ability, as a government, to successfully implement our platform depends on our ability to thoughtfully consider the professional, non-partisan advice of public servants" [Trudeau, Mandate Letter].

25 *Ibid* at para 6. "I expect that our work will be informed by performance measurement, *evidence, and feedback from Canadians.*" [Emphasis added.]

judgment which held that that aspects of the *AHRA* were unconstitutional and fell under provincial jurisdiction.[26]

1) The *Assisted Human Reproduction Act* Prohibits Trade in Reproductive Capabilities

The *AHRA* was enacted on 29 March 2004. Its aim was to provide a comprehensive federal legislative framework for assisted reproduction in Canada.[27] The Act drew a clear line between prohibited and controlled activities and, among other principles, declared that "trade in the reproductive capabilities of women and men and the exploitation of children, women and men for commercial ends raise health and ethical concerns that justify their prohibition."[28] This principle was based on the 1993 report of the Royal Commission on New Reproductive Technologies,[29] which stated:

> the activities that we see as *ethically unacceptable* on the basis of the *principle of non-commercialization* are the buying and selling[[30]] of gametes,

26 See, for example, *Reference re AHRA*, above note 21 at summary, Cromwell J: "Sections 10, 11, 13, 14 to 18, 40(2), (3), (3.1), (4) and (5), and 44(2) and (3) exceed the legislative authority of the Parliament of Canada under the *Constitution Act, 1867*"; LeBel, Deschamps, Abella, and Rothstein JJ at summary: "Sections 8 to 19, 40 to 53, 60, 61 and 68 of the Act exceed the legislative authority of the Parliament of Canada under the *Constitution Act*, 1867"; *Jobs, Growth and Long-term Prosperity Act*, SC 2012, c 19, ss 713–45, summary: "Division 56 of Part 4 amends the *Assisted Human Reproduction Act* to respond to the Supreme Court of Canada decision in *Reference re Assisted Human Reproduction Act* that was rendered in 2010, including by repealing the provisions that were found to be unconstitutional and abolishing the Assisted Human Reproduction Agency of Canada."

27 See, for example, *AHRA*, above note 8; Health Canada, above note 8; Center for Genetics and Society, above note 8; Jones & Salter, above note 8 at 425–26; Ontario Law Reform Commission, *Report on Human Artificial Reproduction and Related Matters* (Toronto: Ontario Law Reform Commission, 1985); Law Reform Commission of Canada, *Medically Assisted Procreation*, Working Paper 65 (Ottawa: Minister of Supply and Services Canada, 1992).

28 *AHRA*, above note 8, s 2(f).

29 Royal Commission on New Reproductive Technologies, *Proceed with Care: Final Report of the Royal Commission on New Reproductive Technologies* (Ottawa: Minister of Government Services Canada, 1993) [*Proceed with Care*].

30 *AHRA*, above note 8, s 6(1). "6(1) *No person shall pay consideration* to a female person to be a surrogate mother, *offer to pay* such consideration or *advertise that it will be paid* . . . . 7(1) No person shall *purchase, offer to purchase or advertise for the purchase* of sperm or ova from a donor or a person acting on behalf of a donor." [Emphasis added.] Ultimately,

> zygotes, embryos, or fetuses, and the use of *financial incentives* in preconception or adoption arrangements. *To allow commercial exchanges of this type would* undermine respect for human life and dignity and *lead to the commodification of women and children.*[31]

Reflecting these concerns respecting commercial exploitation and incentivization, sections 6 and 7 of the *AHRA* enshrine and enforce the principle of prohibiting the trade in the reproductive capabilities of women and men.[32] Nonetheless, these prohibitions are subject to exceptions associated with reimbursement of expenditures for donation, storage,[33] and surrogacy, as well as reimbursement of loss of work-related income for surrogacy under section 12 of the *AHRA*.[34]

Subsection 12(1) of the *AHRA* restricts the reimbursement of expenditures directly related to assisted reproduction except in accordance with the regulations, explicitly stating:

> [n]o person shall, except in accordance with the *regulations* . . . reimburse a donor for an expenditure incurred in the course of donating sperm or an ovum; . . . reimburse any person for an expenditure incurred in the maintenance or transport of an in vitro embryo; or reimburse a surrogate mother for an expenditure incurred by her in relation to her surrogacy.[35]

Importantly, section 12(2) of the *AHRA* addresses the issue of incentivization and requires that expenditures under section 12(1) be receipted in order to qualify for reimbursement. Specifically, "[n]o person shall *reimburse* an expenditure . . . unless a *receipt* is provided to that person for the expenditure.[36] Therefore, where a woman, man, couple, surrogate, or fertility clinic cannot provide a receipt for an expenditure, the reimbursement is explicitly prohibited.

---

sections (6) and (7) of the *AHRA* based the prohibition on the buyer, with respect to gametes and surrogacy, and not the seller.

31 *Proceed with Care*, above note 29 [emphasis added].

32 *AHRA*, above note 8, ss 6(1) and 7.

33 *Ibid*, s 12(1)(b). In the context of this article, storage includes the maintenance or transport of an *in vitro* embryo.

34 *Ibid*, s 12.

35 See, for example, *ibid*, s 12(1) [emphasis added]; *Reference re AHRA*, above note 21 at para 110.

36 See, for example, *AHRA*, above note 8, s 12(2) [emphasis added]; *Reference re AHRA*, above note 21 at para 110.

Lastly, subsection 12(3) of the *AHRA* allows for reimbursement for a loss of work-related income by a surrogate mother. Specifically, "[n]o person shall reimburse a *surrogate mother* for a loss of *work-related income* incurred *during* her pregnancy, unless . . . the reimbursement is made in accordance with the *regulations*."[37] As section 12(3)(a) of the *AHRA* explicitly refers to a "surrogate mother," an ovum donor engaging in an altruistic medical intervention is not entitled to reimbursement for a loss of work-related income.[38] Moreover, reimbursement for loss of work-related income for the surrogate mother is time limited to only the duration of the pregnancy.[39] Therefore, payments related to *post-pregnancy* work-related income do not constitute a reimbursement and are therefore prohibited.

The prohibitions regarding the commodification and incentivization of reproductive activities are enforced by penalties in section 61 of the *AHRA*, including a fine or a term of imprisonment or both. Therefore, sections 6, 7, and 12 of the *AHRA* provide a comprehensive federal legislative framework to protect the reproductive capabilities of women and men and to prevent the commercial exploitation of reproduction. However, presently, there are no comprehensive regulations authorized under section 65 of the *AHRA* with respect to section 12 of the Act.

2) The *Assisted Human Reproduction Act* Allows the Use of Static and Ambulatory Incorporation by Reference to Promulgate Regulations

When Parliament confers power to make regulations under a legislative act, this power is usually exercised by the regulation-maker through drafting

37 See, for example, *AHRA*, above note 8, s 12(3) [emphasis added]; *Reference re AHRA*, above note 21 at paras 110 and 112.

38 *Reference re AHRA*, *ibid* at para 110: "The section also prohibits reimbursement for expenditures without receipts, *and the reimbursement of surrogate mothers for the loss of work-related income* without medical certification that work may pose a risk to her health or that of the embryo" [emphasis added]; and at para 220, Lebel and Deschamps JJ: "To give another example, ss. 12(1)(c) and *12(3) of the AHRA address the reimbursement of surrogate mothers* for expenditures incurred and *for the loss of work-related income*." [Emphasis added.] Canadian Bar Association, "Reimbursement of Expenditures Under the *Assisted Human Reproduction Act*" (2007), online: www.rainbowhealthontario.ca/wp-content/uploads/woocommerce_uploads/2014/08/AHRA%20Canadian%20Bar%20Association.pdf.

39 *AHRA*, above note 8, s 12(3).

the text of the regulation(s) to be enacted.[40] For example, the Governor in Council is responsible under sections 65(1)(e)–(e.1) of the *AHRA* for developing regulations regarding the reimbursement of receipted expenditures and for loss of income.[41] In addition, section 65(1)(e) of the Act provides the Governor in Council with legislative authority to make regulations respecting the types of expenditures that may be reimbursed.[42]

Importantly, section 65(2) of the *AHRA* states that, during the development of regulations, "[t]he regulations may incorporate any document by reference, regardless of its source, either as it reads on a *particular date* or as it is *amended from time to time*."[43] The phrase "incorporate any document by reference" (hereinafter referred to as "incorporation by reference") has potentially profound public policy consequences. It is used to describe a drafting technique whereby the regulation-maker can simply refer to the title of the document in the regulation, such that the content of any external technical or non-technical standards, methods, guidelines, or any other documents (hereinafter referred to as the "reference document") generated by a third party, which is not in the text of the incorporating legislation or regulation, is incorporated by reference.[44] More specifically, incorporation by reference is used to supplement legislation or regulations by importing and codifying the reference document such that essential rights, powers, obligations, and penalties are self-contained and have legal effect.[45]

40 "Second Report," above note 2 at para 2.

41 *AHRA*, above note 8, s 65(1). "The Governor in Council *may make regulations* for carrying into effect the purposes and provisions of this Act and, in particular, may make regulations . . . (e) respecting the *reimbursement of expenditures* for the purposes of subsection 12(1), including providing for the expenditures that may be reimbursed; (e.1) for the purposes of subsection 12(3), respecting the *reimbursement of a loss of income . . .*" [emphasis added].

42 *Ibid.*

43 *Ibid.*, s 65(2) [emphasis added].

44 See, for example, *Incorporation by Reference in Regulations Act*, above note 2, summary. "This enactment amends the *Statutory Instruments Act* to provide for the express power to incorporate by reference in regulations"; Health Canada, above note 5; New Zealand House of Representatives, *Inquiry into Material Incorporated by Reference*, Report of the Regulations Review Committee, 47th Parliament (Richard Worth, Chairperson) (2004), online: www.parliament.nz/resource/en-nz/47DBSCH_SCR2794_1/fa349b1c81f369bef6395cf6bcdcd0e4e211a2ec; "Second Report," above note 2 at para 2.

45 See, for example, *Incorporation by Reference in Regulations Act*, above note 2; Health Canada, above note 5; New Zealand House of Representatives, above note 44; Canadian Food Inspection Agency, above note 6.

Therefore, any reference document incorporated under section 65(2) of the *AHRA* has the force of law that defines the rights, powers, and obligations of donors, surrogates, fertility clinics, and other interested parties, with any breach of the *AHRA* related to reimbursement of expenditures enforced by penalties under section 61 of the *AHRA*,[46] including a fine or a term of imprisonment or both.[47]

Notably, section 65(2) of the *AHRA* allows for two types of incorporation by reference — namely, static and ambulatory. That this section allows for static incorporation (i.e., incorporating a specific version of a reference document at a defined date) is evidenced by the phrase "as it reads on a particular date." With static incorporation, if the reference document is amended by a third party after its incorporation into regulation, such amendments are not automatically incorporated.[48] In order to adopt the subsequent amendment to the reference document, the government would have to amend the incorporating regulation.[49] Section 65(2) of the *AHRA* also allows for ambulatory incorporation (i.e., a reference document that may be amended from time to time by a third party with said future amendments automatically incorporated into regulation), as evidenced by the phrase "as it is amended from time to time."[50] In effect, with ambulatory incorporation, amendments to the reference document automatically become part of the incorporating regulation.[51] The fact that section 65(2) allows incorporation by reference, and more particularly, ambulatory incorporation, raises significant concerns, as will be discussed below.

3) The *Assisted Human Reproduction Act* Is Fundamentally Important to Canadian Society

Prior to the Government of Canada drafting regulations related to reimbursement of expenditures, the Supreme Court held that particular sections

46 See, for example, *AHRA*, above note 8, s 61.

47 *Ibid*, s 65(4).

48 "Second Report," above note 2 at para 3.

49 *Ibid*.

50 *AHRA*, above note 8, s 65(2). "The regulations may incorporate any document by reference, regardless of its source, either *as it reads on a particular date* or *as it is amended from time to time*." [Emphasis added.]

51 "Second Report," above note 2 at para 4.

of the *AHRA* were unconstitutional and fell under provincial jurisdiction.[52] At issue in the case of *Reference re Assisted Human Reproduction Act*[53] was whether several provisions of the *AHRA* fell within the scope of the federal criminal law power under section 91(27) of the *Constitution Act, 1867*.[54] In order to determine whether the *AHRA* was a valid criminal law, the Supreme Court examined the three requirements for such a law, which are (1) a prohibition; (2) backed by a penalty; (3) with a criminal law purpose.[55]

While the Attorney General of Quebec conceded that the absolute prohibitions under sections 6 to 7 of the *AHRA* were valid criminal law,[56] the majority of the Supreme Court in a 4:4:1 decision (McLachlin CJ and Binnie, Fish, and Charron JJ; Cromwell J concurring in part and determinative with respect to section 12 of the *AHRA*) held that section 12 was

52 *Reference re AHRA*, above note 21. See above note 26.

53 Above note 21.

54 See, for example, *Reference re AHRA, ibid* at para 35; *Attorney General of Quebec v Attorney General of Canada*, 2008 QCCA 1167 at paras 35–44; *Reference re Assisted Human Reproduction Act*, 2010 SCC 61 (Respondent's Factum and Schedule, Attorney General of Quebec at para 36): "36. The Attorney General of Canada argues that the impugned provisions constitute a valid exercise of Parliament's jurisdiction over criminal law: the legislation creates crimes, imposes sanctions for a legitimate public objective, namely, the protection of public health and morality, and establishes an exemption regime through a regulatory scheme. Since health is not a field assigned exclusively to one level of government, he maintains there is no colourable encroachment on the jurisdictions of the provinces"; *Reference re Firearms Act (Can)*, 2000 SCC 31 at para 27; Ian B Lee, "The *Assisted Human Reproduction Act Reference* and the Federal Criminal Law Power" (2011) 90 *Canadian Bar Review* 471, online: www.law.utoronto.ca/utfl_file/count/documents/lee/Lee_AHRA_CanBarRev.pdf; Alison Harvison Young & Angela Wasunna, "Wrestling with the Limits of Law: Regulating New Reproductive Technologies" (1998) 6 *Health Law Journal* 239; Patrick Healy, "Statutory Prohibitions and the Regulation of New Reproductive Technologies under Federal Law in Canada" (1995) 40 *McGill Law Journal* 905; Timothy Caulfield, Marie Hirtle, & Sonia LeBris, "NRGTs: Is Criminalization the Solution for Canada?" (1997) 18 *Health Law Canada* 3; Ubaka Ogbogu, "The *AHRA Reference* and the Thin Line between Health and Crime" (2013) 22:1 *Constitutional Forum* 93; *Proceed with Care*, above note 29 at 13: "A field with such wide-reaching social, ethical, and public policy implications could never be dealt with adequately by a single government ministry or department."

55 See, for example, *Reference re AHRA*, above note 21 at para 35; *Reference re Firearms Act (Can)*, above note 54 at para 27.

56 See, for example, *Reference re AHRA*, above note 21 at paras 10, 15, 17, 26, 87, 91, 111, 288, and 290.

an extension of the regime established by sections 6 and 7.[57] Furthermore, section 12 formed an "exemption from the strictness of the regime which they impose[d] and, to some extent, define[d] the scope of the prohibitions provided for in those sections."[58] Therefore, the majority of the Supreme Court held that Parliament under section 12 of the *AHRA* had selectively prohibited reprehensible and harmful conduct to particular factual situations related to reimbursement of receipted expenditures.[59] This satisfied the first requirement of a valid criminal law—a prohibition.

Secondly, the Supreme Court determined that the prohibitions under section 12 of the *AHRA* are enforced by penalties in section 61,[60] including a fine or a term of imprisonment or both.[61] This satisfied the second requirement of a valid criminal law—a penalty.

Chief Justice McLachlin then examined the third requirement, that of a criminal law purpose, which in this case centred on morality, health, and security.[62] Specifically, the question was whether the *AHRA* met the modern conception of a valid criminal law objective by serving "a public purpose" like "[p]ublic peace, order, security, health … [and] morality."[63] Chief Justice McLachlin recognized that morality, security, and avoiding or containing

---

57 See, for example, *ibid* at paras 110–12, McLachlin CJ and Binnie, Fish, and Charron JJ; at paras 290–92, Cromwell J.

58 *Ibid* at paras 290–92.

59 *Ibid* at para 26.

60 *AHRA*, above note 8, s 61.

61 See, for example, *Reference re AHRA*, above note 21 at para 110, McLachlin CJ and Binnie, Fish, and Charron JJ. "The prohibitions in s. 12 are backed by the penalties in s. 61."

62 See, for example, *ibid* at para 21; Françoise Baylis, "Supreme Court of Canada Decision on the *Assisted Human Reproduction Act* Creates Urgent Need for Action" (2011) 33:4 *Journal of Obstetrics and Gynaecology Canada* 317; Françoise Baylis, "The Regulation of Assisted Human Reproductive Technologies and Related Research: A Public Health, Safety and Morality Argument" (2006) at 492, online: https://cdn.dal.ca/content/dam/dalhousie/pdf/sites/noveltechethics/nte-Appendix%202_Regulation%20of%20AHR%20Technologies%20&%20Related%20Research-Clean%20Copy.pdf: "From an ethical perspective this challenge is deeply problematic as the federal legislation is clearly needed to protect and promote public health, safety, and morality for current and future generations of Canadians through the pursuit of ethical and therapeutic science and technologies."

63 See, for example, *Reference re AHRA*, above note 21 at para 41, McLachlin CJ and Binnie, Fish, and Charron JJ; *Reference re Validity of Section 5(a) of the Dairy Industry Act*, [1949] SCR 1 at 50, Rand J; Lee, "The *Assisted Human Reproduction Act Reference* and the Federal Criminal Law Power," above note 54.

public health evils were capable of supporting criminal laws in Canada.[64] Specifically, she recognized that Parliament had power to enact general norms for the whole of Canada in order to meet the pressing moral concerns raised by assisted reproduction, including conduct contrary to our central moral precepts, with the prohibition of legitimate public health evils[65] and the promotion of personal security playing supporting roles.[66]

Legitimate public health evils under the purview of criminal law comprise acts or conduct that may have an injurious or undesirable effect on public health,[67] including, in this case, serious physical and psychological harms to donors of sperm or ova, surrogate mothers, and/or persons created through misuse of assisted reproduction.[68] Chief Justice McLachlin held that the techniques surrounding assisted reproduction as well as any conduct that abuses these processes pose "risks to the health of the population and may *legitimately be considered a public health evil to be addressed by the criminal law*."[69] This satisfied the third requirement of a valid criminal law — a criminal law purpose.

Of prime importance with respect to protecting the health, well-being, safety, dignity, and rights of Canadians, and also the high-water mark in McLachlin CJ's reasoning with respect to gamete and embryo donors, as well as surrogates, was the following:

---

64 See, for example, *Reference re AHRA*, above note 21 at para 47, McLachlin CJ and Binnie, Fish, and Charron JJ. "In this case, the Attorney General of Canada relies mainly on the objectives of upholding morality and avoiding or containing potential public health evils. Mingled with these are overtones of security insofar as the practices may harm participants and offspring. *It has been recognized that morality, public health evils and security are, in principle, capable of supporting criminal laws.* We are not therefore confronted with the need to determine whether a new type of objective can be recognized as a valid criminal law purpose. The question is simply whether the legislative scheme falls within the ambit of the objectives that the Attorney General of Canada has identified." [Emphasis added.]

65 See, for example, *ibid* at paras 48 and 51, McLachlin CJ and Binnie, Fish, and Charron JJ: "I conclude that *upholding morality is the principal criminal law object of the* Act .... In summary, morality constitutes a valid criminal law purpose." [Emphasis added.] *Schneider v British Columbia*, [1982] 2 SCR 112 at 142; *RJR-MacDonald Inc v Canada (Attorney General)*, [1995] 3 SCR 199 at para 32.

66 *Reference re AHRA*, above note 21 at paras 48 and 51, McLachlin CJ and Binnie, Fish, and Charron JJ.

67 *Ibid* at para 62, McLachlin CJ and Binnie, Fish, and Charron JJ.

68 *Ibid*.

69 *Ibid* [emphasis added].

> *Parliament has a strong interest* in ensuring that basic moral standards govern the creation and destruction of life, as well as their *impact on persons like donors and mothers*. Taken as a whole, the Act seeks to avert serious damage to the fabric of our society by *prohibiting practices that tend to devalue human life and degrade participants*. This is a valid criminal law purpose, grounded in *issues that our society considers to be of fundamental importance*.[70]

Subsequent to this Supreme Court case, the first criminal charges, prosecution, and conviction under the *AHRA* occurred on 13 December 2013 in relation to ovum donation and surrogacy.[71] The company Canadian Fertility Consultants and its owner, who were charged on twenty-seven counts under the *AHRA*[72] and *Criminal Code*, pled guilty to purchasing ova, paying women to act as surrogates, and accepting payments for arranging the services of a surrogate in contravention of sections 6 and 7 of the *AHRA*. As a result of a guilty plea, the Court imposed a combined fine of $60,000. Although it may be argued that a fine was not a severe consequence and just the "cost of doing business,"[73] the case does highlight that donors, surrogates, fertility clinics, and other interested parties are at risk of prosecution for breaches of the *AHRA*.[74]

70 *Ibid* at para 61 [emphasis added].

71 See, for example, Tom Blackwell, "Canadian Fertility Consultant Received $31K for Unwittingly Referring Parents to U.S. 'Baby-Selling' Ring" *National Post* (15 December 2013), online: http://nationalpost.com/wcm/f413a24a-479e-4a76-96be-6e31265a75f7; Alison Motluk, "First Prosecution Under *AHRA* Ends in Conviction" (14 February 2014), online: CMAJ www.cmaj.ca/content/186/2/E75.full; *R v Picard and Canadian Fertility Consulting Ltd*, Agreed Statement of Facts (2016), online: Novel Tech Ethics www.dal.ca/content/dam/dalhousie/pdf/sites/noveltechethics/AHRA_Facts.pdf.

72 See, for example, Blackwell, above note 71; Motluk, above note 71.

73 Françoise Baylis & Jocelyn Downie, "Wishing Doesn't Make It So" *Impact Ethics* (17 December 2013), online: https://impactethics.ca/2013/12/17/wishing-doesnt-make-it-so: "There is much to be concerned about with this case, not the least of which is the small financial penalty. Indeed, the penalty is so low that others involved in similar activities might just consider fines a 'cost of doing business,' factor this cost into their price, and not modify their behaviour."

74 Robert Cribb & Emma Jarratt, "Canada's Vague Surrogacy Laws May Be Doing More Harm Than Good" *Toronto Star* (8 September 2016), online: www.thestar.com/news/canada/2016/09/18/canadas-vague-surrogacy-laws-may-be-doing-more-harm-than-good.html.

C. CONCERNS ABOUT USING INCORPORATION BY REFERENCE TO PROMULGATE REGULATIONS

As noted above, the possible use of incorporation by reference with respect to the *AHRA* raises significant concerns. First, it allows a non-elected body that is not directly and democratically accountable to the Canadian public, as are members of Parliament, to determine the content of regulations made by the Governor in Council, which donors, surrogates, fertility clinics, and other interested parties have to abide by. Second, it may reduce the transparency in the policy-making process that is essential for government accountability. Third, it may lead to the creation of ineffectual policy, as federal departments, such as Health Canada, may not be required to draft policy in order to achieve regulatory objectives. Fourth, it may create barriers to public participation during the rule-making period if normative procedures such as notice and comment are not undertaken. Fifth, it may create barriers to public accessibility to Canadian law, thus failing to provide meaningful assurance that regulations will be reasoned and democratically responsive. Finally, when used in conjunction with other provisions of the *AHRA*, it may create exceptions to parliamentary control and oversight of sub-delegated law-making.[75] Exploration of these concerns, as described below in the context of eligible reimbursable expenses under the *AHRA*, suggests incorporation by reference is not essential, necessary, and appropriate in this context.

1) Sub-delegation of Rule-Making Power by Incorporation by Reference

The basic legal principle in constitutional and administrative law is that incorporation by reference of external documents should, in the absence of clear authority, be seen to be illegal, as it is an unlawful sub-delegation of

75 See, for example, Erin L Nelson, "Comparative Perspectives on the Regulation of Assisted Reproductive Technologies in the United Kingdom and Canada" (2006) 43:4 *Alberta Law Review* 1023 at 1033; Nina A Mendelson, "Private Control over Access to Public Law: The Perplexing Federal Regulatory Use of Private Standards" (2014) 112:5 *Michigan Law Review* 737 at 747. Judicial review, popular sovereignty, and constitutionality are other concerns related to incorporation by reference; however, these elements are outside the scope of this paper.

regulation-making power.[76] This principle is based upon the Latin maxim *delegatus non potest delegare*, "one to whom power is delegated cannot himself further delegate that power."[77] Updating this maxim to the modern context, a person to whom a power to legislate has been delegated may not thereafter re-delegate that power to another party unless clearly authorized to do so by law.[78] Nonetheless, section 65(2) of the *AHRA* gives authority to do so: that section empowers the Governor in Council to incorporate a reference document into regulations by authorizing and sub-delegating regulation-making power to another person or body to act in its stead.[79] More specifically, the sub-delegated body, and not the authority on whom the rule-making power

76 See, for example, "Second Report," above note 2 at para 46; Andrew J Kania, "Incorporation by Reference in Canadian Federal Delegated Legislation: Contention, Concerns and Possible Reform" (Paper delivered at Australia–New Zealand Scrutiny of Legislation Conference: Scrutiny and Accountability in the 21st Century, Parliament House, Canberra, 6–8 July 2009), online: www.aph.gov.au/About_Parliament/Senate/Whats_On/Conferences/sl_conference/papers/kania; John Willis, "*Delegatus non potest delegare*" (1943) 21 *Canadian Bar Review* 257 at 259; *Comeau's Sea Foods Ltd v Canada (Minister of Fisheries and Oceans)*, [1997] 1 SCR 12 at para 28: "At the time of the initial enactment of s. 7, the prima facie presumption of statutory construction which grew up around the Latin maxim *delegatus non potest delegare* that '[a] discretion conferred by statute is . . . intended to be exercised by the authority on which the statute has conferred it and by no other authority' may have operated more strongly. Express delegation was generally thought necessary." *Ramawad v Canada (Minister of Manpower and Immigration)*, [1978] 2 SCR 375.

77 Mark Aronson & Matthew Groves, *Judicial Review of Administrative Action*, 5th ed (Sydney: Lawbook Co, 2013) at para 6.50: "An examination of the cases shows this strong presumption to exist only where the primary repository of power is a court, or a disciplinary body distinct from a department or other large institution. It is trite law that a large degree of devolution of functions is permitted to institutional and departmental decision-makers, even though they are bound by the rules of natural justice."

78 "Second Report," above note 2 at para 6.

79 *Ibid* at para 44. "In assessing the desirability of this sort of blanket approach, it should be kept in mind that the incorporation by reference technique, when it provides for the incorporation of material as amended from time to time, means that Parliament's delegate is in effect permitted to select another person or agency to perform a part of its law-making power in its place. *When a delegate incorporates not only an existing document, but also future amendments to it, the delegate is effectively subdelegating the law-making power granted by Parliament to the person or body that will amend the material that is incorporated by reference.*" [Emphasis added.]

has been conferred under the *AHRA*, will have the power to determine the content of these regulations.[80] Supporting this proposition, the Canadian House of Commons Standing Committee for the Scrutiny of Regulations (the "standing committee") stated in 2008 that

> [i]t has always been the view of the Committee that the incorporation by reference of external material into regulations "as amended from time to time" amounts to a subdelegation of regulation-making power, in that *it will be the body amending the incorporated material*, and not the authority on whom the power to make the regulations has been conferred, *that will determine the content of the regulations.*[81]

This statement by the standing committee is supported by various academics, with Salembier opining that a regulation-making authority sub-delegates the future evolution of a rule to the author of the incorporated document when ambulatory incorporation by reference is used.[82] Moreover, Pearce and Argument state that

> [t]he inclusion in delegated legislation of requirements stipulated by another organization means that the other organization is, in effect, stating the law on the topic. This may not be so if the incorporation is of a document as in force at a particular time. But if the incorporation is of the document as in force from time to time, *this enables the organization writing the document to determine the content of the delegated legislation.*[83]

While many jurisdictions utilize incorporation by reference, this power has been criticized. The standing committee, in "Report No 90—Accessibility of Documents Incorporated by Reference in Federal Regulations," stated that

> *incorporation by reference should be used only where it would be impracticable to do otherwise.* Further, that regulation-making authorities should be required to state in the Regulatory Impact Analysis Statement accompanying the

80 *Ibid* at para 6.

81 *Ibid* [emphasis added].

82 J Paul Salembier, *Regulatory Law and Practice in Canada* (Markham, ON: LexisNexis Butterworths, 2004) at 258.

83 Dennis C Pearce & Stephen Argument, *Delegated Legislation in Australia*, 2d ed (Sydney: Butterworths, 1979) at 279–80 [emphasis added].

> instrument the *reasons why avoiding the incorporation by reference was considered impracticable.*[84]

Although this statement by the standing committee is not a legal standard or test in Canada, one other jurisdiction has made a public statement on this issue. Specifically, the Regulations Review Committee of the New Zealand House of Representatives expressed similar concerns in 2004 by stating that incorporation by reference should be used sparingly and only where essential, necessary, and appropriate for the purpose.[85] More specifically, the use of incorporation by reference should be used only in a limited number of cases where it is impracticable to do otherwise.[86]

I opine that, in the case of the *AHRA*, it is not impracticable to do otherwise. Reliance on a Task Force is not essential when expertise and experience in developing policy at the intersection between health and criminal law matters already resides within Health Canada and the Department of Justice, respectively. Health Canada can develop regulations related to eligible reimbursable expenses internally to ensure the principles stated in the *AHRA* are upheld in order to promote the health, well-being, safety, dignity, and rights of Canadians.

2) Threats to Openness and Transparency in Government

In a mandate letter to the minister of health, Prime Minister Justin Trudeau stipulated that the federal government is "committed to set a higher bar for openness and transparency in government" and that "information should be *open by default*."[87] The prime minister also indicated that he expects Canadians to hold him and his government accountable for delivering on their commitments.[88] This commitment has also been supported by Health Canada, which has launched the Regulatory Transparency and Openness

84 Government of Canada, Standing Joint Committee for the Scrutiny of Regulations, "Accessibility of Documents Incorporated by Reference in Federal Regulations, Report No 90," online: www.parl.ca/DocumentViewer/en/42-1/REGS/report-2.

85 New Zealand House of Representatives, above note 44.

86 *Ibid.*

87 Trudeau, Mandate Letter, above note 24 at para 8 [emphasis added].

88 *Ibid* at para 4. "*I expect Canadians to hold us accountable for delivering these commitments*, and I expect all ministers to do their part — individually and collectively — to improve economic opportunity and security for Canadians." [Emphasis added.]

Framework in order to provide "greater transparency and openness to further strengthen trust in our regulatory decisions."[89]

The importance of openness and transparency in government cannot be overstated. Specifically, openness and transparency on the part of policy-makers[90] allow citizens of a functioning democracy to hold their government accountable through examination and scrutiny.[91] In turn, this fosters public trust and confidence. Furthermore, transparency allows for the free dissemination of information as well as the sharing and facilitation of knowledge that leads to societal progress.[92] Transparency as it relates to democratic government consists of three elements: (1) the institution that possesses the information, (2) the information that is to be made transparent, and (3) the person(s) to whom the information will be available.[93] An examination of these three elements suggests that the possible promulgation of regulations related to eligible reimbursable expenses under the *AHRA* via incorporation by reference may contradict the declared commitment to openness and transparency by Prime Minister Trudeau.

If we examine the CSA Group standards, the document states it was prepared by a task force serving under the Subcommittee on Reproductive Tissues and the Technical Committee on Safety of Cells, Tissues, and Organs for Transplantation and Assisted Reproduction[94] (the "task force").

---

89 Health Canada, "Regulatory Transparency and Openness" at para 2, online: http://hc-sc.gc.ca/home-accueil/rto-tor/index-eng.php.

90 See, for example, Frederick Schauer, "Transparency in Three Dimensions" (2011) 4 *University of Illinois Law Review* 1339; Cary Coglianese et al, "Transparency and Public Participation in the Federal Rulemaking Process: Recommendations for the New Administration" (2009) 77 *George Washington Law Review* 924; William Funk, "Public Participation and Transparency in Administrative Law: Three Examples as an Object Lesson" (2009) 61 *Administrative Law Review* 171; Jacob E Gersen & Anne Joseph O'Connell, "Hiding in Plain Sight? Timing and Transparency in the Administrative State" (2009) 76 *University of Chicago Law Review* 1157.

91 Schauer, above note 90 at 1347–350.

92 *Ibid* at 1350.

93 *Ibid*.

94 CSA Group standards, above note 19. "This Standard was prepared by the Subcommittee on Reproductive Tissues, under the jurisdiction of the Technical Committee on Safety of Cells, Tissues, and Organs for Transplantation and Assisted Reproduction and the Strategic Steering Committee on Health Care Technology, and has been formally approved by the Technical Committee. *Annex A was prepared by a Task Force serving under the Subcommittee and Technical Committee. This Standard has been approved as a National Standard of Canada by the Standards Council of Canada.*" [Emphasis added.]

Presently, the identity of the members of the task force and the authors of the CSA Group standards is confidential and not public information. The task force and the CSA Group are the only entities that possess this information and it is unknown whether this information will be made accessible to the public. One very specific consequence of the lack of openness and transparency regarding members of the task force is that there can be no independent assessment of the expertise available to the task force or of any potential conflicts of interest (real or apparent). For example, was there expertise in health law, ethics, reproductive medicine, and the social sciences? Were gamete donors, surrogates, as well as other women adequately represented?[95] Were member of related industries, such as sperm and egg banks, fertility clinics, importers and exporters, as well as brokers represented? Were real or apparent conflicts of interests disclosed by members before deliberations? For instance, a broker who serves both a couple and the surrogate may have a conflict of interest with respect to payments for arranging the surrogacy relationship. Surely, the legitimacy of the task force must be questioned if those who would be directly affected by the standards—donors, surrogates, fertility clinics, and other interested parties—were not members of the task force or, at the very least, were not extensively consulted.

In addition to the lack of information regarding the identity of the members of the task force, donors, surrogates, fertility clinics, and other interested parties have no knowledge of the materials or groups who were consulted (and relied upon) during their deliberations. For example, the task force does not describe, outline, or make freely available documents and testimony considered in its deliberations or any policy document developed as a result of these deliberations. Once more, the task force and the CSA Group are the only entities that possess this information and it is unknown whether this information will be made accessible to the public. As a result, the Canadian public does not know *who* considered *what* information in developing the CSA Group standards. This is inconsistent with the public's interest in knowing whether task force members were overly dependent on information from a narrow range of stakeholders.[96] Consequently, donors,

95 Mendelson, above note 75 at 759.

96 *Ibid* at 779.

surrogates, fertility clinics, and other interested parties cannot assess the legitimacy of the task force deliberations and decisions.

To be clear, as a third party, there is no legal obligation on the CSA Group to disclose information to the Canadian public regarding members of the task force or documents or policy underlying the CSA Group standards. Additionally, there is no legal obligation on the task force or the CSA Group to provide any assurances that an underlying policy document was even developed.[97] The task force and the CSA Group do not have a self-imposed transparency mechanism, and, moreover, they are not subject to the *Access to Information Act*,[98] which applies to government agencies (including Health Canada). Consequently, if the CSA Group standards are incorporated by reference, the lack of transparency with respect to the members and expertise of the task force, as well as the materials or groups who were consulted, may not be defensible and would be inconsistent with the federal government's commitment to openness and transparency (in an effort to promote accountability).

3) Incorporation by Reference and the Risk of Ineffectual Policy

Regulations should not include unnecessary or confusing material and must be expressed in terms that impose clear obligations on the Canadian public, especially when criminal law penalties are involved. The promulgation of unclear regulations, whether incorporated by reference or not, leads to confusion, thereby making it impossible for Canadians to undertake their activities according to the rule of law. Furthermore, unclear regulations create an environment that thrusts the legal system in the direction of uncertainty and moves a society under law to a regime of official discretion.[99] This would be especially so when a conflict arises between the enacting legislation, regulations, and a reference document.

Upon this background of requiring clarity in the law, there is also a necessity to have clear policy and policy objectives, regardless of the legislative vehicle used (i.e., legislation or regulations), to underpin and implement obligations on the Canadian public. In the present context, policy

97 *Ibid* at 760.

98 RSC 1985, c A-1.

99 Anthony D'Amato, "Legal Uncertainty" (1983) 71 *California Law Review* 1.

development would include researching, identifying, analyzing, and synthesizing information to produce a policy document containing options and recommendations related to eligible reimbursable expenses. This robust policy process would provide a solid foundation for discourse and engagement between the public and government via consultation and would provide advice and guidance to government ministers.

However, the possible promulgation of regulations related to eligible reimbursable expenses via incorporation by reference could undermine this norm. Specifically, if Health Canada promulgates such regulations by incorporation by reference, who is required to develop policy to support the regulations? Is Health Canada required to draft policy in order to achieve their regulatory objectives? If Health Canada does not draft policy supporting the content of the regulations, who is the third party that will? Or, alternatively, is a third party required to assist Health Canada in the drafting of policy? Most importantly, what may be the repercussions of any such approaches?

Under section 20(1) of the *AHRA*, the minister of health "is *responsible for the policy* of the Government of Canada respecting assisted human reproduction."[100] While the minister is responsible for policy, no comprehensive and overarching policy or guidance documents, directives, draft regulations, or other significant documents related to eligible reimbursable expenses have been published to date. For example, Health Canada has published only two minor directives with respect to reimbursement of expenditures as it relates to (1) reproductive material and embryos and (2) surrogacy.[101] Specifically, the directive for reproductive material and embryos states that, if a

100 Above note 8 [emphasis added]; see also *AHRA*, *ibid*, s 25(1). Prior to s 25(1) being repealed, this subsection evidenced the role of the minister in the creation of policy under the *AHRA* by empowering the minister to issue policy directions to the agency in relation to any matter under the *AHRA*.

101 Government of Canada, "Prohibitions," above note 17:

> Although paying a surrogate mother is a crime, a surrogate mother may be repaid for out-of-pocket costs directly related to her pregnancy (i.e., maternity clothes, medications) .... Repayment of a particular expense must not involve financial or other gain to the surrogate mother and normally occurs after receipts for costs are provided to the person making the repayment; ... Payment of 'anticipated expenses' or an 'unexplained allowance' would be seen as violating the prohibition in the *AHR Act*; ... Whether or not a particular cost is directly related to the surrogacy depends on the circumstance(s) of each surrogacy arrangement. This means that a surrogate mother can only be repaid for out-of-pocket costs if they

donor has out-of-pocket costs, that person may be repaid for pain medication or for travel to the clinic where pre-screening and donation takes place. In addition, the directive for surrogacy states that surrogates can be repaid only for out-of-pocket costs, including costs for maternity clothes, travel for medical appointments, medications, and loss of work wages.[102] The scarcity of information regarding eligible reimbursable expenses in these directives indicates the dire need to address this issue in a robust policy document.[103]

As Health Canada has not currently published such a policy document in relation to eligible reimbursable expenses, there is a possibility that the CSA Group may voluntarily draft an explanatory document, akin to a policy statement, supporting the CSA Group standards if they are incorporated by reference. Health Canada could subsequently adopt this explanatory document. Nonetheless, the CSA Group is not legally obligated to do so. This lack of obligation on behalf of the CSA Group is supported by the fact that no accompanying explanatory document was published alongside the CSA Group standards in order to support the provisions contained within it.

The possible repercussions of promulgating regulations without a robust supporting policy are numerous: among other considerations, they may not support the regulatory objectives of Health Canada, or an explanatory document may be inconsistent with the *AHRA*. A brief examination of the CSA Group standards supports this contention and, in some cases, highlights that inconsistencies between the CSA Group standards and the *AHRA* may border on incentivization (see, e.g., clauses 3.2.1, 3.4, and 3.5.1).[104]

The first example of ineffectual policy and the possibility of legal uncertainty concerns the description of eligible reimbursement recipients under section 12(1)(b) of the *AHRA* and clause A.1 of the CSA Group standards.

---

are directly related to the surrogacy and usually when a receipt is attached. For instance, a surrogate mother may be repaid for loss of work wages if a doctor certifies, in writing, that bed rest is necessary for her health and/or the health of the embryo or fetus. However, costs related to the surrogacy also depend on each surrogate mother's situation.

102 *Ibid.*

103 The author acknowledges that Health Canada may not develop regulations related to eligible reimbursable expenses, but instead may simply "clarify" and expand the list of expenses in these two directives. There has been no definitive statement from Health Canada that this is the course of action it will take, thereby leading to more uncertainty on this issue.

104 CSA Group standards, above note 19.

Subsection 12(1)(b) of the *AHRA* states that "[n]o person shall, except in accordance with the regulations ... reimburse any *person* for an expenditure incurred in the maintenance or transport of an *in vitro* embryo." As the term "person" is not defined under the *AHRA*, the *Interpretation Act*[105] may be utilized. It defines a person to include a corporation. Therefore, under the *AHRA* in conjunction with the *Interpretation Act*, an incorporated fertility clinic may be defined as a person that is eligible for reimbursement of receipted expenditures incurred in the maintenance or transport of an *in vitro* embryo. Nonetheless, the CSA Group standards omit fertility clinics as an eligible reimbursement recipient and state that "[c]ategories of potential recipients [of reimbursements] ... include ... *donor* of ova[,] ... *donor* of sperm[,] ... *donor(s)* of in vitro embryos; and ... *person* who acts as a surrogate."[106] The CSA Group standards thereby suggest that fertility clinics, which may incur significant expense in the maintenance or transport of an *in vitro* embryo, should not be reimbursed for providing these essential services under any circumstance. It is unclear whether regulations will state unequivocally that fertility clinics are an eligible reimbursement recipient, or whether it is necessary to state it at all in light of section 12(1)(b) of the *AHRA* and the *Interpretation Act*, and what controls will be in place to set limitations on possible fee schedules in order to negate incentivization.

A second example of ineffectual policy and a possibility of legal uncertainty relates to reimbursement for loss of work-related income by a surrogate mother under sections 12(1) and (3)(a) of the *AHRA* and clause A.3.2.2 (in conjunction with A.2.1.2) of the CSA Group standards. Subsection 12(1)(c) of the *AHRA* states, "No person shall, except in accordance with the regulations, ... reimburse a *surrogate mother* for an *expenditure* incurred by her in relation to her surrogacy."[107] Furthermore, section 12(3)(a) of the *AHRA* states, "No person shall reimburse a *surrogate mother* for a *loss of work-related income incurred during her pregnancy* ... unless ... continuing to work may pose a risk to her health or that of the embryo or foetus."[108]

105 RSC 1985, c I-21. The *Interpretation Act* is *An Act Respecting the Interpretation of Statutes and Regulations*.

106 See, for example, CSA Group standards, above note 19, clause A.1; *AHRA*, above note 8, s 3: "*donor* means (a) in relation to human reproductive material, the individual from whose body it was obtained, whether for consideration or not; and (b) in relation to an *in vitro* embryo, a donor as defined in the regulations . . . ."

107 See, e.g., *AHRA*, above note 8, s 12(1) [emphasis added].

108 See, e.g., *ibid*, s 12(3) [emphasis added].

Payments related to post-pregnancy work-related income do not constitute a permissible reimbursement under section 12(3)(a) of the *AHRA* and are prohibited. Importantly, as section 12(3)(a) of the *AHRA* is explicitly limited to a "surrogate mother," this means that an ovum donor engaging in an altruistic medical intervention is not entitled to loss of work-related income.

Nonetheless, clause A.3.2.2 (in conjunction with A.2.1.2) of the CSA Group standards expands the eligible recipients of reimbursement for loss of work-related income to include ovum donors.[109] It appears that the task force has taken it upon itself to include a further eligible recipient group for reimbursement of work-related income, one that is not promulgated under the *AHRA*. The task force is wordsmithing the *AHRA* such that "reimbursement of expenditures" for an ovum donor may also mean "loss of work-related income." This interpretation of the *AHRA* by the task force potentially instructs that it is permissible to reimburse an ovum donor for loss of work-related income, which is inconsistent with and in contravention to the current *AHRA*. The lack of an explanatory document negates any inquiry into the reasoning behind clause A.3.2.2 (in conjunction with A.2.1.2).

Although the CSA Group standards have expanded the categories of eligible recipients, I would argue that the Government of Canada should indeed consider amending the *AHRA* to allow ovum donors engaging in an altruistic medical intervention to be eligible for loss of work-related income. Such donors are required to attend multiple medical appointments prior to donation. These appointments are associated with initial screening, interviews with clinical coordinators and physicians, as well as testing and assessment of general health matters. Thereafter, donors have to attend a fertility clinic for a retrieval procedure(s) under sedation. They may also have to return to the fertility clinic for a post-retrieval checkup. During this process, there is a risk that donors may suffer from an iatrogenic complication called ovarian hyperstimulation syndrome, which can be mild, moderate, or severe and can lead to serious illness or death. Donors

109 CSA Group standards, above note 19, clause A.3.2.2: "A donor may be reimbursed for net loss of work-related income due to being unable to work as a result of her participation in the donation process if a qualified medical practitioner certifies, in writing, that work might pose a risk to her health and safety." *Ibid*, clause A.2.1: "An ova donor or surrogate shall only be reimbursed for a loss of work-related income if a qualified medical practitioner certifies, in writing, that continuing to work might pose a risk to the donor or surrogate's health and safety or that of the embryo or fetus. Such reimbursements shall be made in accordance with Clauses A.2.2 and A.3."

suffering from ovarian hyperstimulation syndrome may require acute or long-term medical care. Consequently, it would be prudent to amend the *AHRA* and proposed regulations to expressly allow an ovum donor to be reimbursed for loss of work-related income incurred as a result of medical appointments, treatment, and retrieval procedure(s).

A third example of ineffectual policy and a possibility of legal uncertainty relates to financial receipts under section 12(2) of the *AHRA* and clause A.2.2.1 of the CSA Group standards. Subsection 12(2) addresses the issue of incentivization and requires that only receipted expenditures can be reimbursed.[110] The Supreme Court in the *Reference* decision upheld this provision, explicitly stating that "section [12] also *prohibits reimbursement for expenditures without receipts*."[111] The law is unequivocal and unquestionable on this point. Therefore, where a woman, man, couple, surrogate, or fertility clinic cannot provide a receipt related to assisted reproduction, the reimbursement of expenditures is explicitly prohibited. Nonetheless, clause A.2.2.1 of the CSA Group standards indicates that, in order for allowable reimbursements of expenditures to be made, a receipt or "verifiable claim" for each expenditure must be presented.[112] In accordance with clause A.2.2.3, the claimant must also provide "a signed declaration" confirming that the expenditures have not been and will not be otherwise reimbursed.[113] However, section 12(2) of the *AHRA* does not contemplate a verifiable claim and a signed declaration. Moreover, the term "verifiable claim" is ambiguous. It is not certain the term "verifiable claim" assists reimbursement recipients in understanding their obligations regarding receipts.

The CSA Group may base the inclusion of the term "verifiable claim" on recent caselaw in areas such as consumer-product class actions, whereby

110 See, for example, *AHRA*, above note 8, s 12(2). "No person shall reimburse an expenditure referred to in subsection (1) unless a receipt is provided to that person for the expenditure": *Reference re AHRA*, above note 21 at para 110 [emphasis added].

111 *Ibid* [emphasis added].

112 CSA Group standards, above note 19, clause A.2.2.2. "In order for allowable reimbursements of expenditures to be made, the following documentation shall be submitted to the person issuing the reimbursement: (a) a receipt or *verifiable claim* for each expenditure; (b) the relevant certificate from the regulated health care professional, where applicable; and (c) with every claim for reimbursement, a *signed declaration* in accordance with Clause A.2.2.3." [Emphasis added.]

113 *Ibid*, clause A.2.2.3: "The signed declaration shall (a) be signed by the person who is claiming reimbursement; and (b) confirm that the expenditures or the loss of work-related income have not been and will not be otherwise reimbursed."

parties who were seeking court approval of a settlement did not require a receipt as proof of purchase. For example, in *Wiggins v Mattel Canada Inc*,[114] settlement class members, in order to be paid under the terms of a settlement agreement, were required to have a receipt. Nonetheless, the court held that the "threshold for making claims is very low, reflecting the realities of consumer conduct, for example, in not *retaining receipts*."[115] Importantly, caselaw surrounding class action lawsuits and other forms of law has developed and evolved over many years. Arguing the same untested principles or interpretation in relation to the *AHRA* may be ultimately unsuccessful in a court of law. A lower court may be influenced by a literal interpretation of section 12(2) of the *AHRA*, as well as the Supreme Court reasoning that "section [12] also *prohibits reimbursement for expenditures without receipts*."[116] The reasoning of the court in not requiring receipts in *Wiggins v Mattel Canada Inc*, along with other similar cases, may not apply with respect to the *AHRA*.

The disparity between the CSA Group standards' references to a verifiable claim linked to a signed declaration, on the one hand, and section 12(2) of the *AHRA* supported by a legal ruling from our highest court, on the other, creates an unclear obligation. In doing so, it does not protect the interests of donors, surrogates, fertility clinics, and other interested parties, and potentially instructs the Canadian public to break the law. No amount of wordsmithing by the task force can amend the substance of the law as promulgated or ruled upon.

Although this chapter is not exhaustive of the issues related to ineffectual policy, it does highlight the risks that arise when a third party develops a reference document. Moreover, it also highlights that the absence of a freely published explanatory document leads to speculation as to the reasoning used to support provisions in a reference document. As Health Canada has not published a robust policy document in relation to eligible reimbursable expenses or provided a valid rationale or public statement addressing the CSA Group coincidentally publishing the CSA Group standards, we are faced with questions as to whether Health Canada will sub-delegate its responsibility.

In my opinion, the Parliamentary process of rule-making requires robust development of policy consistent with its underlying basis, purpose,

114 2011 ONSC 2964 at para 13.

115 *Ibid*.

116 *Reference re AHRA*, above note 21 at para 110 [emphasis added].

and objectives. Expertise and experience in developing policy at the intersection between health and criminal law matters reside within Health Canada and the Department of Justice, respectively. Both departments have developed policy documents related to numerous facets of the *AHRA*, and have developed and promulgated the *Consent Regulations*. The semblance of institutionalized exhaustion at Health Canada would not be a justification for sub-delegating that department's responsibility.

4) Creating Barriers to Public Participation

Of paramount importance to donors, surrogates, fertility clinics, and other interested parties (and the prime challenge of possibly incorporating by reference the CSA Group standards) is public participation during the rule-making period. During the development of the CSA Group standards, there was no legislative requirement imposed upon the CSA Group to allow public inspection or consultation. The CSA Group did have a voluntary "inquiry stage" consistent with its own internal development process. According to that process, "[o]nce a draft is complete, we put the *draft standard out for public review and comment*. Then, the technical committee reaches consensus and our internal staff conducts a quality review. Finally, a pre-approval edit of the standard is completed."[117] Although the CSA Group had a voluntary "inquiry stage" in June 2015, the majority of Canadian donors, surrogates, fertility clinics, and other interested parties may not have been aware of this third-party process. Consequently, notice and comment may have been limited, thereby creating a barrier to meaningful public participation.[118]

The robustness of the process undertaken by the task force in drafting the CSA Group standards is relatively thin when compared to the normative instrument, namely, the *Canada Gazette*. The *Gazette* is the normative instrument allowing the Canadian public to review and publicly comment on proposed regulations. This instrument supports the notion that greater public accessibility is required during the rule-making period, as opposed to after promulgation, in order to promote citizen engagement in policy-making. The normative procedure with respect to the enactment of regulations is drafting, review, and public consultation. This includes, but is not limited

117 CSA Group, "How Standards Are Developed" (2016), online: www.csagroup.org/codes-standards/standards-development [emphasis added].

118 Mendelson, above note 75 at 747.

to, the minister of health drafting a regulatory impact analysis statement and producing a proposed regulation that is reviewed by the clerk of the Privy Council in consultation with the deputy minister of justice. Following review and forwarding to the Privy Council Office and the Treasury Board, the proposed regulation is published in the *Canada Gazette*, Part I, thereby giving the Canadian public notice of the proposed regulation while also allowing the public an opportunity to comment. Following this, the regulation is reviewed and may be revised. Once in final form, a draft order in council is prepared for signature by the governor general. The regulation is then published in the *Canada Gazette*, Part II.[119]

This process of drafting, review, and public consultation is a fundamental mechanism to prevent abuse and safeguard against malfeasance. Any deviation from this established process, such as utilizing the CSA Group internal development process including a voluntary "inquiry stage," does not amount to robust public consultation, which is profoundly inconsistent with our core assumptions about democratic government.[120] In the present case, this barrier to access can be overcome only if the CSA Group standards are either published in the *Canada Gazette* or, in the alternative, further developed by Health Canada and thereafter published in the *Canada Gazette*.

Regulations related to eligible reimbursable expenses are likely to affect only a narrow group of the Canadian public, including gamete donors, surrogates, intended parents, and fertility clinics. It may be prudent to impose a specific obligation in the *AHRA* or the regulations relating to eligible reimbursable expenses to consult with those groups in addition to a requirement to consult publicly with Canadians.[121] There is precedent to have a duty to consult particular groups that may be affected by legislation or regulations in Canada. In addition, due to the contested legal history of the *AHRA*,

119 See, for example, Government of Canada, "Guide to the Federal Regulatory Development Process" (2014), online: www.tbs-sct.gc.ca/hgw-cgf/priorities-priorites/rtrap-parfa/guides/gfrpg-gperf/gfrpg-gperftb-eng.asp.

120 Mendelson, above note 75 at 796.

121 *Green Energy and Green Economy Act, 2009*, SO 2009, c 12, Schedule B, s 5(1), which amends the *Electricity Act, 1998*, SO 1998, c 15, s 25.32 by adding s 4.4: "The Minister may direct the OPA to implement procedures for *consulting aboriginal peoples* and other persons or groups as may be specified in the direction, on the planning, development or procurement of electricity supply, capacity, transmission systems and distribution systems and the direction may specify the manner or method by which such consultations shall occur and the timing within which such consultations shall occur." [Emphasis added.]

particularly the Supreme Court decision,[122] specific obligations in the Act or regulations to consult with the provinces and territories may also be prudent in order to, in the words of the prime minister, "deliver real results and professional government to Canadians."[123] Finally, precedence of consultation in the field of assisted reproduction, with particular attention to the extensive public consultation and review procedure utilized during the development and promulgation of the *Consent Regulations*, which will be discussed below, also supports the contention that barriers to meaningful public participation should be eliminated.

5) Incorporation by Reference May Create Barriers to Accessibility to the Law

The fundamental concept of an orderly Canadian society is that the public has a duty to act in accordance with the law. If Canadians have a duty to obey the law, they must know the content of the law.[124] "Rudimentary justice requires that those subject to the law must have the means of knowing what it prescribes."[125] Therefore, the law related to assisted reproduction needs to be published for public scrutiny, be transparent, and be readily and publicly accessible,[126] and it must leave donors, surrogates, fertility clinics, and other interested parties, including intended parents, no doubt as regards their rights and obligations. Barriers to accessibility to the law diminish meaningful assurances that regulations will be reasoned and democratically responsive,[127] while also undermining agency procedures, political oversight, public deliberation, as well as future voting potential as a means of effective accountability.[128] Consequently, access to the law cannot be "incidental, occasional, or selective."[129]

122 *Reference re AHRA*, above note 21.

123 Trudeau, Mandate Letter, above note 24 at para 5 [emphasis added].

124 Mendelson, above note 75 at 774.

125 Antonin Scalia, "The Rule of Law as a Law of Rules" (1989) 56 *University of Chicago Law Review* 1175 at 1179.

126 Mendelson, above note 75.

127 *Ibid* at 748 and 777.

128 See, for example, *ibid* at 747 and 789; New Zealand House of Representatives, above note 44; Leslie Green, "Law and Obligations" in Jules L Coleman & Scott J Shapiro, eds, *The Oxford Handbook of Jurisprudence and Philosophy of Law* (Oxford: Oxford University Press, 2002).

129 Mendelson, above note 75 at 748 and 774.

In the case of the *AHRA*, the *Incorporation by Reference in Regulations Act* imposes a further obligation on the minister of health to ensure that documents incorporated by reference, which may include the CSA Group standards, are accessible.[130] Nevertheless, the *Incorporation by Reference in Regulations Act* is silent on the statutory definition of "accessibility," as well as when a reference document should be made accessible to the public. The question that must be asked of the minister of health is, When and where will donors, surrogates, fertility clinics, and other interested parties, including intended parents, gain access to information about their rights and obligations under the law if a document is incorporated by reference? For example, does accessibility under the *Incorporation by Reference in Regulations Act* mean making the reference document readily available for free during its development and drafting by a third-party organization prior to promulgation? Alternatively, does it mean making the most up-to-date version of the reference document readily available from a third-party organization at a per access fee after promulgation? Does it mean making the most up-to-date version of the reference document readily available for free on the Health Canada website only after promulgation? Should the reference document containing all incorporated material be available in an electronic format on the Government of Canada website, or at government offices in hard copy for free inspection by persons likely to be affected by, or interested in, it?[131] If donors, surrogates, fertility clinics, and interested parties, including intended parents, have to find the reference document outside of normative legislative or regulatory sources, this not

---

130 *Incorporation by Reference in Regulations Act*, above note 2, s 18.3(1): "The regulation-making authority shall ensure that a document, index, rate or number that is incorporated by reference is accessible."

131 See, for example, New Zealand House of Representatives, above note 44; Government of Canada, above note 84:

> With the foregoing in mind, while the Joint Committee welcomes the new requirement in section 18.3 of the *Statutory Instruments Act* that material incorporated by reference be made accessible, the Joint Committee is of the view that this requirement must include, in order to be effective, the following safeguards: . . . Recommendation 3 That the *Statutory Instruments Act* be amended to require that regulation-making authorities make all incorporated materials available for consultation by the public, free of charge, including all former versions of the incorporated materials. Recommendation 4 That the *Statutory Instruments Act* be amended to establish a central repository for incorporated materials and require regulation-making authorities to provide, on an annual basis, a list of all incorporated documents.

only creates a barrier to access but also highlights the limitations of incorporation by reference.[132]

A further barrier to access is the possibility that the CSA Group may impose a fee for access to review the full text of the CSA Group standards, future amendments of the standards, and related documents (i.e., supporting policy documents or explanatory documents, if they exist) as a result of copyright restrictions imposed by third parties. Unless an executed contract is undertaken between Health Canada and the CSA Group to permit future publication of the CSA Group standards, amendments, and related documents, the CSA Group is under no obligation to continue to provide access at any price and may revoke this access at will. For example, access to the related CSA Group document entitled "CAN/CSA-Z900.1-17—Tissues for Assisted Reproduction" requires a payment of CAD $168.[133] This fee provides a substantial financial obstacle to accessibility that is inconsistent with core democratic values.[134] Without purchasing this document, donors, surrogates, fertility clinics, and other interested parties will be unaware of whether it is related to the CSA Group standards or whether it contains policy or explanatory reasoning supporting the clauses in the standards. Furthermore, requiring the public to purchase this document undermines open discussion of public affairs and accountability of government power.[135]

Some private-sector bodies argue that the copyright of standards-developing organizations should be protected and that reasonable accessibility does not mean accessible for free.[136] More specifically, they argue that reasonable accessibility should mean a fair, proper, or moderate fee in order to allay the cost of developing the standards. Moreover, private-sector bodies state that, if iterations of standards in the future are required to be accessible for free, the long-term sustainability of standards-developing

132 See, for example, *AHRA*, above note 8; Mendelson, above note 75 at 795.

133 CSA Group standards, above note 19.

134 Mendelson, above note 75 at 769.

135 *Ibid.*

136 See, e.g., *Veeck v Southern Building Code Congress International, Inc*, 241 F3d 398 (5th Cir 2001); Mendelson, above note 75; CSA Group, above note 117; ANSI, Government Affairs, "Incorporation by Reference, Reasonable Availability, and the U.S. Standardization System," online: www.ansi.org/ibr; Jessica Bassett, "OFR Responds to Petition on Incorporation by Reference" (14 October 2013), online: the Regulatory Review www.regblog.org/2013/10/14/14-bassett-ofr-responds.

organizations would be endangered, and that, if such organizations cease to exist, then this resource will be lost to related industries, regulators, and government clients.[137]

In order to negate the issue of reasonable accessibility, one solution is for the minister of health to simply avoid incorporating a document by reference, including the CSA Group standards. The minister recently stated that she is "convinced that we have an obligation as a government of Canada . . . to do more than simply open up the federal wallet."[138] From this perspective, contracting the CSA Group to develop a possible reference document would appear to be contradictory, at the very least. Alternatively, the minister could acquire the copyright from the CSA Group, which may be prohibitively expensive and is not an option that I support. Health Canada could request that the CSA Group negotiate a licence or waive copyright of the CSA Group standards as a condition of incorporation into the regulations. Finally, Health Canada could argue that the reference document should not be eligible for copyright, especially if incorporated verbatim into the regulations.[139]

6) Loss of Parliamentary Control over Future Amendments to Regulations if Incorporated by Reference

Subsection 66(1) of the *AHRA* adds another unique level of oversight to the regulation-making process, stating that "[b]efore a regulation is made . . . the Minister shall lay the proposed regulation before each House of Parliament." Consequently, any regulation, including a proposed regulation that incorporates by reference, needs to be laid before both houses of Parliament and thereafter referred to the appropriate committee of each house for review.[140] This requirement was created in response to concerns by the House of Commons Standing Committee on Health about the broad regulation-making power of the Governor in Council. More particularly, as the Standing Committee on Health noted, because assisted reproduction "is

137 Aerospace Industries Association, "Standards — Incorporation by Reference" (28 January 2015), online: www.aia-aerospace.org/report/standards-incorporation-by-reference.

138 Susan Lunn, "Health Minister Vows to Do More Than Just 'Open the Federal Wallet'" *CBC News* (27 September 2016), online: www.cbc.ca/news/politics/philpott-health-minister-provinces-funding-accord-1.3780633.

139 New Zealand House of Representatives, above note 44.

140 See, for example, *AHRA*, above note 8, ss 66(2)–(2.1); Nelson, above note 75 at 1032.

such a highly sensitive and controversial area, we strongly feel that a parliamentary safeguard of this nature is necessary. Elected representatives should have the opportunity to shape essential regulations to ensure that they reflect the best interest of Canadians."[141] In addition to this parliamentary oversight, Health Canada has also stated unequivocally that the process for the development of regulations that involves the *Canada Gazette*, Part I, described above, will not be abandoned.[142]

Although section 66(1) of the *AHRA* adds another unique level of oversight, section 67 of the Act does contain exceptions to such oversight: if the minister of health is of the opinion that (1) any amendment to an existing regulation is so immaterial or insubstantial, or (2) the regulation must be made immediately to protect health or safety,[143] the regulation may be made without being laid before either House of Parliament. Even though these exceptions exist, they do not apply in this case. Specifically, regulations related to reimbursement of expenditure are not an amendment to an existing regulation. Moreover, they cannot be said to be required immediately to protect health or safety. However, there are no guarantees that future amendments to a reference document, caused by changing social opinion or if the standards become outdated or incomplete, will undergo the same scrutiny before either house of Parliament.

This proposition is supported by the CSA Group document amendment process. The CSA Group has an amendment process that includes

---

141 House of Commons, Standing Committee on Health, *Assisted Human Reproduction: Building Families* (Ottawa: Standing Committee on Health, 2001).

142 Government of Canada, "Plans to Introduce," above note 9:

> To uphold the Government's commitment to these recommendations and ensure that the latest scientific and technological advancements are considered, Health Canada plans to: update the regulations for the safety of donor semen, and move them from the *Food and Drugs Act* to the *AHRA*; develop regulations for testing and screening the donors of ova, as well as for tracing donations for the purposes of monitoring adverse events and recalls; and *clarify eligible reimbursable expenses* for parties involved in surrogacy arrangements, and semen and ova donation. Once regulations are in place, the Department will assign inspectors to administer and enforce this important piece of legislation. The Government encourages Canadians to read the Notice of Intent and provide their comments to the Department by November 29, 2016. At a later stage, *interested stakeholders will have another opportunity to provide feedback following the pre-publication of the regulatory proposals in the* Canada Gazette, *Part I*. [Emphasis added.]

143 *AHRA*, above note 8, s 67(1).

what it terms a "maintenance stage." Specifically, the CSA Group standards undergo systematic review and amendment no less than every five years to ensure they stay current and technically valid.[144] Consequently, there is a risk that the minister of health may proclaim future amendments to the reference document immaterial or insubstantial under section 67 of the *AHRA* so that it can bypass further scrutiny before each house of Parliament under section 66(1). Importantly, the Canadian public has no idea what the subjective terms "immaterial" or "insubstantial" mean, as that meaning will be determined at the official discretion of the minister of health. Accordingly, any possible "immaterial" or "insubstantial" future amendment made to the CSA Group standards that are incorporated by reference relegates responsibility for the drafting and review of the content of the law from the legislative authority of parliamentarians, who will not be notified, to those of a future iteration of the task force.[145]

Some might argue that a task force may be more responsive to social change than Parliament, that it can potentially act as a focal point for debate and is an independent organization theoretically insulated against political pressures. Regardless, the possible role of a task force in drafting the content of regulations still raises significant issues related to parliamentary control over sub-delegated law-making. Specifically, such a process would allow a non-elected body that is not directly and democratically accountable to the Canadian public, as are members of Parliament, to have the power to determine the content of regulations made by the Governor in Council.[146]

In addition to the aforesaid risk that a future regulation may be made without being laid before either house of Parliament, section 18.4 of the *Incorporation by Reference in Regulations Act* also provides for the express power to incorporate by reference a future regulation without publication in the *Canada Gazette*.[147] The legislative summary of Bill S-2 (*Incorporation by Reference in Regulations Act*) states that this power "reflect[s] the understanding that one of the advantages of incorporation by reference is

144 CSA Group, above note 117.

145 This is so, even if amendments may not have automatic effect but may be separately reviewed, either with or without modification, by the Standing Joint Committee for the Scrutiny of Regulations.

146 "Second Report," above note 2 at para 6.

147 *Incorporation by Reference in Regulations Act*, above note 2, s 18.4.

... that the formal requirements of the Act with respect to registration and publication may not need to be met."[148]

Upon a holistic examination, section 67 of the *AHRA* may be used in conjunction with section 18.4 of the *Incorporation by Reference in Regulations Act* to allow future amendments to a reference document that are "immaterial" or "insubstantial" to be exempt from scrutiny before each house of Parliament,[149] as well as from publication and printing requirements.[150] In fact, scrutiny, publication, and printing may be at the behest of the minister of health.[151] Effectively, the minister may, in his or her opinion under the powers authorized under section 67, direct final rule-making power to amend the content of regulations to a parallel mechanism that truncates the legislative process.[152] Donors, surrogates, fertility clinics, and other interested parties who are supposed to know their rights and obligations, and parliamentarians who are supposed to scrutinize the law, will not be able to do so.[153] In

148 Parliament of Canada, "Legislative Summary of Bill S-2: An Act to Amend the *Statutory Instruments Act* and to Make Consequential Amendments to the *Statutory Instruments Regulations*" (29 October 2013), online: https://lop.parl.ca/About/Parliament/LegislativeSummaries/bills_ls.asp?Language=E&ls=S2&Mode=1&Parl=41&Ses=2&source=library_prb [emphasis added].

149 *AHRA*, above note 8, s 66(1).

150 *Ibid*, s 67(1).

151 *Ibid*: "A regulation may be made without being laid before either House of Parliament *if the Minister is of the opinion that* (a) the changes made by the regulation to an existing regulation are so immaterial or insubstantial that section 66 should not apply in the circumstances; or (b) the regulation must be made immediately in order to protect the health or safety of any person." [Emphasis added.]

152 See Elizabeth May, Saanich–Gulf Islands, BC on "Bill S-2 (Historical), *Incorporation by Reference in Regulations Act*," above note 6: "I have seen it referred to in the media as a 'sleeper law,' something that appears so dry that it does not gain public attention, but which does have deeply anti-democratic implications." Craig Scott, Toronto-Danforth, ON, *ibid*: "In my capacity not only as a former professor of law but also as the official opposition critic for democratic and parliamentary reform, I believe that this bill could end up being an anti-democratic reform. It could be a step backward for accountable government. Essentially, it would give carte blanche to the executive branch to use incorporation by reference of an open sort with very few, if any, serious constraints."

153 *Ibid*. Ève Péclet, La Pointe-de-l'Île, QC: "This means that these amendments will never be reviewed by parliamentarians. That is a problem. Canadians, who are supposed to know the law, and parliamentarians, who are supposed to study it, will not be able to do so. They will not necessarily be aware of all of the changes made to the hundreds of thousands of regulations pertaining to legislation in other countries. In addition, incorporations by reference will not even have to be published in the *Canada Gazette*."

fact, this possible mechanism negates the opportunity for these interested parties to meaningfully comment, prior to promulgation, on the content of regulations they have to meet. Importantly, this process is diametrically opposed to section 66(1) of the *AHRA*, which offers Parliament an ongoing role in the policy process to debate and amend regulations.[154] Future discussion and access to the text of the reference document should not be just a formality, but it must be readily and meaningfully available to the public.[155]

In addition to the aforesaid risks related to sub-delegated law-making, there are several risks related to the strong incentive for Health Canada to adopt the CSA Group standards as a whole, rather than amending them, prior to promulgation.[156] For example, amending the CSA Group standards may be criticized as creating complexity and unnecessary duplication.[157] Furthermore, if Health Canada has depended on the task force to develop a reference document, it may continue to rely on these privately generated clauses even if it is not advisable to do so.[158] For example, there is no guarantee that any future amendment to the reference document will further Health Canada's goal or purpose, and it may in fact move away from its mandate or policy in this field to serve the public interest, as required and defined by statute.[159] Moreover, as the reference document would be enshrined in the regulations, the task force might become the *de facto* agent to develop future amendments via sub-delegation. In effect, the task force could become entrenched in the regulatory content-making and amendment process of the *AHRA*. Clearly, such a process, and the overall process of incorporating by reference diminishes the authority of the minister of health and of parliamentarians.

D. A TROUBLING JUXTAPOSITION OF THE CONSENT TO USE REGULATIONS

Following the enactment of the *AHRA*, successive Parliaments under Liberal (Paul Martin, 2004–6) and Conservative (Stephen Harper, 2006–15) governments failed to draft and promulgate comprehensive regulations authorized

154 *AHRA*, above note 8, s 66.

155 Mendelson, above note 75 at 806.

156 *Ibid* at 782.

157 *Ibid*.

158 *Ibid* at 785.

159 *Ibid* at 776.

under section 65 of the Act,[160] with the exception of the *Consent Regulations*, which came into force on 1 December 2007.[161] By examining the robust consultation process undertaken in the drafting and promulgation of the *Consent Regulations*, I argue that the same process should be followed with respect to clarifying reimbursement of expenditures under the *AHRA*, rather than utilizing incorporation by reference of third-party CSA standards.

The principle of free and informed consent is described in section 8 of the *AHRA*,[162] which states that no person shall make use of human reproductive material (e.g., ova, sperm) for the purpose of creating an embryo unless the donor of the material has given written consent,[163] and that no person shall make use of an *in vitro* embryo for any purpose unless the donor has given written consent.[164] Equivalent to sections, 6, 7, and 12 of the *AHRA*, the prohibitions outlined in section 8 are also enforced by penalties in section 61,[165] including a fine or a term of imprisonment or both.

Importantly, the regulatory impact analysis statement related to the development of the *Consent Regulations* stated that the regulations were to affect the following groups, (1) donors of human reproductive material and donors of *in vitro* embryos, (2) establishments and persons involved

---

160 *AHRA*, above note 8, s 65(1).

161 *Consent Regulations*, above note 20.

162 *AHRA*, above note 8, s 3. "'Consent' means fully informed and freely given consent that is given in accordance with the applicable law governing consent and that confirms to the provisions of the *Human Pluripotent Stem Cell Research Guidelines* released by the Canadian Institutes of Health Research in March 2002, as detailed in the Regulations.'" This definition was subsequently repealed, SC 2012, c 19, s 713.

163 *AHRA*, above note 8, s 8(1): "No person shall make use of human reproductive material for the purpose of creating an embryo unless the donor of the material has given written consent, *in accordance with the regulations*, to its use for that purpose." [Emphasis added.]

164 See, for example, *ibid*, s 8(3): "No person shall make use of an *in vitro* embryo for any purpose unless the donor has given written consent, in accordance with the regulations, to its use for that purpose." Section 8(2) also addresses posthumous use without consent of the donor, as "[n]o person shall remove human reproductive material from a donor's body after the donor's death for the purpose of creating an embryo unless the donor of the material has given written consent, in accordance with the regulations, to its removal for that purpose . . . ." Health Canada, "Consent to Use Human Reproductive Material and In Vitro Embryos," online: www.hc-sc.gc.ca/dhp-mps/brgtherap/legislation/reprod/consent-eng.php; *Evans v the United Kingdom*, Application No 6339/05 (7 March 2006) (ECHR).

165 *AHRA*, above note 8, s 61.

in collecting human reproductive material for the purpose of creating an embryo, and (3) establishments and persons who make use of an *in vitro* embryo, whether in an assisted reproduction procedure or for research.[166] These groups will also be affected by the proposed regulations related to reimbursement of receipted expenditure.

In sharp contrast with recent practice of clarifying eligible reimbursable expenses, an extensive public consultation and review procedure was undertaken by Health Canada with respect to the development and promulgation of the *Consent Regulations*. Specifically, public servants developed and drafted the *Consent Regulations*. As well, numerous high-level technical briefings were held between September 2004 and January 2005 with provincial and territorial officials to outline the regulatory-development process being undertaken. A notice of intent was thereafter published in the *Canada Gazette*, Part I, on 30 October 2004.[167] The *notice* explained that Health Canada was developing the components of the regulatory framework and noted that the department planned to "undertake public involvement activities and to provide interested parties the opportunity to participate"[168] and that it would subsequently post a consultation discussion paper related to the proposed regulation. The consultation discussion paper was subsequently posted on the Health Canada website on 8 November 2004 and sent to provincial and territorial officials.[169] In addition, the paper was sent to 376 individuals and organizations identified as interested parties by the department. According to information on the Health Canada website, 43 written submissions were received and there were 622 consultations.[170]

The proposed *Consent Regulations* were then pre-published in the *Canada Gazette*, Part I, on 24 September 2005.[171] Following this, ten additional

166 See, for example, "*Assisted Human Reproduction (Section 8) Regulations* Regulatory Impact Analysis Statement," (2005) C Gaz I, 3037 & 3038 [Regulatory Impact Analysis Statement].

167 (2004) C Gaz I, 3003, online: www.gazette.gc.ca/rp-pr/p1/2004/2004-10-30/pdf/g1-13844.pdf.

168 *Ibid*.

169 Health Canada, "Seeking Input on a Proposed Approach for Regulations Concerning Section 8 (Consent) and the Section 3 Definition of an *In vitro* Embryo Donor under the *AHRA*," online: www.hc-sc.gc.ca/hl-vs/pubs/reprod/index-eng.php.

170 Regulatory Impact Analysis Statement, above note 166 at 3045.

171 *Ibid* at 3037 & 3038. The Regulatory Impact Analysis Statement to the *Assisted Human Reproduction (Section 8) Regulations* published in (2005) C Gaz I, 3037–57

submissions were received. Between November 2004 and March 2006, Health Canada also had extensive public consultations and received a further 53 submissions from stakeholders and the general public, including federal parliamentary committees, provincial governments, professional associations, and experts in the field of assisted reproduction, human rights, and health law.

Following pre-publication in the *Canada Gazette*, Part I, the proposed *Consent Regulations* were amended and a revised document was laid before both houses of Parliament. It was reviewed by the House of Commons Standing Committee on Health on 27 October 2006,[172] and the Senate Committee on Social Affairs, Science and Technology on 30 October 2006.[173] Thereafter, the proposed *Consent Regulations* were published in the *Canada Gazette*, Part II, on 27 June 2007[174] and came into force on 1 December 2007.

Clearly, the development and promulgation of the *Consent Regulations* by Health Canada included extensive public consultation and review procedures. This process contrasts markedly with that currently undertaken in clarifying eligible reimbursable expenses. Importantly, Health Canada did not utilize a third-party for-profit organization, such as the CSA Group, to develop or draft the *Consent Regulations* and did not utilize section 65(2) of the *AHRA* to incorporate any such document by reference.

E. CONCLUSION

Given the importance of regulations related to eligible reimbursable expenses and the risks associated with a third party developing a reference document, it is not essential, necessary, and appropriate to engage a for-profit private organization such as the CSA Group (and associated task force) to serve and protect the public interest in this area. The regulations related to eligible reimbursable expenses explore issues such as public health, ethics, and morality, as well as physical and psychological harms, rather

contained paragraphs in an incorrect sequence. The corrected Regulatory Impact Analysis Statement was re-published on 24 September 2005.

172 *AHRA*, above note 8, s 66.

173 Library of Parliament, "Assisted Human Reproduction and Informed Consent" (2006) at 1, online: www.lop.parl.gc.ca/content/lop/ResearchPublications/prb0635-e.pdf.

174 See, for example, *Assisted Human Reproduction (Section 8 Consent) Regulations*, (2007) C Gaz II, 1520–46, online: http://publications.gc.ca/gazette/archives/p2/2007/2007-06-27/pdf/g2-14113.pdf.

than issues that require external expertise in matters such as engineering or laboratory safety. The CSA Group has previously developed consensus-based standards such as "CAN/CSA-Z900.1-12 — Tissues for Assisted Reproduction," which provides minimum requirements for the verification of safe practices for organ-donation organizations, tissue-retrieval organizations, tissue banks, and the like. Arguably, the CSA Group could also provide similar consensus-based standards for the testing, screening, and safety of sperm and ovum donors. However, testing, screening, and safety in the laboratory context differ substantially from issues related to ethics, morality, and harm.

The established legislative process involving rule-making by Health Canada and subsequent public consultation would promote our open, balanced, and consensus-based system. More specifically, Health Canada must actively engage provincial and territorial officials, professional associations, experts in the field of assisted reproduction, bioethicists, donors, surrogates, fertility clinics, and other interested parties via robust public consultation. Doing so would increase the legitimacy of the process — and its outcome — in the eyes of the Canadian public, particularly when compared to the process adopted by a standards-developing organization. In contrast, sub-delegating the responsibility to determine the content of regulations to the task force would not allow for the best participation and the most accepted legislative-making approach on an issue that affects donors, surrogates, fertility clinics, and other interested parties on a daily basis.

Reliance on expertise, if any, of a task force as it relates to eligible reimbursable expenses is not essential when expertise and experience in developing policy at the intersection between health and criminal law matters already resides within Health Canada and the Department of Justice, respectively. Health Canada does not lack the breadth and depth of expertise and resources needed to draft the regulations. Health Canada can and should develop regulations related to eligible reimbursable expenses internally to ensure that the principles stated in the *AHRA* are upheld in order to promote the health, well-being, safety, dignity, and rights of Canadians.

Finally, by possibly sub-delegating the critical responsibility of developing the content of regulations to a third party, including future variants of reference documents that may contain "immaterial" or "insubstantial" amendments, Health Canada puts at risk "meaningful engagement . . . and

... constructive dialogue with Canadians, civil society, and stakeholders."[175] This potential process does not meet the highest ethical standards and Canadians' well-founded expectations of our government.[176] Admittedly, there has been little political movement on this issue, and a major Supreme Court decision has scuttled the *AHRA* and subsequent regulation development. Nevertheless, if the Government of Canada promulgates regulations related to reimbursement of expenses under the *AHRA* using the mechanism of incorporation by reference, it would not be what Canadians deserve.[177]

175 *Ibid* at para 14. "[I] will expect you to work with your colleagues and through *established legislative, regulatory, and Cabinet processes* to deliver on your top priorities" [emphasis added].

176 *Ibid* at para 19. "When dealing with our Cabinet colleagues, Parliament, stakeholders, or the public, *it is important that your behaviour and decisions meet Canadians' well-founded expectations of our government*." [Emphasis added.]

177 *Ibid* at para 5.

5

Should Canada Implement a Flat-Rate Reimbursement Model for Surrogacy Arrangements?

LEGAL AND ETHICAL RECOMMENDATIONS FOR A REVISED APPROACH TO REIMBURSEMENT

Angel Petropanagos, Vanessa Gruben, & Angela Cameron

A. INTRODUCTION

In 2016, Health Canada announced its intention to proceed with bringing into force sections 10, 12, and 45 to 58 of the *Assisted Human Reproduction Act* (*AHRA*)[1] and to draft the supporting regulations.[2] The completion of these sections of the *AHRA* has been long awaited by many providers, users, and researchers of third-party reproduction.[3] In particular, these groups have been awaiting section 12 regulations, which concern the reimbursement of expenditures for surrogates and donors of reproductive materials. In their absence, there has been considerable confusion with respect to the legal permissibility of reimbursements of receipted expenses for surrogates and donors of reproductive materials.[4] In practice, surrogates and

1 *Assisted Human Reproduction Act*, SC 2004, c 2 [*AHRA*].

2 Notice (Department of Health), (2016) C Gaz I, 2818 (*Assisted Human Reproduction Act*).

3 Dave Snow, Françoise Baylis, & Jocelyn Downie, "Why the Government Won't Regulate Assisted Human Reproduction: A Modern Mystery" (2015) 9:1 *McGill Journal of Law and Health* 1.

4 Robert Cribb & Emma Jarratt, "Canada's Vague Surrogacy Laws May Be Doing More Harm Than Good" *Toronto Star* (18 September 2016), online: www.thestar.com/news/canada/2016/09/18/canadas-vague-surrogacy-laws-may-be-doing-more-harm-than-good.html [Cribb & Jarratt, "Canada's Vague Surrogacy Laws"]; Françoise Baylis, Jocelyn Downie, & Dave Snow, "Fake It Till You Make It: Policymaking and Assisted

gamete donors are often reimbursed for expenses related to their involvement in third-party reproduction.[5] At present, these reimbursements occur with little to no legal guidance on which receipted expenses should qualify for reimbursement. If and when completed, the section 12 regulations would provide a list of the types of receipted expenses that could be legally claimed by surrogates and donors.

While the section 12 regulations will provide stakeholders with more guidance and legal certainty, the implementation of the model for reimbursement, as it is currently drafted, creates several practical, ethical, and legal challenges. In this chapter, we revisit the model for receipted expenses outlined in section 12 of the *AHRA* and discuss its limitations. In response to these limitations, we propose an alternative model for reimbursement that organizes expenses into three separate groups. We call this approach the "three baskets" flat-rate model for reimbursement.

Our flat-rate model stems from practical, ethical, and legal concerns about the receipted-expense model established under section 12 that were voiced during a round table meeting of feminist academics and activists from across the country held in November 2016 in Ottawa. At this meeting, some participants began to explore alternative models for reimbursement, one of which was eventually called the "three baskets" approach. Under this approach, surrogates and donors would receive flat-rate reimbursements in three separate categories.

Since we first began discussing these ideas for flat-rate reimbursement of women acting as surrogates, the political and legal climate in Canada regarding the regulation of surrogacy has shifted. At the time, we were working under the assumption that Health Canada would move forward with the proposed regulatory scheme, and we were exploring ways to improve the proposed framework within the confines of the altruistic framework of the *AHRA*. The guiding principles of the *AHRA* state that "commercial ends raise health and ethical concerns that justify their

Reproduction in Canada" (2014) 36:6 *Journal of Obstetrics and Gynecology Canada* 510 [Baylis, Downie, & Snow, "Fake It Till You Make It"].

5 Alison Motluk, "The Human Egg Trade: How Canada's Fertility Laws Are Failing Doctors, Donors, and Parents" *The Walrus* (12 April 2010), online: https://thewalrus.ca/the-human-egg-trade/ [Motluk, "The Human Egg Trade"]; Tom Blackwell, "Canada's Murky Legal World of Surrogate-Consultants and Human-Egg Buyers" *National Post* (9 March 2012), online: http://nationalpost.com/wcm/f7a8b71e-97cb-4b58-9027-10e07adaodfd.

prohibition," and it is within this framework and for these reasons that we propose here a model for reimbursement, not compensation.[6]

In the meantime, there have been new calls to move to a model based on "compensation" for surrogacy, in which surrogates could receive payment for their services beyond the reimbursement of expenses. For example, in May 2017, the Canadian Fertility and Andrology Society issued a position statement that called for the "reasonable compensation" of women who act as surrogates.[7] Furthermore, in March 2018, member of Parliament Anthony Housefather announced that he intended to table a private member's bill that would decriminalize payment for surrogacy.[8]

It is important to note that we, the authors of this paper, do not share a common position on the legitimacy of a payment-based model. We do, however, share the position that, in the context of the altruistic framework put forth by the *AHRA* (as it exists at the time of writing), a flat-fee model would be an improvement on the reimbursement of receipted expenses currently laid out in section 12. Therefore, for the purposes of this chapter, we do not advocate for either an altruistic or a commercial model for surrogacy, but, rather, we focus on how to improve the existing framework for altruistic reimbursement through an amendment to section 12.[9]

---

6 *AHRA*, above note 1, s 2.

7 This is distinct from the approach advocated by the Canadian Fertility and Andrology Society (CFAS), which has proposed compensation for donors and surrogates: CFAS, Position Statement, "Compensation for Third Party Reproduction" (May 2017), online: https://cfas.ca/public-affairs/position-statements/.

8 Kathleen Harris, "Liberal MPs, Advocates Want to Legalize Fees for Surrogate Moms and Sperm Donors" *CBC News* (27 March 2018), online: www.cbc.ca/news/politics/decriminalization-surrogate-mothers-sperm-donors-1.4594733.

9 For a detailed discussion of the arguments in favour of a reimbursement model, see, for example, Anne Phillips, *Our Bodies, Whose Property?* (Princeton, NJ: Princeton University Press, 2013) at 65; Françoise Baylis, "Brickbats and Bouquets for the Draft Legislation on Assisted Human Reproduction" (2001) 10:1 *Health Law Review* 3; Gwynne Basen, Margrit Eichler, & Abby Lippman, eds, *Misconceptions: The Social Construction of Choice and the New Reproductive and Genetic Technologies* (Hull, QC: Voyageur, 1993); Françoise Baylis, "Transnational Commercial Contract Pregnancy in India" in Françoise Baylis & Carolyn McLead, eds, *Family-Making: Contemporary Ethical Challenges* (Oxford: Oxford University Press, 2014) 265 at 266 (in the transnational context). For critical, intersectional engagement with questions of commercialization in a transnational context, see France Winddance Twine, *Outsourcing the Womb: Race, Class and Gestational Surrogacy in a Global Market*, 2d ed (New York: Routledge, 2015); Amrita Pande, *Wombs in Labor: Transnational Commercial*

In what follows, we argue for our three baskets flat-rate approach to reimbursement of expenses incurred by women who act as surrogates. Although our discussion is focused on the reimbursement of surrogates, a similar model for reimbursements could be applied to gamete and embryo donation. We focus our attention on surrogacy because it is the most involved and cost-intensive form of third-party reproduction and thus serves as an appropriate test model for our proposed approach to reimbursement.

In Section B of this chapter, we summarize various approaches to the reimbursement (as opposed to compensation) of women who act as surrogates from different jurisdictions. This section illustrates the various ways that surrogacy has been managed, and illustrates points of comparison and difference between current models and our proposed flat-rate reimbursement model. In Section C, we argue that the current reimbursement model established by section 12 of the *AHRA* faces a range of ethical and practical limitations. In Section D, we outline our flat-rate reimbursement model, which captures three categories of surrogacy-related expenses: (1) base expenses, (2) legal and counselling fees, and (3) extraordinary expenses for which a receipt and/or approval by a designated third party would be required. Although a minor statutory amendment would be required to institute this flat-rate approach, our proposed model would be consistent with the overall Act, which is premised on reimbursement rather than compensation.[10] In our view, this proposal addresses the limitations that exist with the current model that permits reimbursements of only those expenses for which a receipt is provided.[11] To conclude, we propose mechanisms for the oversight and enforcement of the proposed model.

Surrogacy in India (New York: Columbia University Press, 2014). For a discussion of the arguments in favour of and against a compensation or paid model, see, for example, Nelson, Chapter 6, this volume; Alana Cattapan, "Risky Business: Surrogacy, Egg Donation and the Politics of Exploitation" (2014) 29:3 *Canadian Journal of Law and Society* 361; Suze G Berkhout, "Buns in the Oven: Objectification, Surrogacy and Women's Autonomy" (2008) 34:1 *Social Theory and Practice* 95; Debora Spar, "For Love and Money: The Political Economy of Commercial Surrogacy" (2005) 12:2 *Review of International Political Economy* 287; Stephen Wilkinson, "The Exploitation Argument Against Commercial Surrogacy" (2003) 17:2 *Bioethics* 169 [Wilkinson, "Exploitation Argument Against Commercial Surrogacy"].

10 As is discussed below, section 12 currently requires receipts for reimbursement. See also Terry Murray, "Support Grows for Paying Surrogates" (2017) 189:30 *Canadian Medical Association Journal* E1004.

11 With the exception of loss of work-related income: *AHRA*, above note 1, s 12(3).

B. CURRENT APPROACHES TO REIMBURSEMENT FOR WOMEN WHO ACT AS SURROGATES

Different jurisdictions have adopted a variety of approaches to reimbursing or compensating women who act as surrogates.[12] Our objective here is not to consider whether Canada should move to a paid surrogacy model but rather to examine the different ways women are reimbursed for acting as a surrogate.[13] Before turning to the various approaches adopted by different jurisdictions that allow altruistic surrogacy, we first clarify what we mean by "reimbursement" as opposed to "compensation."

On the one hand, there are jurisdictions that have adopted an altruistic model of surrogacy and allow for surrogates to be reimbursed by intended parents only for expenses related to the surrogacy.[14] Such an approach ensures that women who act as surrogates do not suffer an economic disadvantage—that they are not out of pocket. A reimbursement model should be revenue neutral for the surrogate. Under a reimbursement model, the surrogate neither loses nor makes money; she is paid back only for expenses that she would not have incurred, *but for* the surrogacy. Take, for example, a woman who spends $15,000 on extra food, vitamins, and travel to medical appointments as a result of the pregnancy. Under a reimbursement model, she would only receive $15,000: the amount spent in order to carry the pregnancy to term. On the other hand, there are jurisdictions that have adopted a compensation (sometimes referred to as a commercial) model, which allows a surrogate to receive payment in exchange for her services that totals more than what she spends on surrogacy-related expenses.[15] In other

12 See, generally, E Scott Sills, ed, *Handbook of Gestational Surrogacy: International Clinical Practice and Policy Issues* (Cambridge: Cambridge University Press, 2016).

13 Nelson, Chapter 6, this volume; Cattapan, above note 9; Berkhout, above note 9; Spar, above note 9; Wilkinson, "Exploitation Argument Against Commercial Surrogacy," above note 9.

14 Altruistic surrogacy is allowed and regulated in the United Kingdom, Greece, South Africa, New Zealand, Australia, and a number of US states: Katarina Trimmings & Paul Beaumont, "General Report on Surrogacy" [Trimmings & Beaumont, "General Report on Surrogacy"] in Katarina Trimmings & Paul Beaumont, eds, *International Surrogacy Arrangements: Legal Regulation at the International Level* (London: Hart, 2013) 438 at 454 [Trimmings & Beaumont, eds, *Legal Regulation*].

15 A few jurisdictions permit commercial surrogacy by judicial precedent, including California, Massachusetts, and Ohio: Trimmings & Beaumont, "General Report on

words, under a compensation model, a woman acting as a surrogate may earn a profit, depending on the market for surrogacy services. Returning to our same example, if a woman spends $15,000 on extra food, vitamins, and travel to medical appointments, but the intended parents pay her $20,000, the woman would make a profit of $5,000. This for-profit payment would be permitted under a compensation or payment model.

1) Some International Approaches to Reimbursement

There are a number of jurisdictions that demonstrate a commitment to altruism and explicitly restrict payments to women acting as surrogates to reimbursements.[16] Some offer a broad definition of what constitutes an authorized expense related to the surrogacy, while others have enumerated the expenses that may be reimbursed.[17] Not only do the regulatory frameworks differ, but the scope of expenses that may be claimed varies from place to place.[18] This brief comparison illustrates some of the different approaches to reimbursement. Our proposal is a departure from these approaches and recommends a completely novel approach to reimbursement.

The United Kingdom appears to take the broadest approach. In that country, it is not an offence to pay a surrogate. However, a court must be satisfied that no payments have been made other than for "expenses reasonably incurred" or must authorize a payment that does not meet this criterion before transferring parentage as part of a parental order application.[19] Notably, there is no specific statutory definition of what qualifies as an expense that is "reasonably incurred," nor is there a list of enumerated expenses. These have been left to judicial interpretation, and no court has refused an order on the basis of the reimbursement to the surrogate.[20] The

Surrogacy," above note 14 at 449. Several jurisdictions, including Ukraine and Russia, allow commercial surrogacy by statute: *ibid* at 451.

16 These include the United Kingdom, Greece, Australia, New Zealand, South Africa, Israel, and several US states: *ibid* at 454.

17 See, generally, Erin Nelson, *Law, Policy and Reproductive Autonomy* (London: Hart, 2013).

18 Trimmings & Beaumont, "General Report on Surrogacy," above note 14 at 454.

19 Nathalie Gamble, "A Better Legal Framework for United Kingdom Surrogacy" in Susan Golombok et al, eds, *Regulating Reproductive Donation* (Cambridge: Cambridge University Press, 2016) 140 at 152.

20 *Ibid* at 153.

failure to clearly define what qualifies as a permissible expense may result in women deriving some profit from the surrogacy arrangement.

For example, in *J v G*, a UK court concluded that payments totaling USD$56,750 (including USD$2,750 as an allowance for unspecified "incidental expenses," USD$1,000 as an inconvenience fee for the IVF transfer, and USD$53,000 as a pregnancy compensation fee) fell within the definition of "expenses reasonably incurred." The court concluded that the payments were "not so disproportionate to expenses reasonably incurred that the granting of an order would be an affront to public policy," nor were they of "such a level to overbear the will of the surrogate."[21] In our view, such an approach is not consistent with altruistic surrogacy but rather results in a compensatory payment to the woman who acts as a surrogate.

To address some of the uncertainty generated by broad regulatory language, a number of jurisdictions have sought to provide more detailed statutory definitions of what constitutes an expense eligible for reimbursement.[22] For example, in Greece, we find a statutory definition, albeit a broad one, of what expenses or costs may be reimbursed. Greek law prohibits a surrogate from earning a "financial gain" and clarifies that "the payment of expenses involved in the achievement of a pregnancy, the gestation, delivery and postpartum period" as well as reimbursement for "any incidental

---

21 *J v G*, [2013] EWHC 1432 at para 22 (Fam).

22 For example, in South Africa, section 301 of the *Children's Act*, No 38 of 2005, provides:

> 301. *Payments in respect of surrogacy prohibited*
>
> (1) Subject to subsections (2) and (3), no person may in connection with a surrogate motherhood agreement give or promise to give to any person, or receive from any person, a reward or compensation in cash or kind.
>
> (2) No promise or agreement for the payment of any compensation to a surrogate mother or any other person in connection with a surrogate motherhood agreement or the execution of such an agreement is enforceable, except a claim for—
>
> (a) compensation for expenses that relate directly to the artificial fertilisation and pregnancy of the surrogate mother, the birth of the child and the confirmation of the surrogate motherhood agreement;
>
> (b) loss of earnings suffered by the surrogate mother as a result of the surrogate motherhood agreement; or
>
> (c) insurance to cover the surrogate mother for anything that may lead to death or disability brought about by the pregnancy.

For a discussion of the South African model, see Melodie Slabbert & Christa Roodt, "South Africa" in Trimmings & Beaumont, eds, *Legal Regulation*, above note 14, 325 at 335.

loss of profit by the child-bearing woman because of absence from work, or the loss of remuneration for salaried employment which she has missed because of absence related to the purpose of pregnancy, gestation, labour or post-partum period" do not constitute a financial gain.[23]

Other jurisdictions seek to provide clarity by offering both a definition and specific examples of what constitutes an expense or cost that may be reimbursed. For example, in New South Wales, Australia, the *Surrogacy Act 2010* provides that a woman acting as a surrogate may be reimbursed for the "reasonable costs associated with . . . (a) becoming or trying to become pregnant, (b) a pregnancy or a birth, (c) entering into and given effect to a surrogacy arrangement."[24] The *Surrogacy Act 2010* offers a non-exhaustive list of examples of such reasonable costs, including medical costs associated with the pregnancy or birth, travel or accommodation costs associated with the pregnancy or birth, cost of reimbursing the birth mother for a loss of earnings as a result of unpaid leave for a predefined period, and counselling and legal costs in relation to the surrogacy.[25] These costs vary from state to state in Australia. For example, in the state of South Australia, women who act as surrogates are not allowed to receive reimbursement for lost income.[26] In New Zealand, "reasonable and necessary expenses" related to certain purposes, including for independent legal advice, are permitted.[27]

These approaches have been subject to a range of criticisms. As mentioned above, the UK approach has been criticized as permitting compensation rather than restricting payment to reimbursements.[28] The Australian

23 Article 13 of Greek Law 3305/2005 defines in detail that the surrogacy agreement, which is to be concluded by and between the commissioning parents and the surrogate woman, must have no financial benefit for the latter: Charalampos Amoiridis & Anastasia Akritidou, "Surrogacy Proceedings in Greece After the Implementation of Law 4272/2014" *Greek Law Digest* (7 November 2016), online: www.greeklawdigest.gr/topics/aspects-of-greek-civil-law/item/217-surrogacy-proceedings-in-greece-after-the-implementation-of-law-4272-2014.

24 *Surrogacy Act 2010* (NSW), s 7. A similar approach is adopted in Queensland (*Surrogacy Act 2010* (Qld), s 11), Tasmania (*Surrogacy Act 2012* (Tas), s 9) and Western Australia (*Surrogacy Act 2008* (WA), s 6(3)(b)).

25 *Surrogacy Act 2010* (NSW), s 7.

26 *Family Relationships Act 1975* (SA), s 10HA.

27 *Human Assisted Reproductive Technologies Act 2004* (NZ), s 14.

28 Michael Wells-Greco, "United Kingdom" in Trimmings & Beaumont, eds, *Legal Regulation*, above note 14, 367 at 379. See also Kirsty Horsey & Sally Sheldon, "Still Hazy After All These Years: The Law Regulating Surrogacy" (2012) 20:1 *Medical Law Review* 67.

approach has been criticized for being "complex and confusing," as the regulations "vary significantly in how they define commercial surrogacy as well as what practices they prohibit and the penalties attached."[29] Millbank argues that, not only do these definitions result in confusion, they can result in arbitrary or unfair outcomes. For example, she explains that "the nadir of fine distinctions was reached in [New South Wales] by a law that renders an unpaid advertisement for an unpaid surrogacy arrangement lawful, but a paid advertisement for an unpaid surrogacy arrangement a criminal offence."[30] The confusion and inconsistencies among states become more complex and difficult to navigate where parties reside in different Australian states and must seek to reconcile the different statutory regimes.[31] Scholars have argued that this confusion, coupled with a lack of available women willing to act as surrogates, has prompted many Australians to engage in surrogacy arrangements outside the country.[32]

Many scholars who criticize these reimbursement models call for the adoption of a compensation or paid model for surrogacy.[33] This chapter takes a different approach: it examines the shortcomings of a receipted-expenses model of reimbursement and offers a reform proposal that falls within a reimbursement model. In doing so, our critique calls for an improvement within the existing legal framework. While the United Kingdom has adopted a flat-rate reimbursement model for egg donors, no country has sought a flat-rate reimbursement model for surrogates.[34] Before turning to the details

---

29 Jenni Millbank, "Rethinking 'Commercial' Surrogacy in Australia" (2015) 12:3 *Journal of Bioethical Inquiry* 477 at 479.

30 *Ibid.*

31 *Ibid.*

32 Kelton Tremellen & Sam Everingham, "For Love or Money? Australian Attitudes to Financially Compensated (Commercial) Surrogacy" (2016) 50:6 *Australian and New Zealand Journal of Obstetrics and Gynecology* 558 at 559. See also Ainsley J Newson, "Compensated Transnational Surrogacy in Australia: Time for a Comprehensive Review" (2016) 204:1 *Medical Journal of Australia* 33, who argues that altruistic surrogacy increases the desire for Australians to travel for commodified or paid surrogacy for a number of reasons.

33 Millbank, above note 29; Newson, above note 32. See also Anita Stuhmcke, "The Regulation of Commercial Surrogacy: The Wrong Answers to the Wrong Questions" (2015) 23:3 *Journal of Law and Medicine* 333.

34 This approach is described in Stephen Wilkinson, "Is the HFEA's Policy on Compensating Egg Donors and Egg Sharers Defensible?" (2013) 21:2 *Medical Law Review* 173 [Wilkinson, "HFEA's Compensation Policy"].

of our proposed model, we describe the current Canadian approach to reimbursement proposed under section 12 of the *AHRA*.

2) The Canadian Approach

At present, the *AHRA* prohibits payment to women who act as surrogates and for brokering surrogacy arrangements but allows for surrogates to be reimbursed for receipted expenses for costs incurred during the surrogacy.[35] This approach upholds altruism or non-commercialization and ensures that surrogates are not financially penalized by being out of pocket for surrogacy-related expenses.[36] Section 12 provides:

> 12 (1) No person shall, except in accordance with the regulations,
>
> (a) reimburse a donor for an expenditure incurred in the course of donating sperm or an ovum;
>
> (b) reimburse any person for an expenditure incurred in the maintenance or transport of an in vitro embryo; or
>
> (c) reimburse a surrogate mother for an expenditure incurred by her in relation to her surrogacy.
>
> *Receipts*
>
> (2) No person shall reimburse an expenditure referred to in subsection (1) unless a receipt is provided to that person for the expenditure.
>
> *No reimbursement*
>
> (3) No person shall reimburse a surrogate mother for a loss of work-related income incurred during her pregnancy, unless
>
> (a) a qualified medical practitioner certifies, in writing, that continuing to work may pose a risk to her health or that of the embryo or foetus; and
>
> (b) the reimbursement is made in accordance with the regulations.

---

35 *AHRA*, above note 1, s 6.

36 This approach is consistent with the recommendations of the Royal Commission on New Reproductive Technologies, *Proceed with Care: Final Report of the Royal Commission on New Reproductive Technologies* (Ottawa: Minister of Government Services Canada, 1993) at 668. The Standing Committee on Health also recommended against a paid system of surrogacy. See House of Commons, Standing Committee on Health, *Assisted Human Reproduction: Building Families* (December 2001) at 12–13. For a detailed discussion of the history of regulation of surrogacy, see Cattapan, Gruben, & Cameron, Introduction, this volume.

Section 12 requires receipts to be provided for reimbursements related to expenditures incurred by the surrogate in relation to her surrogacy.[37] Receipts are to be given to the party providing the reimbursement.[38]

Unfortunately, because regulations have never been promulgated, there appears to be a lack of clarity on what expenses are eligible for reimbursement. Indeed, the legality of reimbursing surrogates at all under this incomplete legal framework has been the subject of debate. Professors Françoise Baylis and Jocelyn Downie, for example, maintain that, in the absence of the section 12 regulations, legal reimbursement is impossible.[39] In contrast, Health Canada's website indicates that reimbursement of certain expenses is permitted. In explaining the types of reimbursements permissible, the website provides:

> A surrogate mother can only be repaid for out-of-pocket costs if they are directly related to the surrogacy and usually when a receipt is attached. For instance, a surrogate mother may be repaid for loss of work wages if a doctor certifies, in writing, that bed rest is necessary for her health and/or the health of the embryo or fetus. However, costs related to the surrogacy also depend on each surrogate mother's situation.[40]

The reimbursement of expenses is further complicated by variance in provincial law.[41] In practice, it is quite common for many intended parents

---

37 This is why we refer to this model as a "receipted expense" model.

38 This chapter does not address the legality of payments to third parties or agencies who facilitate surrogacy arrangements. However, agencies that arrange egg donation and surrogacies are quite common in Canada. See Alison Motluk, "After Pleading Guilty for Paying Surrogates, Business Is Booming for This Fertility Matchmaker" *Globe and Mail* (28 February 2016), online: www.theglobeandmail.com/life/health-and-fitness/health/business-is-booming-for-fertility-matchmaker-leia-swanberg/article28930242/ [Motluk, "Business Is Booming"]. For a critique of the role played by agencies, see Nelson, Chapter 6, this volume.

39 Françoise Baylis & Jocelyn Downie, "Wishing Doesn't Make It So" (17 December 2013), *Impact Ethics* (blog), online: https://impactethics.ca/2013/12/17/wishing-doesnt-make-it-so/. See also Baylis, Downie, & Snow, "Fake It Till You Make It," above note 4.

40 Health Canada, "Prohibitions Related to Surrogacy" (18 July 2013), online: www.canada.ca/en/health-canada/services/drugs-health-products/biologics-radiopharmaceuticals-genetic-therapies/legislation-guidelines/assisted-human-reproduction/prohibitions-related-surrogacy.html.

41 The *Constitution Act, 1867* (UK), 30 & 31 Vict, c 3, reprinted in RSC 1985, Appendix II, No 5, gives provinces jurisdiction over contract and as such we see variation from province to province as to whether such contracts are enforceable.

and surrogates to enter into a contract that lays out reimbursable surrogacy-related expenses.[42] However, these contracts are not enforceable in all provincial and territorial jurisdictions, and not all provinces and territories have relevant regulations.[43] Regardless of whether such a contract is enforceable under provincial or territorial law, these contracts cannot, of course, violate the *AHRA*'s prohibition against compensation for surrogacy. In this climate of uncertainty and little or no oversight, some individual lawyers, intended parents, and surrogates have interpreted the law on receipted expenses in overly broad or liberal ways.[44]

In short, surrogates, intended parents, and their lawyers in Canada have argued that they are operating in a legal grey zone concerning receipted expenses while trying to ensure that surrogates are not out of pocket with respect to surrogacy-related expenses as they await the section 12 regulations.[45]

C. CONCERNS WITH SECTION 12 OF THE *AHRA*

In general, the implementation of section 12 is (and will continue to be) fraught with practical, ethical, and legal challenges. In particular, the lack of regulations detailing which expenses are allowable under the *AHRA* is highly problematic. As a result, surrogates and intended parents are left to guess and negotiate what and how much can be reasonably reimbursed. In

42 Alison Motluk, "Anatomy of a Surrogacy" *Hazlitt* (6 November 2017), online: https://hazlitt.net/longreads/anatomy-surrogacy [Motluk, "Anatomy of a Surrogacy"].

43 For example, in Ontario, surrogacy agreements are not binding and can be used only as evidence of an intention to parent. A surrogacy agreement is unenforceable in law, but it may be used as evidence of an intended parent's intention to be a parent of a child contemplated by the agreement, and a surrogate's intention not to be a parent of a child contemplated by the agreement: *Children's Law Reform Act*, RSO 1990, c C.12, s 10(9) [*CLRA*]. See Lavoie & Côté, Chapter 3, this volume for a discussion of the legal framework in Quebec and the need for reform. For a general discussion, see Erin Nelson, "Global Trade and Assisted Reproductive Technologies: Regulatory Challenges in International Surrogacy" (2013) 41:1 *Journal of Law, Medicine and Ethics* 240 [Nelson, "Global Trade and Assisted Reproductive Technologies"]; Karen Busby, "Of Surrogate Mother Born: Parentage Determinations in Canada and Elsewhere" (2013) 25:2 *Canadian Journal of Women and the Law* 284.

44 Motluk, "Business Is Booming," above note 38; Motluk, "Anatomy of a Surrogacy," above note 42. Payment to surrogates may also be increasing because of the federal government's reluctance to enforce clear breaches of the Act. See Motluk, "The Human Egg Trade," above note 5.

45 Cribb & Jarratt, "Canada's Vague Surrogacy Laws," above note 4.

June 2015, at the request of Health Canada, the Canada Standards Association (CSA) drafted an Annex entitled "Reimbursement of Expenses for Donors and Surrogates" ("CSA standards"), which it published in October 2016.[46] As McLeod discusses in Chapter 4 in this volume, parts of the CSA standards could be incorporated by reference as regulations[47] or could be used as a template for the section 12 regulations.[48] These standards set out broad categories of expenses.[49] Although it is beyond the scope of this chapter to critique the CSA standards, the proposed list of allowable expenses alone cannot resolve all of the uncertainty, confusion, and dissatisfaction with the receipted-expenses model.

We maintain that, even if the regulations for section 12 were to be completed and put into effect and Health Canada were to clarify and enforce the oversight and corresponding penalties of the *AHRA*, the current receipted-expenses model established by this section will continue to suffer from several practical, ethical, and legal limitations that can negatively impact women who act as surrogates as well as intended parents.

First, the receipted-expenses model established by section 12 requires that women acting as surrogates pay for the surrogacy-related expenses up front; obtain, keep, and manage receipts for these expenses; and then submit them to the appropriate party (such as the intended parents) for reimbursement. Such expenses might include transportation to medical appointments, certain food expenses, and maternity clothes.[50] (In the absence of the regulations for section 12, we can only speculate which receipted expenses would be permissible). These upfront costs can burden

46 CSA Group, "Annex A (Informative): Reimbursement of Expenses for Donors and Surrogates" (October 2016), online: http://shop.csa.ca/content/ebiz/shopcsa/resources/documents/Z900_2_1-12EN_Annex_A.pdf [CSA standards].

47 In his chapter, McLeod discusses the possibility that Health Canada may incorporate the CSA standards by reference as regulations under section 12 and the concerns that may arise as a result.

48 Importantly, some of the CSA standards included reimbursements for costs incurred following pregnancy, which would fall outside the current statutory language of section 12 of the *AHRA*.

49 CSA standards, above note 46.

50 These examples are reflected in an annex entitled "Reimbursement of Expenses for Donors and Surrogates" prepared by a Task Force of the Canadian Standards Association Group at the request of Health Canada in June 2015: CSA standards, above note 46. For more information about the CSA Annex, see McLeod, Chapter 4, this volume.

surrogates and unfairly put them at a financial disadvantage.[51] While the current model is intended to ensure that surrogates are reimbursed for certain categories of expenses,[52] any surrogacy model or arrangement that requires upfront payment by surrogates puts these women at risk of not receiving the reimbursement or of shouldering additional financial costs, such as credit card interest, while waiting for their reimbursement. As a result, some surrogates may be unable to meet their own personal expenses in order to pay for these surrogacy-related expenses.

Second, in the current model, surrogates face additional burdens related to administration and oversight. There is unaccounted, unpaid time involved in engaging in the administrative and managerial tasks described above, in addition to the delay between receipt submission and reimbursement for surrogacy expenses. Obtaining or verifying receipts can pose practical challenges. Receipts for some items may not contain the appropriate identifying information. For example, items bought at second-hand stores, dollar stores, smaller retailers, and farmers' markets may not have receipts that indicate what product or service was purchased. In addition, some costs associated with surrogacy, such as time lost from work, may not be easily quantified or verified. Such an issue may be a more general problem with reimbursement or taxation systems, yet it is reasonable to propose ways for avoiding this added complication in a reimbursement model for surrogacy, particularly where surrogates are employed in service industries where one relies to a large extent on tips.[53] Under the current model, surrogates who are students and whose grades or education suffer as a result of the surrogacy would likely have no way of capturing, quantifying, or verifying the associated costs under the receipted-expenses model. As a result, women who participate in surrogacy risk financial exploitation under the current model. Indeed, Alison Motluk recently documented this exploitation in her article, "Anatomy of Surrogacy," which describes the financial difficulties a surrogate in Canada recently experienced under such

51 While this may not be universally true, the view was expressed in the presentation of three surrogates who attended the November 2016 workshop.

52 Glen Rivard & Judy Hunter, *The Law of Assisted Human Reproduction* (Markham, ON: LexisNexis, 2005) at 120.

53 Indeed, this concern was highlighted in Motluk's recent article, "Anatomy of a Surrogacy," above note 42 (where Gil's employment consisted of looking after children and housekeeping).

an approach. She describes tension between Gil, the woman acting as the surrogate, and the intended parents. Motluk writes:

> What followed were some testy exchanges about money. "… I just want to make sure that you know that I know that taking me on as a surrogate has been an extra expense for you. This affects all the decisions I make …," Gil wrote. She was living from paycheque to paycheque, and in the lag between paying out of pocket for the high-priced fertility drugs and doctors' visits and being reimbursed for them, she found herself completely broke…. Then she mentioned that almost everyone she knew who'd carried twins needed bed rest toward the end of their pregnancies, and she worried in an email that the couple would not be able to afford to pay for her lost wages if that happened to her. "Thank you for your concern, but we can manage with our finances," the mom shot back.[54]

This risk is antithetical to the *AHRA*'s guiding principles against the harm and exploitation of women.[55] Unfortunately, there are reports of such exploitation within Canada.[56]

Further, oversight of the current framework through potential audit under section 12 raises important practical concerns for both surrogate and intended parents. The current approach under section 12 requires one of the parties (either the surrogate, the intended parent(s), or the clinic) to keep the receipts in order to justify the claimed expense.[57] Should Health Canada wish

54 Motluk, *ibid*.

55 *AHRA*, above note 1, s 2.

56 Motluk, "Anatomy of a Surrogacy," above note 42. Other Canadian women have also reported harms and coercion as a result of their surrogacy arrangements. See, for example, Tom Blackwell, "This Ontario Surrogate Wanted to Help Another Woman Have a Child, but the Decision Nearly Killed Her" *National Post* (15 October 2015), online: http://nationalpost.com/wcm/24d8b74c-a7de-4136-8204-af1a46acb296 [Blackwell, "Ontario Surrogate Nearly Killed"]; Tom Blackwell, "Canadian Surrogate Eliminated Baby from Triplet Pregnancy at Urging of Overseas Couple" *National Post* (9 September 2015), online: http://nationalpost.com/wcm/42d4b695-333a-49ef-99a2-226b2e7057e7 [Blackwell, "Canadian Surrogate Eliminated Baby"].

57 The most recent consultation document from Health Canada seems to indicate that the intended parent(s) will be required to keep the receipts for a period of six years. See Health Canada, "Toward a Strengthened *Assisted Human Reproduction Act*: A Consultation with Canadians on Key Policy Proposals" (11 July 2017) at 4.2.6, online: www.canada.ca/en/health-canada/programs/consultation-assisted-human-reproduction/document.html.

to conduct audits to ensure compliance with the regulations, it will need to undertake a relatively onerous process of matching receipts with payments received. Such audits may be time consuming and require inspectors with specialized accounting expertise to conduct the audits.[58] Since some surrogacy arrangements do not involve third parties, such as clinics or agencies, presumably these detailed audits will be left up to inspectors with Health Canada. Given the limited enforcement of the *AHRA* to date, some may question whether Health Canada has the willingness and the resources available to undertake such detailed audits.[59] Indeed, Health Canada has made few attempts to enforce these provisions, even when faced with complaints about actions that are in clear breach of the Act.[60] As we discuss below, our proposed model would require a less onerous oversight process.

Third, it is likely that there will be uncertainty and inconsistency in the scope of allowable reimbursements and that this will create variation between surrogacy arrangements and give rise to inequity among surrogates and intended parent(s). For example, some surrogates may agree to participate in surrogacy arrangements that provide less security or opportunity for the reimbursement of expenses. Similarly, some intended parents may incur greater costs than others because of the type or number of receipted expenses claimed by the surrogate. Variation in the reimbursement amounts provided to women acting as surrogates is a problem that is seemingly inherent to reimbursement systems.[61] Under the current section 12 reimbursement model, as we discuss below, it is possible to reimburse surrogates differently depending on how much they choose to spend on, say, maternity clothes. Under our proposed model, variation would be less likely to occur, because all women acting as surrogates would be reimbursed

58 Notably, the now defunct Assisted Human Reproduction Agency of Canada would likely have played an important role in overseeing the reimbursement model. See Rivard & Hunter, above note 52 at 181–82.

59 To date, there has been only one set of charges laid under the *AHRA*: Alison Motluk, "First Prosecution Under *Assisted Human Reproduction Act* Ends in Conviction" (2014) 186:2 *Canadian Medical Association Journal* E75. This has caused scholars and the media to question the willingness of Health Canada to enforce the *AHRA*: Baylis, Downie, & Snow, "Fake It Till You Make It," above note 4.

60 Tom Blackwell, "Health Canada All but Ignores Illegal Ad for Surrogate, Cash for Egg Donors, Internal Documents Reveal" *National Post* (13 December 2015), online: http://nationalpost.com/wcm/d369b3ec-1d7f-46df-ac5d-ad3e63464a4b.

61 Compensation models also suffer from a similar variation problem: each surrogate would be compensated different amounts depending on what was negotiated.

exactly the same amount for their basic surrogacy-related expenses. We argue that, with prior knowledge of the amount of the monthly budgeted flat rate, surrogates could better plan for their expenses. Further, a flat rate would better support consistency and fairness related to the amount of reimbursement that surrogates receive and it could also reduce the variation among the costs of surrogacy arrangements for intended parents.

Under the current section 12 model, there is nothing to limit the amount that surrogates spend on certain products and services, such as food or maternity clothing. As a result, there may be opportunities for some surrogates to claim much better quality food, goods, or services in their surrogacy arrangement as compared to other surrogates (e.g., organic food and designer clothing). Surrogates and intended parents have been able to claim expenses, such as cars or other "gifts," that well exceed what is a reasonable surrogacy-related expense and should be understood as compensation.[62] Inappropriate "reimbursements" have occurred, in part, because the regulations for section 12 have not yet been drafted. However, even when the regulations are completed and provide a list of allowable receipted expenses, the practical challenges associated with the oversight and enforcement of a receipted approach seem to make it quite possible (and perhaps easy) for inappropriate reimbursements to occur.[63]

In our view, the proposed flat-rate model would eliminate much, but not all, of the uncertainty regarding the potential costs associated with a surrogacy. Under the current legislative framework, some intended parents may pay considerably more for surrogacy than others. Variation of "allowable expenses" in surrogacy arrangements may lead to concerns about fairness and equity in access in surrogacy, particularly if such differences occur along race, class, or geographic lines within Canada. As discussed below, the proposed model would bring greater certainty to the costs associated with a surrogacy arrangement, which would benefit both the women who act as surrogates and the intended parents. The flat-rate reimbursement model would render the cost of an "average" surrogacy transparent to both intended parents and surrogates. Absent exceptional circumstances, dealt with under the third "basket," all parties could budget for and anticipate expenses with more precision across surrogacy arrangements.

62 Motluk, "Anatomy of a Surrogacy," above note 42.

63 See Lavoie & Côté, Chapter 3, this volume.

Importantly, the *AHRA* currently provides no mechanism for surrogates, intended parent(s), or clinics to inquire about the scope or limits of the expenses that may be reimbursed. As a result, and given the significant penalties associated with a breach of section 12 of the *AHRA*, some parties may be cautious about taking an expansive approach to interpreting these provisions, with the result that surrogates may well be left out of pocket.[64] Yet, the lack of enforcement or oversight may also encourage others to take risks and allow for/incur expenses that could be considered compensatory.

Fourth, the current model may also prevent some surrogates from accessing important counselling services and much-needed legal advice. The upfront financial burden on surrogates is especially problematic with respect to these services, which are very expensive but also vital to a healthy and fair surrogacy arrangement. Indeed, the Canadian Fertility and Andrology Society's "Guidelines on Third Party Reproduction" cite the importance of ensuring that surrogates have access to independent medical and legal counselling.[65] If the surrogate cannot afford the associated costs, she will be less likely to receive independent legal advice, putting her at risk of entering into a contract that does not adequately address her interests.[66] Examples include agreements that restrict the surrogate's ability to engage in activities perceived as being risky, such as travelling, eating certain foods, and living in a particular location. Surrogates are also at risk of entering into agreements that mistakenly give others, such as the intended parents, control over their own health care treatment decisions.[67] Similarly, financial constraints that limit access to and use of independent legal counsel can harm

64 *AHRA*, above note 1, ss 60–61.

65 Canadian Fertility and Andrology Society, "Guidelines for Third Party Reproduction" (April 2016), online: https://cfas.ca/clinical-practice-guidelines/ [CFAS, "Guidelines for Third Party Reproduction"].

66 See, generally, Motluk, "Anatomy of a Surrogacy," above note 42.

67 For example, there are concerns that women who act as surrogates could be coerced into selectively reducing a multiple pregnancy or other medical procedures: Blackwell, "Canadian Surrogate Eliminated Baby," above note 56. This coercion may exist despite a physician's fiduciary obligation toward the surrogate as his patient and the legal and ethical requirement that the surrogate must consent to any medical procedure: Deborah L Forman, "Abortion Clauses in Surrogacy Contracts: Insights from a Case Study" (2015) 49:1 *Family Law Quarterly* 29. See, generally, Katherine Drabiak-Syed, "Currents in Contemporary Bioethics: Waiving Informed Consent to Prenatal Screening and Diagnosis? Problems with Paradoxical Negotiation in Surrogacy Contracts" (2011) 39:3 *Journal of Law, Medicine and Ethics* 559.

or burden the intended parents. The surrogate or the intended parents may find that they lack information or protection relating to parentage rights and obligations resulting from the surrogacy arrangement. Similarly, the inability to access counselling services can exacerbate the risk of exploitation or harm to the surrogate, the intended parents, or both parties, who may lack the necessary information for participating in a surrogacy arrangement.[68] There is currently nothing in section 12 that would help ensure that the parties in a surrogacy arrangement have access to independent legal and counselling services.[69] Placing the financial burden on surrogates with respect to legal and counselling fees not only raises important equity and access issues but also poses a risk of harm to surrogates.

The current receipted-expenses model puts surrogates and intended parents at risk of burden, harm, or exploitation, it may lead to uncertainty and inconsistency in the scope of allowable expenses, and it fails to protect and promote independent legal and counselling options for surrogates. Accordingly, in our view, it fails to promote the guiding principles of the *AHRA*, namely, "the protection and promotion of human health, safety, dignity and rights" in the use of assisted reproductive technologies as well as the "health and well-being of women" and "free and informed consent."

D. OUR PROPOSAL: THE FLAT-RATE REIMBURSEMENT MODEL

In our view, a flat-rate reimbursement model for surrogates would go a long way to addressing many of these issues. Although no country has adopted such a system with respect to surrogacy, we note that egg donors in the United Kingdom are provided with a flat fee, based on the average, notional expenses incurred as a result of the donation process.[70] This approach has

68 Jolly Joy, "The Role of Counselling in the Management of Patients with Infertility" (2015) 17:2 *Obstetrician and Gynecologist* 83 at 85.

69 Although the *AHRA* is silent on the need for counselling and legal advice, the CFAS recommends that both be present for surrogates: "Guidelines for Third Party Reproduction," above note 65 at 11–12.

70 The decision to shift from a reimbursement-based model to a flat-rate model was taken after a consultation process in 2007 led by the Human Fertilisation and Embryology Authority (HFEA): HFEA, *SEED Report: A Report on the Human Fertilisation & Embryology Authority's Review of Sperm, Egg and Embryo Donation in the United Kingdom* (London: HFEA, 2005).]

received mixed reviews. It has been lauded for promoting "administrative efficiency" and for acknowledging that it may be "petty and offensive" to expect someone to donate her eggs but then refuse to pay her expenses unless she is able to produce a receipt.[71] On the other hand, there is the concern that such a model may not be revenue neutral: because actual expenses are not being reimbursed, some donors will be overcompensated and others will be undercompensated.[72]

The flat-rate approach described in this chapter is intended to support a reimbursement model, rather than compensation. As described above, a reimbursement model puts the woman acting as a surrogate back in the same economic position she would have been but for the surrogacy. This is consistent with the current altruistic model under the *AHRA*, which criminalizes the commercialization of surrogacy.[73] The proposed flat-rate model ensures that surrogates have their surrogacy-related expenses covered by receiving regularly scheduled reimbursements directly from the intended parent(s). This model avoids the risk of market-driven commercialization or commodification, thereby complying with the legislation as it stands. In our view, a flat-rate compensation model with upfront payment for independent legal and counselling and allowable exceptions for additional costs is best suited for managing the reimbursement of expenses incurred by surrogates in the Canadian context. This model would require a minor statutory amendment as well as the development of the regulatory model and accompanying oversight mechanisms detailed below.[74]

71 Emily Jackson, "Compensating Egg Donors" in Sumi Madhok, Anne Phillips, & Kalpana Wilson, eds, *Gender, Agency and Coercion* (Basingstoke, UK: Palgrave Macmillan, 2013) 181 at 187–88. See also Wilkinson, "HFEA's Compensation Policy," above note 34.

72 *Ibid*.

73 *AHRA*, above note 1, ss 6–7.

74 To allow for the proposed flat-rate model, sections 12(2) and (3) could be amended as follows:

Section 12(2): No person shall reimburse an expenditure referred to in subsection (1) except in accordance with the regulations.

Section 12(3): No person shall reimburse a surrogate mother for a loss of work-related income incurred in relation to her surrogacy, except in accordance with the regulations.

1) Base Rate

In this model, the first basket would be a mandatory monthly flat rate, which would be paid to a woman who acts as a surrogate, likely over the course of twelve months (before, during, and after the pregnancy). We propose that the reimbursements be made in monthly (or bimonthly) installments, so surrogates do not bear the burden of covering pregnancy-related costs up front. Further, the payment of a monthly reimbursement rate would also serve to protect the interests of the intended parents. If the surrogate decided to end the surrogacy arrangement or in the event of miscarriage, the reimbursement payments would be prorated. We would note that, in an effort to ensure that surrogates are not left with any out-of-pocket expenses for a failed attempt at pregnancy, miscarriage, pregnancy termination, or termination of the surrogacy agreement, reimbursement payments could not be retracted under this proposal.

The reimbursement rate would be determined based on the base expenses associated with surrogacy,[75] which would expect to be incurred by all women who act as surrogates. These could include vitamins, supplements, medication, medical supplies, and medical services; (home) pregnancy tests; alternative or complementary health care services; travel and accommodation; dependent care for time spent travelling to and attending related appointments or during the recovery period after birth; communication (e.g., long distance charges, internet, and phone use) directly related to the surrogacy; meals on any day on which the surrogate attends an appointment; a portion of food during pregnancy or increased costs in food-related expenses; clothing required during the pregnancy and post-birth recovery; costs in exercise-related expenses (e.g., gym or fitness facility membership rates); obtaining or confirming relevant medical and other records; and supplemental health and life insurance.

This list is intended to be illustrative rather than exhaustive. The determination of which items would be included on this list should be accomplished in partnership with stakeholders, including surrogates, intended parents, and people who have already had children via surrogacy. Including the voice

---

75 This list is derived, in part, from the CSA standards Annex, above note 46. While the authors do not endorse the overall approach adopted by the CSA Task Force, the Annex itself provides a starting point for considering the types of expenses incurred during a surrogacy.

and perspectives of surrogates in decision making about the flat-rate basket items and amounts is particularly important. It is essential that we understand from women who have acted as surrogates (as well as intended parents) what expenses are incurred in the typical course of a surrogacy as well as the potential risks associated with the proposed reimbursement process. Although speculation on the types of expenses and risks is unavoidable, first-hand knowledge is absolutely necessary to ensure this legislative framework is responsive and meets the needs of those involved in surrogacy arrangements. Further, the dollar amount of reimbursement should be determined in consultation with qualified experts, such as actuaries and cost estimators,[76] and should be based on the Consumer Price Index assessment of the average costs in Canada (or provincially) for these base expenses. A similar process was used in the development of the *Child Support Guidelines*, which establish child support in Canada based on the notional expenses incurred in raising children, and may be a useful starting point in this context.[77] Finally, we recommend that this rate be laid out in the regulations to the *AHRA*, rather than the Act itself, to facilitate changing the rates responsively, based on, for example, annual inflation or increases in the costs of food or transportation.

The proposed flat rate would also help ensure that surrogates have funds allocated toward the payment of their basic surrogacy-related needs prior to these expenses arising, thus not leaving them at risk for being out of pocket for these costs. It would simultaneously eliminate the surrogate's need to collect and submit receipts for these costs and the need of the intended parent(s) to manage and reimburse for these receipts. The creation of a flat rate for these base expenses would also reduce opportunities for unwittingly slipping into "compensation" and would provide clarity for all those involved. Intended parents and surrogates alike would be able to budget for monthly or bimonthly payments and plan for the basic expenses over the full twelve months.

2) Legal and Counselling Fees

The second basket would include a flat rate covering a mandatory, one-time reimbursement payment to women for legal and counselling fees.

76 See International Cost Estimating and Analysis Association, online: ICEAA www.iceaa.ca.

77 *Federal Child Support Guidelines*, SOR/97-175.

Given the importance of legal advice and counselling services at the outset of the arrangement, it is critical that these are provided once the intended parent and surrogate are considering entering into a surrogacy arrangement together. In our view, these are important expenses that should be kept separate from base expenses in order to ensure that women receive payment at the outset for these costs and that they are financially able to seek legal and counselling services as required. The flat rate could be based on an interprovincial survey of such services, completed by a qualified cost estimator, similar to the calculations undertaken for child support payments mentioned above. This process would ensure that regional differences (between provinces and between urban and rural areas) were taken into account in estimating a fair rate for all surrogacy arrangements.

Legal counselling is essential for women acting as surrogates. While there is some provincial variation, many intended parent(s) and surrogates enter into a surrogacy contract.[78] These contracts address a range of issues, not simply parentage. Contracts are negotiated despite the fact that the family law statutes in many provinces stipulate that they are not binding and, in some cases, may be used only as evidence of the parties' intentions regarding parentage.[79] Contracts may include clauses restricting the surrogate's diet to foods that pose no risk to the fetus, requiring the surrogate to undergo certain types of prenatal testing, or prohibiting the surrogate from travelling to certain jurisdictions where family laws may be unclear about the recognition of parentage in surrogacy arrangements.[80] Given the significance of these contracts and their potential to be highly intrusive, we believe it is essential that women who act as surrogates are provided with independent legal advice. In other words, a potential surrogate should

78 Nelson, "Global Trade and Assisted Reproductive Technologies," above note 43. See Lavoie & Côté, Chapter 3, this volume. See also Stefanie Carsley, "Tort's Response to Surrogate Motherhood: Providing Surrogates with a Remedy for Breached Agreements" (2013) 46:1 *University of British Columbia Law Review* 1; Motluk, "Anatomy of a Surrogacy," above note 42 (where a woman signed a surrogacy contract in the absence of independent legal advice; arguably, some of the problems that subsequently arose between the parties could have been addressed at the outset if she had been represented by a lawyer).

79 Stefanie Carsley, "Reconceiving Quebec's Laws on Surrogate Motherhood" (2018) 96 *Canadian Bar Review* 121.

80 See Lavoie & Côté, Chapter 3, this volume, where the authors report on participants' descriptions of the surrogacy contracts they entered into.

receive legal advice from a lawyer who represents only her interests and does not also represent the intended parents. Independent legal advice seeks to ensure that a woman understands her rights and responsibilities under the contract and is also advised whether certain clauses are legally binding or may be considered contrary to public policy. Finally, independent legal advice can ensure that protective clauses are in place, such as ensuring that there is disability and life insurance coverage for the surrogate should disability or death result from the pregnancy. Indeed, certain provincial governments have recognized the importance of independent legal advice for women considering surrogacy by including it as a necessary condition of a legally recognized surrogacy agreement for the purpose of parentage.[81]

Given the importance of legal advice in these circumstances, we believe a separate amount is warranted and should be earmarked for this purpose. The legal rates associated with reviewing a surrogacy agreement can be quite high, ranging from $1,500 to $3,000.[82] The proposed approach ensures that there is money available at the outset to pay the lawyer's fee and thereby promotes access for a woman who is considering acting as a surrogate. Notably, the legal advice still qualifies as independent, even though payment is made by a third party, as the retainer would be between the potential surrogate and the lawyer.

Second, this basket would also include funds allocated for counselling and support services. Professional counsellors, including social workers and psychologists, can, for example, help surrogates manage stress, anxiety, and relationships with intended parents and fertility clinics. Notably, the CFAS Counselling Special Interest Group has developed practice guidelines that recommend counselling in third-party reproduction generally, including surrogacy. These guidelines recommend that all individuals, including surrogates, undergo separate counselling sessions.[83] The length and number of sessions will inevitably vary in response to individual surrogates' situations.

Under this proposed model, the costs of the surrogates' independent legal and counselling rates should be paid directly to the law firm or counsellor on the surrogate's behalf. This payment should be paid prospectively. Women who are considering surrogacy or who are acting as surrogates

81 *CLRA*, above note 43, s 10.

82 This is based on an informal telephone poll with a handful of lawyers who regularly negotiate such contracts in Ottawa and Toronto.

83 CFAS, "Guidelines for Third Party Reproduction," above note 65 at 11.

should not incur any upfront costs in these two areas. Prospective, direct payment seeks to ensure that the surrogate can access legal and mental health counselling support that is independent from such sought by the intended parents (or offered by the clinic) and that cost is not a barrier to access. Prospective payment also ensures that the surrogate is not charged should she decide not to proceed with the surrogacy arrangement after obtaining legal advice or counselling. While we recognize that these fees may be high and beyond the reach of some intended parents within the current for-profit medical model for assisted reproduction services, we believe that the payment of these fees is a necessary precondition to family building through surrogacy, as they protect and promote the interests of the surrogate, the intended parent(s), and any resulting children.

The second basket would afford surrogates legislated financial protection for legal and counselling services. This targets the kinds of documented exploitation of surrogates[84] that has occurred within Canada. Provincial schemes for surrogacy contracts vary, and not all provinces require independent legal advice, particularly prior to conception. No provinces require counselling prior to, during, or after surrogacy. With funds specifically allocated to independent legal and counselling services, many if not all surrogates will be able to gain access to these important services.

3) Exceptional Expenses

The third basket provides a mechanism for surrogates to claim additional reimbursement for exceptional expenses that may arise as a result of the pregnancy. These payments are not mandatory: they would be made by intended parents on a case-by-case basis. In our view, a woman should not be out of pocket as a result of exceptional expenses arising from her choice to act as a surrogate, so this basket provides an opportunity for surrogates to claim expenses that go beyond the base rate and legal and counselling fees.[85] Or they may arise from complications after the pregnancy, such as post-partum depression, which may require counselling and drug coverage, or physical conditions such as hip dysplasia, which may require ongoing

84 Motluk, "Anatomy of a Surrogacy," above note 42; Blackwell, "Ontario Surrogate Nearly Killed," above note 56.

85 Luana Coco, Tania Giannone, & Giuseppe Zarbo, "Management of High-Risk Pregnancy" (2014) 66:4 *Minerva Ginecologica* 383.

physiotherapy.[86] Surrogates may also suffer additional complications from pregnancy, given the higher incidence of multiple embryo transfer among Canadian surrogates and the accompanying health risks for the pregnant woman carrying multiple embryos.[87] In order to be eligible, these types of expenses must be supported by a certificate from a health professional that attests to their exceptional nature. As is discussed in the following section, these exceptional expenses would require approval from an ombudsperson either at Health Canada or through a third party charged with overseeing the distribution of these reimbursement payments to the surrogate. We recognize that oversight of any reimbursement model will be complex, but we believe it is more manageable than the current model, even when Health Canada's regulatory process is completed. In our view, such an approach would be less onerous and require less auditing expertise than the current proposal under section 12. We believe this to be the case as the current model would require auditing for each surrogacy arrangement, while our proposed model would primarily require auditing of arrangements that include costs that go beyond the basic and legal and counselling reimbursements. Although a full discussion of auditing and oversight is beyond the scope of this chapter, we would simply note here that the federal government could draw on other enforcement models in complex regulatory environments such as income taxation.[88]

Importantly, the legal recognition of exceptional expenses would support the opportunity for more surrogates to access reimbursement for the unexpected costs that they incurred as a result of their surrogacy. This third basket recognizes that women who have unexpected complications should not be left out of pocket, and it ensures that they are reimbursed should such complications arise. This category also alerts intended parents to the fact that, beyond basic expenses and legal and counselling fees, they may bear the financial burden of unforeseen circumstances that arise

86 Erin K Smith et al, "Postpartum Depression Screening: A Review for Psychiatrists" (2016) 24:3 *Harvard Review of Psychiatry* 173.

87 Kiran M Perkins et al, "Trends and Outcomes of Gestational Surrogacy in the United States" (2016) 106:2 *Fertility and Sterility* 435.

88 See, for example, *Income Tax Act*, RSC 1985, c 1 (5th Supp), s 152(4), where taxpayers are presumed to comply with the Act, and, after initial processing and correction of obvious errors made in completing the return, the return may be selected for audit and thus subjected to a detailed examination.

before, during, and after the pregnancy of the woman acting as their surrogate. This basket will not only give a sense of security to surrogates, but it will also help intended parents to plan for exceptional payments as they undertake their family-building project.

4) Oversight and Enforcement

Finally, we recommend rigorous oversight of the proposed model. As discussed above, the current framework for the reimbursement of expenses places a significant administrative burden on surrogates. Further, there is no mechanism within the current framework for surrogates, intended parents, or other stakeholders to seek clarification about the scope of coverage or raise concerns about non-compliance with the *AHRA*.

We recommend that oversight of this model, whether through Health Canada or the creation of an independent ombudsperson,[89] be multifaceted. First, there must be oversight of the disbursement of the fees, which would include conducting sample audits to ensure that the flat rates have been dispensed as required by the *AHRA*. This oversight would be accomplished through spot audits, similar to Canada's income tax compliance regime, rather than an administrative regime requiring scrutiny of each individual reimbursement payment; such a process would, in our view, be significantly less onerous. Second, there must be a mechanism for individuals to make inquiries about the application of the rates, especially exceptional expenses, as well as a mechanism for surrogates, intended parents, and other stakeholders to make complaints about the distribution of rates under the Act. These complaints could arise from non-payment, underpayment, or overpayment under the Act.

In addition, Health Canada or the ombudsperson would be responsible for approving claims for extraordinary expenses made by surrogates. As discussed above, there may be circumstances where a woman's pregnancy

89 The current iteration of the *AHRA* anticipates some kind of oversight body or individual, inasmuch as it requires documentation from a medical professional to validate a claim by a surrogate to lost employment income: *AHRA*, above note 1, s 12(3). Fully activating the regulations under section 12 will already require some verification mechanism for this documentation, and these could be extended to include the verification role we discuss in this section. Also, Nelson, Chapter 6, this volume, suggests the creation of an ombudsperson with a larger, more complex role.

or childbirth has given rise to complications that may result in her incurring expenses that are out of the ordinary and are not notionally included in the flat rate. Health Canada would be responsible for determining whether these expenses were legitimate and should be reimbursed. This determination would include evaluating the documentation supporting the surrogate's claim. We note that a proactive approach to inquiries regarding such expenses is preferable than a system based on retrospective audits. The question of oversight and enforcement also arises in other aspects of assisted reproduction. Although this question is beyond the scope of this paper, we note that the oversight and enforcement of section 12 is an integral part of the regulation and oversight of the Act in general.[90]

E. CONCLUSION

As Health Canada continues to seek stakeholder feedback and works toward completing the section 12 regulations of the *AHRA*, it is important to acknowledge the practical, ethical, and legal challenges with the current model. In this chapter, we have proposed an alternative reimbursement model for surrogates (which could possibly be extended to gamete and embryo donors) who participate in third-party reproduction. Our flat-rate reimbursement model addresses some of the concerns that arise from the existing model. It aims to do so by removing the upfront or out-of-pocket costs for surrogates; minimizing administrative, managerial, and oversight burdens; limiting and standardizing the amounts for reimbursement; allocating a separate basket for legal and counselling rates; and creating an oversight mechanism. Our model seeks to address the upfront payments and administrative burdens borne by surrogates, the inconsistency that leads to variability and uncertainty between surrogates and intended parents, the critical importance of counselling and independent legal advice for women who are considering acting as surrogates, and the lack of oversight and enforcement of the current approach.

The proposed flat-rate model for reimbursement is consistent with the framework that underpins the *AHRA* and is intended to be a response to the current lived reality of Canadian surrogates and intended parents. It is

90 See Nelson, Chapter 6, this volume, for further suggestions regarding the oversight of assisted reproduction.

a proposal that seeks to introduce certainty and fairness in the reimbursement of women who act as surrogates. The full development of our proposed model must be based on meaningful engagement and collaboration with the various stakeholders, including surrogates. The inclusion of the various stakeholders, particularly surrogates, is a necessary component for the completion of the *AHRA* regulations, and more generally for the ethical legislation, provision, and oversight of assisted reproduction. Clearly, our model will not resolve all of the challenges related to third-party reproduction in general, or surrogacy more specifically. While we recognize that the proposed model is likely to experience some challenges and unintended consequences, we maintain that it improves upon the existing model insofar as it would alleviate many of the practical, ethical, and legal concerns related to the current approach under section 12.

6

Surrogacy in Canada

TOWARD PERMISSIVE REGULATION

*Erin Nelson**

A. INTRODUCTION

Surrogacy is an age-old practice and one with varying degrees of social acceptability. The original form of surrogacy, traditional surrogacy, involves fertilization (via sexual intercourse or assisted insemination) of the surrogate mother's egg with the intended father's sperm. In traditional surrogacy, the surrogate mother of a child is also the child's biological (genetic) mother. When fertility treatments such as in vitro fertilization ("IVF") became available, it became possible to separate gestation from genetics which, in theory at least, made surrogacy potentially more appealing as a mode of family formation. In gestational surrogacy, the egg cell comes from either the intended mother or a donor. The surrogate is the child's birth mother, but she is not genetically related to the child. In turn, this arguably leads to more clarity around genetic parentage and, in particular, motherhood.

The ability to separate genetics from gestation in the context of surrogacy did not lead readily to greater acceptance of surrogacy. If anything, it led to heightened concern due to the perceived ease with which women's bodies

* I would like to thank Daniel Howitt for assisting with research on this chapter. I also wish to thank my colleague Ubaka Ogbogu and the editors and anonymous peer reviewers of this chapter for their helpful comments on earlier drafts. Finally, I gratefully acknowledge the financial support of the University of Alberta Faculty of Law.

could be used (and potentially exploited) to advance the aims of those who could not conceive naturally but wished to have genetically related children. Some feminists raised concerns about the very availability of IVF, given the emphasis it places on women's reproductive roles.[1] Others worried about exploitation of women and children, and about the notion that a woman might be forced to relinquish a child toward whom she had developed a maternal bond.[2] This latter concern was fuelled by the *Baby M* case, in which the child's surrogate mother (genetic and gestational) refused to relinquish the child to the intended parents. The intended parents successfully sought custody of the child, while the surrogate mother (who was also the child's biological mother) was granted access to the child.[3]

The arguments for and against surrogacy as a method of family building are well known and have been canvassed at length elsewhere.[4] My aim here is not to consider these concerns in depth, but to provide a foundation for the assertion that surrogacy is contested and that the legal rules around surrogacy in Canada (and other jurisdictions) reflect a substantial degree of discomfort with the practice. I would go so far as to say that Canadian law seeks to discourage surrogacy and perhaps thereby avoid dealing with the legal and policy challenges it creates.

1 See, for example, Renate Klein, "From Test-Tube Women to Bodies Without Women" (2008) 31:3 *Women's Studies International Forum* 157; Joan C Callahan & Dorothy E Roberts, "A Feminist Social Justice Approach to Reproduction-Assisting Technologies: A Case Study on the Limits of Liberal Theory" (1995–96) 84:4 *Kentucky Law Journal* 1197 at 1227; Susan Sherwin, *No Longer Patient: Feminist Ethics and Health Care* (Philadelphia: Temple University Press, 1992) at 128–29.

2 Joseph F Sullivan, "Brief by Feminists Opposes Surrogate Parenthood" *New York Times* (31 July 1987), online: https://nyti.ms/2FC1A3L; Phyllis Chesler, *Sacred Bond: The Legacy of Baby M* (New York: Times Books, 1988).

3 *In the Matter of Baby M*, 217 NJ Super 313 (Ch Div 1987), rev'd 109 NJ 396 (1988).

4 See, for example, Chesler, above note 2; Stephen Wilkinson, "The Exploitation Argument Against Commercial Surrogacy" (2003) 17:2 *Bioethics* 169; Suze Berkhout, "Buns in the Oven: Objectification, Surrogacy, and Women's Autonomy" (2008) 34:1 *Social Theory and Practice* 95; Jennifer Damelio & Kelly Sorensen, "Enhancing Autonomy in Paid Surrogacy" (2008) 22:5 *Bioethics* 269; MM Tieu, "Altruistic Surrogacy: The Necessary Objectification of Surrogate Mothers" (2009) 35:3 *Journal of Medical Ethics* 171; Peter Gaffney, "Why the 'Widespread Agreement' Is Wrong: Contesting the Non-harm Arguments for the Prohibition of Full Commercial Surrogacy" (2009) 17:2 *Journal of Law and Medicine* 280; Elizabeth Anderson, "Is Women's Labor a Commodity?" (1990) 19:1 *Philosophy and Public Affairs* 71; R Jo Kornegay, "Is Commercial Surrogacy Baby-Selling?" (1990) 7:1 *Journal of Applied Philosophy* 45; Alan Wertheimer, "Two Questions About Surrogacy and Exploitation" (1992) 21:3 *Philosophy and Public Affairs* 211.

In this chapter, I explore Canadian surrogacy law, briefly outlining the law's evolution and providing a snapshot of current regulation. I argue that Canada should reform surrogacy law and policy by decriminalizing commercial surrogacy. Instead, both altruistic and commercial forms of surrogacy should be permitted, with oversight. I then consider how Canada might be able to achieve oversight of surrogacy and explain why regulation must be thoughtfully and carefully approached.

B. REGULATION AND RATIONALES

1) Background: The Evolution of Canadian Law

The news that babies could be conceived via IVF was greeted with a mixed reception. Women and couples who stood to benefit from the availability of assisted reproduction took a positive view, as did those who wished to be able to provide assisted reproductive technology (ART) services. The wider public was less optimistic about the emerging technology, with many commentators expressing grave concern about its potential to disrupt the family and society more generally.[5] The worry paralleled that which is seen when any significant new medical technology becomes available but was paired with moral and religious concerns around the meaning of motherhood and family.[6]

Soon after it became possible to treat infertility with IVF, several countries (including Canada) studied the legal and ethical implications of ARTs and surrogacy, with a view to informing policy development.[7] Many of these

5 Erin Nelson, *Law, Policy and Reproductive Autonomy* (Oxford: Hart, 2013) at 326.

6 *Ibid*.

7 See, for example, UK, Warnock Committee, *Report of the Committee of Inquiry into Human Fertilisation and Embryology*, Cmnd 9314 (London: Her Majesty's Stationery Office, 1984); Royal Commission on New Reproductive Technologies, *Proceed with Care: Final Report of the Royal Commission on New Reproductive Technologies* (Ottawa: Ministry of Supply and Services Canada, 1993); New York State Task Force on Life and the Law, *Assisted Reproductive Technologies: Analysis and Recommendations for Public Policy* (New York: New York State Task Force on Life and the Law, 1998); US, President's Council on Bioethics, *Reproduction and Responsibility: The Regulation of New Biotechnologies* (Washington, DC: President's Council on Bioethics, 2004); Ontario Law Reform Commission, *Report on Human Artificial Reproduction and Related Matters* (Toronto: Ontario Law Reform Commission, 1985); New South Wales Law Reform Commission, *Artificial Conception: Human Artificial Insemination (Report 49)* (Sydney: The Commission, 1986); Select Committee of the Legislative Council, *Report of the*

studies led to policy recommendations for cautious regulation (indeed, Canada's own royal commission into these issues titled its report *Proceed with Care*[8]). The general tone of the recommendations of the royal commission reflected concern about the implications of the lack of research into the safety and efficacy of reproductive technologies and, in particular, their potential to cause harm to women and children.[9] Another significant concern that shaped the commission's views related to stability and certainty around families.[10]

The commission took an especially pessimistic and disapproving view of surrogacy. The commissioners were particularly worried about commercial surrogacy, insisting that the practice is an affront to human dignity because it commodifies reproduction.[11] They also claimed that surrogacy was harmful to women, that it is incompatible with women's autonomy,[12] and that it harms children who are born via the process.[13] In concluding its discussion of surrogacy, the commission was clear in condemning the practice, explaining that "the extent to which the Commissioners deplore the practice of preconception arrangements is evident in our determination to recommend strong measures to discourage these arrangements .... Our goal is to halt commercial practices entirely and to discourage others from participating in these arrangements."[14]

In addition to endorsing a careful and restrictive approach to regulation, the commission was strongly in favour of national regulation.[15] As the

Select Committee of the Legislative Council on Artificial Insemination by Donor, In-Vitro Fertilisation and Embryo Transfer Procedures and Related Matters in South Australia (Adelaide: Government Printer, 1987); New South Wales Law Reform Commission, *Discussion Paper 15 (1987): Artificial Conception: In Vitro Fertilisation* (Sydney: The Commission, 1988); New South Wales Law Reform Commission, *Artificial Conception: Surrogate Motherhood (Report 60)* (Sydney: The Commission, 1988); Victoria Committee to Consider the Social, Ethical and Legal Issues Arising from In Vitro Fertilization, *Consolidated Reports of the Victorian Inquiry into IVF and Related Issues, 1982–1984* (Melbourne: Committee to Consider the Social, Ethical and Legal Issues Arising from In-vitro Fertilisation, 1990).

8 Royal Commission on New Reproductive Technologies, *Proceed with Care*, above note 7.

9 *Ibid* at 35–42.

10 *Ibid* at 42–44.

11 *Ibid* at 683.

12 *Ibid* at 684.

13 *Ibid* at 686. The commission provides little detail as to what the harms to children are.

14 *Ibid* at 692.

15 *Ibid* at 17–22 and 108–9.

commission itself acknowledged, the difficulty with that position is that the federal government lacks jurisdiction over medical practice.[16] The commission offered the power over peace, order, and good government and the federal spending power as alternative foundations for federal jurisdiction, but ultimately the most convincing route to federal jurisdiction proved to be the criminal law power.[17]

Canada's current law on surrogacy is found in the *Assisted Human Reproduction Act* (*AHRA*). The *AHRA* originated as legislation that included both criminal prohibitions and a regulatory component.[18] Not long after the legislation was passed, the government of Quebec challenged its constitutional validity. The challenge to the *AHRA* asked the Supreme Court of Canada to give an opinion as to the constitutional validity of the regulatory component of the Act. The regulatory aspects of the legislation included the creation and operation of an agency designed to comprehensively regulate clinical and research uses of ARTs.[19] The agency would have been responsible for licensing, inspection, and enforcement, advising the minister of health about developments in assisted reproduction practice, and collecting, analyzing, and maintaining health information related to assisted reproduction, including surrogacy.[20] The Supreme Court concluded that, while the prohibitions within the *AHRA* were a valid exercise of Parliament's criminal law power, the regulatory aspects were invalid, as they infringed on provincial jurisdiction.[21] As a result, most of the regulatory aspects of the law were repealed, leaving only the criminal prohibitions and a minimal regulatory component aimed at enforcement and compliance with the Act.[22]

---

16 *Ibid* at 18–22.

17 See, for example, Timothy Caulfield, "Clones, Controversy, and Criminal Law: A Comment on the Proposal for Legislation Governing Assisted Human Reproduction" (2001) 39:2 *Alberta Law Review* 335; Alison Harvison Young & Angela Wasunna, "Wrestling with the Limits of Law: Regulating New Reproductive Technologies" (1998) 6 *Health Law Journal* 239.

18 *Assisted Human Reproduction Act*, SC 2004, c 2 [*AHRA*].

19 *Ibid*, s 21.

20 *Ibid*, s 24.

21 *Reference re Assisted Human Reproduction Act*, 2010 SCC 61.

22 *Ibid*. There is also a section dealing with distribution and testing of gametes for use in assisted reproduction (*AHRA*, above note 18, s 10). The repealing legislation is the *Jobs, Growth and Long-Term Prosperity Act*, SC 2012, c 19, ss 713–52.

The *AHRA* prohibits commercial (or paid) surrogacy, but does not preclude altruistic surrogacy.[23] Women who provide surrogacy services may be reimbursed for their surrogacy-related expenses, but questions remain about what expenses count as legitimate for this purpose.[24] A person offering to pay or providing payment for surrogacy services is subject to a fine (to a maximum of $500,000), a term of imprisonment (up to ten years), or both. The same penalty applies to a person who accepts payment for arranging surrogacy services (or who offers payment to a person to arrange for surrogacy services).[25] Notably, it is not a criminal offence for a woman to accept payment for providing surrogacy services.

There are some additional legal rules relevant to surrogacy outside of the *AHRA*, including provincial laws related to how parentage is assigned after a child is born via a surrogacy arrangement.[26] The lack of clarity around surrogacy in some province's laws arguably contributes to the general discouragement of surrogacy, but as these laws do not prohibit or directly restrict surrogacy, they will not be discussed in depth here.

Although not specific to surrogacy, one province (Quebec) also has legislation governing ART practice.[27] A number of other provinces have explored the need for regulation, but to date no other province has translated that interest or concern into action. In some provinces, medical regulatory

---

23 *AHRA*, above note 18, s 6.

24 *Ibid*, s 12(1)(c) provides that reimbursement to surrogate mothers can be made only in accordance with the regulations. No such regulations yet exist. Health Canada provides advice on its website as to what types of expenses may be reimbursed, explaining that a surrogate can be "repaid for out-of-pocket costs directly related to her pregnancy and usually a receipt is needed." Such costs can include "maternity clothes, travel for medical appointments, and medications [and] . . . loss of work wages if a doctor certifies, in writing, that bed rest is necessary for her health and/or the health of the embryo or fetus." See Health Canada, "Prohibitions Related to Surrogacy," online: www.canada.ca/en/health-canada/services/drugs-health-products/biologics-radiopharmaceuticals-genetic-therapies/legislation-guidelines/assisted-human-reproduction/prohibitions-related-surrogacy.html.

25 *AHRA*, above note 18, ss 6(2)–(3).

26 For a discussion of parentage laws in Canada, see Erin Nelson, "Global Trade and Assisted Reproductive Technologies: Regulatory Challenges in International Surrogacy" (2013) 41:1 *Journal of Law, Medicine and Ethics* 240 [Nelson, "Global Trade and Assisted Reproduction"]. At least one province has a law governing surrogacy contracts. Quebec law provides that such contracts are null and void (Art 541 CCQ).

27 *An Act Respecting Clinical and Research Activities Relating to Assisted Procreation*, CQLR c A-5.01.

bodies have established professional guidelines relevant to ART practice.[28] Nationally, clinical practice guidelines addressing some aspects of ART practice (including third-party reproduction) have been produced by professional organizations such as the Society of Obstetricians and Gynaecologists of Canada (SOGC) and the Canadian Fertility and Andrology Society (CFAS).[29]

2) Canada's Current Regulatory Approach: Can We Justify the Status Quo?

Canada's legal approach to surrogacy cannot be justified. In my view, current Canadian law is neither effective nor necessary and should be reformed. Surrogacy—whether engaged in altruistically or for compensation—requires oversight, not prohibition. Oversight should focus on issues of health and safety and should be designed to facilitate rather than frustrate surrogacy. In addition, an oversight mechanism should include as a key priority the collection of data on surrogacy practice to ensure that future policy decisions are informed by evidence.

Before outlining my objections to the law itself, it is important to consider the legitimacy, and the consequences, of the objectives promoted by the royal commission, and which underlie Canadian surrogacy law and policy—that surrogacy should be understood as a harmful practice and should be discouraged. While altruistic surrogacy is permitted in Canada, the prohibitions directed at commercial surrogacy are backed by extraordinary sanctions. The combined effect of the prohibitions and the lack of clarity around the types of expenses that can legitimately be reimbursed

---

28 See, for example, College of Physicians and Surgeons of Alberta, *Standards and Guidelines: Assisted Reproductive Technology (ART)* (Edmonton: College of Physicians and Surgeons of Alberta, 2017), online: www.cpsa.ca/wp-content/uploads/2017/11/Assisted-Reproductive-Technology-Standards-and-Guidelines.pdf.

29 See, for example, Jason K Min et al, "Joint SOGC-CFAS Clinical Practice Guideline: Elective Single Embryo Transfer Following In Vitro Fertilization" (April 2010) 32:4 *Journal of Obstetrics Gynaecology Canada* 363 [Min et al, "SOGC-CFAS"]; Jon Havelock et al, *Clinical Practice Guidelines: Guidelines for Third Party Reproduction* (Montreal: Canadian Fertility and Andrology Society, April 2016), online: https://cfas.ca/clinical-practice-guidelines; Jason Min & Camille Sylvestre, *Clinical Practice Guidelines: Guidelines on the Number of Embryos Transferred* (Montreal: Canadian Fertility and Andrology Society, 2013), online: https://cfas.ca/clinical-practice-guidelines.

means that participants are often unsure about their rights and afraid to ask for clarification.[30] In this way, the law not only discourages surrogacy, it also discourages participants from trying to protect their rights. The law thereby ensures that when surrogacy takes place in Canada, it occurs in conditions of fear and uncertainty. In part at least, the fear and uncertainty seem to be the result of participating in a practice that skirts an undefined boundary between legal and criminal behaviour, a point made clear by anecdotal accounts of the experiences of surrogate mothers in Canada.[31] These accounts make it hard to avoid the conclusion that some women who participate in surrogacy arrangements are harmed by their participation. But they also illustrate the extent to which the law itself is to blame for that harm.

It is essential to acknowledge as well that our law puts in place a set of prohibitions aimed at discouraging a particular method of family building. In effect, the law impedes the ability of certain individuals and groups within society (gay male couples, single or partnered women who cannot carry a pregnancy themselves) to have and raise children who are biologically related to them. Whatever one's views about the importance (or not) of being able to have the experience of raising biologically related children, this approach interferes with a profoundly personal decision. It is undeniable that our legal and policy approach to surrogacy denies these individuals the opportunity for a significant life experience that many of us take for granted. The reasons provided in defence of the law are based on the harm that will result from a less restrictive approach. Is this justification legitimate? If not, I am at a loss as to how we can defend the law. Even if I could be persuaded that the use of law to discourage surrogacy and the formation of particular families is legitimate, I would still conclude that law reform is required, as I explain below.

The principles articulated in the *AHRA* provide some signals as to the rationale for the law related to surrogacy. These refer to the importance of protecting and promoting "human health, safety, dignity and rights" and highlight in particular the need to protect women's health and well-being.[32] The principles also emphasize that the health and ethical concerns raised by

---

30 See Karen Busby & Delaney Vun, "Revisiting *The Handmaid's Tale*: Feminist Theory Meets Empirical Research on Surrogate Mothers" (2010) 26:1 *Canadian Journal of Family Law* 13 at 65–66; Alison Motluk, "Anatomy of a Surrogacy" *Hazlitt* (6 November 2017), online: https://hazlitt.net/longreads/anatomy-surrogacy.

31 Alison Motluk's article makes this point eloquently (see Motluk, *ibid*).

32 *AHRA*, above note 18, ss 2(b)–(c).

"trade in the reproductive capabilities of women and men and the exploitation of children, women and men for commercial ends" justify the prohibition of such trade.[33] The law's objective, then, is to safeguard health and well-being and to prevent exploitation and harm by discouraging the potential emergence of a market for reproductive services, including surrogacy.

These objectives may have been justifiable when the *AHRA* was passed in 2004. At that time, we knew little about the safety of ARTs in general and of the practice of surrogacy in particular. More than a decade later (and nearly twenty-five years after the royal commission concluded its work), we have considerably more evidence about how surrogacy affects women, children, and families. And that evidence (albeit not entirely conclusive) suggests that the predictions of exploitation and harm resulting from the use of ARTs and surrogacy in building families were overblown. To be sure, some uses of ARTs can cause harm (for example, permitting anonymous sperm donation—a policy that many countries have now retreated from[34]). But the initial concerns about the negative impact that non-traditional methods of family formation would have on society have simply not been borne out. While it is true that an increasing number of Canadian families do not conform to the "heterosexual couple with children" norm that was the profile of the traditional Canadian family, Canadian society has by and large accepted and adapted to the many modern variations on family structure.[35] Law has been somewhat slow to catch up, meaning that many families still lack the legal security that is automatically

33 *Ibid*, s 2(f).

34 See, for example, Brigitte Clark, "A Balancing Act? The Rights of Donor-Conceived Children to Know Their Biological Origins" (2012) 40:3 *Georgia Journal of International and Comparative Law* 619; Eric Blyth & Lucy Frith, "Donor-Conceived People's Access to Genetic and Biographical History: An Analysis of Provisions in Different Jurisdictions Permitting Disclosure of Donor Identity" (2009) 23:2 *International Journal of Law, Policy and the Family* 174; Ilke Turkmendag, "The Donor-Conceived Child's 'Right to Personal Identity': The Public Debate on Donor Anonymity in the United Kingdom" (2012) 39:1 *Journal of Law and Society* 58.

35 See, for example, Nicholas Bala & Christine Ashbourne, "The Widening Concept of 'Parent' in Canada: Step-Parents, Same-Sex Partners, and Parents by ART" (2012) 20:3 *Journal of Gender, Social Policy and the Law* 525. For a description of the changing types of families in Canada, see Statistics Canada, *Portrait of Families and Arrangements in Canada: Families, Households and Marital Status, 2011 Census of Population* (Ottawa: Minister of Industry, 2012) at 3 and 6–7, online: www12.statcan.gc.ca/census-recensement/2011/as-sa/98-312-x/98-312-x2011001-eng.pdf.

granted to the traditional family, but progress is being made in most Canadian jurisdictions.[36]

In contrast to the fears expressed by the royal commission and by the lawmakers responsible for the *AHRA*, the evidence as to the effects of participating in surrogacy arrangements indicates that women who provide surrogacy services are not exploited or harmed by their participation. Rather, they are well-adjusted women seeking to help others to welcome children into their families.[37] In general, women serving as surrogates do not have difficulty relinquishing the child to the care of the intended parents.[38] Many describe the sense that the child is very clearly not theirs, and, although they feel a sense of responsibility toward the child (and the intended parents), they do not wish to remain responsible for the care of the child.[39] Research into families built via surrogacy shows that such families do not suffer from problems or concerns that are distinct from (or more pronounced than) those that typically arise in families.[40] It is important to

36 See, for example, Vanessa Gruben & Angela Cameron, "Donor Anonymity in Canada: Assessing the Obstacles to Openness and Considering a Way Forward" (2017) 54:3 *Alberta Law Review* 665 at 674 (where the authors discuss the need for comprehensive family law reform to assure the security of women-led families from sperm donors who might at some point seek to become legal parents of offspring conceived through AI).

37 Busby & Vun, above note 30; Janice C Ciccarelli & Linda J Beckman, "Navigating Rough Waters: An Overview of Psychological Aspects of Surrogacy" (2005) 61:1 *Journal of Social Issues* 21; Vasanti Jadva et al, "Surrogacy: The Experience of Surrogate Mothers" (2003) 18:10 *Human Reproduction* 2196; Elly Teman, "The Social Construction of Surrogacy Research: An Anthropological Critique of the Psychosocial Scholarship on Surrogate Motherhood" (2008) 67:7 *Social Science and Medicine* 1104.

38 See sources cited *ibid*.

39 At the Ottawa workshop that led to this book, we met with some women who had provided surrogacy services, and this was the view expressed by all of them.

40 Susan Golombok et al, "Families Created through Surrogacy Arrangements: Parent-Child Relationships in the 1st Year of Life" (2004) 40:3 *Developmental Psychology* 400; Susan Golombok et al, "Surrogacy Families: Parental Functioning, Parent-Child Relationships and Children's Psychological Development at Age 2" (2006) 47:2 *Journal of Child Psychology and Psychiatry* 213; Susan Golombok et al, "Non-Genetic and Non-Gestational Parenthood: Consequences for Parent-Child Relationships and the Psychological Well-Being of Mothers, Fathers and Children at Age 3" (2006) 21:7 *Human Reproduction* 1918; Susan Golombok et al, "Families Created Through Surrogacy: Mother-Child Relationships and Children's Psychological Adjustment at Age 7" (2011) 47:6 *Developmental Psychology* 1579; Katherine H Shelton et al, "Examining Differences in Psychological Adjustment Problems Among Children Conceived by Assisted Reproductive Technologies" (2009) 33:5 *International Journal of Behavioral Development* 385.

acknowledge that such research into family functioning cannot reach conclusions about long-term implications, given the time frame within which it has been conducted.[41]

As to the effect of surrogacy on the children who are born through such arrangements, the evidence that has emerged in the last decade (or so) on surrogacy outcomes for children suggests that children are not harmed. Rather, they are developmentally and psychosocially very similar to their non–surrogate conceived peers.[42] Again, it is not possible at this stage to reach firm conclusions about the complete absence of harm, given that the studies done to date have tracked children only up to roughly age ten. My point in noting the limits of the existing data is not to suggest that we cannot make laws without conclusive evidence establishing that a practice is harmful, but simply to reflect the limitations of our current knowledge.

In addition to the academic literature about surrogacy, we have some anecdotal evidence about how surrogacy is currently practised in Canada. One of the commission's most significant concerns was the potential for growth of a market for surrogacy (and other reproductive) services. The *AHRA* is geared toward preventing commercialization of surrogacy and the involvement of third-party brokers. To that end, the law prohibits third parties from accepting payment for arranging for the services of a surrogate mother.[43] In spite of this prohibition, there are several for-profit surrogacy consultants doing business in Canada, including Canadian Surrogacy Options,[44] Canadian Fertility Consultants,[45] ANU Fertility Consultants,[46] Surrogacy in Canada Online,[47] and Proud Fertility.[48] These organizations charge intended parents thousands of dollars for their consulting services, which include coordinating various appointments with professionals (psychologists, lawyers, fertility specialists) for both the surrogate and the intended parents, assisting the surrogate in obtaining additional life insurance, and providing a generic surrogacy contract for the parties to work

41 See sources cited *ibid.*

42 *Ibid.*

43 *AHRA*, above note 18, ss 6(2)–(3).

44 See online: www.canadiansurrogacyoptions.com.

45 See online: http://fertilityconsultants.ca.

46 See online: www.surrogacyincanada.com.

47 See online: https://surrogacy.ca.

48 See online: http://proudfertility.com.

from.[49] Since all of these services are available without the need for a consultant, the primary purpose of these consulting operations seems to be to connect intended parents with women willing to provide surrogacy services (in other words, "arrange for the services of a surrogate mother"). To date, there has been one prosecution of such agencies under the *AHRA*,[50] which suggests that there is little enthusiasm for enforcing the law. In any case, the clear conclusion that emerges from the existence of such organizations is that the law is not effective in preventing them from profiting from surrogacy.[51]

The evidence about how women, children, and families are affected by their participation in surrogacy cannot assure us that there is no potential for harm or exploitation arising from participation in surrogacy arrangements.[52] It does, however, suggest that Canada's ultra-cautious and restrictive approach to regulation is not necessary in order to prevent these effects. The evidence also shows that the law does not seem to be achieving its aims. Anecdotal evidence tells us that increasing numbers of children are born via surrogacy,[53] raising questions about whether the law is succeeding in deterring Canadians from participating in surrogacy. In addition, media reports intimate that at least some of the surrogacy

---

49 See, for example, Surrogacy in Canada Online, online: https://surrogacy.ca/about-us/about-sco.html; Canadian Surrogacy Options, online: https://surrogacy.ca/about-us/faq.html#how-long-has-sco-been-in-business.

50 See Alison Motluk, "First Prosecution Under *Assisted Human Reproduction Act* Ends in Conviction" (2014) 186:2 *Canadian Medical Association Journal* E75; Alison Motluk, "After Pleading Guilty for Paying Surrogates, Business Is Booming for This Fertility Matchmaker" *Globe and Mail* (28 February 2016), online: www.theglobeandmail.com/life/health-and-fitness/health/business-is-booming-for-fertility-matchmaker-leia-swanberg/article28930242 [Motluk, "After Pleading Guilty"].

51 One surrogacy consultant's website indicates that services were provided on a not-for-profit basis from 2001 to 2010, but "due to increasing demands" the organization became a "registered business" in 2011. See Surrogacy in Canada Online, above note 49.

52 And, in any case, I do not take the view that we are required to empirically establish an absence of potential harm in order to take a less restrictive legal stance.

53 In her recent study, Pamela M White notes that, in 2012 in Canada, there were 400 reported gestational surrogacy cycles, resulting in 133 live births. These numbers are fairly low, and they are clearly incomplete if the numbers reported by surrogacy consultants are even close to accurate. Pamela M White, "Hidden from View: Canadian Gestational Surrogacy Practices and Outcomes, 2001–2012" (2016) 24:47 *Reproductive Health Matters* 205 at 207 (Table 1).

arrangements in Canada involve payment beyond the reimbursement of reasonable expenses that the law permits.[54]

My argument that commercial surrogacy should not be criminally prohibited should not be understood as signifying that I have no reservations about commercial or compensated surrogacy — I do. In particular, the role played by third parties (surrogacy agencies or brokers) in commercial surrogacy is cause for concern. Such organizations profit from the anxieties of intended parents and the reproductive labour of surrogate mothers. Yet, although our law was arguably designed to prevent the development and growth of such organizations, surrogacy consultants have long been involved in surrogacy arrangements in Canada, and these businesses are increasing in number.

3) Should We Regulate Surrogacy?

My argument that Canada should abandon the criminal prohibition on paid surrogacy is part of a larger project of law reform. Although surrogacy should not be criminalized, the interests at stake demand oversight aimed at safeguarding the well-being of all parties involved — the intended parents, the surrogate mother, and the child.

Surrogacy raises complex policy issues touching on health and health care, family law, the welfare of children, and citizenship and immigration. The basic legal question is whether surrogacy should be freely permitted, permitted with restrictions, or prohibited. But even in jurisdictions where that question is answered (and there are many that have not even taken that step[55]), when children are born as a result of surrogacy arrangements

54 Alison Motluk, "The Baby-Making Business: On the Front Lines of Toronto's Booming, Semi-legal Surrogacy Market" *Toronto Life* (3 February 2014), online: https://torontolife.com/city/baby-making-business-surrogacy-market-toronto; Motluk, "After Pleading Guilty" above note 50; Motluk, "Anatomy of a Surrogacy," above note 30.

55 See Steven J Ory et al, *International Federation of Fertility Societies IFFS Surveillance 2013* (IFFS, October 2013), online: http://c.ymcdn.com/sites/www.iffs-reproduction.org/resource/resmgr/iffs_surveillance_09-19-13.pdf?hhSearchTerms=%222013+and+survey+and+surrogacy%22. A more recent survey on third-party parenting options indicates that surrogacy is not regulated by law in nineteen countries. See Alexandra S Rashedi et al, "Survey of Third-Party Parenting Options Associated with Fertility Preservation Available to Patients with Cancer Around the Globe," online: *Journal of Global Oncology* [forthcoming], online: http://ascopubs.org/doi/full/10.1200/JGO.2017.009944.

that do not comply with the law, the interests of those children become a key consideration for law and policy. Prospective parents are increasingly responding to restrictive surrogacy laws in their home states by pursuing surrogacy in other, more surrogacy-friendly jurisdictions.[56] When such parents seek to return home with their children, a lack of clarity around biological and/or legal parentage can lead citizenship and immigration authorities to refuse to recognize the citizenship of the child.[57] Thus, even if only to protect the interests of these children, it is essential that some aspects of surrogacy—such as parentage and citizenship status—be regulated.

In addition to ensuring that the legal status of the child and family is clear and unambiguous, the primary rationale for oversight is the need to ensure that the interests of all participants are protected. While I have argued that we should have a fairly high degree of comfort that surrogacy is not harmful—at least as practised in affluent societies where women's autonomy and equality are prized[58]—I do not mean to suggest that the practice should be entirely left to market forces. Surrogacy, which involves IVF and other invasive medical procedures undertaken for the benefit of others, cannot be provided in a completely unregulated space. If all goes well, surrogacy results in the birth of a child whose legal status and parentage need certainty and clarity. As with adoption, oversight is needed to ensure the protection of the interests of the child. Regulation aimed at health and safety, informed decision making about participation, and data collection is essential to safeguard the interests of those participating in surrogacy arrangements.

It seems that surrogacy has become increasingly common in the years since the *AHRA* was adopted, although we lack good data as to how

---

56 See, for example, Amrita Pande, "Cross-Border Reproductive Surrogacy in India" in E Scott Sills, ed, *Handbook of Gestational Surrogacy: International Clinical Practice and Policy Issues* (Cambridge: Cambridge University Press, 2016) 143; Olga van den Akker, *Surrogate Motherhood Families* (London: Palgrave Macmillan, 2017) at 199–230. See also Busby & White, Chapter 7, this volume, for a discussion of cross-border reproductive care.

57 See Nelson, "Global Trade and Assisted Reproduction," above note 26.

58 Most of the research that has been done on surrogacy "outcomes" has been conducted in such jurisdictions. Whether the same conclusions could be drawn from research into surrogacy in developing countries, or areas where women's options are more limited, is unknown. My guess is that we would have considerably more cause for concern about surrogacy practice in less affluent parts of the world.

frequently surrogacy occurs in Canada. According to recent research by Pamela M White, based on data from Canada's voluntary ART registry, in 2001, fewer than 100 gestational surrogacy cycles were officially reported, and there were 21 live births to gestational surrogates.[59] In 2012, there were almost 400 reported gestational surrogacy cycles, resulting in 133 live births.[60] In contrast, one surrogacy consultant's website indicates that its organization alone has helped thousands of parents and has been involved in 1,325 births.[61] All of these figures exclude surrogacy arrangements pursued outside of Canada. Clearly, we lack complete and accurate data about how often Canadians turn to surrogacy as a mode of family building. This alone suggests a need for regulation, to make it possible to collect such data. In turn, the data will help to inform evidence-based policy.

White's research findings also raise a potential concern about health risks for women providing surrogacy services. In her study, White found a substantially higher rate of multiple embryo transfer in surrogate IVF cycles compared to non-surrogate cycles.[62] Between 2003 and 2012, 40 percent of non-surrogate IVF patients had two embryos transferred, compared to 60 percent of gestational surrogates. When donor ova were used (i.e., ova from a woman other than the intended mother), 85 percent of gestational surrogates received two or more embryos in each cycle.[63] Multiple embryo transfer leads to an increased risk of multiple gestation pregnancy, which poses numerous health risks for both the mother and the babies. These risks include maternal hypertension, preeclampsia and anemia, intra-uterine growth retardation, low birth weight, premature birth, stillbirth, and neonatal death).[64] In recent years, these risks have been mitigated to a

59 White, "Hidden from View," above note 53 at 207 (Table 1). See also White, Chapter 2, this volume, which highlights the critical lack of data in Canada.

60 White, "Hidden from View," above note 53 at 207 (Table 1).

61 Canadian Fertility Consultants, above note 45. Another consulting business (Canadian Surrogacy Options) claims to have helped build 879 families through surrogacy, above note 44. Another, Surrogacy in Canada Online, states on its website that it estimates the number of surrogacy arrangements in Canada at more than 400 per year, online: https://surrogacy.ca/surrogacy-in-canada/faq-on-surrogacy.html#how-many-surrogacy-arrangements-have-there-been-in-canada.

62 White, "Hidden from View," above note 53 at 206.

63 *Ibid* at 210.

64 See, for example, Tarek El-Toukhy, Yacoub Khalaf, & Peter Braude, "IVF Results: Optimize Not Maximize" (2006) 194:2 *American Journal of Obstetrics and Gynecology* 322; Peter Braude & the Expert Group on Multiple Births after IVF, *One Child at a*

significant degree through clinical practice guidelines aimed at reducing multiple birth rates. And, while it is difficult to know whether surrogates are actually experiencing harm as a result of IVF practice in surrogacy, it is cause for concern to see that women who provide surrogacy services do not appear to be benefiting from the same safety-oriented practices (i.e., elective single-embryo transfer) that non-surrogates receive and that are recommended in Canadian IVF guidelines.[65]

As White acknowledges, the data she analyzed are incomplete and focus on the use of gametes and embryos in assisted reproduction treatments, not on the surrogate mothers themselves.[66] There is limited demographic information collected about the people involved in ART treatment. When treatment outcomes are reported, the outcomes relate to the success of the ART treatments themselves, rather than to health concerns or complications experienced by women who receive the treatments.[67] But, given the potential implications of the data—that surrogate patients are treated differently in the provision of ART services than non-surrogate patients—there is a clear need for oversight to protect the health and safety of surrogate mothers.

A key element of an oversight scheme is to provide for a way to collect data about surrogacy. Sound policy decisions cannot be made without evidence. We do have some facts about how surrogacy is practised in Canada. We know that Canadians are involved, both as intended parents and as surrogates. We also know that Canadian women provide surrogacy services for non-Canadian intended parents[68] and that some Canadian intended parents seek surrogacy services abroad.[69] Surrogacy appears to be increasingly common as a method of family formation.[70] What we lack

Time: Reducing Multiple Births After IVF (London: Human Fertilisation and Embryology Authority, 2006); Siladitya Bhattacharya & Mohan S Kamath, "Reducing Multiple Births in Assisted Reproduction Technology" (2014) 28:2 *Best Practice and Research: Clinical Obstetrics and Gynaecology* 191.

65 Min et al, "SOGC-CFAS," above note 29.

66 White, "Hidden from View," above note 53 at 206.

67 *Ibid.*

68 *Ibid.*

69 Nelson, "Global Trade and Assisted Reproduction," above note 26.

70 White, "Hidden from View," above note 53 at 207 (Table 1). The reported data do not show a large number of surrogacy arrangements, but the information does indicate an increase. Together with the information provided by surrogacy consultants about the numbers of families they help with surrogacy (see above note 61), it is difficult to deny that surrogacy is being practised with increasing frequency in Canada.

is information to show who participates in surrogacy arrangements, how they are affected by their involvement in surrogacy either at home or outside of Canada, how surrogate-formed families function in the long term, and whether the law is being complied with or ignored. In other words, we lack the data that would provide insight into the form of oversight needed to minimize the potential for harm to participants.

C. A CANADIAN REGULATORY MODEL

Before exploring regulatory approaches, I want to note that there is one reason for maintaining a criminal prohibition related to surrogacy—namely, to preserve the federal government's ability to make laws related to surrogacy. The Supreme Court of Canada's ruling in *Reference re Assisted Human Reproduction Act* makes it clear that any attempt by the federal government to regulate aspects of fertility practice—including surrogacy—will fall outside of Parliament's legislative jurisdiction.[71] It seems that, for now, the only way to preserve any regulatory boundaries around surrogacy is to maintain criminal prohibitions of some kind. Absent these prohibitions, unless and until the provinces and territories take steps to regulate surrogacy, there will be no legal rules in place. As noted above, only one province (Quebec) has legislation governing ART practice, and that law does not address surrogacy.[72]

As outlined earlier, the existence of professional guidelines around facility requirements and clinical practice means that there is some degree of oversight in place even without the *AHRA*.[73] While such regulatory and professional guidelines are useful to a point, they do not provide a complete or ideal structure for oversight. At the very least, they are guidelines and rules put in place by the group that benefits from being able to provide ART treatment services. The clear conflict of interest here suggests that arm's length oversight is needed.[74] Moreover, when regulation is left entirely to professional organizations, we have no assurance as to the validity of the

71 *Reference re Assisted Human Reproduction Act*, above note 21.

72 See above note 27.

73 See above notes 28 & 29.

74 See Debora L Spar, *The Baby Business: How Money, Science, and Politics Drive the Commerce of Conception* (Boston: Harvard Business School Press, 2006) at 51; Nelson, *Law, Policy and Reproductive Autonomy*, above note 5 at 264–66.

regulation-making process or the extent to which the interests of patients have been prioritized.[75] The clinical practice guidelines crafted by the SOGC and the CFAS have not traditionally been readily available to the public;[76] even when they are accessible, the process for creating them is not open or transparent, and it is therefore unclear whose input was sought during that process.[77] And, in any case, regulations and guidelines adopted by medical regulators or professional organizations are incomplete, in that they address only the medical aspects of the practice they target.

Turning to consider regulatory models for Canada, one option worth exploring is incremental change within the existing model. The government could, for example, alter the law to criminalize some other aspect of surrogacy. A possibility might be to create an offence of pursuing commercial surrogacy arrangements without the approval of a government or, preferably, arm's-length regulator. That would allow for the maintenance of a federal role without needing to criminalize payment to surrogates or commercial arrangements specifically. Another option might be to create a payment system with a capped amount and criminalize payments beyond that amount. Again, the arrangements would have to be monitored by a regulatory body to ensure oversight with a view to minimizing or eliminating the possibility of harm or exploitation.[78]

While the suggestion to criminalize some other aspect of surrogacy lacks the virtue of decriminalizing surrogacy, it would have the significant

75 See Vanessa Gruben, "Freezing as Freedom? A Regulatory Approach to Elective Egg Freezing and Women's Reproductive Autonomy" (2017) 54:3 *Alberta Law Review* 753 at 763.

76 CFAS began making its clinical practice guidelines public in July 2016, online: www.newswire.ca/news-releases/the-canadian-fertility-and-andrology-society-releases-clinical-practice-guidelines-on-assisted-reproduction-to-the-public-585036481.html. The SOGC has made clinical practice guidelines available to the public in the past but has announced that, as of January 2017, all content published in the *Journal of Obstetrics and Gynaecology Canada* from January 2016, including clinical practice guidelines, policy statements, and technical updates, is available only to members of the SOGC as a benefit of membership: see online: https://sogc.org/clinical-practice-guidelines.html.

77 See Dylan Kozlick, "Clinical Practice Guidelines and the Legal Standard of Care: Warnings, Predictions, and Interdisciplinary Encounters" (2011) 19 *Health Law Journal* 125 at 134.

78 On the theory that the best way to prevent exploitation is to ensure that all parties understand their rights and obligations throughout the process.

advantage of permitting commercial and altruistic surrogacy and enabling the collection of data on both. If the evidence shows that either or both of these practices are actually causing harm, the approach or degree of permissiveness could be modified. Another potential downside of this approach is that it could fail to provide sufficient justification for federal legislation, as it might not focus on practices that are properly within the criminal law power.

If it proves to be impossible to ensure that federal regulatory authority can be maintained in the context of surrogacy, it will become necessary for provinces and territories to implement a mechanism for oversight. This will undoubtedly prove challenging. While most Canadian provinces have clinics offering fertility treatment, many have just one or two such clinics.[79] As a result, it is difficult to imagine provinces taking on the task of regulating. Although social views have changed since the introduction of assisted reproduction, there is still considerable resistance, and the political cost involved in regulating assisted reproduction and surrogacy may be high.

One middle-ground possibility is that of federal-provincial co-operation. This approach to regulation is well-suited to the context: some provinces have a more pressing need to regulate than others, but almost all provinces need some form of regulation. And, given the ease with which Canadians can cross provincial borders to obtain private health care services, a national approach to regulating in this area is preferable to variable regional regulation. A national approach would also be far more efficient (particularly if a regulatory body is set up, as one such organization will cost far less than multiple organizations with overlapping or identical functions).

Canadian constitutional history in general, and specifically in the context of assisted reproduction and surrogacy regulation, gives us few reasons to be confident that a co-operative or collaborative approach to regulation is achievable.[80] That said, there are two health-related contexts in which

79 The CFAS website lists clinics in eight provinces: British Columbia (5), Alberta (2), Saskatchewan (2), Manitoba (1), Ontario (23), Quebec (8), New Brunswick (1), Nova Scotia (1). Canadian Fertility and Andrology Society, "IVF Clinics," online: https://cfas.ca/ivf-clinics.

80 For a general discussion of the issues see, for example, Richard Simeon, "Intergovernmental Relations and the Challenges to Canadian Federalism" (1980) 23:1 *Canadian Public Administration* 14. See also Constance MacIntosh, "The Governance of Indigenous Health" in Joanna N Erdman, Vanessa Gruben, & Erin Nelson, eds, *Canadian Health Law and Policy*, 5th ed (Toronto: LexisNexis Canada, 2017) 135; Dayna Nadine Scott, "The Environment, Federalism, and the *Charter*" in Peter Oliver, Patrick Macklem,

Canadian federal and provincial/territorial governments are progressing toward co-operative models—medical assistance in dying (MAID) and cannabis possession for personal consumption. Both are areas that involve the intersection of the criminal law with health policy and, as such, require involvement of both levels of government to ensure that adequate safeguards against harm and abuse are in place.

Oversight of cannabis use will involve shared responsibility among the federal and regional governments. The federal role will entail responsibility for setting rules and standards for production of cannabis and outlining the "types of cannabis products that will be allowed for sale, packaging and labelling requirements for products, standardized serving sizes and potency, prohibiting the use of certain ingredients, . . . tracking of cannabis from seed to sale to prevent diversion to the illicit market, [and] restrictions on promotional activities."[81] Provinces and territories will "license and oversee the distribution and sale of cannabis, subject to federal conditions."[82] The provinces and territories will also have the ability to make specific rules related to minimum age for use of cannabis, the limit permitted for personal possession, the growing of cannabis at home (e.g., how many plants per residence are permitted), and restricting locations where cannabis can be consumed.[83]

In the context of MAID, the federal government has amended the *Criminal Code* to provide for MAID in the circumstances outlined within the Code.[84] The provisions address who can provide or assist with providing MAID, how MAID can be provided (either by assisting suicide or by directly administering the medications that will end the person's life), and what conditions must be present in order for a patient to be eligible to access MAID.[85] The provinces and territories can make rules regulating assisted dying on matters within their jurisdiction, including rules related

& Natalie Des Rosiers, eds, *The Oxford Handbook of the Canadian Constitution* (New York: Oxford University Press, 2017) 493.

81 Health Canada, "Legalizing and Strictly Regulating Cannabis: The Facts," online: www.canada.ca/en/services/health/campaigns/legalizing-strictly-regulating-cannabis-facts.html.

82 *Ibid.*

83 *Ibid.*

84 *Criminal Code*, RSC 1985, c C-46, ss 241.1–241.4.

85 Health Canada, "Medical Assistance in Dying," online: www.canada.ca/en/health-canada/services/medical-assistance-dying.html.

to training for providers and to the process of requesting or carrying out MAID.[86]

Both of these contexts involve overlapping jurisdiction, and, in both, there is a clear expectation and need that the two levels of government will work together to achieve optimal oversight and regulation. It is too early to evaluate the success of either of these regulatory models, but perhaps these examples mean that we can be optimistic about the prospects for co-operation in regulating surrogacy.

D. TOWARD A REGULATORY STRUCTURE

1) Lessons from Abroad

When considering new ways to achieve oversight, it is often helpful and informative to look to the experiences of other jurisdictions that have adopted a similar approach. The tricky part in the context of surrogacy is finding other models to consider. Even where surrogacy is legal and regulated to some extent, most jurisdictions do not have a well-developed approach to oversight. For example, the United Kingdom has in place a robust regulatory system for ARTs (the Human Fertilisation and Embryology Authority, or HFEA) but does not have a regulatory model specific to surrogacy arrangements.[87] Two jurisdictions that are exceptional in this respect are Israel and the state of Victoria in Australia. The two models share some similar features but are quite different in focus and approach. They also serve as cautionary tales to an extent, in that they are more useful as examples of how not to approach regulation and oversight than as models to emulate.

Israel was the first country to recognize surrogacy arrangements as legally valid.[88] It passed its surrogacy law in 1996, legalizing surrogacy at

86 Alberta Health, "Medical Assistance in Dying," online: www.health.alberta.ca/health-info/medical-assistance-dying.html.

87 Law reform may be on the horizon in the United Kingdom. The Law Commission has initiated a review of the law related to surrogacy, see: Law Commission, "Surrogacy," online: www.lawcom.gov.uk/surrogacy/.

88 *Agreements for the Carriage of Fetuses (Approval of Agreement and Status of the Newborn) Law*, 5756-1996, SH No 1577 [Surrogacy Agreements Law]. The legislation is available only in Hebrew, and I thank my colleague Professor Eran Kaplinsky for his assistance in explaining the meaning of several sections of the Act. See also Law Library of Congress, "Israel Reproduction and Abortion: Law and Policy" (2012-007460), online: www.loc.gov/law/help/israel_2012-007460_IL_FINAL.pdf; Elly Teman, "Surrogacy in

a time when many countries were prohibiting at least some forms of the practice. But although surrogacy (including commercial surrogacy) is legal in Israel, the regulatory structure is extremely restrictive. The law creates a complex set of eligibility criteria and requires approval of all surrogacy arrangements by an interdisciplinary Surrogacy Agreement Approvals Committee.[89] Participants must meet numerous conditions before a surrogacy agreement will be approved; these relate to age, residency,[90] marital status,[91] religion,[92] and the source of gametes to be used.[93]

Before it will approve a surrogacy arrangement, the committee must be satisfied that there is a medical justification for pursuing surrogacy.[94] It must also agree that all parties are medically and psychologically suitable and that all have received counselling.[95] The committee must be satisfied that the agreement does not place the health of the surrogate or the potential child at risk and that the agreement does not include conditions that could infringe the rights of the potential child or any of the parties to the agreement.[96] In addition to the formal requirements of the legislation, the committee has adopted several policies that guide its own practice, relating to such matters as the acceptable age for the surrogate, health stipulations for the surrogate (including those related to pregnancy as well as other health issues), and the number of children the surrogate has delivered.[97]

Israel: State-Controlled Surrogacy as a Mechanism of Symbolic Control" in Sills, ed, *Handbook of Gestational Surrogacy*, above note 56, 165 at 165 [Teman, "Surrogacy in Israel"].

89 Surrogacy Agreements Law, above note 88, § 3; "Israel Reproduction and Abortion," above note 88 at 11. The composition of the committee is specified in the legislation.

90 Surrogacy Agreements Law, above note 88, § 2; "Israel Reproduction and Abortion," above note 88 at 10.

91 Surrogacy Agreements Law, above note 88, § 2. The criteria specify that surrogates should be single women, although the committee can approve a surrogacy arrangement involving a married surrogate, if satisfied that the intended parents were not able to find a single woman willing to provide surrogacy services after making reasonable efforts to do so.

92 *Ibid.*

93 *Ibid.*

94 Surrogacy Agreements Law, above note 88, § 4; "Israel Reproduction and Abortion," above note 88 at 11.

95 *Ibid.*

96 *Ibid.*

97 Teman, "Surrogacy in Israel," above note 88 at 169.

Victoria, like all other Australian states (except the Northern Territory, which has no law on surrogacy), permits altruistic surrogacy but prohibits commercial or paid surrogacy.[98] Victoria's regulatory model is unique within Australia and involves approval of surrogacy arrangements by a Patient Review Panel (PRP).[99] Individuals or couples who wish to pursue surrogacy must apply to the PRP for approval of their proposed surrogacy arrangements. Before approving a surrogacy arrangement, the panel must be satisfied that eligibility criteria are met and that legislative requirements have been fulfilled. Eligibility criteria include requirements that the intended parents are medically or socially infertile or unable to carry a pregnancy;[100] in addition, limits are placed on the age and pregnancy history of potential surrogates.[101] The law precludes the use of the surrogate's own oocytes.[102] In addition to the eligibility criteria, the legislation sets out a number of other requirements that must be met in order for a surrogacy arrangement to be approved. All parties must have received counselling and legal advice[103] and must demonstrate that they are able to make informed decisions about proceeding.[104]

Both Israel and Victoria are examples of restrictive regulation of surrogacy. Both permit the practice, subject to significant constraints. And both involve processes that are extremely invasive to the lives of those involved. Victoria's PRP requires a report from the counsellor who provided counselling, a report from an independent psychologist who assessed the parties, certified copies of criminal record checks, certified copies of child

98 *Assisted Reproductive Treatment Act 2008* (Vic), s 44; *Surrogacy Contracts Act 1993* (Tas), s 4; *Parentage Act 2004* (ACT), s 41; *Surrogacy Act 2008* (WA), s 8; *Surrogacy Act 2010* (NSW), s 8; *Surrogacy Act 2010* (Qld), s 56; *Family Relationships Act 1975* (SA), s 10HA(2a)(i).

99 The Patient Review Panel (PRP) is part of the Victorian Assisted Reproductive Treatment Authority (VARTA). The panel was established by the *Assisted Reproductive Treatment Act 2008* (Vic), s 82.

100 *Ibid*, s 40(1)(a)(i).

101 *Ibid*, ss 40(1)(b) and 40(1)(ac).

102 *Ibid*, s 40(1)(ab).

103 *Ibid*, s 40(1)(c). Section 43 provides further details about the counselling and legal advice required.

104 *Ibid*, s 40(1)(f). The legislative requirements have been further explained by the PRP in its Guidance Note on approval of surrogacy arrangements: Patient Review Panel, *Guidance Note 1: Approval of Surrogacy Arrangements in Victoria* (Melbourne: Patient Review Panel, November 2015), online: www2.health.vic.gov.au/about/publications/policiesandguidelines/patient-review-panel-guidance-note-1-surrogacy-arrangements.

protection order checks, proof of age of the surrogate mother, proof of live birth by the surrogate mother, and evidence of independent legal advice.[105] In Israel, all parties must submit to "an in-depth psychological evaluation, including intelligence tests and interviews with a psychologist. The psychologist's report must attest to their mental stability and suitability for the surrogacy process."[106]

In Israel, as Elly Teman explains, the statutory and informal conditions for approval mean that surrogacy is very much understood to be an option of last resort.[107] Her description of her years-long work with those involved in surrogacy—surrogates, intended parents, physicians, lawyers, and other key players—gives rise to a sense that surrogacy is discouraged and that the approval process itself, with its length and demands, is in some ways a test of commitment.[108] Even before embarking on the surrogacy process, Israeli intended parents who have unexplained infertility or have experienced multiple miscarriages likely feel that they have endured a significant ordeal, as the committee requires multiple unsuccessful IVF attempts and/or miscarriages before it will approve a surrogacy arrangement in such cases.[109]

One could argue that the processes adopted in Israel and Victoria make the case against oversight of surrogacy.[110] I disagree. Oversight is not inevitably restrictive. The tenor of the regulatory processes adopted in these jurisdictions is dictated by the history of ART regulation in these jurisdictions and by the social and cultural concerns around ARTs particular to these states. Israeli law handles surrogacy uniquely, in comparison

105 Victoria Health, "Applications to the Patient Review Panel," online: www2.health.vic.gov.au/hospitals-and-health-services/patient-care/perinatal-reproductive/assisted-reproduction/applications.

106 Teman, "Surrogacy in Israel," above note 88 at 169. As Teman goes on to explain, a potential surrogate mother is required to wait a year after any type of traumatic event in her life to undergo the psychological evaluation. And a surrogate mother will not be approved by the committee if she has "been hospitalized in a psychiatric unit in the past; the committee also has disqualified surrogates who have had past experience with depression, intensive therapy, or have used antidepressants such as Prozac."

107 *Ibid* at 170.

108 *Ibid*.

109 *Ibid* at 169. Teman notes that the committee seems to expect that the intended mother will have experienced seven miscarriages and have attempted IVF seven to ten times.

110 As did one of the anonymous peer reviewers of this chapter.

with its approach to other reproductive technologies. In contrast to the liberal rules around most ARTs, including who may use reproductive technologies (same-sex couples, single women) and which technologies may be used (pre-implantation genetic diagnosis, sex selection), surrogacy is restricted in availability. In Australia, the initial legal stance taken toward surrogacy was highly restrictive. Surrogacy in all forms was prohibited, and, in some states, eligibility for ARTs such as IVF was limited to heterosexual married couples.[111] While the eligibility rules have been relaxed to a degree, there remains intense concern around ARTs and family formation, and that explains, to an extent at least, the degree of invasiveness that the surrogacy approval process entails.[112]

I noted at the beginning of this section that the regulatory approaches used in Israel and Victoria may serve as cautionary tales as to the unintended effects of regulation. In Israel, the regulatory approach is in fact well suited to its aim — to permit the practice of surrogacy in a manner that is consistent with the objective of increasing the birth rate for Jewish, heterosexual nuclear families.[113] In Victoria, the regulatory scheme is perhaps more restrictive in practice than was intended, but its aim was never to create a permissive, open approach to surrogacy. What these examples show is that we must approach regulation thoughtfully and with a clear sense of our objectives in putting an oversight mechanism in place.

2) A Canadian Regulatory Model

I have argued that surrogacy should be permitted but subject to oversight to minimize the potential for harm and to promote the interests of children, surrogate mothers, and intended parents. In my view, the critical issue is to ensure that there is a mechanism in place to supervise surrogacy arrangements so that participating in surrogacy does not lead to disadvantage or harm to any of the participants. This could be accomplished by an

111 See Nelson, *Law, Policy and Reproductive Autonomy*, above note 5 at 273–75; Helen Szoke, "Regulation of Assisted Reproductive Technology: The State of Play in Australia" in Ian Freckelton & Kerry Petersen, eds, *Controversies in Health Law* (Sydney: Federation Press, 1999) 240 at 246.

112 Nelson, *Law, Policy and Reproductive Autonomy*, above note 5 at 275.

113 Teman, "Surrogacy in Israel," above note 88 at 166.

arm's-length oversight body that reviews and monitors surrogacy agreements and/or the provision of services by surrogacy consultants or agencies.

Surrogacy arrangements are complex interpersonally, medically, legally, and practically. In the end, if all goes as planned, there will be a child who needs secure, stable parenting and who stands to benefit from a healthy relationship between the surrogate and intended parents, or who stands to be harmed if the relationship among the adult participants is destructive. Those who wish to form families using surrogacy should be able to obtain unbiased professional advice and assistance without having to pay thousands of dollars to an agent or broker. All of the tasks that brokers assist with are available directly from the service providers (insurers, lawyers, counsellors) without a surcharge imposed by brokers. The primary value-added provided by surrogacy consultants or brokers is to match surrogates with intended parents, in spite of the reality that it is an offence under the *AHRA* to "accept consideration for arranging for the services of a surrogate mother."[114]

One possible role for an oversight agency or body would be to have that organization offer the services currently being provided by surrogacy consultants. The organization could maintain a list of professionals (counsellors, psychologists, lawyers) who work in third-party reproduction and who have experience dealing with surrogacy arrangements. It could also provide basic information to women who are considering offering surrogacy services and to intended parents. It could be a liaison between fertility treatment providers and patients. And it could almost certainly offer these services for a small fee oriented toward cost recovery. This is no doubt possible; surrogacy agencies in the United Kingdom operate on a not-for-profit basis.[115]

E. CONCLUSION

We are at a crossroads in terms of surrogacy regulation. The royal commission's ultra-cautious approach to regulation no longer seems necessary, as the evidence indicates that the social and individual harms speculated about in early days of assisted reproduction have not materialized. This suggests

114 *AHRA*, above note 18, s 6(2).

115 See, for example, Brilliant Beginnings, online: www.brilliantbeginnings.co.uk; Surrogacy UK, online: www.surrogacyuk.org; COTS (Childlessness Overcome Through Surrogacy), online: www.surrogacy.org.uk.

that many, perhaps most, of the activities that are criminally prohibited in the *AHRA* could safely be decriminalized and regulated.[116] But, absent the criminal law, there is no legitimate way for the federal government to retain any regulatory presence in the context of assisted reproduction. To date, the only province that regulates ART practice is Quebec.[117] Other provinces have considered regulating, but none have taken steps to implement a regulatory scheme.[118] In practical terms, if the federal government repeals the prohibitions around paid surrogacy, the result will be an almost completely unrestricted market for surrogacy in Canada. Although I view the heavy-handed regulatory approach adopted in the *AHRA* to be unnecessary there is, as I have argued, strong justification for regulation and oversight of surrogacy, as a practice that touches on both health care and family law.

Health Canada is currently contemplating updating and clarifying some aspects of the *AHRA* through the development of regulations.[119] The importance of this timing is difficult to overstate—apart from repealing numerous sections of the *AHRA* after the Supreme Court stated that most of the Act was *ultra vires* Parliament, the federal government has taken no steps in respect of the *AHRA* in the thirteen years since it was enacted.[120] The time to suggest a significant overhaul to the regulation of surrogacy in Canada is now.

---

116 For a discussion of the effect of Canada's current law on embryo and ART research, see Ubaka Ogbogu, "Genetics and the Law" in Erdman, Gruben, & Nelson, eds, *Canadian Health Law and Policy*, above note 80, 281 at 285–87.

117 Above note 27.

118 See, for example, University of Alberta Health Technology and Policy Unit, *Assisted Reproductive Technologies (ARTs): Final Report* (Edmonton: Alberta Health Technologies Decision Process, 2014); Shannon O'Neill & Jeff Blackmer, *Assisted Reproduction in Canada: An Overview of Ethical and Legal Issues and Recommendations for the Development of National Standards* (Ottawa: Canadian Medical Association, 2015); Ontario Ministry of Health and Long-Term Care, Advisory Process for Infertility Services, *Advisory Process for Infertility Services Key Recommendations Report* (Toronto: Ministry of Health and Long-Term Care, 2015).

119 Health Canada, "Toward a Strengthened *Assisted Human Reproduction Act*: A Consultation with Canadians on Key Policy Proposals" (2017), online: www.canada.ca/en/health-canada/programs/consultation-assisted-human-reproduction/document.html.

120 *AHRA*, above note 18.

7

Desperately Seeking Surrogates

THOUGHTS ON CANADA'S EMERGENCE AS AN INTERNATIONAL SURROGACY DESTINATION

Karen Busby & Pamela M White

A. SEEKING SURROGATES

As most countries have laws restricting or prohibiting surrogacy, participants in surrogacy arrangements can be caught up in a legal tango. Applicable legal regimes may include those of the jurisdiction where a surrogate or the intended parents reside and where a surrogate-born baby is delivered. At play are immigration and citizenship rules; criminal, family, and parentage law; and assisted reproduction legislation and professional guidelines, especially those governing sperm donation, egg retrieval, and the creation, evaluation, manipulation, donation, and implantation of embryos. Moreover, as assisted reproduction laws are frequently under legislative review, participants may find that a carefully developed plan is no longer feasible.

Even though many countries prohibit in-country surrogacy, only a small number of jurisdictions, including Turkey and New South Wales, expressly prohibit their residents from engaging in cross-border surrogacy. The Canadian *Assisted Human Reproduction Act* (*AHRA*) prohibits or restricts various assisted reproduction activities but, as this Act is not expressly stated to have extraterritorial effect, it applies only to activities engaged in within Canada's borders.[1] As most restrictive or prohibitive

1 SC 2004, c 2 [*AHRA*]. On extraterritoriality see, for example, Erin Nelson, "Global Trade and Assisted Reproductive Technologies: Regulatory Challenges in International

assisted reproduction laws do not have extraterritorial effect, people seeking to expand their families through surrogacy or gamete donation are free to figure out which combination of legal regimes is most helpful and then access care in those jurisdictions.

Intended parents always need to keep in mind status laws (especially regarding parentage and citizenship) in their country of residence to ensure that children born offshore to a surrogate do not end up either parentless or stateless by virtue of incompatible legal regimes.[2] If the intended parents and surrogate both reside in one of the twenty-six European countries that have signed the Schengen Agreement, the child can cross national borders without a passport, thereby obviating the need for immediate determination of status.[3] Otherwise, for example, a gay couple needs to find a surrogate who will give birth in a jurisdiction that will recognize the couple's parentage. Some would-be parents may want to ensure that the child will be a particular sex or that the embryo carries, or does not carry, certain genetic traits. Some intended parents will calculate whether, for example, lower medical costs or lax approaches to the number of embryo transfers in one jurisdiction are worth the trouble of that jurisdiction's slower and less certain status determinations.[4] Intended parents for whom cost is not a deterrent will look for surrogacy regimes that allow them to pay surrogates or, at least, have some loopholes, making it easier to find willing participants.

It has been estimated that, by 2012, as many as 25,000 babies were born to surrogates in India and that half of these babies ended up in Western countries.[5] Researchers have voiced concerns about the potential for social injustice and exploitation when North Americans, Europeans, and Australians obtain surrogacy services from women living in low-income countries,

Surrogacy" (2013) 41 *Journal of Law, Medicine and Ethics* 240; Sharon Bassan, "Shared Responsibility Regulation Model for Cross-Border Reproductive Transactions" (2016) 37 *Michigan Journal of International Law* 299.

2 See Stefanie Carsley, "DNA, Donor Offspring and Derivative Citizenship: Redefining Parentage Under the *Citizenship Act*" (2016) 39 *Dalhousie Law Journal* 525.

3 See Laurence Brunet et al, *A Comparative Study on the Regime of Surrogacy in EU Member States* (European Parliament, 2013) at para 3.1.2.2, online: www.europarl.europa.eu/RegData/etudes/STUD/2013/474403/IPOL-JURI_ET(2013)474403_EN.pdf.

4 See Families Through Surrogacy's website for examples of the legal and medical considerations being contemplated by intended parents choosing surrogacy, online: www.familiesthrusurrogacy.com/surrogacy-by-country and www.familiesthrusurrogacy.com/agency-ratings.

5 Priya Shetty, "India's Unregulated Surrogacy Industry" (2012) 380 *The Lancet* 1633.

especially those in the Global South.[6] Particularly troubling were findings that fertility clinics denied surrogates decisional autonomy and other basic rights, took advantage of their illiteracy and economic vulnerability, and provided poor post-natal health care. Recently, Mexico (Tabasco) as well as most of the South and Southeast Asian countries (India, Thailand, Cambodia, Nepal) that were once destinations for those seeking surrogates have responded to these concerns by, effectively, prohibiting international surrogacy.[7]

Yet reproductive activities have proven to be economically footloose and adaptable. As once-robust destinations close down, others open up. California and Canada appear to have emerged as preferred jurisdictions for those seeking surrogates outside their home country. In California, where commercial surrogacy is legal regardless of the marital status or sexual orientation of the intended parents and pre-birth parental contracts are binding, 44 percent of gestational surrogate *in vitro* fertilization (IVF) treatment cycles in 2015 were undertaken on behalf of international intended parents. Information obtained from the BC Vital Statistics Agency

6 One of the first large empirical studies on surrogates in India was Ranjana Kumari, "Final Report: Surrogate Motherhood — Ethical or Commercial" (2012), online Centre for Social Research drive.google.com/file/d/0B-f1XIdg1JC_Uio4RmlYUkNsTFE/view. More recent book-length empirical studies include Amrita Pande, *Wombs in Labor: Transnational Commercial Surrogacy in India* (New York: Columbia University Press, 2014) and Sharmila Rudrappa, *Discounted Life: The Price of Global Surrogacy in India* (New York: New York University Press, 2015).

7 Regarding India, Thailand, Cambodia, Nepal, and Mexico, see, respectively, Government of India, Ministry for Home Affairs (Foreigners Division), "Circular No 462, Re: Foreign Nationals [Including Overseas Citizens of India (OCI) cardholders] Intending to Visit India for Commissioning Surrogacy" (3 November 2015) [Circular No 462], online: www.mea.gov.in/images/attach/surrogacy03112016.pdf, directing that no visas should be issued to foreign nationals or permissions granted to OCIs to commission surrogacy in India and no exit permission should be granted to children born through surrogacy in India to foreign nationals and OCI cardholders; Jonathan Head, "Thailand Bans Commercial Surrogacy for Foreigners" *BBC News* (20 February 2015), online: www.bbc.com/news/world-asia-31546717; Lauren Crothers, "Cambodian Surrogacy Crackdown: Move to Reassure Pregnant Women and Families" *Guardian* (23 November 2016), online: www.theguardian.com/world/2016/nov/24/cambodian-surrogacy-crackdown-move-to-reassure-pregnant-women-and-families; Rachel Abrams, "Nepal Bans Surrogacy, Leaving Couples with Few Low-Cost Options" *New York Times* (2 May 2016), online: https://nyti.ms/2HLLLxH; Victoria Burnett, "As Mexican State Limits Surrogacy, Global System Is Further Strained" *New York Times* (23 March 2017), online: https://nyti.ms/2nJ9UKm.

indicates that more than one-third of all babies born to surrogates in 2015 were recorded on their birth registration form as the children of parents who did not live in Canada.[8] With the recent prohibitions on surrogacy in South and Southeast Asia, these numbers could rise dramatically.

We start this chapter by exploring why Canada is emerging—and being touted[9]—as an international surrogacy destination. We then consider whether Canadians should be concerned about this development. We ask whether the concerns about consent, distributive justice, exploitation, and commodification raised about reproductive medicine practices in the Global South apply now that Canada has emerged as a site of international reproductive offshoring. We then explore whether there are other reasons for Canadians to feel uneasy about international intended parents seeking surrogates in Canada, which leads into a discussion on whether Canada should introduce residency restrictions on surrogacy. We close by noting some research gaps and suggesting that Canadian lawmakers consider prohibiting international surrogacy in Canada or, at least, level the playing field between international and local surrogacy by permitting surrogates to be paid a fee by Canadian intended parents.

B. WHY HAS CANADA BECOME AN INTERNATIONAL SURROGACY DESTINATION?

Most jurisdictions prohibit all forms of surrogacy within their borders. Canada is among the small number of jurisdictions that allow non-residents to participate in surrogacy. (Other permissive jurisdictions include Greece, Ukraine, Russia, Georgia, Kenya, and some US states.) Other surrogacy-permitting jurisdictions, including India, Israel, South Africa, the United Kingdom, and some American and Australian states, restrict the availability of surrogacy to citizens, resident nationals, state residents, or those having domicile.

Canadian law also confers various status advantages that draw to this country those seeking to become parents via surrogacy. It robustly prohibits

8 Pamela M White, "Canada's Surrogacy Landscape Is Changing: Should Canadians Care?" (2017) 39:11 *Journal of Obstetrics and Gynecology Canada* 1046, online: www.jogc.com/article/S1701-2163(17)30575-3/fulltext.

9 Families Through Surrogacy, above note 4, online: www.familiesthrusurrogacy.com/surrogacy-by-country.

discrimination based on sexual orientation or marital status. Queer people or those who are not in a marriage-like relationship cannot be denied the ability to enter a surrogacy arrangement and can be legally recognized as parents. Additionally, many Canadian provinces have implemented speedy parentage-determination processes.[10] Once intended parents are named as parents on the child's birth certificate, a Canadian passport can be issued, and, in most cases, depending on the laws of the country of domicile, the new family can return home. Every child born in Canada is automatically a Canadian citizen, a status many prospective parents would consider desirable.[11]

Some intended parents desire multiple embryo implants or want to ensure that their children are of a particular sex or have, or do not have, certain genetic traits. As Canadian law on the use and manipulation of gametes and embryos is quite conservative, Canadians travel to the United States to take advantage of permissive reproductive practices in many American states.[12] Those participating in surrogacy who seek less regulatory oversight or who desire more radical interventions can simply ask the potential surrogate to cross the border into the United States to have IVF performed following sex selection or pre-implantation genetic testing. Nearly two-thirds of Canadians live within a one-hour drive of the Canada–US border and most passport-holding Canadians can cross this border with ease. Between 2006 and 2013, Canadian residents were the most numerous non-US resident group to obtain treatments such as donor oocytes, pre-implantation genetic diagnosis and screening, and intra-cytoplasmic sperm injection. Canadian intended parents were the fourth most numerous group after those from the People's Republic of China, France, and the United Kingdom to have treatments involving gestational surrogacy

10 Karen Busby, "Of Surrogate Mother Born: Parentage Determinations in Canada and Elsewhere" (2013) 25 *Canadian Journal of Women and the Law* 284 [Busby, "Of Surrogate Mother Born"]. Quebec is more restrictive than the other provinces; see Régine Tremblay, "Surrogates in Quebec: The Good, the Bad and the Foreigner" (2015) 27 *Canadian Journal of Women and the Law* 94.

11 See Lyndsie Bourgon, "Why Women Are Coming to Canada Just to Give Birth" *Maclean's* (8 August 2017), online: www.macleans.ca/society/health/why-women-are-coming-to-canada-just-to-give-birth; Justin Bachman, "The Most Desirable Passports on Earth Don't Include America's" *Bloomberg* (3 March 2017), online: www.bloomberg.com/news/articles/2017-03-03/the-most-desirable-passports-on-earth-don-t-include-america.

12 Edward G Hughes & Denise DeJean, "Cross-Border Fertility Services in North America: A Survey of Canadian and American Providers" (2010) 94 *Fertility and Sterility* e16.

in the United States.[13] The attractiveness of Canada's proximity to the United States, where it is possible to obtain a greater range of reproductive services, coupled with Canada's price advantage (discussed below) have become significant components of what promoters are calling the "blended Canada/US surrogacy option."[14]

International intended parents can realize significant financial advantages in Canada. Canadian women and the children they bear are entitled to access publicly funded prenatal, delivery, and post-natal care, and surrogates' fertility treatments are partially funded in some provinces.[15] No province has laws expressly requiring or facilitating recovery of publicly funded health care costs related to surrogates' fertility treatments, pregnancy, delivery, or post-natal care from international intended parents. There is no information online from governments in any province or territory about recovery of the newborn child's health care costs, although media have reported on a case where the foreign intended parents left Canada with unpaid medical bills and the hospital sought to make the Canadian surrogate pay for care received by the sickly baby.[16] An extensive internet search supports the observation that provincial policies (including those of health authorities) for the recovery of infant care costs are poorly publicized and may be uncommon.[17] It is not clear how such policies, if they exist, are enforced against intended parents once they have left the country.

---

13 Aaron D Levine et al, "Assessing the Use of Assisted Reproductive Technology in the United States by Non–United States Residents" (2017) 108:5 *Fertility and Sterility* 815 (Table 3), online: https://doi.org/10.1016/j.fertnstert.2017.07.1168.

14 Families Through Surrogacy, above note 4, online: www.familiesthrusurrogacy.com/surrogacy-by-country.

15 Ontario funds IVF and AI for surrogates but keeps no records on the number of surrogates obtaining treatment under the Ontario Fertility Program. FOI request A-2017-00-00166 made by Pamela M White to Ontario Ministry of Health and Long-Term Care (1 September 2017).

16 Tom Blackwell, "Canadian Surrogates Get Hefty Bills as Hospitals Start Charging When Babies Heading to Foreign Parents" *National Post* (21 February 2013), online: http://nationalpost.com/news/canada/ontario-surrogate-gets-1400-bill-after-giving-birth-as-hospitals-start-charging-third-party-carriers-for-post-natal-care.

17 We found only two such policies: Quinte Hospital Surrogacy Policy, online: http://policyandorders.cw.bc.ca/resource-gallery/Documents/BC%20Women%27s%20Hospital%20-%20Fetal%20Maternal%20Newborn/WW.07.19%20Surrogacy%20Policy.pdf; and BC Women's Hospital, online: http://policyandorders.cw.bc.ca/resource-gallery/Documents/BC%20Women%27s%20Hospital%20-%20Fetal%20Maternal%20Newborn/Surrogacy%20Policy-WW.07.19-Sep-27-2016.pdf.

Nonetheless, some agencies and lawyers now advise their clients that they may be responsible for the newborn's health care expenses.

Most Canadian women who are employed at the time they become pregnant, including surrogates, are entitled to partial reimbursement of the income lost during confinement and post-delivery through the national employment insurance regime.[18] Such payments can reduce the amount of lost income for which intended parents may need to reimburse a surrogate. As well, the value of the Canadian dollar is low compared to the US dollar. This further reduces expenses associated with surrogacy, including the surrogate's reimbursable expenses, legal and IVF costs incurred in Canada, and the intended parents' travel and post-birth living expenses.

It is a criminal offence for anyone to pay or offer to pay a fee to a surrogate in Canada. However, Canadian law does not criminalize payment of the surrogacy-facilitating service provider, and this business activity is permitted as long it does not actively recruit surrogates.[19] Canada's well-established information and support networks for surrogates, clinics, agencies, and lawyers stretch across the country. These networks help ensure that surrogates are identifiable and healthy and that they and intended parents are well matched and properly informed. Increasingly, social media is used to link up, from around the world, surrogates, intended parents, and facilitating agencies to share experiences and to exchange information about treatment options.[20] It is not uncommon for a would-be Canadian surrogate to review numerous requests before making the decision that she and the intended parents are a good match.[21]

18 Canada, "EI Maternity and Parental Benefits: Overview," online: www.canada.ca/en/services/benefits/ei/ei-maternity-parental.html. The very first line in this online overview notes that "EI [Employment Insurance] maternity benefits are offered to biological mothers, including surrogate mothers, who cannot work because they are pregnant or have recently given birth."

19 Erin Nelson, *Law, Policy and Reproductive Autonomy* (Oxford: Hart, 2013) ch 6.

20 Emily Jackson et al, "Learning from Cross-Border Reproduction" (2017) 25 *Medical Law Review* 23 at 29. See the study of SMO, the largest moderated US public surrogacy site, which examines what surrogates say about their expectations, experiences, matching processes, and relationships with intended parents: Zsuzsa Berend, "The Romance of Surrogacy" (2012) 27 *Sociological Forum* 913.

21 Denise Balkissoon, "It's Illegal to Pay a Surrogate Mother in Canada: So What Would Motivate a Woman to Do It?" *Globe and Mail* (12 February 2015), online: www.theglobeandmail.com/life/parenting/an-inside-look-at-the-difficult-process-of-surrogacy/article22953150.

While there are no data on the number of Canadian women willing to act as altruistic surrogates, it is probably safe to conclude this number does not meet domestic, much less international, demand. Indeed, news articles documenting the searches made by intended parents seeking surrogates[22] and websites[23] devoted to matching surrogates and intended parents attest to the unmet wants of domestic and international intended parents.

We have reason to believe, from anecdotal evidence, that some Canadian surrogates are receiving compensation. Media stories support this observation[24] as do other sources. For example, in a case on spousal support, a husband alleged that his wife was being paid to be a surrogate. The court found that monthly payments of $1,950 were reimbursement for expenses, and not income, even though no receipts or reports were required to establish the amounts owing.[25] Academics conducting empirical research in Canada have avoided asking surrogacy participants about payments for either permissible expense reimbursement or prohibited fee-like compensation because such questions are ethically fraught. However, some researchers believe that, or know of specific instances in which, compensatory payments are being made by non-Canadian intended parents, thus encouraging Canadian women to become surrogates for foreigners rather than for Canadians.[26] Canadian criminal law does not apply to extraterritorial acts, so, as long as payments

22 Tom Blackwell, "Health Canada All but Ignores Illegal Ad for Surrogate, Cash for Egg Donors, Internal Documents Reveal" *National Post* (13 December 2015), online: http://nationalpost.com/wcm/d369b3ec-1d7f-46df-ac5d-ad3e63464a4b; Patricia Kozicka, "Surrogacy in Canada: What You Need to Know" *Global News* (12 August 2016), online: http://globalnews.ca/news/2879259/surrogacy-in-canada-what-you-need-to-know.

23 See the following selection of websites used by intended parents seeking surrogates: https://ivf.ca/forums/page/donor/_/surroip; www.surrogatefinder.com/surrogate_couples/Canada/Ontario/Toronto; https://surrogacy.ca/services/intended-parents.html; and www.findsurrogatemother.com/intended-parents/canada/toronto.

24 CBC News, "Paid Surrogacy Driven Underground: CBC Report" *CBC News* (1 May 2007), online: www.cbc.ca/news/technology/paid-surrogacy-driven-underground-in-canada-cbc-report-1.691254.

25 *JR v CR*, 2015 BCPC 54.

26 Many of the researchers who attended the Surrogacy in Canada: Critical Perspectives Workshop held 16–18 May 2017 at the University of Ottawa Faculty of Law [Surrogacy in Canada Workshop], which was the catalyst for this edited collection, indicated that they knew of instances where such payments had been made. Researchers working on qualitative research — work that has not yet been published — also said that they avoid the ethical quandaries inherent in getting information about possibly illegal activities by not asking questions about money during the formal interview.

are made outside of Canada, an argument can be made that no Canadian law has been violated.[27] Complicating the matter is the long-standing Canadian government policy to facilitate the issuance of passports to children born offshore to surrogates for intended Canadian parents. This practice has occurred in spite of the fact that almost all of these offshore arrangements involve a fee for surrogacy services and therefore would have been criminally prohibited had the arrangement been executed in Canada.[28]

In sum, factors contributing to Canada's emergence as a destination for non-Canadians hoping to become parents through surrogacy include the following: laws allowing non-Canadians to participate in altruistic surrogacy; laws prohibiting discrimination on the basis of sexual orientation or marital status and facilitating recognition of parentage and granting citizenship; proximity to the United States, which allows easy access to a range of reproductive technologies; various financial advantages, especially access to publicly funded health care and income recovery; and the availability of informed and interested potential surrogates and networks of support. Given these advantages and the lack of other options, especially following the shutdown of international surrogacy in most of South and Southeast Asia, the attraction of Canada as an international surrogacy hub is likely to grow.

C. IS THE INTERNATIONAL DEMAND FOR CANADIAN SURROGATES TROUBLING?

When serious ethical issues started to emerge in the early 1980s related to assisted reproduction, especially surrogacy, Canadians received conflicting advice from policy bodies. The Ontario Law Reform Commission advised in 1985 that regulation of commercial surrogacy by provinces (who have jurisdiction over family status, contracts, and regulation of health care professionals) would best protect the interests of those touched

27 Susan G Drummond & Sara R Cohen, "Eloquent (In)Action: Enforcement and Prosecutorial Restraint in the Transnational Trade in Human Eggs as Deep Ambivalence About the Law" (2014) 26 *Canadian Journal of Women and the Law* 206. *Contra* Jocelyn Downie & Françoise Baylis, "Transnational Trade in Human Eggs: Policy, Law and (In)Action in Canada" (2013) 41 *Journal of Law, Medicine and Ethics* 224.

28 Kristin Lozanski, "Transnational Surrogacy: Canada's Contradictions" (2015) 124 *Social Science and Medicine* 383.

by surrogacy.[29] The commission cautioned against relying on prohibition and criminalization as the dominant responses to assisted reproduction, especially surrogacy. In contrast, almost a decade later, the Royal Commission on New Reproductive Technologies recommended that the federal government criminally prohibit all surrogacy and that provinces make surrogacy arrangements unenforceable.[30] The royal commission was deeply influenced by and reflected feminist thinking of the time. It opined that women could not give meaningful consent to surrender prior to the delivery of a child and that surrogacy was exploitative of vulnerable women and commodified the bodies of women and the children they carried. It also voiced concerns about the alteration to normative family structures that assisted reproductive technology would bring.[31] The federal government ultimately pursued a middle ground, criminalizing commercial surrogacy but permitting altruistic surrogacy.[32] While article 541 of the Quebec *Civil Code* affirms the absolute nullity of surrogacy agreements, other Canadian provinces have revised their parentage laws to accommodate surrogacy, or courts, including Quebec courts, have stepped in to fill the legislative gaps. [33] However, few steps have been taken in any province toward regulating surrogacy arrangements, including setting terms, such as a requirement for independent medical or legal advice;[34] developing health care practices,

29 Ontario Law Reform Commission, *Report on Human Artificial Reproduction and Related Matters* (Toronto: Ontario Law Reform Commission, 1985) at 102, online: www.ontla.on.ca/library/repository/mon/27010/40633-1.pdf.

30 Dave Snow, "Criminalizing Commercial Surrogacy in Canada and Australia: The Political Construction of 'National Consensus'" (2016) 51 *Australian Journal of Political Science* 1 at 4.

31 Royal Commission on New Reproductive Technologies, *Proceed with Care: Final Report of the Royal Commission on New Reproductive Technologies* (Ottawa: Minister of Government Services Canada, 1993) vol 1 at 42–44.

32 *AHRA*, above note 1, ss 6(1) and 12(2).

33 See Tremblay, above note 10; Busby, "Of Surrogate Mother Born," above note 10.

34 A notable exception is Ontario, *All Families Are Equal Act (Parentage and Related Registrations Statute Law Amendment)*, SO 2016, c 23, which requires that the parties obtain independent legal advice before entering into a surrogacy agreement. Both Ontario and Quebec have placed limits on the number of embryos that should be transferred. In 2016, the Ontario Fertility Program funding IVF established that one embryo was to be transferred per funded cycle. See online: www.ontario.ca/page/get-fertility-treatments. In Quebec, see *An Act Respecting Clinical and Research Activities Relating to Assisted Procreation*, CQLR c A-5.01, s 10.3, which states: "In the course of an *in vitro* fertilization activity, only one embryo may be transferred into a

such as restricting the number of embryos that can be implanted or requiring reporting on activities;[35] or pursuing cost recovery from international intended parents. We find these regulatory gaps deeply troubling.

Little qualitative or quantitative research has yet been published in peer-reviewed journals on the experiences of those involved in surrogacy in Canada.[36] However, research conducted in the United States and the United Kingdom demonstrates that fears about the exploitative nature of surrogacy that so preoccupied policy-makers, legislators, and ethicists in the 1980s and 1990s have proven to be largely unfounded.[37] Systematic

woman. However, taking into account the quality of embryos, a physician may decide to transfer two embryos if the woman is 37 years of age or over. The reasons for the decision must be entered in the woman's medical record." This requirement was first put in place in 2015 by Bill 20, SQ 2015, c 25, s 3.

35 Embryo transfer guidelines have been developed: Jason Min & Camille Sylvestre, *Guidelines on the Number of Embryos to Transfer* (Montreal: Canadian Fertility and Andrology Society, 2013). Research indicates that embryo transfer guidelines are not always being followed when the patient is a gestational surrogate. Research by Pamela M White, "'One for Sorrow, Two for Joy?' American Embryo Transfer Guideline Recommendations, Practices and Outcomes for Gestational Surrogate Patients" (2017) 34 *Journal of Assisted Reproduction and Genetics* 431; Pamela M White, "Commercialization, Altruism, Clinical Practice: What Explains Similarities and Differences in Californian and Canadian Gestational Surrogacy Outcomes" *Women's Health Issues*, online: https://doi.org/10.1016/j.whi.2018.01.004, shows that, while single embryo transfer has increased, it is less likely to occur for surrogates and when donor oocyte embryos are used. Lawyers practising in this area advise that, as provinces move to recover the health care costs of surrogates and newborns, intended parents will not be able to obtain insurance coverage for multiple births and therefore will seek only single embryo transfers.

36 See Surrogacy in Canada Workshop, above note 26. We are aware of only a few published studies: Shir Dar et al, "Assisted Reproduction Involving Gestational Surrogacy: An Analysis of the Medical, Psychosocial and Legal Issues — Experience from a Large Surrogacy Program" (2015) 30:2 *Human Reproduction* 345; Pamela M White, "Hidden from View: Canadian Gestational Surrogacy Practices and Outcomes, 2001–2012" (2016) 24 *Reproductive Health Matters* 205; Stu Marvel et al, "Listening to LGBTQ People on Assisted Human Reproduction: Access to Reproductive Material, Services, and Facilities" in Trudo Lemmens et al, eds, *Regulating Creation: The Law, Ethics, and Policy of Assisted Human Reproduction* (Toronto: University of Toronto Press, 2016) ch 13; Sophia Fantus, "The Path to Parenthood Isn't Always Straight: A Qualitative Exploration of the Experiences of Gestational Surrogacy for Gay Men in Canada — Perspectives of Gay Fathers and Surrogates" (PhD Thesis, University of Toronto, Faculty of Social Work, 2017) [unpublished], online: https://tspace.library.utoronto.ca/handle/1807/80680.

37 Berend, "The Romance of Surrogacy," above note 20; Zsuzsa Berend, "'We Are All Carrying Someone Else's Child': Relatedness and Relationships in Third-Party

meta-reviews and empirical studies of surrogacy practices and outcomes reveal that, overall, the experience has been positive for almost all participants in these two countries; nothing in the research supports the assertion that surrogates are being exploited or that they change their minds about surrendering the child after birth.[38] While there are some media stories on surrogacy gone wrong in Canada,[39] these accounts are few and far between. Evidence obtained from longitudinal studies examining relationships among UK surrogates, intended parents, and surrogate-born children reveals the development of strong familial ties and positive outcomes.[40] While research on queer families created through surrogacy and assisted reproduction has been less common, the findings generally reveal positive results for all participants.[41] Many Canadians have come to view surrogacy as a legitimate way to create families. A 2012 Canadian survey indicates that 40 percent of childless men and 25 percent of childless women would use surrogacy if they were unable to have a biological child.[42]

Reproduction" (2016) 118 *American Anthropologist* 24; Marcin Smietana, "Affective De-Commodifying, Economic De-Kinning: Surrogates' and Gay Fathers' Narratives in US Surrogacy" (2017) 22 *Sociological Research Online* 5.

38 Karen Busby & Delaney Vun, "Revisiting *The Handmaid's Tale*: Feminist Theory Meets Empirical Research on Surrogate Mothers" (2010) 26 *Canadian Journal of Family Law* 13; Angela Campbell, "Law's Suppositions About Surrogacy Against the Backdrop of Social Science" (2012) 43 *Ottawa Law Review* 29; Viveca Söderström-Anttila et al, "Surrogacy: Outcomes for Surrogate Mothers, Children and the Resulting Families — A Systematic Review" (2016) 22 *Human Reproduction Update* 260; Anna Maria Tallandini et al, "Parental Disclosure of Assisted Reproductive Technology (ART) Conception to Their Children: A Systematic and Meta-Analytic Review" (2016) 31 *Human Reproduction* 1275. Berend, "The Romance of Surrogacy," above note 20 and "'We Are All Carrying Someone Else's Child,'" above note 37.

39 See, for example, Cynthia Vukets, "Surrogate Mother's Nightmare" *Toronto Star* (9 September 2011), online: www.thestar.com/news/canada/2011/09/09/surrogate_mothers_nightmare.html.

40 See, for example, Vasanti Jadva et al, "Surrogates and Intended Parents in the UK" (2016) 4 *Journal of Medical Law and Ethics* 215; Jennifer Readings et al, "Secrecy, Disclosure and Everything In-Between: Decisions of Parents of Children Conceived by Donor Insemination, Egg Donation and Surrogacy" (2011) 22 *Reproductive Biomedicine Online* 485.

41 See, for example, Marvel et al, above note 36, and Lucy Blake et al, "Gay Father Surrogacy Families: Relationships with Surrogates and Egg Donors and Parental Disclosure of Children's Origins" (2016) 106 *Fertility and Sterility* 1503.

42 Judith C Daniluk & Emily Koert, "Childless Canadian Men's and Women's Childbearing Intentions, Attitudes Towards and Willingness to Use Assisted Human Reproduction" (2012) 27 *Human Reproduction* 2405.

One of Canada's significant debates about surrogacy turns on differing views about the moral evil and social harm of paid surrogacy. When the *AHRA* was passed in 2004, prohibition of commercial surrogacy was consistent with other national narratives about the benefits of publicly funded health care, fears about commercialization and trade in the reproductive capabilities of women and men, and a "desire to avoid 'American style' social policy."[43] Canadians were opposed to the commodification of the human body, choosing instead to privilege the altruistic donation of organs, blood, and blood products. However, Canada's altruistic surrogacy regime has developed into a regime that ambivalently straddles a commercial/non-commercial divide.[44] All those involved, with the exception of the surrogate, receive payment for their services: IVF clinicians, counsellors, legal advisers, and surrogacy agency facilitators.

In our view, conceptualizing surrogacy as the delivery of a good rather than the provision of a service creates yet another justification for under-compensating women's labour.[45] Furthermore, the notion that exploitation is reserved for those paid as surrogates fails to recognize that the way surrogacy is undertaken can contribute to or reduce whether it is harmful. For example, if altruistic surrogates lack information on which to base decisions, if treatments are not tailored to their specific medical needs, and if arrangements fail to recognize the satisfaction they may derive from the service they provide, they may experience harm.[46] Reimbursement for expenses versus compensation for the service is not the feature defining exploitation, though it can be argued convincingly that it is exploitative to prevent a surrogate from receiving compensation when all other actors in the process are paid.

Canadian law is premised on the assumption that commercial surrogacy is more harmful than altruistic surrogacy, but research conducted

43 Jenni Millbank, "Rethinking 'Commercial' Surrogacy in Australia" (2015) 12 *Journal of Bioethical Inquiry* 477; Snow, above note 30.

44 Millbank, above note 43 at 480.

45 Julie Shapiro, "For a Feminist Considering Surrogacy, Is Compensation Really the Key Question?" (2014) 89 *Washington Law Review* 1345 at 1392; Louise Langevin, "Réponse jurisprudentielle à la pratique des mères porteuses au Québec: une difficile réconciliation" (2010) 26 *Canadian Journal of Family Law* 171 at paras 30–38.

46 Alana Cattapan, "Risky Business: Surrogacy, Egg Donation and the Politics of Exploitation" (2014) 29 *Canadian Journal of Law and Society* 361. See also Nelson, Chapter 6, this volume.

in Western countries provides no support for this premise. In the United States, for example, payment for surrogacy does not appear to pressure women who are in financial need into the practice. Findings show that surrogates are middle class, married, and college educated.[47] Indeed, American fertility clinics screen out women who undertake the activity solely for financial reasons.[48] As numerous study findings reveal, surrogates are motivated by altruism, not payment, and what matters most to many surrogates is the quality of the relationship with intended parents during the pregnancy and the sense that their role was valued.[49]

By contrast, empirical findings from research on paid surrogacy in India have highlighted how advanced reproductive technologies and rising Western demand for infertility treatment amplified global inequalities, reinforced neo-colonialism, and supported existing gendered conditions.[50] Indian surrogates, for example, had little to no legal protection and operated from a position of disadvantage due to their illiteracy, financial and physical vulnerability, and lack of effective bargaining power.[51] Researchers

47 Smietana, above note 37 at paras 6.2–6.6.

48 Practice Committee of the Society for Assisted Reproductive Technology and the American Society for Reproductive Medicine, "Recommendations for Practices Utilizing Gestational Carriers: A Committee Opinion" (2015) 103 *Fertility and Sterility* e1.

49 See, for example, Melinda M Hohman & Christine B Hagan, "Satisfaction with Surrogate Mothering: A Relational Model" (2001) 4 *Journal of Human Behavior in the Social Environment* 61; Fiona MacCallum et al, "Surrogacy: The Experience of Commissioning Couples" (2003) 18 *Human Reproduction* 1334; Janice C Ciccarelli & Linda J Beckman, "Navigating Rough Waters: An Overview of Psychological Aspects of Surrogacy" (2005) 61 *Journal of Social Issues* 21; Susan Imrie & Vasanti Jadva, "The Long-Term Experiences of Surrogates: Relationships and Contact with Surrogacy Families in Genetic and Gestational Surrogacy Arrangements" (2014) 29 *Reproductive BioMedicine Online* 424; and Berend, "The Romance of Surrogacy," above note 20 and "'We Are All Carrying Someone Else's Child,'" above note 37. For comprehensive reviews of empirical studies on the experiences of surrogates, intended parents, and surrogate-born children, see Busby & Vun, above note 38; Campbell, above note 38; Söderström-Anttila et al, above note 38; and Tallandini, above note 38.

50 See, for example, France Winddance Twine, *Outsourcing the Womb*, 2d ed (London: Routledge, 2015); Generations Ahead, "A Reproductive Justice Analysis of Genetic Technologies: Report of a National Convening of Women of Colour and Indigenous Women" in Miranda Davies, ed, *Babies for Sale? Transnational Surrogacy, Human Rights and the Politics of Reproduction* (London: Zed Books, 2017) at 276; and Maneesha Deckha, "Situating Canada's Commercial Surrogacy Ban in a Transnational Context: A Postcolonial Feminist Call for Legalization and Public Funding" (2015) 61 *McGill Law Journal* 31 at 54.

51 See, generally, Kumari, above note 6; Pande, above note 6; and Rudrappa, above note 6.

critical of the paid surrogacy arrangements undertaken in India identified the unfair advantage that Western intended parents had relative to the local surrogate, although others argued that there is a difference between harmful exploitation and mutually advantageous exploitation, a situation where both parties benefit.[52]

These images of cross-border surrogacy have the power to conjure up negative thinking about its emergence in Canada. But if we pay close attention to the lessons learned from research on cross-border surrogacy experiences, we find that the commercial nature of the practice is not necessarily its most exploitative component. More important issues include ensuring surrogates have the ability to give informed and voluntary consent, to exercise agency in decision making, and to develop a meaningful relationship with the intended parents that is reciprocated in a mutually acceptable manner. Once exploitation is understood in this context, the dichotomy between paid and altruistic surrogacy becomes a false one, especially when it revolves around notions of a "fair amount" and whether the amount exerts a coercive influence on surrogate participation. Given the large sums being demanded by others involved in the fertility treatment business, it does seem hypocritical to demand minimal or no financial compensation to surrogates when all of the other players reap substantial rewards, often at public expense.[53]

The argument that financial compensation is exploitative is difficult to sustain in the context of North American surrogacy. Non-payment and reliance on altruistic surrogacy is also a "risky business" that includes exploitative opportunities.[54] Harmful practices have the potential to render surrogacy practices exploitative regardless of the altruistic/commercial regime. These practices may include enforceable pre-birth contracts; restrictive and prescriptive behavioural requirements used to control surrogate conduct during pre-pregnancy and prenatal periods; and non-compliance with fertility treatment guidelines regarding access to independent medical advice, single embryo transfer, and consent to medical treatment.[55]

52 Alan Wertheimer, *Exploitation* (Princeton, NJ: Princeton University Press, 1996) ch 4.

53 Millbank, above note 43 at 482; Langevin, above note 45 paras 30–38.

54 Cattapan, above note 46 at 365–66.

55 On these practices, see Hillary Berk, "The Legalization of Emotion: Managing Risk by Managing Feelings in Contracts for Surrogate Labor" (2015) 49 *Law and Society Review* 143. However, compare Dan R Reilly, "Surrogate Pregnancy: A Guide for Canadian Prenatal Health Care Providers" (2007) 176 *Canadian Medical Association Journal* 483 at 484; Jon Havelock et al, *Guidelines for Third Party Reproduction* (Montreal:

Problems with the current federal and provincial legal regimes governing surrogacy, including the lack of regulatory attention to how fertility medicine is practised, and uneven provincial family law have greater potential than payment to harm surrogates and children born to them. Failure to permit compensation for surrogacy services places a surrogate in an unenviable and unfair situation where she is the only service provider in the chain of interventions not permitted to accept consideration. It is against this backdrop that we examine how other countries have used law and policy to deter and prevent non-residents from accessing surrogacy services. We then explore whether Canada should seek self-sufficiency in surrogacy services, noting that striving to meet domestic needs would also address the problem of Canadians going abroad for surrogacy services, a practice that often occurs in exploitative conditions.

D. SHOULD CANADA INTRODUCE RESIDENCY RESTRICTIONS?

1) A Comparison of Residency Restrictions in Other Countries

Some jurisdictions, including Israel, South Africa, the United Kingdom, India, and some states in the United States and Australia, permit surrogacy but restrict its availability to citizens or those who are domiciled or habitually resident in the jurisdiction. Methods used to enforce such prohibitions against non-resident participation in surrogacy include not only the threat of criminal sanctions, but also entry visa restrictions applicable to intended parents, screening out ineligible participants during pre-conception approval processes, prohibitions restricting clinics from attempting to achieve a pregnancy for surrogacy participants until approvals are received, exit restrictions applicable to surrogate-born children, and restrictions on the establishment of parentage. In this section, we examine the reasons articulated in these jurisdictions for non-resident prohibitions and then consider whether Canada should restrict or prohibit surrogacy arrangements involving international intended parents.

Canadian Fertility and Andrology Society, 2016) regarding access to independent medical advice; and Tom Blackwell, "Canadian Surrogate Eliminated Baby from Triplet Pregnancy at Urging of Overseas Couple" *National Post* (9 September 2015), online: http://nationalpost.com/health/canadian-surrogate-pressured-to-eliminate-baby-from-triplet-pregnancy-by-couple.

The 1996 Israeli *Agreements to Carry Embryos (Approval of Agreements and Status of the Newborn Child) Law* requires that all surrogacy agreements be approved by a committee before IVF is attempted. Agreements will be approved only for adults habitually resident in Israel.[56] According to one researcher,

> In light of the prohibition of such agreements in other countries and the possibility of forum shopping for a convenient jurisdiction, the Commission [charged with making recommendations on surrogacy law] recommended that the proposed statutory scheme should apply only if all the parties were residents of Israel and if the agreement was to be carried out in its entirety inside Israel. The intention was to eliminate the potential for reproductive tourism and to ensure that the statutory committee could fulfill its function as a supervisory mechanism to prevent mishaps in the performance of surrogacy agreements.[57]

The 2010 South African surrogacy law found in the *Children's Act No 38*, like the Israeli law, requires pre-conception approval by a committee; such agreements will be approved only between parties domiciled in the country unless there is a compelling reason not to follow this rule.[58] These restrictions were proposed by three different reports[59] and, according to one researcher,

> the domicile requirement is clearly an attempt to discourage international surrogacy and, especially, to avoid South Africa becoming a destination for reproductive tourism. It also precludes the parties from selecting a different legal system or court for the determination of any legal disputes that may arise in connection with the surrogate motherhood agreement. It is

56 Carmel Shalev, "Halakha and Patriarchal Motherhood: An Anatomy of the New Israeli Law" (1998) 32 *Israel Law Review* 51.

57 *Ibid*. See also Carmel Shalev, "Insights on the Report of the Commission in the Matter of In Vitro Fertilisation" (1995) 3 *HaMishpat* 53 [references omitted].

58 Jacqueline Heaton, "The Pitfalls of International Surrogacy: A South African Family Law Perspective" (2015) 78 *Journal of Contemporary Roman-Dutch Law* 24.

59 South African Law Reform Commission, *Report on Surrogate Motherhood*, Project 65 (Pretoria, SA: The Commission, 1993); Parliamentary Ad Hoc Select Committee on the Report of the South African Law Reform Commission on Surrogate Motherhood, *Draft Final Report* (October 1998); and South African Law Reform Commission, *Discussion Paper on the Report and Draft Children's Bill on the Review of the Child Care Act*, Project 110 Discussion Paper 103 (Pretoria, SA: The Commission, 2002).

> important to note that the domicile requirement applies at the time when the surrogate motherhood agreement is entered into. Thus, the agreement may not be concluded before the commissioning parent has established a domicile in South Africa.[60]

In the United Kingdom, a surrogate is the legal mother of the child she bears. Parentage can be legally transferred by means of a parental order or, in the case of a single intended parent, by adoption. However, only persons domiciled in the United Kingdom, the Isle of Man, or the Channel Islands can apply for a parental order under the *Human Fertilisation and Embryology Act 1990*.[61] The *Adoption and Children Act 2002*[62] prevents non–UK resident individuals from legally adopting a UK-born child. As a surrogate-born child cannot be removed from the jurisdiction unless a parental order or adoption has been granted, surrogacy is effectively restricted to permanent residents.[63] A 1997 legislative review of the *Surrogacy Arrangements Act 1985* determined that, contrary to previous expectations, research found positive relationships were being developed among UK-resident surrogates, intended parents, and surrogate-born children. Concern was expressed at that time that the United Kingdom might become a destination for surrogacy tourists, especially given that its European neighbours were taking steps to ban surrogacy. In recommending that stiffer residency restrictions be imposed, the Brazier Report commented:

60 Heaton, above note 58.

61 *Human Fertilisation and Embryology Act 1990* (UK), c 37, s 30; *Human Fertilisation and Embryology Act 2008* (UK), c 22, s 54. See judgment in *Re G (Surrogacy: Foreign Domicile)*, [2007] EWHC 2814 (Fam) [*Re G*], and Deborah Cullen, "Surrogacy: 'Commissioning' Parents Not Domiciled in UK — Matters to Be Borne in Mind by Those Contemplating Surrogacy Arrangements" (2008) 32:1 *Adoption and Fostering* 75.

62 *Adoption and Children Act 2002* (UK), c 38, ss 84 & 85. See *G (A Child) v C & Ors*, [2008] EWCA Civ 105 (CA) and Deborah Cullen, "Child Leaving Country for Purposes of Adoption: Interpretation of Section 84 *Adoption and Children Act* (ACA) 2002 and *Adoption with a Foreign Element Regulations 2005*" (2008) 32:1 *Adoption and Fostering* 76.

63 *In Re C (A minor) (Wardship: Surrogacy)*, [1985] FLR 846 (also known as the "Baby Cotton" case), which occurred prior to the *Surrogacy Arrangements Act (UK) 1985*. A child was born to a UK surrogate as a result of a commercial arrangement made with US intended parents. The UK court determined that it was in the best interests of the child to grant the intended parents wardship, thereby enabling them to take Kim Cotton to the United States. In *Re G*, above note 61, the court permitted a Turkish couple to return home with a surrogate-born child but cautioned that others in the future should not expect this outcome.

> It is important to note developments elsewhere in the European Union. There is … evidence of a growing number of commissioning couples from other countries seeking to find a surrogate in the United Kingdom. Transnational surrogacy arrangements pose special difficulties. Linguistic and cultural differences may impair understanding between the couple and the potential surrogate. Enlightening the child in later years on his or her origins may be more problematic. Couples with no connection with the United Kingdom cannot apply for a parental order. Agencies concerned with the welfare of the child may be unable to ensure that after the child is entrusted to the commissioning couple, adequate measures will be taken to ensure his or her legal status in the family once abroad.[64]

In India, administrative restrictions imposed by a November 2015 circular issued by the Ministry of Home Affairs effectively ban anyone other than a domiciled Indian citizen from engaging in surrogacy. The circular directs that visas not be issued to those seeking to commission surrogacy and that exit permission not be granted to children born through surrogacy to foreign nationals and non-domiciled Indian citizens.[65] If the *Surrogacy (Regulation) Bill 2016*, is passed, not only will the residency requirement be maintained but the bill will also restrict surrogacy to altruistic arrangements between family members domiciled in India. The 2016 bill came about because, according to government officials,

> the Indian government believes the ban will check unethical practices …. We are concerned about the health of the surrogate mother and that the legal and financial rights of the child are protected …. India wants to be on par with developed and developing nations that do not legitimise commercial surrogacy.[66]

Some Australian and US state laws also impose residency requirements. To prevent "regime shopping," legislators in the Australian Central

64 Margaret Brazier, Alastair Campbell, & Susan Golombok, *Surrogacy: Review for Health Ministers of Current Arrangements for Payments and Regulation* (London: Department of Health, 1997) at 27 online: http://webarchive.nationalarchives.gov.uk/+/http://www.dh.gov.uk/en/Publicationsandstatistics/Publications/PublicationsLegislation/DH_4009697.

65 Circular No 462, above note 7.

66 "India: Impending Surrogacy Ban Provokes Surge in Demand" *Asian Correspondent* (19 January 2017), online: http://po.st/SHDkGw.

Territory, South Australia, Victoria, and Tasmania have passed laws preventing anyone who had not lived in the state for ninety days from being recognized as the parent of a child born to a surrogate.[67] While these laws affect would-be international parents, who need a parentage determination in order to get a passport, they have less impact on out-of-state intended parents, as they may not be concerned about the formal legal status of their relationship to the child.[68] State governments in Alabama, Maine, Texas, and Utah also impose state residency restrictions (usually ninety days) on would-be intended parents from other states or other countries. They also make it an offence to "cross state lines" to engage in surrogacy.[69]

Finally, it is worth noting that 2002 Greek reproductive legislation required that, prior to commencement of a surrogacy arrangement, the intended mother and the surrogate-to-be were domiciled in Greece,[70] a restriction imposed to eliminate reproductive tourism and international surrogacy. However, in 2014 these restrictive residency conditions were amended,[71] allowing non-residents to be intended parents and surrogates. Parentage of the child born in Greece to a surrogate now can be assigned to intended parents who are not domiciled in Greece. This change rendered Greece an attractive destination for international surrogacy, although only for heterosexual couples and single infertile women, as surrogacy is not permitted for same-sex intended parents. While Greek surrogacy

67 Mary Keyes, "Cross-Border Surrogacy Agreements" (2012) 26 *Australian Journal of Family Law* 28, citing the Standing Committee of Attorneys-General, Australian Health Ministers' Conference, Community and Disability Services Ministers' Conference Joint Working Group, "A Proposal for a National Model to Harmonise Regulation of Surrogacy" (Sydney: Attorney General: 2009) at 14, which confidently assumed that the inclusion of residency requirements would "prevent exploitation" of forum shopping in Australia.

68 Jackson et al, above note 20.

69 Paul G Arshagouni, "Be Fruitful and Multiply, by Other Means, If Necessary: The Time Has Come to Recognize and Enforce Gestational Surrogacy Agreements" (2012) 61 *De Paul Law Review* 799. See also Richard F Storrow, "Surrogacy: American Style" in Paula Gerber & Katie O'Byrne, eds, *Surrogacy, Law and Human Rights* (New York: Routledge, 2016) 193 at 202.

70 Article 8 of Greek Law 3089/2002, referenced by Kirsty Horsey & Katia Neofytou, "The Fertility Treatment Time Forgot: What Should Be Done About Surrogacy in the UK?" in Kirstey Horsey, ed, *Revisiting the Regulation of Human Fertilisation and Embryology* (London: Routledge, 2015) 117 at 124–25.

71 Article 17, Greek Law 4272/2014. Horsey & Neofytou, above note 70 at 125.

is altruistic, there is no mechanism to ensure that compensation does not occur.[72]

2) Rationale for Residency Restrictions

Surrogacy laws everywhere are designed to ensure respect for the diverse values that lawmakers perceive as important, such as eschewing commodification, reducing gender inequality, assessing the best interests of the child, monitoring financial arrangements, overseeing gamete manipulation, enforcing heteronormativity, implementing religious norms about permissible relationships, or restricting the use of surrogacy to situations where the intended mother cannot carry a pregnancy. Our review of the reasons for imposing residency restrictions reveals that international and interstate surrogacy arrangements are prohibited for three reasons. Most often the involvement of non-residents is simply perceived as obviously and inherently undesirable. Legislators also fear that the involvement of international intended parents might compromise protective processes such as pre-implantation review and lead to practices inconsistent with local values. Finally, and uniquely, it appears that, for lawmakers in the United Kingdom, a significant justification for imposing domicile restrictions was to protect ongoing relationships between the child, the surrogate, and the intended parents.

These justifications are not well developed in the available literature on these laws. Nor is there consistency across assisted reproductive procedures. For example, in the United Kingdom, non-domiciled ova and sperm donors are not prevented from donating gametes or from collecting the regulated payment for the altruistic gift. (Egg donors receive £750 per donation, and sperm donors receive £35 per donation up to a maximum of £750.)[73] Complicating legislative restrictions on surrogacy are citizenship rules. For example, in Canada, the United States, and Australia, citizenship is attained by birth, regardless of the citizenship of the birth mother. Depending on the immigration rules, it may be relatively easy for pregnant visitors to enter the country and give birth while there, and, as a result, the newborn obtains

72 Horsey & Neofytou, above note 70 at 127.

73 Human Fertilisation and Embryology Authority, *Code of Practice*, ch 13, online: www.hfea.gov.uk/code-of-practice/13.

citizenship-by-birth. This factor encourages Mexican surrogates to give birth in California[74] or Chinese women to give birth in Canada.[75]

3) Justifying Residency Restrictions in Canada

In this section, we explore whether more specific justifications can be articulated for adopting laws restricting or prohibiting international surrogacy in Canada. In so doing, we recognize that in closing Canada off to international surrogacy, intended parent-sending countries may be forced to reconsider their own legal and policy stance on surrogacy, as they will be less able to depend on Canada playing a "safety valve" role.[76] We do not consider that it is part of Canada's international duties to offer the services of Canadian surrogates to non-residents, especially when medical costs are borne by Canadians. Moreover, by meeting the needs of international intended parents, childless Canadians are rendered less likely to find a Canadian surrogate to bear their children.

We suggest that regulation and stewardship of the health system are critical state actions,[77] the operation of which is so important to overall social well-being that it should not be left to market forces. Health regulation and stewardship have a special importance in Canada: "universal health care is almost universally loved – 94 percent of Canadians calling it an important source of collective pride and 74 percent stating that is 'very important.'"[78] Canadians expect their provincially funded health care system to meet domestic needs, not the needs of non-Canadians.

Fertility clinics in Canada, which in most provinces operate outside of provincially funded health care systems, cannot meet domestic demand for

74 Families Through Surrogacy, above note 4.

75 Bourgon, above note 11.

76 Guido Pennings et al, "ESHRE Task Force on Ethics and Law 15: Cross-Border Reproductive Care" (2008) 23 *Human Reproduction* 2182.

77 Dominique Martin & Stefan Kane, "National Self-Sufficiency in Reproductive Resources: An Innovative Response to Transnational Reproductive Travel" (2014) 7 *International Journal of Feminist Approaches to Bioethics* 10, special issue on transnational reproductive travel, online: www.utpjournals.press/doi/abs/10.3138/ijfab.7.2.0010.

78 Bruce Cheadle, "Universal Health Care Much Loved Among Canadians, Monarchy Less Important: Poll" *Canadian Press* (25 November 2012), online: www.theglobeandmail.com/news/national/universal-health-care-much-loved-among-canadians-monarchy-less-important-poll/article5640454.

fertility treatments. Many have waiting lists,[79] especially when treatments become provincially funded.[80] The Ontario Fertility Program, which aims to fund assisted reproduction for about 5,000 patients per year, also includes IVF and assisted insemination treatments for surrogates. When Quebec was directly funding assisted reproduction, it also paid for reproductive treatments for surrogates.[81] However, Ontario officials acknowledge that they do not have mechanisms for tracking whether a woman who receives IVF is a surrogate, nor do they collect information on the residency of intended parents.[82]

All prenatal, delivery, post-natal, and infant health care costs for care received by Canadians is publicly funded, except special supplements such as private hospital rooms. Most provinces have policies and programs designed to recover the costs of health care provided to non-residents.[83] However, as it is resident surrogates and their infants who are receiving care—not the intended parents—the mechanisms designed to recover health care costs from international patients appear to be ineffective or, in most cases, non-existent. The desire to conserve scarce health care resources and to control who ultimately benefits from publicly funded health care systems could justify a ban on international intended parents working with Canadian surrogates. At the very least, provincial governments should implement robust health care cost–recovery regimes for the costs associated with surrogate arrangements involving international intended parents.

79 Anecdotal comments to the authors.

80 Online: http://nationalpost.com/health/huge-demand-for-ivf-treatment-in-ontario-where-its-fully-funded-has-wait-lists-stretching-to-2018.

81 Joël Legendre successfully sued the Quebec government to obtain funded IVF for the surrogate he and his partner arranged to carry their children. See "Quebec to Reimburse Gay Men for Surrogacy Costs" *CBC News* (24 April 2014), online: www.cbc.ca/news/canada/montreal/quebec-to-reimburse-gay-men-for-surrogacy-costs-1.2620309.

82 FOI request, above note 15.

83 Examples of coverage details of several provinces' health legislation: Ontario, online: www.health.gov.on.ca/en/public/publications/ohip/travel_another_province_territory.aspx; Alberta, online: www.health.alberta.ca/AHCIP/outside-coverage.html; Manitoba, online: www.gov.mb.ca/health/mhsip/leavingmanitoba.html; Quebec, online: www.ramq.gouv.qc.ca/en/citizens/temporary-stays-outside-quebec/health-insurance/Pages/services-covered.aspx. In cases where, for example, Quebec residents regularly use Ontario health services, some hospitals have developed policies for service provision. See, for example, Montfort Hospital: https://hopitalmontfort.com/en/information-quebec-residents-visiting-emergency-0.

Such actions would ensure distributive justice for Canadians while at the same time meeting the health care needs of Canadian surrogates and infants. As it is possible to limit and, indeed, charge out-of-province residents for medical care received in another provincial jurisdiction,[84] provinces should be encouraged or required to develop a fee regime for international surrogacy. Until provinces can determine an appropriate costing regime, surrogacy undertaken on behalf of international intended parents should be actively discouraged, if not banned.

The UK Longitudinal Study of Assisted Reproduction Families has followed surrogates, intended parents, and surrogate-born children for more than fourteen years.[85] Its research findings show that surrogate-born children do not have negative feelings about the circumstances of their birth and that positive and enduring relationships exist among the parties involved.[86] Yet, even as surrogacy has become a global enterprise, we know nothing about the long-term development of children born abroad to surrogates.[87] For those families who choose to stay in contact with their surrogate, how do they maintain a relationship across different countries and cultures? Does contact taper off over time?[88] While acknowledging research gaps on international surrogacy outcomes and the difficulty of doing such research, it is worth observing that giving priority to surrogacy arrangements between Canadian residents may be in the best long-term interests of all parties, especially the surrogate-born child. Research in other Western countries as well as anecdotes in Canada indicate that surrogates do not see themselves as mothers but they do care about the child's well-being and want to be acknowledged for their unique contribution to bringing the child into the world. Some, perhaps many, surrogates want an enduring relationship with the new family, such as occasional letters, emails, and photographs to show how the child is doing, or they want the child to know who they are and the role they played. Some surrogates report that they are disappointed

84 *Ibid.*

85 Jadva et al, above note 40.

86 Imrie & Jadva, above note 49; Jadva et al, above note 40.

87 Jadva et al, above note 40. See also Vardit Ravitsky, "The Right to Know One's Genetic Origins and Cross-Border Medically Assisted Reproduction" (2017) 6:3 *Israel Journal of Health Policy Research* 1 at 1; Robert Leckey, "Identity, Law, and the Right to a Dream" (2015) 38 *Dalhousie Law Journal* 525.

88 Smietana, above note 37 at paras 5.7–5.9, discusses intentions, expectations, and realities of cross-border post-birth surrogate and intended parent contacts.

when these expectations are unmet after they were agreed to in the surrogacy agreement.[89] Despite such problems, we expect such relationships may be easier to encourage and sustain if all the parties live in Canada.

In the past decade, Canadian law has moved, through legislative reform and caselaw and by relying on the "best interests of the child" doctrine, toward recognizing and supporting diverse family forms. This recognition includes families with one parent or more than two parents, queer parents, and parents who have never been in a sexual relationship.[90] Given this openness, Canadian law is likely to be flexible enough to recognize and support a range of ongoing relationships between surrogates and the children they bear. Recognition of diverse family arrangements is more likely to occur if surrogate-born children remain in Canada.

Seeking reproductive self-sufficiency is another rationale for residency restrictions. While we do not have robust research on this point, those who have been involved in surrogacy in Canada will say that there are not enough Canadian surrogates to meet domestic needs.[91] If the number of Canadians who want to establish their families through surrogacy is significantly greater than the number of willing altruistic Canadian surrogates,

89 Imrie & Jadva, above note 49; Berend, "The Romance of Surrogacy," above note 20 and "'We Are All Carrying Someone Else's Child,'" above note 37.

90 See, generally, Nicholas Bala & Christine Ashbourne, "The Widening Concept of Parent in Canada: Step-Parents, Same-Sex Partners, and Parents by ART" (2012) 20 *American University Journal of Gender, Social Policy and the Law* 525 and, for example, *All Families Are Equal Act (Parentage and Related Registrations Statute Law Amendment)*, above note 34; on queer people as parents, see, for example, Fiona Kelly, "Equal Parents, Equal Children: Reforming Canada's Parentage Laws to Recognize the Completeness of Women-Led Families" (2013) 64 *University of New Brunswick Law Journal* 253; and Robert Leckey, ed, *After Legal Equality: Family, Sex, Kinship* (London: Routledge, 2015); on number of parents, see, for example, *Chartier v Chartier*, [1999] 1 SCR 242 and *AA v BB*, 2007 ONCA 2; on non-sexual families, see Amanda Jerome, "Ottawa Lawyers' Declaration of Parentage Illustrates Shift in Family Law" *Lawyer's Daily* (28 February 2017), online: www.thelawyersdaily.ca/it/articles/2610/ottawa-lawyers-declaration-of-parentage-illustrates-shift-in-family-law-; and Martha Albertson Fineman, *The Neutered Mother, the Sexual Family, and Other Twentieth Century Tragedies* (New York: Routledge, 1995).

91 See comment "40–50 intended parents competing for 7 available surrogates" reported by Robert Cribb & Emma Jarratt, "Canada's Vague Surrogacy Laws May Be Doing More Harm than Good" *Toronto Star* (18 September 2016), online: www.thestar.com/news/canada/2016/09/18/canadas-vague-surrogacy-laws-may-be-doing-more-harm-than-good.html.

it is worth considering ways to address the demand within our own borders. Canadian scholars have suggested that there are various ways to achieve national self-sufficiency for human biological materials, such as reproductive materials, though law reform, public policy, and public attitudinal change.[92] An obvious step toward national self-sufficiency for surrogacy would be to prohibit international intended parents from entering into arrangements with would-be Canadian surrogates. This might increase the number of surrogates willing to work with other Canadians, while decreasing the number of Canadians who travel abroad, and it might reduce the risk of Canadian intended parents exploiting foreign surrogates.[93]

Countries with low birth rates, such as Canada, try to bolster their populations through policies designed to encourage Canadians to have more children. Such policies include funded access to assisted reproduction, financial incentives (such as baby bonuses and tax credits), generous income replacement and leave options before and after the arrival of a child, and subsidized daycare.[94] In our view, the adoption of laws and policies that at least discourage international surrogacy in Canada, with a view to increasing the number of children who will stay in the country, is consistent with this country's pro-family policy objectives.

The prohibition on compensatory payment leaves Canadian surrogates and intended parents in an uncertain legal position. Altruism paradoxically encourages international intended parents to see Canada as an attractive surrogacy destination. Yet international intended parents are unlikely to be prosecuted by Canadian authorities should they compensate a Canadian surrogate, especially if the payment is made outside the country. Moreover, altruistic surrogacy lowers their costs compared to commercial surrogacy undertaken in the United States. Thus, compared with Canadian intended parents, those from abroad have greater opportunity to compensate a surrogate without incurring the risk of legal penalty. In this respect, it could

92 Dominque Martin, "Medical Travel and the Sale of Human Biological Materials: Suggestions for Ethical Policy Development" (2010) 10:3 *Global Social Policy* 377; GKD Crozier & Dominque Martin, "How to Address the Ethics of Reproductive Travel to Developing Countries: A Comparison of National Self-Sufficiency and Regulated Market Approaches" (2012) 12 *Developing World Bioethics* 45.

93 Crozier & Martin, above note 92, and Deckha, above note 50.

94 Other examples include splitting of employment insurance–funded maternity benefits between parents and the Quebec government's provision of paternity benefits, online: www.rqap.gouv.qc.ca/travailleur_salarie/types/paternite_en.asp.

be argued that international intended parents are taking unfair advantage of an unfair situation, one that sees everyone but the surrogate receiving compensation for their services and where domestic, but not international, intended parents will face criminal penalties if they compensate a surrogate. In the quasi-commercial reproductive medicine and surrogacy legal landscape identified by researchers,[95] lifting the ban on payment of surrogates would address the unfair position experienced by Canadian surrogates.

Regardless of whether the federal government moves to lift the ban on commercial surrogacy in Canada or restrict international surrogacy, provincial legislatures need to put in place protections for surrogates, their offspring, and intended parents. Canadian nationalism often causes us to disparage reforms made south of the border, but the US states that have surrogacy legislation offer some innovative ways to protect all parties. While this chapter is not the place to review and assess these measures, we note the incorporation of professional best practices into law, requirements for intended parents to fund maternity leave for the surrogate post-delivery, and provisions that acknowledge the surrogate's rights to protect her health and that of the fetus.[96]

In sum, there are many reasons why Canadian law should prohibit non-residents from participating in surrogacy arrangements in Canada, in addition to the vaguely asserted rationales (inherent undesirability or facilitating compliance with local protective regimes) in other jurisdictions. Residency restrictions would promote a fairer use of scarce health care resources, ensure that Canadians reap the broad benefits of our publicly funded health care system, and avoid introducing market ideology into the system. Some research supports the assertion that it is in the long-term best interests of all the participants in a surrogacy arrangement to be in proximity to each other — an outcome more likely to be frustrated if the intended parents and surrogate-born child quickly leave Canada. Giving preference to Canadian intended parents also promotes national self-sufficiency and distributes the benefits to domestic residents who, for financial, ethical, or availability reasons, cannot travel abroad for assisted reproduction.

95 Millbank, above note 43.

96 Storrow, above note 69.

E. RECOMMENDATIONS FOR RESEARCH AND LAW REFORM

It is surprising how little we know about surrogacy in Canada.[97] This chapter is premised on two beliefs that have proved difficult to substantiate empirically: international demand for surrogacy is increasing in Canada and the number of willing surrogates in Canada is smaller than the number of Canadians seeking a surrogate. Moreover, we do not know how many babies have been born to traditional and gestational surrogates, who the intended parents are, or how often the blended Canada/US option is used. We cannot say how many surrogate-born babies are being brought into the country by Canadian intended parents or being taken out by international parents. We do not know the proportion of non-resident to resident intended parents. Canada's assisted reproductive registry, unlike the one in the United States, does not record the permanent place of residence of intended parents, even though the international organization on assisted reproduction registries supported by the World Health Organization recommends this practice.[98] No single entity is charged with collecting Canada-wide data about surrogacy practices and outcomes, and provincial and territorial data collection on parental changes recorded by vital statistics registries is incomplete and may use non-comparable variables. We know little about how surrogates make treatment decisions, whether they receive independent counselling and medical care, their degree of long-term satisfaction, and the difficulties they encounter.[99] We recognize that some of the research that needs to be undertaken may be difficult to accomplish, including studies of money matters or longitudinal comparisons of outcomes for children who stay in Canada and those who are removed. While we can probably safely extrapolate findings from UK and US research about the

97 See White, Chapter 2, this volume.

98 Fernando Zegers-Hochschild et al, "The International Committee for Monitoring Assisted Reproductive Technology (ICMART) and the World Health Organization (WHO) Revised Glossary on ART Terminology" (2009) 24:11 *Human Reproduction* 2683. See recent studies by Levine et al, above note 13, and Kiran M Perkins et al, "Differences in the Utilization of Gestational Surrogacy Between States in the USA" (2018) 5 *Reproductive Biomedicine and Society Online* 1.

99 Erika L Fuchs & Abbey B Berenson, "Screening of Gestational Carriers in the United States" (2016) 106 *Fertility and Sterility* 1496; Berend, "The Romance of Surrogacy," above note 20 and "'We Are All Carrying Someone Else's Child,'" above note 37.

characteristics of participants and their level of satisfaction, it remains baffling that next to no research has been done on these topics in Canada.

We know from recent events that, while many countries have prohibited non-resident intended parents from engaging in surrogacy, the demand has not diminished. We expect Canada to experience increased pressure to accommodate growing international demand for surrogacy. Based on the very limited knowledge that exists, it appears that most of the demand seems to come from international parents living in Europe, the United Kingdom, and Australia. In the future, demand may swell to include intended parents from other places, including Taiwan and the People's Republic of China, especially as the latter recently lifted its one-child policy and has been unable to meet needs through domestic fertility services.[100] Research from countries where women live with forms and levels of sex inequality similar to those experienced by Canadian women (i.e., the United Kingdom and the United States) demonstrates that, overwhelmingly, surrogates are not exploited but rather are satisfied with the experience.[101] Therefore, there is no reason to move toward prohibiting surrogacy altogether in Canada. But there are good reasons why Canadian lawmakers should move to prohibit non-residents from participating in surrogacy arrangements in this country.

We argue that residency restriction would promote fairer use of scarce health care resources and would help ensure that Canadians reap the broad benefits of our publicly funded health care system. We also believe that restrictions may be in the long-term best interests of all the participants, especially the children. Giving preference to Canadian intended parents promotes national self-sufficiency in assisted reproduction. Given

---

100 Carolyn Zhang, "Chinese Women Head Overseas to Freeze Their Eggs" *New York Times* (31 August 2016), online: https://nyti.ms/2HNTxqS; Kalee Thompson, "Whoa Baby! Why American Surrogates Are in Demand for Chinese Families" *Hollywood Reporter* (4 November 2016), online: www.hollywoodreporter.com/features/whoa-baby-why-american-surrogates-are-demand-chinese-families-942832; Wang Xiaodong & Shan Juan, "Birth by Surrogacy to Remain Prohibited" *China Daily News* (9 February 2017), online: www.chinadaily.com.cn/china/2017-02/09/content_28144123.htm.

101 See, for example, Hohman & Hagan, above note 49; MacCallum et al, above note 49; Ciccarelli & Beckman, above note 49; Imrie & Jadva, above note 49. For comprehensive reviews of empirical studies on the experiences of surrogates, intended parents, and surrogate-born children, see Busby & Vun, above note 38; Campbell, above note 38; Söderström-Anttila et al, above note 38; Tallandini et al, above note 38; Berend, "The Romance of Surrogacy," above note 20; Berend, "'We Are All Carrying Someone Else's Child,'" above note 37; and Smietana, above note 37.

that international bans on foreign surrogacy will prevent Canadians from going abroad and participating in often-exploitative surrogacy in the Global South, domestic demand is likely to rise. Increasing pressure exerted by international intended parents, if left unchecked, will only add to the already overloaded capacity of Canadian surrogates. Moreover, the prioritization of relationships that produce children who remain in Canada is also consistent with Canada's pro-family stance. Finally, placing restrictions on international intended parents addresses the unfair advantage that they enjoy if they offer fees payable offshore.

It is beyond the scope of this chapter to elaborate on the legislative and regulatory challenges posed by our recommendation that international intended parents be actively discouraged, if not prevented, from seeking the services of Canadian surrogates. We do note that unitary states such as the United Kingdom, Israel, and South Africa have legislative abilities to institute parentage rules that work alongside citizenship, health care, and entry provisions to discourage non-domiciled intended parents from accessing domestic surrogacy services. Multi-state nations such as Australia and the United States where criminal law operates at the individual state level can seek to limit surrogacy to domiciled individuals on a state-by-state basis, though such an approach creates uneven surrogacy laws. In Canada, where vital statistics, family law, and health care are provincial responsibilities but border controls and criminal law are federal matters, a much more co-operative approach between all levels of government is needed to establish pan-national policy whereby Canadian surrogacy needs would be given priority.

Concomitant with placing restrictions on international intended parents exists the larger issue of the unfair disadvantage experienced by Canadian surrogates who are the only actors in the surrogacy arena unable to receive compensation for their services. This unfair disadvantage could be eliminated by permitting commercial surrogacy in Canada, which would likely, in turn, increase the number of women willing to be surrogates and help alleviate the current shortage, which is exacerbated by growing international demand.

Surrogacy is an accepted way to found a family. Surrogacy will not go away; rather, it is on the increase.[102] The growing domestic and international

102 "As Demand for Surrogacy Soars, More Countries Are Trying to Ban It" *The Economist* (13 May 2017), online: www.economist.com/ news/international/21721926-many-feminists-and-religious-leadersregard-it-exploitation-demand-surrogacy.

demand calls for legal reform. The overall situation of assisted reproduction, but especially surrogacy, presents major challenges for population health funding and research. Ignoring the importance of these issues and being satisfied with half-way measures will once again result in misplaced law and imperfect restrictions. One of the first priorities should be enabling Canadians to achieve their desires for family and for this to be accomplished in a manner consistent with the best health care practices.

8

Self-Sufficiency for Surrogacy and Responsibility for Global Structural Injustice

Katy Fulfer

A. INTRODUCTION

In this chapter, I present an argument for self-sufficiency for surrogacy. In the context of health care, "self-sufficiency" refers to meeting a community's needs for a medical product or service, usually with unpaid donations from community members rather than commercial payments or sourcing products and services from outside of the community.[1] Because self-sufficiency makes use of unpaid, or altruistic, donations, it is often positioned as a direct contrast to commercialization.[2]

My defence of self-sufficiency responds to the limited ability of Canada's *Assisted Human Reproduction Act*[3] (*AHRA*) to address ethical challenges that arise with transnational surrogacy, where people travel across national borders to hire a surrogate. Following recent arguments in the literature,

1 GKD Crozier & Dominique Martin, "How to Address the Ethics of Reproductive Travel to Developing Countries: A Comparison of National Self-Sufficiency and Regulated Market Approaches" (2012) 12:1 *Developing World Bioethics* 45 at 48; Dominique Martin & Stefan Kane, "National Self-Sufficiency in Reproductive Resources: An Innovative Response to Transnational Reproductive Travel" (2014) 7:2 *IJFAB: International Journal of Feminist Approaches to Bioethics* 10 at 11.

2 John Keown, "The Gift of Blood in Europe: An Ethical Defence of the EC Directive 89/381" (1997) 23:2 *Journal of Medical Ethics* 96 at 97.

3 *Assisted Human Reproduction Act*, SC 2004, c 2 [*AHRA*].

I take as a starting assumption the claim that Canada has a moral-political responsibility to address ethical challenges raised by transnational surrogacy.[4] I offer self-sufficiency as a mechanism for taking responsibility.

Second, I articulate the key concepts grounding self-sufficiency. Most significantly, I argue for an interpretation of self-sufficiency that is grounded in a relational conception of persons, which recognizes that persons are constituted "in and through relationships."[5] I also seek to expand the way responsibility has been theorized in self-sufficiency. Although reducing reliance on transnational surrogacy has been an important goal of self-sufficiency,[6] rectifying global injustice has not been central to conceptualizing responsibility in this framework. My primary contribution is broadening the scope of collective responsibility within self-sufficiency to include responsibilities for global structural injustice. Because self-sufficiency includes obligations to address global structural injustice, it provides a mechanism for Canada to take responsibility for its role in maintaining injustices within transnational surrogacy.

Next, I defend self-sufficiency as an ethical way to govern surrogacy domestically, pointing to ways in which self-sufficiency can address ethical challenges within surrogacy in Canada. Although I do not argue against commercialization per se, I raise points of contrast between the non-relational foundation of commercialization and the relational foundation of self-sufficiency.

In this chapter, I advocate a particular relational interpretation of the foundation for self-sufficiency. While self-sufficiency may be practical for Canada insofar as it is consistent with the legalization of unpaid surrogacy in the *AHRA*,[7] outlining how self-sufficiency might be implemented in

4 Maneesha Deckha, "Situating Canada's Commercial Surrogacy Ban in a Transnational Context: A Postcolonial Feminist Call for Legalization and Public Funding" (2015) 61:1 *McGill Law Journal* 31 at 38; Katy Fulfer, "Cross-Border Reproductive Travel, Neocolonialism, and Canadian Policy" (2017) 10:1 *IJFAB: International Journal of Feminist Approaches to Bioethics* 225 at 240 [Fulfer, "Cross-Border Reproductive Travel"].

5 Jennifer J Llewellyn & Jocelyn Downie, "Introduction" in Jocelyn Downie & Jennifer J Llewellyn, eds, *Being Relational: Reflections on Relational Theory and Health Law* (Vancouver: UBC Press, 2012) 1 at 4.

6 Crozier & Martin, above note 1 at 48; Martin & Kane, above note 1 at 11; Françoise Baylis & Jocelyn Downie, "Achieving National Altruistic Self-Sufficiency in Human Eggs for Third-Party Reproduction in Canada" (2014) 7:2 *IJFAB: International Journal of Feminist Approaches to Bioethics* 164 at 167 [Baylis & Downie, "Altruistic Self-Sufficiency"].

7 *AHRA*, above note 3, s 6.

this country is beyond the scope of this chapter. To conclude, I flag concerns related to developing self-sufficiency in Canada that require further exploration.

Before turning to my argument, let me explain some assumptions that inform my discussion. First, because I situate my defence of self-sufficiency within the Canadian context, I do not make general claims about whether self-sufficiency would offer an ethical approach in other national contexts. With this qualification in mind, I do understand my defence to provide an outline for a more general argument about the moral and political good of self-sufficiency. However, given the need to attend to particularities in national contexts, such a general argument is beyond the scope of this chapter.

Second, let me clarify how I interpret the connections between altruism, commercialization, and exploitation. In the *AHRA*, commercialization and exploitation are taken to be necessarily linked.[8] The connection between these two then justifies the criminalization of commercial payments for surrogacy.[9] Yet, in my view, exploitation can occur in unpaid or paid surrogacy.[10] Thus, "commercialization" should not be assumed to be a stand-in term for "exploitation." Further, there is increasing skepticism in the surrogacy literature that commercial payments are necessarily exploitative, especially in Global Northern countries.[11] Therefore, readers should not equate my defence of self-sufficiency with supporting the link made between commercialization and exploitation. Because I advocate for the principles of self-sufficiency rather than a specific instantiation of those principles, my defence is consistent with the non-commercialization stance

8 *Ibid*, s 2.

9 The *AHRA* also prohibits payments for gametes and embryos and for arranging payments for the aforementioned. *Ibid*, ss 6–7.

10 Rakhi Ruparelia, "Giving Away the 'Gift of Life': Surrogacy and the Canadian *Assisted Human Reproduction Act*" (2007) 23:1 *Canadian Journal of Family Law* 11 at 13 (many problems with commercial surrogacy may also appear, or be made worse in some cases, in unpaid surrogacy).

11 Erin Nelson, "Global Trade and Assisted Reproductive Technologies: Regulatory Challenges in International Surrogacy" (2013) 41:1 *Journal of Law, Medicine and Ethics* 240 at 247; Alana Cattapan, "Risky Business: Surrogacy, Egg Donation, and the Politics of Exploitation" (2014) 29:3 *Canadian Journal of Law and Society* 361 at 373; Nicole F Bromfield, "'Surrogacy Has Been One of the Most Rewarding Experiences in My Life': A Content Analysis of Blogs by US Commercial Gestational Surrogates" (2016) 9:1 *IJFAB: International Journal of Feminist Approaches to Bioethics* 192 at 210.

adopted in the *AHRA*. However, some of the more specific recommendations I make — for example around the reimbursement of expenses — may be in tension with sections of the *AHRA*.

B. THE *AHRA* AND TRANSNATIONAL SURROGACY

The *AHRA* bans payment to surrogates.[12] However, Canadians do engage in commercial surrogacy abroad. Some observers have argued that restrictive legislation might encourage seeking surrogacy abroad,[13] particularly when the federal government does not seek to enforce the ban on commercial payments in such cases.[14] Children who are born to Canadians as a result of commercial transnational surrogacy receive citizenship, provided there is a genetic link to a parent.[15] Canadians, as well as other people residing in the Global North, pursue transnational surrogacy for a host of reasons, including the lack of available service providers in the home country, success rates, waiting times, and cost.[16] Specifically, lower costs in Global Southern destinations may make surrogacy abroad more accessible than seeking a surrogate in one's home country.[17] Given the South Asian

12 For more on the history of this prohibition, see the Introduction to this volume.

13 Nelson, above note 11 at 241.

14 Raveena Aulakh, "Couple Fights Federal Surrogacy Policy to Bring Their Boy Back to Canada" *Toronto Star* (20 August 2011), online: www.thestar.com/news/gta/2011/08/20/couple_fights_federal_surrogacy_policy_to_bring_their_boy_back_to_canada.html; Tara Carman, "IVF Babies Born Abroad Test Canada's Citizenship Laws" *Vancouver Sun* (6 January 2015), online: www.vancouversun.com/News/10706565/story.html.

15 Immigration, Refugees and Citizenship Canada, "Assessing Who Is a Parent for Citizenship Purposes Where Assisted Human Reproduction (AHR) and/or Surrogacy Arrangements Are Involved" Operational Bulletin 381 (8 March 2012), online: www.cic.gc.ca/english/resources/manuals/bulletins/2012/ob381.asp.

16 Eric Blyth, "Fertility Patients' Experiences of Cross-Border Reproductive Care" (2010) 94:1 *Fertility and Sterility* e11 at e13.

17 Nelson, above note 11 at 241. Referring to originating points for intended parents in the "Global North" and surrogacy destinations in the "Global South" can be a useful heuristic to emphasize the stratification of reproduction and differential power dynamics. Although Global Southern destinations such as India and Thailand have received much attention, some destinations in the Global North, such as the Ukraine or the Czech Republic, may also exhibit stratification and differential power dynamics. For example, re the comparison between cross-border reproductive care in Thailand and in the Czech Republic, see Andrea Whittaker & Amy Speier, "'Cycling Overseas': Care, Commodifcation, and Stratification in Cross-Border Reproductive Travel" (2010) 29:4 *Medical Anthropology* 363.

diaspora in Canada, for example, some people may travel to countries in the Global South because they have cultural or family ties there.[18]

Transnational surrogacy raises a host of ethical concerns, especially when destinations for surrogacy are located in the Global South. In addition to concerns around exploitation via commodification, transnational surrogacy raises concerns around the exploitation of economic and other vulnerabilities,[19] human trafficking,[20] health risks to surrogates,[21] devaluation of surrogates' labour,[22] denials of autonomy or agency,[23] and the reinforcement of gendered, racialized, and colonialist stereotypes.[24] Although there is disagreement about the severity or nature of these harms, this list suffices to show that transnational surrogacy carries with it risks of harm that disproportionately affect surrogates.

Feminist bioethicists and legal scholars have argued that the *AHRA* cannot be considered apart from the realities of transnational surrogacy. In alignment with principles in the *AHRA*, Jocelyn Downie and Françoise Baylis argue that Canada ought to enforce the *AHRA*'s prohibitions on payment when Canadians seek gametes across national borders.[25] Other

18 Whittaker & Speier, above note 17 at 371.

19 Alison Bailey, "Reconceiving Surrogacy: Toward a Reproductive Justice Account of Indian Surrogacy" (2011) 26:4 *Hypatia* 715; Jyotsna Agnihotri Gupta, "Reproductive Biocrossings: Indian Egg Donors and Surrogates in the Globalized Fertility Market" (2012) 5:1 *IJFAB: International Journal of Feminist Approaches to Bioethics* 25; Vida Panitch, "Global Surrogacy: Exploitation to Empowerment" (2013) 9:3 *Journal of Global Health Ethics* 329.

20 Gupta, above note 19.

21 Bailey, above note 19; Emma Ryman & Katy Fulfer, "The Patient-Worker: A Model for Human Research Subjects and Gestational Surrogates" (2017) (Early View Articles) *Developing World Bioethics* 1 at 8.

22 GKD Crozier, Jennifer Lane Johnson, & Christopher Hajzler, "At the Intersections of Emotional and Biological Labor: Understanding Transnational Commercial Surrogacy as Social Reproduction" (2014) 7:2 *IJFAB: International Journal of Feminist Approaches to Bioethics* 45.

23 Serene Khader, "Intersectionality and the Ethics of Transnational Commercial Surrogacy" (2013) 6:1 *IJFAB: International Journal of Feminist Approaches to Bioethics* 68; Katy Fulfer, "Commercial Contract Pregnancy in India, Judgment, and Resistance to Oppression" (2015) 30:4 *Hypatia* 846.

24 Khader, above note 23; Amrita Banerjee, "Race and a Transnational Reproductive Caste System: Indian Transnational Surrogacy" (2014) 29:1 *Hypatia* 113.

25 Jocelyn Downie & Françoise Baylis, "Transnational Trade in Human Eggs: Law, Policy, and (In)Action in Canada" (2013) 41:1 *Journal of Law, Medicine and Ethics* 224 [Downie & Baylis, "Transnational Trade"]. Downie and Baylis focus on egg donation, but their

proposals require revising the *AHRA*. Erin Nelson argues that restrictive legislation makes it difficult for intended parents to access surrogacy domestically, which encourages transnational surrogacy, thereby contributing to the ethical problems.[26] Further, revising domestic regulation in sending and in destination countries for surrogacy may be the most effective way to address calls for international regulation.[27] Both Maneesha Deckha and I have argued that Canada's current regulatory scheme reinforces imperialist or colonial power relations, and we both advocate lifting the commercial ban in the *AHRA*.[28] Deckha further argues in favour of a government-run system that provides surrogacy under provincial health care, and she advocates allowing payments to surrogates.[29]

From this brief overview, it is clear that the *AHRA as currently applied* provides insufficient resources to address the ethical challenges emerging from transnational surrogacy. I will assume for the sake of argument that transnational surrogacy, as it currently exists, is a site of injustice (the discussions cited here provide support for this assumption). In what follows, I argue that Canada has a responsibility to address transnational surrogacy and that a regulatory framework informed by self-sufficiency enables us to do so.

C. A RELATIONAL CONCEPTION OF SELF-SUFFICIENCY

As previously stated, in health care, self-sufficiency refers to the goal of meeting a community's need for a medical resource or service with voluntary, usually unpaid, donations from community members.[30] Self-sufficiency emerged as a policy option in the 1970s and 1980s in response to a need for safe, non-exploitative blood donation procedures.[31] Blood donation is likely the most recognized example of self-sufficiency, and arguments have

argument can reasonably apply to surrogacy because of similar concerns around exploitation.

26 Nelson, above note 11 at 246. See also Busby & White, Chapter 7, this volume.

27 Nelson, above note 11 at 248–49.

28 Deckha, above note 4 at 63; Fulfer, "Cross-Border Reproductive Travel," above note 4 at 242.

29 Deckha, above note 4 at 70.

30 Dominique Martin, "Medical Travel and the Sale of Human Biological Materials: Suggestions for Ethical Policy Development" (2010) 10:3 *Global Social Policy* 377 at 386; Martin & Kane, above note 1 at 11.

31 Martin, above note 30 at 386.

emerged for applying self-sufficiency to organ donation, gamete donation, surrogacy, and stem cell therapies, especially with the rise of transnational medical travel.[32]

In addition to serving the practical goal of meeting a community's need for a medical product or service, self-sufficiency refers to a particular "social ethos," as Martin and Kane describe it, which includes "social community, shared responsibility for meeting needs, protection of the vulnerable, and the promotion of justice."[33] In this section, I defend a relational conception of self-sufficiency's social ethos. First, I explain my interpretation of "social community" as a national, political community. Second, I describe "solidarity," the term I use to refer to the foundation for a community's responsibility to meet needs in a way that promotes social justice.

My account builds upon defences of self-sufficiency by Martin and Kane, and Baylis and Downie, respectively.[34] I provide a corrective to these defences by contributing a more robust account of a community's responsibility to address global justice. Whereas "responsibility" is usually defined in terms of meeting a nation's demand for a product or service internally, I expand the concept to include mitigating global injustice. Collective responsibilities to groups in other national communities, specifically, in the present context, to women in surrogacy destinations in the Global South, have equal weight to responsibilities to members of one's national community.

1) Community

Martin and Kane list "social community" as part of the ethos of self-sufficiency. In my account, the "social community" is a national, political community. Focusing on national community is partly practical, as nation-states have the authority to create and enforce policy within their borders.[35] Philosophically, focusing on national community establishes what is entailed by "shared responsibility," which Martin and Kane also include within

32 *Ibid*; Crozier & Martin, above note 1; Downie & Baylis, "Transnational Trade," above note 25; Petra Thorn et al, "Cross-Border Reproductive Services: Suggestions for Ethically Based Minimum Standards of Care in Europe" (2012) 33:1 *Journal of Psychosomatic Obstetrics and Gynecology* 1.

33 Martin & Kane, above note 1 at 11 & 14.

34 *Ibid*; Baylis & Downie, "Altruistic Self-Sufficiency," above note 6.

35 Crozier & Martin, above note 1 at 46.

self-sufficiency's ethos. In the Rawlsian tradition of liberal democratic theory, political obligations accrue when people are governed under a common constitution.[36] Thus, obligations to share responsibility for addressing community needs, protecting vulnerable persons, and promoting just relationships are obligations of and between members of the national community. This account of community is my starting point.[37]

In addition to defining community in terms of the nation-state, I emphasize the experiential, deliberative dimensions of membership in a political community. Politics not only involves just institutions but also aims to foster public spaces for citizens to come together to deliberate on questions that affect or matter to them. As Iris Marion Young describes, politics in this sense refers to "public communicative engagement with others for the sake of organizing our relationships and coordinating our actions most justly."[38] Through deliberation, citizens' speech and action constitute politics.[39] Including experiential, deliberative dimensions of political community will enhance the way responsibility is construed. Community members share responsibility for participating in and supporting political deliberation with their peers.

Although there may be some fluidity in the use of "community" in this chapter, "political community" and "national community" serve as approximates for the "social community" dimension of self-sufficiency's social ethos.

2) Solidarity

Martin and Kane list "shared responsibility for meeting needs, protection of the vulnerable, and the promotion of justice" as features of the social ethos of self-sufficiency.[40] I refer to these aspects of self-sufficiency with the term

36 Iris Marion Young, "Responsibility and Global Justice: A Social Connection Model" (2006) 23:1 *Social Philosophy and Policy Foundation* 102 at 103 [Young, "Social Connection Model"].

37 In a following section, I argue that members of a national community may have obligations to members of other political communities (e.g., obligations to surrogates in other nations).

38 Young, "Social Connection Model," above note 36 at 123.

39 Hannah Arendt, *The Human Condition* (Chicago: Chicago University Press, 1958) at 182–83 [Arendt, *The Human Condition*].

40 Martin & Kane, above note 1 at 14.

"solidarity." That term captures the collective responsibility community members undertake to meet the population's need (or demand) for surrogacy.[41] Solidarity includes considerations of distributive and social justice.[42] In other words, self-sufficiency attends to power dynamics as well as need. Economic status, sexuality, and marital or relationship status are often barriers for some people accessing infertility treatments. Although implementing self-sufficiency would require a procedure for determining fair distribution, attention to financial and other social vulnerabilities is part of its ethos.[43]

Thus far, everything I have said about solidarity can be grounded in a traditional liberal account of persons or a relational conception. By a liberal conception of personhood, I refer to a conception of the self as an ideally rational agent, abstracted from context and relationships, who acts to maximize their desires.[44] By a relational conception, I refer to persons as "constituted *in and through* relationship with others."[45] A relational account is better suited to motivate the solidarity upon which self-sufficiency relies. A non-relational account privileges private interests over relational ones, thus limiting the extent to which solidarity is other-regarding.

To contrast a relational and non-relational account of solidarity, consider how solidarity has been defined in the field of public health ethics[46] as "common interests, purposes or sympathies between discrete individuals or among members of a group."[47] Common interests might manifest through "altruism," "reciprocity," "cooperating with others . . . with a common cause and anticipation of mutual advantage" or through "mutual care and

41 Deckha, above note 4 at 74. Given space constraints, I bracket the question of whether surrogacy constitutes a medical need. I refer to surrogacy as a fertility treatment because it is used in conjunction with other fertility interventions to assist child-bearing. See Baylis & Downie, "Altruistic Self-Sufficiency," above note 6; Carolyn McLeod, "The Medical Nonnecessity of In Vitro Fertilization" (2017) 10:1 *IJFAB: International Journal of Feminist Approaches to Bioethics* 78 at 81.

42 Françoise Baylis, Nuala P Kenny, & Susan Sherwin, "A Relational Account of Public Health Ethics" (2008) 1:3 *Public Health Ethics* 196 at 203.

43 Martin & Kane, above note 1 at 27–29.

44 Llewellyn & Downie, above note 5 at 7.

45 *Ibid* at 4.

46 I will not make a claim about whether infertility treatments fall under the rubric of public health. Rather, both self-sufficiency for surrogacy and public health discourses may be grounded in similar accounts of community solidarity. In addition, it may be that infertility constitutes a public health concern. See Martin & Kane, above note 1 at 27.

47 Baylis, Kenny, & Sherwin, above note 42 at 204.

concern."[48] According to Françoise Baylis, Nuala Kenny, and Susan Sherwin, these definitions of solidarity privilege an individual's private interests over a broad understanding of community or the public good. These interpretations of altruism, reciprocity, and co-operation depict solidarity as instrumentally good for facilitating an individual's interests. Although mutual care and concern is relational, it can be understood narrowly in terms of interpersonal relationships rather than communal bonds or relationships of power and privilege. Solidarity is undermined when private interests motivate it, because it is then rendered unable to "reach beyond the intimate or communal bonds to capture distant strangers, many of whom may be among the vulnerable and systematically disadvantaged members of society."[49] According to Baylis, Kenny, and Sherwin, the notion of solidarity requires expansion so it can accommodate and address relationships of vulnerability and power. Otherwise, public health ethics is not sufficiently public.

In contrast to non-relational accounts, conceptualizing solidarity through a relational conception of persons avoids problems of instrumental personal interests or narrowly conceived interpersonal relationships. A central insight of feminist relational theory is that the self is a being-in-relation, which cannot be understood as an atomized, abstract entity outside of relationships. Thus, relationships constitute the self and human community.[50] A relationally grounded conception of community solidarity enables self-sufficiency to bring a relational focus to surrogacy. Consider this relational description of self-sufficiency:

> The self-sufficiency model resituates reproductive resources in a framework of mutual care and relatedness consistent with feminist bioethics. In transnational reproductive travel, efforts to establish or sustain a relational account of surrogacy, for example, struggle to compete with neoliberal discourse .... Within the self-sufficiency model, the social context of procurement and use of reproductive resources is recognized, and relationships in the personal and public spheres are nurtured, consistent with an ethics of care and a relational understanding of bioethics.[51]

48 *Ibid.*

49 *Ibid.*

50 Llewellyn & Downie, above note 5 at 4; Arendt, *The Human Condition*, above note 39 at 9.

51 Martin & Kane, above note 1 at 27.

I interpret this passage in the broader way suggested by Baylis, Kenny, and Sherwin. Mutual care and concern, and attention to relationships of vulnerability and power, inform bonds of solidarity.

Self-sufficiency focuses on bonds of solidarity between members of a national political community. If, in the context of surrogacy, solidarity requires us to attend to vulnerability and power in addition to need, members of a national political community must look beyond their borders to global inequalities that exist between national communities. In the next section, I make this argument with respect to transnational surrogacy. I will expand the notion of responsibility in self-sufficiency to include shared responsibility to mitigate global structural injustice.

D. SELF-SUFFICIENCY AND RESPONSIBILITY FOR GLOBAL STRUCTURAL INJUSTICE

The tension between the criminalization of commercial payments for surrogacy in the *AHRA* and the lack of enforcement arguably contributes to the decision of some Canadians to seek surrogacy abroad.[52] In arguing for reform to address this tension, Deckha encourages feminists and policymakers to think about responsibility globally and domestically:

> As many of the practices comprising transnational surrogacy at the present time in India are exploitative, a postcolonial feminist framework thus prompts sending nations, of which Canada is one, to evaluate the impact of the *AHRA* in inducing Canadians to travel to India or elsewhere in the Global South where commercial surrogacy may develop due to conditions of poverty.[53]

Deckha's answer to this call is to reduce transnational travel by making surrogacy within Canada more accessible, specifically by repealing the ban on commercial payments in the *AHRA* and funding fertility treatments through provincial health care systems.[54] I offer a related but different answer: reduce transnational travel by promoting self-sufficiency.

A relational account of solidarity ensures that self-sufficiency responds to relationships of power and vulnerability. Because self-sufficiency refers

52 Nelson, above note 11.

53 Deckha, above note 4 at 63.

54 *Ibid.*

to a national political community, bonds of solidarity and corresponding responsibilities exist between community members. If a community succeeds in meeting its population's need for surrogacy, then the motivation to pursue transnational surrogacy will disappear. Because responsibility is defined as responsibility to other community members, reducing transnational travel is a benefit of self-sufficiency. However, reducing travel is not a central aspect of taking responsibility for community needs. This point helps make sense of how reducing transnational travel might be "an important [yet] secondary objective" to meeting demands for surrogacy.[55]

In this section, I broaden the scope of community solidarity and its corresponding responsibilities. I draw on the work of political philosopher Iris Marion Young to suggest that a national political community has responsibilities to address global structural injustices. Conceiving responsibility solely in terms of meeting national demands risks casting surrogates in Global Southern locations as distant strangers. In other words, it risks obscuring how transnational surrogacy depends on global relations of power and vulnerability. Reducing reproductive travel is not merely a goal of self-sufficiency but part of how a national political community could take responsibility for global structural injustice.

Responsibility for structural injustice aligns with self-sufficiency's commitment to social justice.[56] Young offers an account of responsibility for structural injustice that is useful for expanding the conception of responsibility within self-sufficiency.[57] According to her, agents are responsible for structural injustice in virtue of how their actions support and maintain social-structural processes that yield injustice. Agents include individual actors, groups, corporate actors, and institutions. Structural injustice is produced through the interplay between personal, collective, and institutional actions within social-structural processes. "Social-structural processes" refer to a complicated interplay of processes that structure society, including economic, legal, and social norms, resource distribution, and schemes of co-operation and competition. When these social-structural processes create power hierarchies, they produce structural injustice, whereby one

55 Crozier & Martin, above note 1 at 49; see also Martin & Kane, above note 1 at 25.

56 Young, "Social Connection Model," above note 36.

57 Iris Marion Young, "Responsibility and Global Labor Justice" (2004) 12:4 *Journal of Political Philosophy* 365 [Young, "Global Labor Justice"]; Iris Marion Young, *Responsibility for Justice* (New York: Oxford University Press, 2011) [Young, *Responsibility for Justice*].

group is under a threat of domination or has restricted opportunities for action, and another group receives social benefits or enhanced opportunities for action.[58]

Agents are responsible for structural injustice by virtue of their social positions and connections to others in social-structural processes. Responsibilities that accrue through social connections are more expansive than models that focus on causal responsibilities for direct harm. Although causing harm directly makes agents responsible, they can also be responsible for structural injustice without directly or intentionally doing wrong or even when they follow accepted laws and norms. Put another way, agents may unintentionally and unknowingly support structural injustice while seeking to achieve their plans or goals. And, as the relevant social connections can extend beyond national borders, responsibilities for structural injustice cut across and between national political communities.

To clarify the notions of structural injustice and responsibility for it, consider the case of sweatshops, Young's paradigmatic example of global structural injustice.[59] Sweatshops involve a number of dispersed social connections between consumers, brands, retailers, manufactures, factory owners, and workers. A number of strands constitute the social-structural processes that produce structural injustice in relation to sweatshops. In the globalized economy, sweatshops operate against a background of regional and international free-trade agreements, national labour policies (or a lack thereof), coercive contracts, poverty, and international financial institutions. Sweatshop workers, in this picture, are subjected to structural injustice. Agents such as factory owners or managers may be causally responsible for harming workers. But, consumers are also connected to workers through the various social-structural processes described. Buying products that result from sweatshop labour helps maintain the social-structural processes that produce the structural injustice. Therefore, consumers have some responsibility to take actions that work to change the structures that produce injustice. Consumers share this responsibility with other agents that contribute to the injustice of sweatshops.

Transnational surrogacy is also a site of structural injustice. As we have seen, the ethical challenges arising from transnational surrogacy include

58 Young, *Responsibility for Justice*, above note 57 at 52.

59 *Ibid*, ch 5.

exploitation, risks to health, undermining of surrogates' rights and autonomy, and reinforcement of gendered, racialized, and colonialist stereotypes. These challenges emerge from social-structural processes involving globalized capitalism, poverty, restrictive legislation in originating points for reproductive travel, lack of access to surrogacy domestically (which could be due to finances or discrimination), and a lack of international regulation of surrogacy. Those engaged in transnational surrogacy participate in and maintain this system, even when they do not violate legal or moral norms that are accepted in their home countries. For example, intended parents may pay all relevant fees, and yet the clinic or agency arranging the surrogacy may not pay the surrogate her full wage.[60]

If transnational surrogacy is a site of structural injustice, and if Canadians participate in social-structural processes that maintain it, then Canadians have responsibilities to address structural injustice within transnational surrogacy. Most obvious, perhaps, are the responsibilities of intended parents who travel abroad for surrogacy or of fertility specialists and brokers who assist in cross-border arrangements. However, participation is not limited to the practice of hiring or directly facilitating transnational surrogacy.

To participate in structural injustice is to occupy social positions that are connected to and accrue benefits from the injustice. In transnational surrogacy, some connections are not straightforward. For example, as a result of ethical protections encoded in the *AHRA*, Canadian women occupy a position of benefit that is not afforded to foreign surrogates. The principles in the *AHRA* indicate that exploitation should be protected against. Because Canada does not enforce the *AHRA* extraterritorially, the ethical protections apply only within Canada. In other words, the tension between law and practice constructs only women within Canada as deserving of protection from exploitation.[61] This benefit is not necessarily one that was intentionally created, but it provides a benefit for Canadians that is not provided for foreign surrogates. It could be that policy-makers have good reasons for not enforcing the ban on payment for surrogacy outside of Canada. For example, it may not be in the best interests of children resulting from surrogacy if they were denied citizenship or if their parents were criminally punished. These explanations for the accrual of benefits

60 Rebecca Haimowitz & Vaishali Sinha, *Made in India* (Brooklyn, NY: Chicken and Egg Pictures, 2010).

61 Fulfer, "Cross-Border Reproductive Travel," above note 4 at 230.

do not mitigate responsibility for structural injustice. Even if justifications for not enforcing the *AHRA* outside of Canada are reasonable, Canadian policy interacts with other factors to yield structural injustice. This interaction exemplifies Young's point about structural injustice emerging from agents who follow accepted norms and rules. Legislation might be intended to regulate a domestic practice, but it interacts within a global social structure to produce structural injustice.

Young argues that responsibility for structural injustice is shared by those who participate in social-structural processes of injustice, including those who benefit from it. This responsibility is forward-looking in that it seeks to address structural injustice rather than locate an agent as blameworthy for it. While there is not one way to discharge responsibilities, changing the systems requires collective action.[62] Because social connections are dispersed, power for change is likewise dispersed; collective action enables people to come together to make change. Government or other institutions may be resources for making change, but responsibility cannot be put solely on the powers of state government.[63] The national political community is also responsible.

Young's account of responsibility for structural injustice, or something akin to it, enriches and elaborates on the ethos expressed by self-sufficiency. It makes a national political community's responsibility for structural injustice just as important as responsibilities between members of the community to meet the need for surrogacy.

E. SELF-SUFFICIENCY AND RELATIONAL BONDS

Self-sufficiency is a mechanism for Canada to address global responsibilities for harms perpetrated by transnational surrogacy, especially in relation to the inconsistencies in how the *AHRA* is enforced. Some may agree that Canada has responsibilities for global structural injustice but be skeptical about whether self-sufficiency is a good mechanism for taking responsibility.[64] To be an effective tool for regulating surrogacy, self-sufficiency must meet domestic demands in an ethical way as well as reduce transnational travel. In this section, I examine ways in which self-sufficiency can meet ethical

62 Young, *Responsibility for Justice*, above note 57 at 143.

63 *Ibid* at 112.

64 Deckha, above note 4.

challenges presented by surrogacy in domestic contexts. The strengths of self-sufficiency, I will argue, are located in its relational foundation.

1) Qualifications

Before proceeding, a note about self-sufficiency, altruism, and commercialization is needed. Commentators have presented altruism as a way to avoid problems that come with commercialization, such as the exploitation of women and the commodification of women and children.[65] Because self-sufficiency typically relies on unpaid donations, it may seem as if self-sufficiency is reducible to altruism. Such a reduction is misleading. For one, "altruism" is an ambiguous term: although it sometimes means "unpaid donation,"[66] it can also refer to a psychological attitude toward donation.[67] In his study of blood donation, for example, Richard M Titmuss examines altruism in paid and unpaid donation. He uses the term to refer to giving to a stranger with no expectation of direct reciprocity. It is a psychological motivation, a desire to help.[68]

Although self-sufficiency should not be conflated with altruism, there is a contrast between commercialization and self-sufficiency that is important to flag. Markets may not be necessarily or inherently exploitative or problematic. However, commercialization is closely associated with a non-relational conception of persons that self-sufficiency explicitly resists. Feminists have identified how economics and contract theory are organized around an idealized economic subject as fully constituted outside of relationships, self-interested, and instrumentally rational.[69] My argument implies that the abstracted rational economic agent that underpins commercialization is an insufficient ground for regulating surrogacy ethically.

65 Keown, above note 2 at 97; Richard M Titmuss, *The Gift Relationship: From Human Blood to Social Policy* (New York: Pantheon Books, 1971).

66 Baylis & Downie, "Altruistic Self-Sufficiency," above note 6 at 171.

67 Titmuss, above note 65 at 198, 212; Gillian J Hewitson, *Feminist Economics: Interrogating the Masculinity of Rational Economic Man* (Northampton, MA: Edward Elgar, 1999) at 173.

68 Titmuss, above note 65 at 198 and 212.

69 Hewitson, above note 67 at 159–61; Drucilla K Barker & Edith Kuiper, "Introduction: Sketching the Contours of a Feminist Philosophy of Economics" in Drucilla K Barker & Edith Kuiper, eds, *Towards a Feminist Philosophy of Economics* (New York: Routledge, 2003) 1 at 2–3.

Although I will not be arguing against commercialization directly, I would suggest that the starting point for many approaches to commercialization will not bolster political community. Whether such a non-relational conception of persons is a necessary foundation for commercial systems is a question I leave open. My goal in this section is to establish ways in which a relational conception of persons and of self-sufficiency bolsters relationships within a national political community. Because I am arguing that self-sufficiency provides a mechanism for Canada to reduce transnational travel for surrogacy, I restrict my discussion to domestic surrogacies.

2) Surrogate–Intended Parent Relationships

Martin and Kane argue that transnational surrogacy "facilitates disconnection rather than fostering intimacy" between surrogates and intended parents.[70] Physical distance in transnational surrogacy may exacerbate possibilities for disconnection, but disconnection poses a similar challenge in domestic surrogacy, especially given Canada's expansive geography.[71] Further, the issue of disconnection may be more acute in surrogacy than in other services within a self-sufficiency framework. Whereas "the stranger" as a recipient of solidarity in blood donation was an organizing concept in Titmuss's study,[72] "the stranger" in surrogacy makes less sense. A surrogate and intended parents may enter the relationship as strangers, but their lives will necessarily be intertwined, to some degree, for (at least) the duration of the surrogacy.

Disconnection may be a barrier to the surrogate–intended parent relationship in a couple of ways. First, surrogacy as an agreement to provide gestational services suggests that the connection between a surrogate and intended parents is temporary and will end with the birth of a child. A commercial agreement specifying that final payments will be rendered at birth — or shortly thereafter (e.g., if a surrogate pumps breast milk) — may entrench this concern. Second, intended parents may seek disconnection as a way to reinforce their identities as social parents over worries about a surrogate's (potential) parental claims.

70 Martin & Kane, above note 1 at 26.

71 Jennifer Parks, "Care Ethics and the Global Practice of Commercial Surrogacy" (2010) 24:7 *Bioethics* 333 at 337.

72 Titmuss, above note 65 at 198.

Surrogates' experiences challenge the presumption of disconnection that gestational agreements may imply. In Nicole Bromfield's analysis of blogs related to commercial surrogacy in the United States, most surrogates viewed their relationship with intended parents as extending beyond the contractual relationship, in robustness and duration.[73] Surrogates often hoped or expected a friendship to develop:

> The relationships with the commissioning parents are viewed by the surrogates as special, loving, and important, which is part of the surrogacy experience, and they feel they are making a sacrifice out of love or compassion for the commissioning parents.[74]

While it seems unlikely that solidarity would require that the intended parents love the surrogate, surrogates' expressed desires for continuing or intimate relationships with intended parents represent a call for the intended parents to respond to and appreciate the surrogate's unique investment (e.g., emotional labour)[75] in their reproductive projects.

Self-sufficiency resists disconnection by fostering connections that are attentive to vulnerability and power. Rather than conceptualizing surrogacy as *primarily* a service arrangement, self-sufficiency structures surrogacy as primarily a relationship of solidarity. In being fellow community members, the surrogate and intended parents are connected through social processes prior to the initiation of the arrangement. Thus, the surrogate is first a fellow member of the national political community before she is a service provider. Approaching surrogacy as a solidarity relationship emphasizes the surrogate as a unique subject, thereby discouraging objectifying her as fungible or instrumentally valuable.

Further, self-sufficiency does not presume that the relationship between intended parents and the surrogate will end at the birth of a child. Although self-sufficiency does not prescribe a norm for their relationship, it opens up space for intended parents and surrogates to negotiate the nature of their

73 Bromfield, above note 11 at 206. In these studies, surrogates reported that their experiences of surrogacy are mainly positive. The main negative aspects of their experiences related to their relationships with intended parents. Negative experiences did not usually overwhelm positive ones. See also Amrita Pande, *Wombs in Labor: Transnational Commercial Surrogacy in India* (New York: Columbia University Press, 2014).

74 Bromfield, above note 11 at 207.

75 Crozier, Johnson, & Hajzler, above note 22 at 48.

continuing relationship, with attention to axes of power and vulnerability. In sum, self-sufficiency provides a starting point that seeks to mitigate challenges surrogates identify in their relationships with intended parents.

This framework for surrogacy helps respond to a criticism that surrogacy enforces pronatalism. Some critics find surrogacy problematic in its current context because it supports stereotypes that women ought to bear children.[76] Further, in unpaid surrogacy, gendered and cultural norms about women as naturally caring or giving may reinforce pronatalism and coercion.[77] For example, Rakhi Ruparelia describes how, in South Asian–Canadian families, marriage is primarily a relationship between families, not between individuals.[78] In such a context, pronatalist ideas that tie women's identity to motherhood may result in childless women experiencing coercion to pursue surrogacy, and/or a fertile woman experiencing coercion to serve as a surrogate for family members.[79]

Because self-sufficiency seeks to address vulnerability, and because gendered vulnerabilities are part of the social background of surrogacy, challenging pronatalism is part of the relational work of self-sufficiency. Although self-sufficiency may not be able to address familial pressures, it would seek to confront vulnerabilities that are part of the social context for the national political community. It seeks to make surrogacy more public. Self-sufficiency mitigates gendered vulnerabilities by refocusing care work as publicly and politically valuable: when a political community values care work as a public good, it will be better situated to provide relational supports to protect a surrogate from harm, disrespect, or exploitation. As this point indicates, fostering a good relationship between the surrogate and intended parents is work performed, in part, by the national political community.

3) The Relational Bonds Between Surrogates and Their Political Communities

Initially, surrogacy seems to be primarily a relationship between a surrogate and intended parents, with contributions from legal advisers and health

76 Debra Satz, "Markets in Women's Reproductive Labor" (1992) 21:2 *Philosophy and Public Affairs* 107 at 127.

77 Ruparelia, above note 10 at 30–31.

78 *Ibid.*

79 *Ibid* at 32.

care professionals. Intended parents certainly have direct responsibilities to surrogates. In self-sufficiency, the national political community also has responsibilities to the surrogate—that is, responsibilities to implement and support a system under which surrogacy needs can be fulfilled ethically.

As indicated in the discussion of valuing care work publicly, community solidarity involves providing relational support for the bonds between a surrogate and intended parents. Martin and Kane state:

> Establishing relationships in the immediate term and facilitating future relationships if and when they become desirable or necessary is likely to be beneficial for all participants, if these relationships are formed within the context of a legal, medical, and social system that provides appropriate psychosocial support and clarity on legal obligations and rights, which help to foster trust.[80]

The network described in this quotation is beneficial for "all participants," meaning surrogates and intended parents.[81] But such a network is also part of the responsibility a community has to meet surrogacy needs ethically.

This responsibility, which is grounded in self-sufficiency's relational conception of persons, requires that care work be publicly affirmed and valued. Doing so represents a radical shift, as caring relations and care work have not typically been valued publicly.[82] To support the surrogate, surrogacy first must be acknowledged as a form of "social reproduction." This term refers to social processes that form the basis of communities and enable traditionally productive forms of work.[83] Biological reproduction and domestic labour are paradigmatic forms of social reproduction. Second, surrogacy, as a form of social reproduction, must be valued as such. In her work on dependency workers, Eva Feder Kittay finds inspiration in doulas, who provide care and support to new mothers rather than relieving them of their own caring opportunities by providing child care.[84]

80 Martin & Kane, above note 1 at 26.

81 *Ibid.*

82 Eva Kittay, *Love's Labor: Essays on Women, Equality, and Dependency* (New York: Routledge, 1999).

83 Crozier, Johnson, & Hajzler, above note 22 at 58.

84 Feder Kittay, above note 82. Kittay defines a dependency worker as anyone who provides care for someone who is "inevitably dependent," whether this work is done voluntarily or paid (*ibid* at ix).

Doula practice helps revise what it means to value caring relations publicly. Doing so means

> that the value of receiving and giving care would be publicly acknowledged; that the burdens and cost incurred by doing the work of caring for dependents would not fall to the dependency worker alone (even when that dependency work is freely assumed); and that the commitment to preserving caring *relations* would be assumed by society.[85]

To ensure that the surrogate is adequately supported in providing a caring service to the intended parents is part of a community's responsibility. In addition, social networks in the community should be attentive to dangers of stereotypes around altruism and giving. They should not compound surrogates' vulnerabilities by using stereotypes to coerce certain modes of behaviour.[86]

In addition, the political community's responsibility to the surrogate involves resisting neoliberal depictions of surrogacy that place the primary locus of responsibility on an individual surrogate. Neoliberal discourses present surrogates as "entrepreneurs of the self" who exercise reproductive autonomy in a rational and responsible manner, especially for their children.[87] A surrogate's body serves as collateral for the entrepreneurial endeavour.[88] She assumes the health risks that come with pregnancy and infertility treatments.[89] The picture of the surrogate as an entrepreneur of the self is inaccurate insofar as it ignores or covers over considerations of vulnerability and power. In some ways, surrogacy in Canada already mitigates this depiction of surrogacy, because Canadian surrogates have access to provincial health care, a circumstance that reinforces the value of self-sufficiency's commitment to shared responsibility.

---

85 *Ibid* at 109 [emphasis in original].

86 Hewitson, above note 67 at 183.

87 Melinda Cooper & Catherine Waldby, *Clinical Labor: Tissue Donors and Research Subjects in the Global Bioeconomy* (Durham, NC: Duke University Press, 2014) at 31; see also Charlotte Halmø Kroløkke & Saumya Pant, "'I Only Need Her Uterus': Neoliberal Discourses on Transnational Surrogacy" (2012) 20:4 *Nordic Journal of Feminist and Gender Research* 233 at 234 and 239.

88 Cooper & Waldby, above note 87 at 84.

89 Ryman & Fulfer, above note 21 at 8.

My claim that the national political community is responsible for supporting surrogates stems from the social connections between surrogates and their fellow community members.

If intended parents fail to meet their responsibility to the surrogate, the political community steps in. This "stepping in" may happen in a number of ways and may involve members of the national political community in different respects. A primary way in which the national political community would exercise this responsibility might be in providing support services for surrogates and ensuring, through democratic dialogue and action, that surrogates can access these services.

What is important for my argument here is not how the community addresses its responsibility to the surrogate but, rather, establishing that shared responsibility exists. It is worth noting that responsibility in self-sufficiency requires a more public organization of surrogacy than we currently have in Canada, where the fertility industry is largely private and there is no consistent data reporting.[90] The surrogate is not an entrepreneur of the self who takes on risks for herself; self-sufficiency entails spreading these burdens among community members.

4) Strengthening Solidarity in the National Political Community

In exercising its responsibility to meet surrogacy needs ethically, self-sufficiency can serve to strengthen bonds of solidarity within the national political community. My definition of political community captures experiential dimensions of political engagement: the political is not just the constitution that governs us but also the activity of engaging with fellow community members to take up matters of political import.[91]

Public deliberation is central to this dimension of political community. Through public deliberation, political community is created and main-

90 Pamela M White, "Hidden from View: Canadian Surrogacy" (28 September 2016) *Impact Ethics* (blog), online: https://impactethics.ca/2016/09/28/hidden-from-view-canadian-surrogacy. See also, White, Chapter 2, this volume.

91 Anya Topolski, *Arendt, Levinas and a Politics of Relationality* (London: Rowman and Littlefield International, 2015) at 57.

tained.[92] Framed in terms of responsibility, members of the political community are co-responsible for their shared world. Public deliberation is left intentionally open. It refers broadly to engaging with fellow community members in speech and action in the public realm.[93] Such activities may include public forums, neighbourhood meetings, citizen action groups, protests, marches, and town hall meetings.[94] There is a feedback loop at work in this conception of politics: public deliberation is part of the way in which a political community exercises its responsibility for our shared world, and enacting public deliberation serves to strengthen the political community. Such deliberation enhances democratic opportunities and resists isolating trends that facilitate political apathy and disconnection.[95]

Self-sufficiency, then, requires more public, political deliberation about surrogacy and related issues. Currently, public engagement around surrogacy in Canada is limited. Policy-makers and fertility professionals tend to dominate these conversations, with little input from surrogates or from the general public.[96] The reasons for the relative silence of surrogates and intended parents around surrogacy in Canada may be due to a number of factors, including a fear or reluctance to discuss experiences, given the ambiguities in the *AHRA*.

Self-sufficiency supports greater opportunities for members of the national political community, and not only policy-makers or fertility professionals, to deliberate about surrogacy. In addition to requiring better empirical information about surrogacy in Canada, the national community may take up questions about the value of surrogacy, assisted reproduction, and related issues.[97] Given self-sufficiency's commitment to social justice, these conversations would involve addressing concerns around adoption

---

92 Young, "Global Labor Justice," above note 57 at 377.

93 Arendt, *The Human Condition*, above note 39 at 198; Young, "Global Labor Justice," above note 57 at 123.

94 Hannah Arendt, *Hannah Arendt: The Last Interview and Other Conversations* (Brooklyn, NY: Melville House, 2013) at 36.

95 Topolski, above note 91 at 51.

96 Alana Cattapan, "Clarifying the AHR Act After 12 Long Years" (18 November 2016), *Impact Ethics* (blog), online: https://impactethics.ca/2016/11/18/clarifying-the-ahr-act-after-12-long-years/ [Cattapan, "Clarifying the AHR Act"]; Charis Thompson, *Making Parents: The Ontological Choreography of Reproductive Technologies* (Cambridge, MA: MIT Press, 2005).

97 White, above note 90.

as a procreative option, the subsidizing of fertility treatments, pronatalism and gender, discrimination against LGBTQ2 families, and histories of colonialism that affect family making in Canada.

Procreation is deeply moral, and moral deliberation about parenthood is worth encouraging. While I do not advocate subjecting to scrutiny the procreative desires of any particular person or group, I wish to point out that questions such as whether it is good to have children, how it is good to have children, and how many children one ought to have are not ones that tend to be taken up publicly or that are used to inform policy. Yet perhaps they should be. Charis Thompson notes that the voices most prominent in political advocacy around assisted reproduction are those groups that have an economic stake in it: current or potential clients of fertility clinics, fertility specialists, and pharmaceutical companies that manufacture infertility drugs and technologies.[98] She describes this narrow site of political engagement that is driven by private interests rather than broader ethical or political questions as contributing to "publics of privacy."[99] That fertility patients, potential consumers, and fertility specialists engage politically around matters that are personal to them is not a problem. What self-sufficiency would encourage, however, it that public discourse around surrogacy should be aimed at public good and not dominated by private interests.

F. TOWARDS A FULL DEFENCE OF SELF-SUFFICIENCY

In this chapter, I have elaborated on previous defences of self-sufficiency to articulate a relational conception of self-sufficiency that has the potential to serve as a mechanism for meeting Canada's responsibilities to mitigate structural injustice abroad. Although my argument has been restricted to Canada, because of the particularities of social-structural processes at work to support structural injustice in transnational surrogacy, the relational social ethos that structures self-sufficiency might be beneficial for other national political communities.

I acknowledge that I have defended a social ethos for self-sufficiency and have not offered a way of implementing self-sufficiency in Canada. I have pointed to some ways in which the status quo would have to change—

98 Thompson, above note 96 at 96.

99 *Ibid.*

for example, around the public value of care work and the social networks needed to support surrogates. In this last section, I outline questions that need to be addressed for a full defence of self-sufficiency, with a focus on implementing its social ethos.

1) Altruism and Commercialization

My defence of self-sufficiency has danced around questions about the value of altruism. I have focused on outlining and defending the relational foundation of self-sufficiency rather than untangling notions of altruism and its role in self-sufficiency. In Canada, considering questions of altruism and commercialization with respect to surrogacy requires examining the fertility industry, which is for-profit and largely unregulated.

Insofar as commercial systems tend to be grounded in a non-relational conception of persons, I am skeptical that ethical challenges related to surrogacy can be addressed better by commercialization than by self-sufficiency.[100] Further, self-sufficiency has the practical benefit of aligning with the *AHRA*'s non-commercialization stance. Nevertheless, if it is the will of the national political community, there may be ways to bring the social ethos of self-sufficiency to inform revisions to commercialization.

2) Payment and Reimbursement

Media reports suggest that surrogates experience financial burdens as a result of surrogacy.[101] Because self-sufficiency attends to relationships of power and vulnerability, it would be important, within such a framework, to mitigate the financial costs to surrogates and their families. Within this framework, *how* to address financial burdens and economic vulnerability would be matters for political deliberation. It seems likely, though, that the *AHRA* would need supplementation or amendment if financial vulnerabilities are to be addressed. Currently, section 12 of the *AHRA*, which governs reimbursements, is not in force, and Health Canada has not provided

100 Hewitson, above note 67 at 159.

101 Robert Cribb & Emma Jarratt, "Attempts to Clarify Surrogacy Rules Could Hurt Altruistic Surrogates in Canada" *Toronto Star* (9 October 2016), online: www.thestar.com/news/world/2016/10/09/attempts-to-clarify-surrogacy-rules-could-hurt-altruistic-surrogates-in-canada.html; see also Lavoie & Côté, Chapter 3, this volume.

clarification about legitimate reimbursable expenses, although, at the time of writing, a regulatory process is underway.[102] Regulations that would meaningfully address financial burdens may require revising the *AHRA*, which allows reimbursements only for out-of-pocket payments and only when receipts are provided.

To date, surrogates have not been consulted widely when regulation around surrogacy has been drafted.[103] If purposefully consulted, surrogates may indicate that an adequate reimbursement framework is sufficient to mitigate their financial burdens. If surrogates overwhelmingly advocate for payment, rather than reimbursement, then the case for self-sufficiency is weakened. Either way, their experiences and knowledge should meaningfully inform how Canada pursues regulating surrogacy.

3) Improving Transnational Surrogacy

My argument began with a premise that Canada has an obligation to reduce transnational surrogacy. *Contra* this premise, some scholars advocate improving transnational surrogacy to address structural injustices therein.[104] As I have argued elsewhere, as long as the prohibitions in the *AHRA* on commercial payments are in force, improving transnational surrogacy will be an ineffective solution for global structural injustice.[105] However, self-sufficiency leaves open the possibility that public deliberation will, all things consider, favour improving transnational surrogacy and implementing some form of commercialization within Canada.

4) Centring Solidarity

My defence of the social ethos of self-sufficiency has centred on solidarity and shared responsibilities among Canada's national political community. By way of conclusion, I suggest that "self-sufficiency" as a term does

102 Dave Snow, Françoise Baylis, & Jocelyn Downie, "Why the Government of Canada Won't Regulate Assisted Reproduction: A Modern Mystery" (2015) 9:1 *McGill Journal of Law and Health* 1.

103 Cattapan, "Clarifying the AHR Act," above note 96.

104 See, for example, Anne Donchin, "Reproductive Tourism and the Quest for Global Gender Justice" (2010) 24:7 *Bioethics* 323 at 331.

105 Fulfer, "Cross-Border Reproductive Travel," above note 4 at 240.

not capture the import of its social ethos. "Self-sufficiency" is intended to highlight distinctive features of the framework. First, "sufficiency" indicates a "commitment to develop and adopt solutions to problems of insufficient supply."[106] Second, "self" indicates that responsibility for sufficiency attaches to the community where the needs arise.[107] In contrast, my argument has suggested that identifying the "self" as a singular community and "sufficiency" as internally focused ignores responsibilities that the national political community has for global structural injustices. Further, the term "self" homogenizes the community. In my account, the community is composed of selves-in-relation who share responsibility for co-creating community through political deliberation. Such deliberation suggests room for diverse voices and difference. The community is not a self, but a plurality.

For these reasons, "self-sufficiency" as a moniker for the governing principles I have defended might be replaced by "community solidarity" for surrogacy. It is the bonds of community that justify the responsibility to meet internal needs and account for global structural injustice. The bonds of community are central to reframing surrogacy as relational, a reframing that commercial systems have limited potential to achieve. Finally, the bonds of community indicate the potential of community members to take up challenges for regulating surrogacy. In short, I suggest that Canada use community solidarity as a guide for re-imagining ethical and socially just regulation for surrogacy.

106 Baylis & Downie, "Altruistic Self-Sufficiency," above note 6 at 169.

107 *Ibid.*

Afterword: Legitimizing Surrogacy — A Social Setback

Maria De Koninck

THIS TEXT IS INCLUDED HERE AS A TRIBUTE TO ABBY LIPPMAN, OUR FRIEND AND A RESPECTED INTELLECTUAL.

A. INTRODUCTION

Dr Abby Lippman, emeritus professor at the Department of Epidemiology, Biostatistics and Occupational Health at McGill University, passed away on 26 December 2017. Her death leaves a great void. As a renowned scholar, Abby made it her mission to raise consciousness, advance knowledge, and mobilize for social justice and respect for human dignity. As a feminist, she used her expertise to advance issues related to women's health, particularly reproductive health, and she was relentless in promoting respect for women's integrity and dignity.

In November 2016, Abby and I co-authored a commentary on surrogacy when the Government of Canada announced that it planned to introduce regulations to strengthen the *Assisted Human Reproduction Act* (*AHRA*). In the summer of 2017, Abby supported me in writing a commentary in response to Health Canada's consultation document entitled "Toward a Strengthened *Assisted Human Reproduction Act*: A Consultation with Canadians on Key Policy Proposals," which included proposals for regulations on surrogacy.[1]

1 I am very grateful to the co-editors of this publication for enabling me to participate and, in so doing, pay a tribute to my lost friend Abby Lippman. I also thank Alana Cattapan for her helpful revision and Diane Guilbault for her support of my work on surrogacy.

The co-editors of the present volume have included the latter commentary[2] as part of this collection to ensure that Abby's and my perspectives on surrogacy are represented and to remind us of Abby's contributions to the debates surrounding reproductive technologies and the issue of surrogacy.[3]

As this Afterword makes clear, we oppose the legitimation of surrogacy. We consider it to be contrary to human dignity, since the mother and the child born are persons and, as such, cannot be the objects of a contract. In the case of the mother, the contract concerns her life for nine months and, in the case of the child, the contract addresses their existence. Following a section that outlines our position on surrogacy, three areas of concern are addressed in this commentary: the infringement on Canadian values by the proposed orientation of the government, the continued "pathologization" of the desire to have children, and perspectives on the evolution of surrogacy in today's society.

B. RATHER THAN DEVELOPING REGULATIONS, CANADA SHOULD BAN SURROGACY

The absence of regulations on the reimbursement of surrogate mothers for their expenditures has, up to now, somewhat shielded Canada from the development of a market in children, even if it has not made it possible to avoid commercial practices in Canadian surrogacy or deterred reproductive tourism on the part of Canadian citizens, a practice that often includes the exploitation of women living in low-income countries. The adoption and implementation of regulations to permit reimbursement of surrogate mothers for expenditures might put an end to this limited protection. Although these regulations would not, strictly speaking, allow a woman to be paid or to make a profit, they would foster the financial evaluation of pregnancy and, in so doing, of a child.[4] By trying to regulate surrogacy, Health Canada follows a path that legitimizes the practice, instead of delegitimizing it, ignoring lessons learned elsewhere. Indeed, many

2 The commentary has been revised for this publication.

3 Diane Beeson, Marcy Darnovsky, & Abby Lippman, "What's in a Name? Variations in Terminology of Third-Party Reproduction" (2015) 31:6 *Reproductive BioMedicine Online* 805.

4 Excerpts from Maria De Koninck & Abby Lippman, "Commentaires sur le projet de règlementer en vertu de la Loi sur la procréation assistée" (submission to Health Canada 21 November 2016).

countries that were previously open to surrogacy now forbid it or refuse its access to foreign couples.[5] Contexts in these countries are different from ours in Canada, but their negative experiences nonetheless underline how surrogacy is problematic and violates women's and children's dignity.[6]

Even if it is authorized in the *AHRA*, there is no consensus in Canada about the legitimacy of the use of surrogacy. Let us recall that, in Quebec, article 541 of the *Civil Code* stipulates: "Any agreement whereby a woman undertakes to procreate or carry a child for another person is absolutely null."[7] Whenever the issue of surrogacy is debated, critics make themselves heard.[8] PDF-Québec (Pour les droits des femmes [For women's rights]),[9] a feminist organization created in 2013, advocates for the universal abolition of surrogacy. In 2017, it published a booklet entitled "Surrogate Motherhood: Modern Day Slavery."[10] In the rest of Canada, feminists have also made their voices heard in opposition to the practice.[11]

Elsewhere, around the world, the campaign against surrogacy continues. Of the twenty-eight member countries of the European Union, twenty ban surrogacy outright.[12] In 2015, Stop Surrogacy Now, an international coalition against surrogacy, launched a campaign and, since then, has been circulating a petition demanding the international abolition of surrogacy.[13] In February

5 "As Demand for Surrogacy Soars, More Countries Are Trying to Ban It" *The Economist* (13 May 2017), online: www.economist.com/news/international/21721926-many-feminists-and-religious-leaders-regard-it-exploitation-demand-surrogacy.

6 On weaknesses inherent to regulating (rather than complete prohibition), see Renate Klein, *Surrogacy: A Human Rights Violation* (North Geelong, AU: Spinifex Press, 2017).

7 *Civil Code of Quebec*, CQLR c CCQ-1991, c 64, art 541, as amended by SQ 2002, c 6, s 30.

8 Yves Boisvert, "Mères porteuses . . . mais bénévoles" *La Presse* (22 February 2016) online: www.lapresse.ca/debats/chroniques/yves-boisvert/201602/19/01-4952356-meres-porteuses-mais-benevoles.php; Céline Lafontaine, "Le remboursement des mères porteuses? Du délire" *Le Devoir* (25 April 2014) online: www.ledevoir.com/opinion/libre-opinion/406482/le-remboursement-des-meres-porteuses-du-delire.

9 PDF Quebec, "A Feminist, Citizens', Mixed, Nonpartisan Group," online: www.pdfquebec.org/index_English.php.

10 Online:www.pdfquebec.org/English/documents/Surrogate_motherhood-PDF_Quebec_Brochure.pdf.

11 For example, see, online: www.feministcurrent.com.

12 Luc Magoutier, "Infographie : Où la GPA est-elle autorisée en Europe?" *La Croix* (7 May 2017), online: www.la-croix.com/Sciences-et-ethique/Ethique/INFOGRAPHIE-Ou-GPA-est-elle-autorisee-Europe-2017-07-05-1200860655.

13 Stop Surrogacy Now, "#StopSurrogacyNow: Add Your Name to the Petition," online: www.stopsurrogacynow.com.

2016, the first international conference for the abolition of surrogacy was held in Paris, supported by fifty-four women's and human rights groups.[14]

In its consultation document, Health Canada's objective regarding surrogacy is stated in terms of the promotion of "an altruistic system."[15] Thus, the department already promotes a specific form of contract pregnancy, one considered adequate and described as altruistic. However, this objective must be questioned, as the use of the word "altruistic" is not neutral; rather, it seeks to draw sympathy by attributing a moral value to contracts binding surrogate mothers, contracts with the object of establishing the terms under which a human being is to be born.

C. HEALTH CANADA'S DIRECTION IS IN OPPOSITION TO CANADIAN VALUES

Canada boasts of being a great place to live, a country where values related to human dignity and equity are respected and where there is a commitment to both individual and collective rights. But what values are upheld when it comes to surrogacy? We suggest that surrogacy poses a threat to human dignity and rights of women and children.

1) A Practice That Threatens the Advancement of Women . . .

There is a long history of struggle by Canadian women to achieve emancipation: to improve their status, to have access to education, to engage in all occupations, and to occupy the halls of power. The success of these endeavours has rested on the need for women to be recognized as persons in their own right, having as many assets and as much potential as men. And, although many struggles continue, women are no longer recognized primarily in terms of their reproductive capacity or their roles as mothers.

By adopting the proposed surrogacy regulations, Canada would institutionalize a practice that brings women back to their position as reproducers,

---

14 Towards the Abolition of GPA, "2018, année de l'abolition de la GPA!" (2018), *Vers l'abolition de la GPA* (blog), online: www.abolition-gpa.org/.

15 Government of Canada, "Toward a Strengthened *Assisted Human Reproduction Act*: A Consultation with Canadians on Key Policy Proposals" (2017) at 23, online: www.canada.ca/en/health-canada/programs/consultation-assisted-human-reproduction/document.html.

since surrogacy means that women are made available to commissioning parties for whom they may bear a child and to whom they are expected to relinquish the child at birth. Women are not mere producers of children and should never be reduced to this function to satisfy others' desires. It is no longer socially acceptable in Canada for a man to appropriate a woman to make sure he has descendants. The use of a surrogate mother is but a "modern" and extended version of this appropriation that Canadian women have completely rejected, and we cannot risk sliding backwards. Although surrogacy is a temporary situation (not one that is lifelong, as in past forms of appropriation), the implications of the child's birth are lifelong, and the relationship established between a surrogate mother and the child's sponsors remains one that appropriates a woman's reproductive potential.

Women have also fought for the humanization of childbirth, arguing correctly that pregnancy and childbirth are first and foremost a human experience that cannot be cut apart nor reduced to a medical and technical intervention. During pregnancy, a woman's relationship to her body changes, since it shelters a child in the making. This experience is a human experience, meaning that the woman's consciousness—notably of this future otherness—is determinant. Pregnancy is definitely not only physiological;[16] it is also psychological and social. As for the child to be born, we now know that, beyond cellular exchanges, the growth *in utero* is far from independent from the woman who carries the fetus and from her personal experiences.[17] The use of surrogate mothers complies with a logic that divides pregnancy and childbirth into pieces and anonymizes this unique human experience, with significant physical and psychosocial consequences for the mother and the child.[18] These consequences are trivialized and the complexity of human experience ignored whenever surrogacy practices are justified.

Many discourses attempt to hide this reality to mislead us into believing that bearing a child is an activity comparable to others, such as caregiving or maintaining a household. This is not the case. A woman who bears a child is involved physically, psychologically, and socially throughout pregnancy to

16 Elseline Hoekzema et al, "Pregnancy Leads to Long-Lasting Changes in Human Brain Structure" (2017) 20:2 *Nature Neuroscience* 287.

17 Natalie MacKinnon et al, "The Association Between Prenatal Stress and Externalizing Symptoms in Childhood: Evidence from the Avon Longitudinal Study of Parents and Children" (2018) 83:2 *Biological Psychiatry* 100.

18 Céline Lemay, *La mise au monde: Revisiter les savoirs* (Montréal: Les Presses de l'Université de Montréal, 2017).

bring that being into this world. The maternal experience of pregnancy and childbirth cannot ever be deemed equivalent to a work activity.[19]

There is abundant evidence adding to our knowledge about how these unique experiences, during which sharing and mother/child exchanges occur, leave both with marks that cannot be erased. And we continue to learn more and more about these exchanges. To minimize the intensity of such a human experience and consider it a process of production is degrading for women, and it is retrogressive for society.

2) ... and Threatens the Advancement of Children's Status and Rights

> In the imagery of biotechnology, a child is only a product fabricated from bits: sperm, oocytes, uterus. Where does that leave us if we forget the dignity of the person and of her body?[20]

The legitimization of surrogacy also jeopardizes values associated with children's human dignity and rights. Canada does not accept the notion that a human can be a product to be sold and rejects turning one into an object of transaction. Why should we weaken these values by accepting that the birth of a child can be planned as a contract between one or more commissioning sponsors and a woman who will have to carry that child for nine months? Ordering a child, even if it does not involve an income or a profit, remains a form of commodification. It is a "social practice that takes childbirth and the child into an exchange system."[21] The child is the object of an exchange, even if there is no remuneration.

Moreover, the great progress we have made in Canada to protect our children—to make sure they are treated as persons in their own right, deserving of respect from their earliest age (e.g., through prohibitions on physical punishment)—would be reversed by a practice such as surrogacy,

19 Many feminist writings deal with the meaning of pregnancy and childbirth, the depth of that experience, and the impact of its medicalization. Authors such as Ann Oakley, Robbie Davis-Floyd, Barbara Katz-Rothman, Emily Martin, and Sheila Kitzinger have published extensively on the subject. I, too, have conducted research on childbirth, caesarean sections, maternal mortality, mothers' experiences with addiction, and the protective reassignment of pregnant workers. This work has produced data on the significance and complexity of the experience of pregnancy and childbirth.

20 Sylviane Agacinski, *Corps en miettes* (Paris: Flammarion, 2013) at 17 [author's translation].

21 *Ibid* at 9.

which turns children into goods that people can simply desire and order for delivery, at the same time potentially erasing the child's maternal origins. Such a child is an orphan of sorts (deprived of their mother), a condition that has been planned, even if the plan is to subsequently attribute the status of mother or of second parent to a sponsor. Planning to make a child motherless to fulfill someone's desire offends our consciences as members of a society that believes human beings should never be treated as commodities. Of course, children can be, for different reasons and in different circumstances, entrusted to adults other than their natural parents, with these other adults becoming their parents. But to plan a birth so that the child will be relinquished essentially alters the child's experience.

We recognize that pressures from different interest groups are strong and that accepting surrogacy might be perceived as a gesture of open-mindedness. But, were the Canadian government to adopt regulations that go further than the tolerance inscribed so far in the law, the government's stated objective of "promot[ing] an altruistic system" could then more accurately be described as a commitment to accepting a social setback for women and children.[22] And this objective is perplexing.[23]

For its part, the media convey messages and reports about surrogacy that are often positive and idealistic, focusing on the happiness made possible by those giving the "gift" of a child, emphasizing the fulfillment of some adults' desire for a child. But what about the child? So much is said and written about the commissioning parents, with so little written about the interests of children. Why, we might ask, does the media generally favour arrangements that attempt to make sure that a parent has a biological link to the child born, while at the same time paying little (if any) attention to the child and their links to their maternal origins? As one observer has said, "In the media there is talk of surrogacy as a way to have children, not a way to lose them, despite the fact that this is what separates surrogacy from any other way of reproducing."[24] Unfortunately, the treatment of these issues

22 Government of Canada, above note 15 at 23.

23 In November 2017, Health Canada released a survey aimed at stakeholders in the "industry" of assisted human reproduction. The survey addresses reimbursement of expenses incurred by surrogates.

24 Kajsa Ekis Ekman, "Cristiano Ronaldo: Women Are Not Your Baby Factories" (2017), *#StopSurrogacyNow* (blog), online: www.stopsurrogacynow.com/cristiano-ronaldo-a-woman-is-not-a-factory.

in the media perpetuates the views of an individualistic society focused on fulfilling desire, with no regard to the consequences.

D. THE CONSTRUCTION AND THE "PATHOLOGIZATION" OF THE DESIRE TO HAVE A CHILD

> A certain sociological vulgate, hardly interested in the symbolical aspects of intergenerational relations or of questions—which are, however, central—of filiation, also takes for granted that in a world where the individual dominates, links between parents and children are based only on individual will and choices. The desire to love a child is thus sufficient to justify the request, and to be loved by a child is a right.[25]

The desire to have a child is a worthy desire, but it is not a right. There is no such thing as a right to a child. One must understand that the desire to have a child is socially supported and is socially constructed. The *pathologization* of subfertility and infertility exemplifies a medical and social drift that creates suffering and distress and can favour the search for solutions at any price. The history of medicine includes many examples of solutions offered to socially constructed problems. Without minimizing the suffering felt by people who realize they cannot have children, it is necessary to question the use of resources to define as pathological situations that should be understood in social terms, and how this might work to maintain or increase the suffering of those involved, while infringing on collective values and/or social rights.

To enable social progress and to identify what kinds of support should be offered to people who wish to have a family, our efforts must be framed in ways that advance human dignity and human rights. Thus, to support adoption, including an end to discrimination in the process (notably against homosexual couples), is a legitimate sign of social progress with respect to practices that enable children who need a home to find one. But to institutionalize the right to reach an agreement with a woman so that she will bear a child to hand over to others is a social setback. This practice is degrading for women. Moreover, it does not respect the rights of children as human beings but rather understands them as products that have been made-to-order

25 Martine Segalen, "Pourquoi la gestation pour autrui dite 'éthique' ne peut être" (2017) 38:2 *Travail, genre et sociétés* 57 [author's translation].

without concern for any emotional risk associated with the planned separation from the mother.

When nature makes it impossible to realize the desire to have a child—and medicine cannot help without putting into question human dignity and rights—society can offer opportunities to satisfy the wish to engage in caretaking, education, and the transmission of knowledge and experience by making it easier to adopt children in need of parents or to engage in different forms of parenting. This is the direction Canada's policies should take.

E. THE EVOLUTION OF A SOCIAL PRACTICE TOWARDS ITS DEFINITION IN MARKET TERMS

Beyond these considerations—which question the practice of using surrogates as a solution—it is important to draw attention to the impact of adopting regulations (such as those proposed in the Health Canada consultation document) that seek social approval through the privileging of discourses of "altruism." On the one hand, the fact that a woman voluntarily accepts becoming a surrogate mother does nothing to alter the negative implications of this practice for the status of women. On the other hand, even if regulations do not permit remuneration, estimating some price that would be an allowable reimbursement opens the door wide to commercial drifts.[26]

Scholarship in the social sciences, particularly in Canada, has demonstrated that, in a social, economic, and political context as ours, once a practice is regulated, it is seen to be legitimate, which then allows it to be redefined in market terms. In other words, approving the practice, as is happening now in an effort to adopt regulations (which had not been done previously), means also approving its growing use and its definition as a perfectly legitimate "solution." The conditions for its normalization are being put into place. Using a surrogate mother becomes legally sanctioned under certain conditions, and it is entirely predictable that the terms under which surrogacy is

26 Interestingly, Vietnam amended its law to allow "altruistic surrogacy" but added an amendment to bar surrogate mothers from being reimbursed for expenses in order to avoid the law's abuse for commercial purposes. "Surrogacy Problem Sneaks Across the Border" *The Nation* (25 April 2017), online: www.nationmultimedia.com/news/opinion/today_editorial/30313268.

practised will evolve over time until it becomes basically a commercial activity, emptying human reproduction of its most profound meaning.[27]

F. CONCLUSION

Are we, in Canada, afraid to assert that women cannot be reduced to their reproductive capacity, and that calling a practice altruistic doesn't alter the situation? Do we not want to protect the status of our children, who under no circumstances should result from contractual arrangements? Do we not wish our laws and regulations to prevent anyone from planning (voluntarily) for a child to be donated to another by the woman who gave birth, the child perhaps never knowing her and unable to trace their origins?

It would be unrealistic to think that, by regulating surrogacy, we will avoid the distorting commercial practices of using surrogate mothers that have been observed around the world, practices that have led several countries to prohibit surrogacy or to shut the door to reproductive tourism. Regulating the practice amounts to its definitive legitimization. And, in a society such as ours, to permit a financial account of pregnancy and childbirth (even if it is limited to the reimbursement of a surrogate's expenses) is another step down the road toward commercialization. Naive optimism has no place here. Market forces and competition[28] in this field will, with the passing of time, continue to erode efforts to protect the rights of women and of children.

Whether it is free, compensated, paid, or profitable, the use of a surrogate mother goes against Canadian values that arose from hard-fought struggles. We need to respect these advances and support, rather than threaten, the progress made with regard to the status of both women and children and in the humanization of childbirth. Pregnancy is not simply a phase in the production of a human being. It is so much more, which cannot and should not be the subject of a contract.

---

27 Céline Lafontaine, *Le corps-marché: La marchandisation de la vie humaine à l'ère de la bioéconomie* (Paris: Éditions du Seuil, 2014).

28 They seem to already be at work: Robert Cribb & Emma Jarratt, "How Canada Is Becoming a Key Player in Global Surrogacy" *Toronto Star* (25 June 2016), online: www.thestar.com/news/world/2016/06/25/how-canada-is-becoming-a-key-player-in-global-surrogacy.html.

Contributors

Karen Busby is a professor of law and the director of the Centre for Human Rights Research at the University of Manitoba. Her research focuses on laws relating to sex, gender, and sexuality including sexual assault, sexual expression, sex work, wife abuse, and assisted reproduction. Throughout her thirty-year career as an academic, Busby has also worked with various litigation and law reform projects with organizations seeking national equality.

Angela Cameron is an associate professor at the University of Ottawa, Faculty of Law. She holds the Shirley E Greenberg Chair for Women and the Legal Profession. Her research is generally in the area of social justice, with particular attention to the equality rights and interests of women. Her research and publications are mainly in the areas of assisted reproductive technologies, violence against women, and Indigenous-settler relations. She is the chair of FAFIA (http://fafia-afai.org), a national feminist NGO, and has worked on a variety of law reform and activism projects within the feminist and LGBTQ+ communities.

Alana Cattapan is an assistant professor at the Johnson Shoyama Graduate School of Public Policy and an associate member of the Department of Community Health and Epidemiology in the College of Medicine at the University of Saskatchewan. A longtime feminist researcher and activist, she studies women's participation in policy making—identifying links between the state, the commercialization of the body, biotechnologies, and reproductive labour. Cattapan's work is funded by the Social Sciences and Humanities Research Council, the Canadian Institutes of Health Research, and the Saskatchewan Health Research Foundation. Her research is interdisciplinary and has been published in journals across a range of fields, including *Studies in Political Economy*, the *Journal of Medical Ethics*, the *Canadian Medical Association Journal*, and the *Canadian Journal of Law and Society*.

Isabel Côté is an associate professor at the Department of Social Work at the Université du Québec en Outaouais and a researcher at the Centre for Studies and Research on Family Intervention, the Familles en mouvance research partnership, and the Réseau québécois en études féministes. Supported by provincial and national funding, her research projects focus on the realization of a parental project with the help of a third party, a sperm donor, or a surrogate. She is particularly interested in the relationship between third parties and intended parents and the resulting children. In collaboration with Kévin Lavoie and Jérôme Courduriès, she directed *Perspectives internationales sur la gestation pour autrui: Expériences des personnes concernées et contextes d'action*, a collective work published by the Presses de l'Université du Québec in 2018.

Maria De Koninck is a professor emerita and an associate professor at the Department of Social and Preventive Medicine, Faculty of Medicine, Université Laval. She was the university's first chair of women's studies. She taught in community health and directed its master's program (2006–2010), lectured medical students on the social determinants of health, and lectured graduate students on research ethics. Her research and publications focus on women's health, pregnancy and work, childbirth, motherhood and drug abuse, reproductive technologies, ethics, midwifery, and women physicians. She was the principal researcher in a multidisciplinary and multi-institutional team studying social health inequalities, poverty, and exclusion (1999–2010). She currently collaborates with Laval Faculty of Medicine on professionalism and ethics, and pursues her work in women's reproductive health.

Katy Fulfer is an assistant professor of philosophy and women's studies at the University of Waterloo. Her research interests are primarily in the field of feminist bioethics. Some of her previous publications, which have appeared in journals such as *Hypatia*, *Developing World Bioethics*, and *IJFAB: International Journal of Feminist Approaches to Bioethics*, examine the ethics of transnational surrogacy. Her current research examines surrogacy in the Canadian context. She is specifically interested in questions of commodification, exploitation, agency, and moral deliberation in assisted reproduction. In addition, Fulfer's research examines these concepts in the context of animal ethics and in the context of the philosophy of Hannah Arendt.

Vanessa Gruben is an associate professor and a member of the Centre for Health Law, Policy and Ethics at the University of Ottawa, Faculty of

Common Law, where she teaches health law and family law. Her research focuses on the legal and ethical aspects of assisted reproduction, including the constitutionality of Canada's *Assisted Human Reproduction Act*, the legal relationship between egg donors and their physicians, the constitutionality of anonymous sperm and egg donation, access to reproductive technologies, and the existing gaps in provincial law for families created through third-party reproduction. Gruben's work is funded by the Social Science and Humanities and Research Council, Canadian Blood Services, and the Foundation for Legal Research. She is a co-editor of the fifth edition of *Canadian Health Law and Policy* (LexisNexis Canada, 2017).

Kévin Lavoie is a PhD candidate in applied human sciences at the Université de Montréal. He received the Vanier Graduate Scholarship from the Social Sciences and Humanities Research Council of Canada. He holds a bachelor's degree from Laval University and a master's degree from the University of Quebec in Outaouais (UQO), both in social work. His current research focuses on assisted human reproduction: sperm donation outside the reproductive health system, as well as the experiences of women involved in egg donation and surrogacy agreements in Canada. With Isabel Côté and Jérôme Courduriès, he co-edited the volume *Perspectives internationales sur la gestation pour autrui: expériences des personnes concernées et contextes d'action* (2018).

Mark C McLeod is a research associate with Impact Ethics, Dalhousie University, Halifax, Nova Scotia. NTE: Impact Ethics is an interdisciplinary research team that does research at the intersection of health, bioethics, and public policy. McLeod previously worked as a policy analyst at the Assisted Human Reproduction Implementation Office (AHRIO) of Health Canada. He developed and identified policy-related issues concerning assisted human reproduction and other related biological sciences under the *Assisted Human Reproduction Act*. He is also a barrister and solicitor.

Christine Overall is a professor emerita of philosophy and holds a University Research Chair at Queen's University, Kingston, Ontario. She is an elected fellow of the Royal Society of Canada and has received two research awards from the Royal Society. She held the Humphrey Professorship in Feminist Philosophy at the University of Waterloo (2003), the Nancy's Chair in Women's Studies at Mount Saint Vincent University (2006–2007), and the Visiting Professorship in Canadian Studies at

Kwansei Gakuin University in Japan (2011–2012). Her research is in the areas of feminist philosophy, applied philosophy, and philosophy of religion. She has published over a hundred articles and book chapters, many of which have been republished. She is the author of six books, including *Why Have Children: The Ethical Debate* (MIT Press, 2012) and the editor of five books, including *Pets and People: The Ethics of Our Relationships with Companion Animals* (Oxford University Press, 2017).

Angel Petropanagos is the quality improvement ethicist at William Osler Health System (Brampton, Ontario). She is also the co-managing editor of the Impact Ethics website (www.impactethics.ca), the co-chair for the Canadian Fertility & Andrology Society's Ethics and Law special interest group, and a board member of the Canadian Bioethics Society. Her primary research explores ethical issues related to fertility preservation and assisted reproduction. She regularly contributes to the review and development of policy and guideline documents, and provides freelance ethics consultation support to fertility clinics.

Pamela M White is a specialist associate lecturer, Kent Law School, University of Kent, where she teaches undergraduate and LLM degree courses in medical law and ethics, and privacy and data protection law. She also teaches undergraduate medical law at Canterbury Christchurch University. Her research interests focus on the interface of medical law, bioethics, regulation, and population health policy. In her published work, she melds qualitative and quantitative data analysis with critical legal studies. Her scholarship draws on her extensive experience in the Canadian federal government where she was a senior director managing health, social, and demographic research. She has held assignments with the Office of Canadian Federal Privacy Commissioner, the Assisted Human Reproduction Agency of Canada, and the Population Health and Genomics Foundation, Cambridge.

Table of Cases

Index

Printed and bound by CPI Group (UK) Ltd, Croydon, CR0 4YY

15/09/2026

14962401-0004